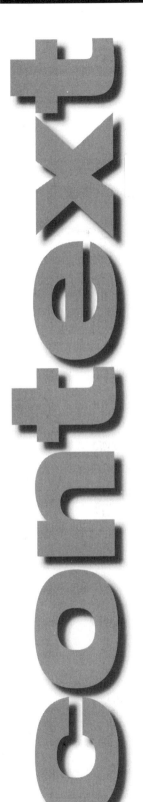

access to history

context

An Introduction to

AMERICAN HISTORY
1860–1990

Alan Farmer and Vivienne Sanders

ASFC LEARNING CENTRE

Hodder & Stoughton

A MEMBER OF THE HODDER HEADLINE GROUP

ACKNOWLEDGEMENTS

The front cover illustration shows John F. Kennedy, reproduced courtesy of the Fitzgerald Kennedy Library, Boston.

The publishers would like to thank the following individuals, institutions and companies for permission to reproduce copyright illustrations in this book: AKG London, pages 36, 53; AP, page 264; © Bettmann/Corbis, pages 60, 92, 111, 118, 162, 166, 168, 173, 182, 183, 191, 225, 231, 273, 285, 287, 291, 293, 302; © Brown Brothers, page 100; IHCi-01816, The Trojan Horse at our Gate by Carey Orr, ChicagoTribune, September 17th, 1935/Chicago Historical Society, page 130 right; © Corbis, pages 26, 28; © Edward Sorrel, page 305; © Hulton Archive, pages 81, 98; Blank Archives/Hulton Archive, page 308; New York Times Co./Carl T. Gossett Jr/Hulton Archive, page 251; Illustrated London News, pages 49 and 50; © Depardon Raymond/Magnum Photos, page 267; Mary Evans Picture Library, page 52 bottom; Peter Newark's Military Pictures, page 52 top; Popperfoto, page 110; © Punch Ltd, pages 130 left, 155 bottom; © May 20th 1936, The Washington Post. Reprinted with permission, page 131.

The publishers would also like to thank the following for permission to reproduce material in this book: Faber and Faber Ltd for extracts from *Kennedy v Khrushchev* by Beschloss, Faber and Faber, 1991; Oxford University Press for the extracts from *Freedom from Fear* by David M. Kennedy, Oxford University Press, 1999 and *American Diplomacy in the Twentieth Century* by R.D. Schulzinger, Oxford University Press, 1994; extracts from Ashton's *In Search of Détente*, 1992, Macmillan, reproduced with permission of Palgrave; extracts from M. Dockrill's *The Cold War*, 1993, Macmillan, reproduced with permission of Palgrave; Pearson Education for the extracts from *A Noble Cause?* By G. DeGroot, Longman, 2000 and *The Origins of the Korean War* by P. Lowe, Longman, 1997; the extracts from *The Impending Crisis 1848-1861* by David Potter, Harper and Row, 1976, reprinted by permission of Pearson Education, Inc.; extract from *Bearing the Cross* by David Garrow published by Jonathan Cape. Used by permission of The Random House Group Limited; Routledge for extracts from *Franklin Rossevelt: The New Deal and War* by Michael Heale, Routledge, 1999; Simon & Schuster for the extract from *Eisenhower: Soldier and President* by Stephen E. Ambrose, Touchstone, 1991.

Every effort has been made to trace and acknowledge ownership of copyright. The publishers will be glad to make suitable arrangements with any copyright holders whom it has not been possible to contact.

Orders: please contact Bookpoint Ltd, 130 Milton Park, Abingdon, Oxon OX14 4SB. Telephone: (44) 01235 827720. Fax: (44) 01235 400454. Lines are open 9.00–6.00, Monday to Saturday, with a 24 hour message answering service. Email address: orders@bookpoint.co.uk

British Library Cataloguing in Publication Data
A catalogue record for this title is available from the British Library

ISBN 0 340 803266

First Published 2002
Impression number   10 9 8 7 6 5 4 3 2 1
Year   2007 2006 2005 2004 2003 2002

Copyright © 2002 Alan Farmer and Vivienne Sanders

Typeset, illustrated and edited by Hardlines, Charlbury, Oxford.
Printed in Great Britain for Hodder & Stoughton Educational, a division of Hodder Headline Plc, 338 Euston Road, London NW1 3BH by Martins The Printers, Berwick upon Tweed.

CONTENTS

List of Figures

List of Profiles

List of Tables

PREFACE

Access to History Context

Structure

In some ways *Access to History: Context* volumes are similar to most textbooks. They are divided into chapters, each of which is focused on a specific topic. In turn, chapters are divided into sections which have self-explanatory headings. As is the case with most textbooks, *Context* authors have organised the chapters in a logical sequence so that, if you start at the beginning of the book and work your way through to the end, everything will make sense. However, because many readers 'dip' into textbooks rather than reading them from beginning to end, care has been taken to make sure that whichever chapter you start with you should not find yourself feeling lost.

Special Features in the Main Text

Points to Consider – at the start of each chapter this shaded box provides you with vital information about how the chapter is organised and how the various issues covered relate to each other.

   Issues boxes are a standard feature of each chapter and, like Points to Consider boxes, are designed to help you extract the maximum benefit from the work you do. They appear in the margin immediately following most numbered section headings. The question(s) contained in each issues box will tell you which historical issue(s) the section is primarily going to cover. If the section you intend to start with has no issues box, turn back page by page until you find one. This will contain the questions the author is considering from that point onwards, including the section you are about to read.

   Boxed sections appear in both the margin and the main column of text. In each of the boxes you will find a self-explanatory heading which will make it clear what the contents of the box are about. Very often, the contents of boxes are explanations of words or phrases, or descriptions of events or situations. When you are reading a chapter for the first time you might make a conscious decision to pay little attention to boxed entries so that you can concentrate your attention on the author's main message.

   Q-boxes appear in the margin and contain one or more questions about the item they appear alongside. These questions are intended to stimulate you to think about some aspect of the material the box is linked to. The most useful answers to these questions will often emerge during discussions with other students.

   Activities boxes – as a general rule, the contents of activities boxes are more complex than the questions in Q-boxes, and often require you to undertake a significant amount of work, either on your own or with others. One reason for completing the task(s) is to consolidate what you have already learned or to extend the range or depth of your understanding.

Profiles – most of these are about named individuals who are central to an understanding of the topic under consideration: some are about events of particular importance. Each Profile contains a similar range of material. The two aspects you are likely to find most useful are:

▼ the dated timeline down the side of the page; and

▼ the source extracts, which provide you with ideas on what made the subject of the Profile especially notable or highly controversial

Profiles also provide useful points of focus during the revision process.

End-of-chapter Sections

The final pages of each chapter contain different sections. It is always worthwhile looking at the **Summary Chart** or **Summary Diagram** first. As their names suggest, these are designed to provide you with a brief and carefully structured overview of the topic covered by the chapter. The important thing for you to do is to check that you understand the way it is structured and how the topics covered inter relate with one another.

The **Working on...** section should be studied in detail once you have finished your first reading of the main text of the chapter. Assuming that you read the Points to Consider section when you began work on the chapter, and that you followed any advice given in it when you read the chapter for the first time, the Working on... section is designed to suggest what form any further work you do on the chapter should take.

The **Answering extended writing and essay questions on...** sections, taken as a whole throughout the book, form a coherent body of guidance on how to tackle these types of examination questions successfully.

The same is true of the **Answering source-based questions on...** sections which have been carefully planned bearing in mind the ways you need to build on the skills you have already developed in this area. You may find these sections particularly helpful during the time you are preparing for an exam.

The last part of each chapter contains a **Further Reading** section. These are of vital importance to you in chapters covering topics you are expected to know about in some detail. To do well in any History course it is essential to read more than one book. However, it is possible to find individual books which can act as your guide and companion throughout your studies, and this is one of them. One of the major ways in which it fulfils this function is by providing you with detailed guidance on the way you can make the most effective use of your limited time in reading more widely.

This book is an integral part of the *Access to History* series. One of its functions is to act as a link between the various topic books in the series on the period it covers, by drawing explicit attention in the Further Reading sections to where, within the series, other material exists which can be used to broaden and deepen your knowledge and understanding. Attention is also drawn to the non-*Access to History* publications which you are likely to find most useful. By using material which has been written based on the same aims and objectives, you are likely to find yourself consistently building up the key skills and abilities needed for success on your course.

Revision

Context books have been planned to be directly helpful to you during the revision period. One of the first things many students do when starting to revise a topic for an examination is to make a list of the 'facts' they need to know about. A safer way of doing this (because it covers the possibility that you missed something important when you originally worked on the topic) is to compile your lists from a book you can rely on. *Context* volumes aim to be reliable in this sense. If you work through the chapter which covers the topic you are about to revise and list the events contained in marginal 'events lists' and in boxed lists of events, you can be confident that you have identified every fact of real significance that you need to know about on the topic. However, you also need to make a list of the historical issues you might be asked to write about. You can do this most conveniently by working through the relevant chapter and noting down the contents of the 'issues boxes'.

For almost everybody, important parts of the revision process are the planning of answers to all the main types of structured and essay questions, and the answering of typical questions (both those requiring extended writing and those based on source material) under exam conditions. The best way to make full use of what this book has to offer in these respects is to work through the two relevant sets of end-of-chapter sections (Answering extended writing and essay questions on… and Answering source-based questions on…) in a methodical manner.

Keith Randell

THE CAUSES OF THE AMERICAN CIVIL WAR

CHAPTER *1*

POINTS TO CONSIDER

This chapter has two main objectives: to examine the 'peculiar institution' of slavery; and to see how slavery helped cause the American Civil War. Two issues are worth keeping in mind as you read the chapter: a) was the war 'irrepressible'? b) who was most responsible for the war?

1 Introduction

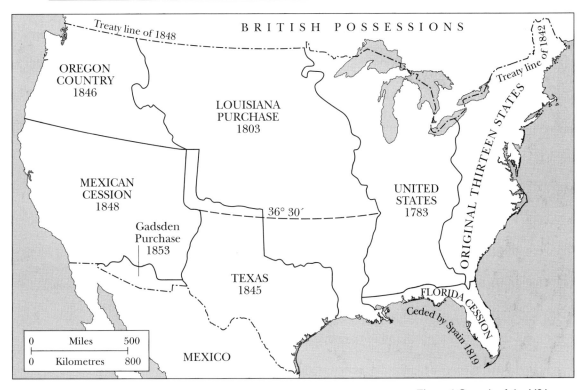

Figure 1 Growth of the USA, 1783–1854.

Before 1861 the history of the USA had been a remarkable success story. The English settlements of the early seventeenth century had grown rapidly, so much so that by 1783 they had been able to win independence. By 1850 the USA extended from the Atlantic to the Pacific and white Americans enjoyed the highest standard of living on earth. The USA's political system was the envy of European radicals. However, not everyone benefited from the 'great experiment', not least Native Americans (who lost much of their land) and African Americans (most of whom were slaves).

a) The American Political System

Slate Rights

The 1787 Constitution had created a system whereby power was divided between the central (or federal) government and individual states. The federal government had executive, legislative and judicial branches, each of which was able to check the actions of the others. State governments tended to replicate the federal government: each had its own governor, its own legislative body, and its own Supreme Court.

Figure 2 The Constitution.

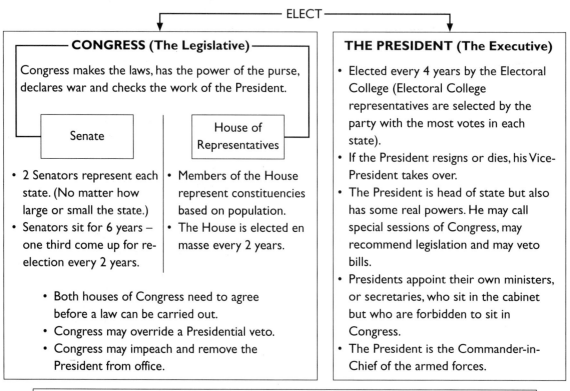

THE AMERICAN PEOPLE

——————— ELECT ———————

CONGRESS (The Legislative)

Congress makes the laws, has the power of the purse, declares war and checks the work of the President.

| Senate | House of Representatives |

- 2 Senators represent each state. (No matter how large or small the state.)
- Senators sit for 6 years – one third come up for re-election every 2 years.

- Members of the House represent constituencies based on population.
- The House is elected en masse every 2 years.

- Both houses of Congress need to agree before a law can be carried out.
- Congress may override a Presidential veto.
- Congress may impeach and remove the President from office.

THE PRESIDENT (The Executive)

- Elected every 4 years by the Electoral College (Electoral College representatives are selected by the party with the most votes in each state).
- If the President resigns or dies, his Vice-President takes over.
- The President is head of state but also has some real powers. He may call special sessions of Congress, may recommend legislation and may veto bills.
- Presidents appoint their own ministers, or secretaries, who sit in the cabinet but who are forbidden to sit in Congress.
- The President is the Commander-in-Chief of the armed forces.

THE SUPREME COURT (The Judiciary)

- This is the highest court. It approves the laws and decides whether they are Constitutional.
- The (usually 9) Supreme Court judges are appointed by the President.
- The Senate ratifies the President's appointments.

By the 1820s almost all white males had the right to vote. The rise of democracy is often associated with President Andrew Jackson (1829–37), a successful soldier, politician and slave-holding landowner who claimed to represent the common man against the interests of privilege. But Jackson benefited from, rather than created, the democratic tide. While there were limits to that tide – women and most blacks, for example, could not vote – the USA was far more democratic than Britain. By the mid-nineteenth century there were two main political parties – the Democrats and the Whigs. The Democrats believed that most issues should be decided at state level. The Whigs, by contrast, favoured federal government intervention. However, neither party was particularly united nor coherent. Each was really an assortment of state parties which only came together every four years to nominate a presidential candidate and devise a set of policies – a platform. Although there was huge interest in politics, government had a limited impact on the lives of most Americans. The Constitution's 'checks and balances' system ensured that there was little likelihood that one party would control the presidency, the Senate, the House of Representatives and the Supreme Court at the same time. It was thus difficult for the federal government to do very much. State governments' actions impinged more on people's lives than those of the federal government.

b) 'A People of Plenty'

In the period 1800–50 the USA's gross national product increased seven fold, and per capita income doubled. Thanks to a high birth rate and immigration from Europe, the population also grew rapidly. By 1860 it had reached 31 million. The population was young (in 1850 over half of all Americans were under 20) and mobile. In the 1840s Americans began crossing the great plains and the Rocky Mountains to settle on the Pacific coast. Most Americans were farmers. Small family farms characterised agriculture, north and south, east and west.

Steamboats revolutionised travel on the USA's great rivers in the early nineteenth century. The country also developed an impressive canal system. However, by 1850 canals were facing competition from railways. By 1860 the USA had over 30,000 miles of track – more than the rest of the world combined. The improved transportation system and the growing food supply encouraged, and were encouraged by, industrialisation. America's industrial 'revolution' mirrored that of Britain. There were important developments in textiles, coal, and iron and steel. The growth of industry led to increased urbanisation. Fewer than one in ten Americans lived in towns (defined as a settlement with more than 2,500 people) in 1820: one in five did so by 1860.

A SOCIETY OF EQUALS?

In the 1830s a perceptive Frenchman, Alexander De Tocqueville, visited the USA and wrote a book recounting his experiences. What struck him was the fact that the country was far more equal than societies in Europe. He noted there was no 'feudal' hierarchy. Instead there were opportunities for men of talent to rise to the top. Historians today are suspicious of this early notion of the 'American dream'. Indians and blacks were far from equal. The nineteenth century also assigned unequal roles to men and women. Essentially seen as home-makers, women were denied the same social and political rights as men.

THE IMPORTANCE OF RELIGION

Mid-nineteenth century Americans were very religious. Most were Protestants – Baptists, Methodists, Presbyterians and Episcopalians. Protestant ministers preached a gospel of hard work, thrift and self-discipline. Worldly success was interpreted as a sign of God's favour. However, in the 1820s there was an upsurge in evangelical Protestantism known as the Second Great Awakening. Preachers fired up people to do battle against the sins of the world.

c) North v. South

Some historians have underplayed North–South differences, stressing instead the similarities between the two sections: the common language; the shared religion; the same legal, political and racial assumptions; the same history. However, other historians believe that there were deep divisions between North and South – divisions which helped bring about war. 'Progressive' historians once claimed that the Civil War was a conflict between an agrarian, planter-dominated South and a capitalist, industrialised, egalitarian North. This view is far too sweeping. There was not one but many 'Souths'. Long-established eastern states like Virginia were very different from new western states like Texas and the lower (or deep) South was different from the upper South. There were also many 'Norths'. Moreover, in many respects, those 'Norths' were not dissimilar economically to the 'Souths'. The North was industrialising, not industrialised. The North, particularly the North-west, was still overwhelmingly rural. Nor was the South economically backward. By the mid-nineteenth century cotton sales made up over half of the USA's total exports. Cotton ensured that Southern society was prosperous and enterprising. The planters (defined as those who owned 20 or more slaves), who made up under 5 per cent of the South's population, did own the major portion of its wealth and did exert political power and social influence. But the same was true of Northern industrialists, bankers and merchants.

Even so, there were economic and social differences between North and South. The North was more industrial. The South, with 35 per cent of the population, produced only 10 per cent of the nation's manufactured goods in the 1850s. The North had twice as much railway track as the South. Only one Southerner in 14 was a town dweller, compared with one in four Northerners. The two sections had different economic interests. The tariff was a source of constant grievance to most Southerners, who argued it benefited Northern industrialists at the expense of Southern farmers. The South felt exploited in other ways. Southerners depended upon Northern credit to finance the growing of cotton, tobacco and sugar: they relied upon Northerners to market these goods; and they were reliant on Northern ships to transport them. Some Southerners, fearing that their section could become little more than a colonial region of the North, stressed the need for the Southern economy to diversify. But most Southerners continued to put their capital into the production of cotton. Many had no wish to industrialise and urbanise.

Between 1830 and 1860 most of the 5 million immigrants to the USA settled in the North. Thus, one in six Northerners in 1860 was foreign-born compared with one in 30 Southerners. There were other differences. Northerners were better educated than Southerners and more responsive to new ideas. While Northerners espoused reform, Southerners tended to condemn all radical 'isms', viewing them as a threat to old values. Historian Wyatt Brown has claimed that Southerners were more concerned about their personal, family, community and sectional honour than Northerners. But the main difference between the two sections and the main reason for the growth of sectionalism was the South's 'peculiar institution' – slavery.

2 The Peculiar Institution

ISSUE:
How benign and profitable was slavery?

The settlement of America was an African as well as a European enterprise. Virtually all the Africans who 'settled' in the seventeenth and eighteenth centuries came as slaves. By 1808, when the African slave trade was declared illegal, there were over a million slaves in the USA. Slavery divided Americans. It continues to divide historians.

a) Slavery pre-1830

In 1776 slavery existed in all the 13 colonies. However, it was of major importance only in the South. In the last decades of the eighteenth century radical Protestants condemned slavery as a moral evil. Others thought it was inconsistent with enlightened ideas which stressed liberty, equality and free enterprise. Northern states abolished slavery, some at a stroke, others gradually. Even some Southerners regarded slavery as an evil (albeit necessary). But 'King Cotton' ensured that slavery survived and throve. In 1790 only 9,000 bales of cotton were produced in the USA. In 1793 Eli Whitney invented the 'gin' which enabled short-fibre cotton to be quickly separated from its seed. Suddenly it became highly profitable to grow cotton and Southern farmers cashed in. By the 1830s the South was producing 2 million bales per year. Cotton production needed a large amount of unskilled labour. Slave labour was ideal.

b) The Abolitionists

Most abolitionists in the first three decades of the nineteenth century supported gradual emancipation, with financial compensation for the slave owners. They also believed that freed slaves should be encouraged to return to Africa. In 1822 the USA purchased Liberia on the west coast of Africa, as a base for returning ex-slaves. However, this policy had little success. Most African Americans regarded themselves as Americans: they had no wish to move to Liberia.

In the early 1830s a new, more strident abolitionist movement developed. This was associated with William Lloyd Garrison. Convinced that slavery was a sin, Garrison rejected the notion of gradual emancipation and demanded (without any notion of how it should be done) immediate abolition. In 1833 a militant National Anti-Slavery Society was established. By 1838 it had nearly 250,000 members and churned out a mass of anti-slavery literature. Many of the leading abolitionists were evangelical Protestants. Most were well-educated. Women played a crucial role. So too did free blacks.

The extent of abolitionists' success must not be exaggerated. The movement had only limited appeal in the North. De Tocqueville wrote: 'The prejudice of race appears to be stronger in the states that have abolished slavery than in those where it still exists'. Many Northerners, fearing a northern exodus of liberated slaves and fearful of the effect that the new crusade would have in the South, hated the abolitionists. Failing to win the support of either the Whig or Democrat Party, abolitionists set up their own Liberty Party. In 1840 its candidate received only 7,000 votes. Not all abolitionists supported the Liberty Party's creation. Nor could abolitionists agree about what strategy to adopt. A plethora of different views resulted in a major schism in the Anti-Slavery Society in 1840.

The abolitionists had no success whatsoever in winning white support in the South. They were not helped by the fact that in 1831 Nat Turner led a slave revolt in which 55 whites were killed. This revolt appalled Southerners who blamed abolitionists for inciting trouble. Abolitionist literature was banned from most Southern states. Abolitionist sympathisers were driven out. Many states placed new restrictions on slaves and there was less talk of the possibility of gradual freedom. Indeed abolitionist attacks goaded Southerners to extol the virtues of their peculiar institution. Nevertheless, if the abolitionists did little in the short term to help the slaves, they did a great deal to polarise opinion. They stirred the consciences of a growing number of Northerners and kept slavery in the forefront of public attention.

c) The Nature of the Peculiar Institution

In 1860 there were nearly 4 million slaves, concentrated mainly in the lower South. By 1860 one in four Southern families owned slaves. Fifty per cent of slave owners owned no more than five slaves. But over 50 per cent of slaves lived on plantations with over 20 slaves. Thus the 'typical' slaveholder did not own the 'typical' slave. Most slaves were held by about 10,000 families. Fifty-five per cent worked in cotton production, 10 per cent in tobacco and 10 per cent in sugar, rice and hemp, while 15 per cent were domestic servants. About 10 per cent lived in towns or worked in industry.

Over the last two centuries there have been major debates about the extent to which Southern slavery was a system of ruthless exploitation. In the early twentieth century Southern historian Ulrich Phillips argued that most slaves were content with their lot. Relationships between slaves and their owners were marked, he thought, by 'gentleness, kind-hearted friendship and mutual loyalty'. In the 1950s Kenneth Stampp claimed that slavery was harsh and he saw little in the way of good relationships between owner and owned. In 1974 Fogel and Engerman, having fed a vast amount of source material into computers, came up with conclusions similar to those of Phillips. In their view, slaves were controlled with minimal force and enjoyed a standard of living comparable to that of Northern industrial workers. The response of historians to Fogel and Engerman's methods and findings was overwhelmingly critical.

In Stampp's view, 'The only generalisation that can be made with relative confidence is that some masters were harsh and frugal; others were mild and generous and the rest ran the whole gamut in between'. Slaves who worked in the rice growing areas of the deep South probably endured the worst conditions. Household servants usually had an easier life than field hands.

FREE BLACKS IN THE SOUTH

By 1860 there were 250,000 free blacks in the South. A high percentage were mulattos, who had been given their freedom by their white fathers.

FREE BLACKS IN THE NORTH

Some 200,000 blacks lived in the North. They suffered from discrimination. Only three states allowed blacks to vote on terms of complete parity with whites in 1860.

Slavery: The Benign View

▼ Slaves did not work harder than most free Americans.

▼ Floggings were rare, if only because slave owners had a vested interest in the care of their property. The evidence suggests that there were few brutal owners and relatively little sexual exploitation. Most whites were restrained in their treatment of slaves by Christian morality and by their own standards of decency.

▼ Most owners preferred the carrot as a source of motivation to the stick. Slaves who worked hard were given extra holidays and more clothing and food.

▼ Given the standards of the day, slaves were reasonably well fed, clothed and housed.

▼ The slave family was the basic unit of social organisation. Slaves usually chose their own partners. Slaves were often traded so that a couple who were fond of each other could live together.

▼ The fact that there was no major slave revolt (apart from Nat Turner's in 1831) suggests that slave conditions were not so bad.

▼ Only a few hundred slaves a year made serious attempts to escape to freedom in the North or in Canada.

▼ Some slaves were granted, or made enough money to buy, their freedom.

Slavery: The Harsh View

▼ Slaves could be sold, punished, sexually exploited, and even killed by their owners.

▼ Firm discipline seems to have been the norm. On plantations, slaves worked in gangs supervised by a black driver and a white overseer, both of whom used the whip if workers fell behind the pace. 'Uppity' slaves were often flogged or branded.

▼ Slaves usually worked longer hours than free Americans.

▼ The slave family unit was far from sacrosanct. Possibly a quarter of slave marriages were broken by forced separation.

▼ By the 1850s few slaves were granted freedom.

▼ The fact that there was no major revolt is not proof that slaves were content with their lot. It is testimony to their realism. A slave revolt was impossible to organise. A minority in most Southern states, slaves were not allowed to own fire-arms or to congregate in large groups. A slave uprising at any time, even during the Civil War, would have been tantamount to mass suicide.

▼ It was difficult for slaves to escape from slavery. Most fugitives were caught and severely punished.

▼ The evidence suggests that most slaves hated slavery. Whenever they had the opportunity of freedom during the Civil War most took it.

---

d) Was Slavery Profitable?

In 1857 a Southerner, Hilton Rowan Helper, published an influential book, *The Impending Crisis of the South*, in which he argued that slavery was responsible for the South's economic decline. 'Slavery, and nothing but slavery', said Helper, 'has retarded the progress and prosperity of our portion of the Union; depopulated and impoverished our cities by forcing the more industrious and enterprising natives of the soil to emigrate to the free states; brought our domain under a sparse and inert population by preventing foreign immigration; made us tributary to the North'. Some historians have followed Helper's line and seen slavery as an economic burden. But most, including Stampp, Fogel and Engerman, argue that slavery was an efficient form of economic organisation which boosted the Southern economy. Given that slave prices doubled in the 1850s, investors in slaves received returns similar to those who invested in industry. The fact that the South lagged behind the North in industrial development can be seen as a sign of its economic health. It was making so much money from cotton it had no incentive to industrialise.

Some historians have argued that once cotton prices fell – as surely they must – then slavery would have died of its own accord: the blood-letting of the Civil War was thus unnecessary. There is little evidence to support this view. In 1860 slavery was flourishing in most parts of the South. There was still a world-wide demand for cotton. Moreover, slavery was not just an economic institution. It was also a system of racial control. It kept blacks in their place. Even poor whites felt they had an interest in preserving slavery: it kept them off the bottom of the social heap. Southerners feared that an end to slavery would result in race war. Thus slave owners and non-slave owners were committed to the peculiar institution: so committed that (ultimately) they were prepared to wage a terrible war in an effort to maintain it. Given this commitment, it is difficult to see how slavery would have withered away without the Civil War.

3 The Impact of the Mexican War

a) The Problem of Western Expansion

As new states applied to join the Union, the key issue was whether they would they be free or slave. The first serious crisis occurred in 1819 when Missouri applied to join the Union as a slave state. Given that this would tilt the balance against them, Northern states opposed Missouri's admittance. The result was a series of furious debates between Southern and Northern Congressmen. In the end, a compromise was worked out. To balance Missouri's admittance, a new free state of Maine was created. It was also agreed, henceforward, that there should be no slavery in the Louisiana Territory, north of latitude 36°30´. South of that line, slavery could exist.

The next problem came in Texas. Americans had settled in Texas, then part of Mexico, from the 1820s. Most were Southerners and many had taken their slaves with them. In 1836 Texas won independence from Mexico. While most Texans hoped to join the USA, many Northerners were opposed to annexation, fearing that this would lead to the spread of slavery and strengthen Southern political power. Given that Texas was a political hot potato, President Jackson and his successor Van Buren shelved the issue. For a few years Texas was an independent republic. Then, in 1844, Democrat James Polk, a slaveholder from Tennessee, was elected president on a platform which promised the annexation of Texas. Outgoing Whig President Tyler, anxious to leave his mark on events, now secured a joint resolution of Congress in favour of the Texas annexation. The result was that Texas was admitted into the Union in 1845.

ACTIVITY

Consider the following question: Was there any truth in the Southern claim that slavery was both a benign and profitable institution?

You might decide slavery was not benign but was profitable, or not profitable but benign, or both benign and profitable or neither benign nor profitable! It is up to you to decide. The important thing is that you have good evidence to support your case.

ISSUE:
What were the main results of the Mexican War?

NEW STATES
In the late eighteenth century the USA devised a system for admitting new states. Areas first assumed territorial status. Once its population had reached 60,000, the territory could submit a proposed constitution to Congress and apply to become a state.

President Polk also had ambitions to annex the Mexican provinces of California and New Mexico. Americans were starting to settle in both areas and the Mexican population was small. In 1845 a Democrat journalist declared, 'it is our manifest destiny to overspread and to possess the whole of the continent which Providence has given us for the development of the great experiment of liberty and federated self-government entrusted to us'. Many Northern Whigs saw this rhetoric as a smoke screen aimed at concealing the evil intent of expanding slavery.

b) Mr Polk's War: 1846–8

The USA's annexation of Texas angered Mexico, which still claimed sovereignty over the state. The fact that there were disputed boundaries between Texas and Mexico was a further problem. Efforts to reach a negotiated agreement failed. Polk's aim was to provoke an incident that would result in war – a war which would lead to the annexation of California and New Mexico. In May 1846 Mexican troops duly ambushed a party of US troops in the disputed area and Polk asked Congress to declare war. Congress obliged. While most Southerners and Westerners fully supported the war, many Northerners saw it as a Southern war of aggression.

In the summer of 1846 US troops annexed New Mexico. They then set off on the long march to California. By the time they arrived American settlers had successfully proclaimed independence from Mexico. In 1847 General Zachary Taylor defeated the Mexicans at Buena Vista while General Winfield Scott captured Mexico City. By the Treaty of Guadalupe Hidalgo (1848) California and New Mexico were ceded to the USA.

c) The Wilmot Proviso

In 1846 David Wilmot, a Northern Democrat, proposed that slavery should be excluded from any territory gained from Mexico as a result of the war. Wilmot was not an abolitionist. Like many Northern Democrats, he resented the fact that Polk seemed to be pursuing a pro-Southern policy. In supporting the Proviso, Northern Democrats hoped to keep blacks out of the new territories and ensure that white settlers would not face competition from slave planters. After a bitter debate, the Proviso passed the House of Representatives. The voting was sectional: every Southern Democrat and all but two Southern Whigs voted against it. Most Northerners voted for it. Senator Toombs of Georgia warned that if Congress passed the Proviso, he would favour disunion rather than 'degradation'. Failing to pass the Senate, the Proviso did not become law.

THE NULLIFICATION CRISIS (1832)

In the late 1820s John C. Calhoun had developed the doctrine of nullification. This had proclaimed the right of any state to overrule any federal law deemed unconstitutional. The crisis over nullification came to a head in 1832 when South Carolina disallowed two tariff acts. President Jackson labelled this action treason and threatened to use force. South Carolina, failing to win support from other Southern states, pulled back from declaring secession.

Northerners believed that Congress had the power to exclude slavery from the territories and should exercise that power. Southerners responded aggressively to this threat, not least John Calhoun of South Carolina. In 1847 he issued a series of resolutions in which he claimed that citizens from every state had the right to take their 'property' to any territory. Congress, he asserted, had no authority to place restrictions on slavery in the territories. If the Northern majority continued to ride roughshod over the rights of the Southern minority, the Southern states would have little option but to secede.

d) The Search for Compromise

Moderate politicians, aware that the problem of slavery expansion threatened to destroy the Union, tried to find a compromise. The most successful idea was the notion of popular sovereignty, associated with two Midwestern Democrat Senators Cass and Douglas. They held that it was not Congress which should decide on whether a territory should allow slaves. That decision should be made instead by the people in the territory. While most Democrats supported popular sovereignty, they did not agree on when exactly a territory should decide on slavery. Northern Democrats saw the decision being made early – as soon as the first territorial assembly met. Southern Democrats saw the decision being made late – near the end of the territorial phase when settlers were seeking admission to the Union. In the interim, they envisaged that slavery would be recognised and protected. Many Americans were opposed to the concept of popular sovereignty. Some Southerners thought they had the right to take their 'property' anywhere. Some Northerners believed that slavery should not be allowed to expand under any circumstances, not even if a majority of settlers wished it to expand.

e) The 1848 Election

The Democrats, rallying around Senator Cass of Michigan, supported popular sovereignty. The Whigs chose Mexican War hero Zachary Taylor, a Southern slave owner, as their candidate. Most Northern Whigs were prepared to endorse him because he seemed a likely winner. To avoid a major split between North and South, the Whigs had no platform on slavery expansion. A new party, the Free Soil Party, which included Northern Democrats who disliked Cass, 'Conscience' Whigs who disliked Taylor, and abolitionists, supported the Wilmot Proviso and nominated former President Van Buren as its presidential candidate. Taylor triumphed, winning 1,360,000 popular votes and 163 electoral college votes. Cass won 1,220,000

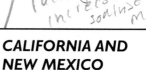

South

North

Political dominance, bearing in mind that gold could increase the south's economic might

votes and 127 electoral college votes. Van Buren won 291,000 votes but no electoral college votes.

f) President Taylor

Taylor was judged by many contemporaries (and by most historians) as a political amateur who was prone to over-simplify complex problems. Although he was a slave owner, he was determined to act in a way that benefited the national interest. His solution to the problem of California and New Mexico was to encourage settlers in both areas to frame constitutions and apply immediately for admission to the Union, without going through the process of setting up territorial governments. In 1849 California duly ratified a constitution prohibiting slavery and applied for admission. Taylor was also prepared to admit New Mexico, even though it did not have enough people to apply for statehood. There was a further problem: New Mexico had a boundary dispute with Texas. Southerners supported Texas's claim: Northerners – and Taylor – supported New Mexico. A clash between the state forces of Texas and the US army suddenly seemed imminent.

Taylor's actions incensed Southerners, Democrats and Whigs alike. There was talk of secession. In October 1849 Mississippi issued a call to all slave states to send representatives to a convention to meet at **Nashville** in 1850. The convention would aim to adopt 'some mode of resistance to Northern aggression'. Bitter sectional divisions were reflected in Congress which met in December 1849. As well as fierce debates over slavery expansion, Southerners also raised the issue of fugitive slaves, claiming that many free states were flouting the law and frustrating slaveholders' efforts to catch runaways.

THE NASHVILLE CONVENTION
In June 1850 delegates from nine of the 15 slave states met at Nashville. The convention displayed little enthusiasm for secession.

g) The 1850 Compromise

Taylor was determined to make no concessions to the South. Talk of secession did not worry him. He was prepared to call (what he saw as) the Southern bluff. But some politicians, including Whig elder statesman Henry Clay, were worried by events and felt that the South had to be placated. In January 1850 Clay offered the Senate a set of resolutions as a basis for a compromise:
▼ California was to be admitted as a free state.
▼ Utah and New Mexico were to be organised as territories without any mention of slavery.
▼ Slave-trading should end in Washington, DC
▼ A more stringent **Fugitive Slave Act** was intended to placate the South.
▼ Texas should surrender the disputed land to New Mexico. In return Congress would assume the $10 million debt which Texas still owed.

THE FUGITIVE SLAVE ACT (1850)
Abolitionists were outraged by the Fugitive Slave Act. Efforts to catch fugitive slaves inflamed feelings further.

The next few months were marked by a series of epic speeches as Clay's proposals, rolled into a single bill, were debated in Congress.

In July 1850 Taylor, who opposed Clay's measure, died. Vice-President Fillmore, a Northern Whig who was sympathetic to the South, became President. Although he supported Clay's bill, he could not prevent it being defeated. Most Northern Congressmen, anxious to escape the charge of bargaining with the 'Slave Power', voted against it. Senator Stephen Douglas now displayed his political skill. Stripping Clay's bill down to its component parts, he submitted each part separately. Southerners voted for those proposals they liked: Northerners did likewise. Moderates, like Douglas himself, swung the balance. By September all the bits of the Compromise had been passed. Douglas and other political leaders hailed the Compromise as a settlement of the issues that threatened to divide the nation. The two years that remained of Fillmore's administration were a period of relative calm. However, some historians have questioned whether the 1850 Compromise was a success or whether it was even a compromise! David Potter thought it was really an 'armistice'. It certainly did not settle the controversy over the status of slavery in the territories.

h) The 1852 Presidential Election

The Democrats chose Franklin Pierce as their presidential candidate. Although he was a Northerner, he was sympathetic to the South. The Democrats campaigned on a platform supporting the 1850 Compromise and popular sovereignty. The Whig Party was divided North against South, both in terms of agreeing to a platform and in terms of choosing a candidate. While most Northerners supported Mexican War hero General Scott (a Southerner), most Southerners hoped to retain Fillmore (a Northerner)! Scott was finally nominated on the 53rd ballot. Although they managed to agree on a leader, the Whigs could not agree on policies. Thus the Whig platform said virtually nothing. The election was a triumph for Pierce who won 1,601,274 votes and carried 27 states. Scott won 1,386,580 votes but carried only four states.

> ### THE IMPACT OF 'UNCLE TOM'S CABIN'
> In 1852 Harriet Beecher Stowe published *Uncle Tom's Cabin*. The novel – a fierce attack on slavery – was a great success, selling over 2 million copies in America over the next ten years. The book helped arouse Northern sympathy for slaves.

> **USA: 1820–50**
>
> **1820** Missouri Compromise;
> **1845** USA annexed Texas;
> **1846** Start of Mexican War (May);
> Wilmot Proviso (August);
> **1848** Treaty of Guadalupe Hidalgo;
> **1850** Compromise.

4 The Rise of the Republican Party

> **ISSUE:**
> Why did the Republican Party emerge as the main challenger to the Democrats?

From the 1830s to the early 1850s US politics had been dominated by the Whigs and Democrats. These parties drew upon national, not sectional, support. The so-called second party system helped contain sectionalism. As long as men placed loyalty to party ahead of sectional loyalty neither North nor South could easily be united one

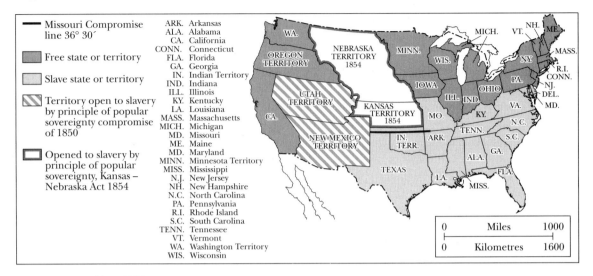

Figure 3 The USA in 1854.

against the other. But in the mid-1850s the second party system collapsed. Northern voters lost faith in the ability of the old parties to tackle the key issues of the day. Two new parties – the Republicans and Know Nothings – appeared, destroying the Whig Party and then stepping into the vacuum left by its demise. Until 1856 it was far from clear which party would dominate the Northern political scene.

a) The Problem of Kansas–Nebraska

Nebraska, part of the Louisiana Purchase, was still unsettled in the early 1850s. Until Congress organised the area into a territory, land could not be put up for sale. While Northerners were keen to see Nebraska developed, Southerners were less enthusiastic. Nebraska lay north of latitude 36°30´. According to the 1820 Missouri Compromise, new states in the area would enter the Union as free states. In January 1854 Stephen Douglas introduced the Kansas–Nebraska bill into Congress. Douglas, architect of the 1850 Compromise, was a man of talent and ambition. He knew that to get a Nebraska bill enacted he needed the support of some Southern senators. They made it clear to Douglas that if he wanted Nebraska organised, his bill must specifically repeal the Missouri Compromise. Douglas accepted this. He also agreed to divide the Nebraska territory into two: Kansas in the south and Nebraska in the north. It was unlikely that slavery would take hold in Nebraska. But there was a possibility that it might spread to Kansas.

Douglas saw no problem in letting the people of Kansas–Nebraska decide their own fate. He was confident that they would not vote for slavery. A supporter of manifest destiny, he did not want the settle-

ment of the West – and the building of a trans-continental railway –
to be stalled by sectional controversy. He hoped that Democrats
would rally behind the idea of popular sovereignty and did not
believe that his bill would heighten sectional tension. This was a serious miscalculation. Douglas's bill, proof to many Northerners that
the Slave Power was still at work, created a 'hell of a storm' in the
North. The ferocity of Northern attacks led to a Southern counter-
attack. Passage of the bill suddenly became a symbol of Southern
honour. President Pierce agreed to make it a test of party loyalty, thus
ensuring that some Northern Democrats would support the measure.
After months of bitter debate, the bill passed both Houses of
Congress, becoming law in May 1854. It had sectionalised Congress:
90 per cent of Southerners voted for it; 64 per cent of Northerners
voted against it. By failing to predict the extent of Northern outrage,
Douglas had weakened his party, damaged his own presidential ambitions and revived North–South rivalry.

b) The Collapse of the Second Party System

In the 1854 elections the Democrats lost all but 23 of their (previously 91) free state seats in Congress. Before 1854 the Whigs would
have benefited. By 1854, however, the Whig Party was no longer a
serious force in many free states. The collapse of the Whig Party has
usually been seen as the direct result of the crisis resulting from the
Kansas–Nebraska Act which set Southern against Northern Whigs.
However, the Whig decline began in several free states in 1853 –
before the Kansas–Nebraska debates. The main problem confronting
Northern politicians at local level in the early 1850s was not slavery
but the issue of immigration.

Between 1845 and 1854 some 3 million immigrants entered the
USA. Over 1 million of these were Irish Catholics. German Catholics
ran the Irish a close second. Fear of a papal plot to subvert and control the USA was deep-rooted among Protestants. Mass immigration
also had unpleasant social and economic consequences. Irish immigrants provided a source of cheap labour, pulling down wage levels.
They were also associated with increased crime and welfare costs.
Given that most Irish and Germans voted Democrat, that party was
unlikely to support anti-immigrant measures. But the Whig Party also
failed to respond to the wishes of nativist voters. Indeed, some Whig
leaders thought the party ought to go out of its way to try to capture
the immigrant vote. Frustrated Northerners began to look to new
parties to represent their views.

c) The Know Nothings and Republicans

As concern about immigration grew, the Know Nothing movement mushroomed. Know Nothing members pledged to vote for no one except native-born Protestants. When asked questions about the order, they were supposed to reply, 'I know nothing', thereby giving the movement its name. The Know Nothing order first entered politics by throwing its support behind suitable candidates from the existing parties. It had so much success that by 1854 it took on the characteristics of a political party. Most Know Nothings wanted checks on immigration and a 21-year probationary period before immigrants could become full American citizens. Northerners joined the movement for a variety of other reasons. Most supported its anti-Catholic stance. Some approved of the fact that it was anti-establishment and promised to return power to the people. The unpopularity of the Kansas–Nebraska Act, associated with the Democrats, also helped the Know Nothings. So many ex-Whigs joined the order that leading Democrats initially thought it was an arm of the Whig Party. But they soon discovered that their own supporters were streaming into Know Nothing lodges as well. By 1854 the order had over a million members and began to wield real political power. In 1854–5 it won control of several Northern states. The order now called itself the American Party.

The Northern electorate was not just concerned with immigration. The Kansas–Nebraska Act awakened the spectre of the Slave Power and many Northerners were keen to give support to parties opposed to slavery expansion. In 1854 a number of anti-slavery coalitions were formed, under a variety of names. It was the Republican name which caught on. By late 1854 it was not clear whether the Know Nothings or Republicans would pick up the tattered Whig mantle in the North. In most Northern states the two parties were not necessarily in competition: indeed they often tried to avoid a contest in order to defeat the Democrats. Many Northerners hated both Catholicism and the Slave Power. Given the Democrat reverses in the North in 1854, it was clear that there would be an anti-Democrat majority in the 1855–6 Congress. But whether the anti-Democrats were more concerned with immigration or slavery expansion remained to be seen. At this stage many Republicans were Know Nothings and vice versa. For those 'pure' Republicans who were opposed to nativism, the 1854 elections were a major setback. Know Nothing strength seemed to block the establishment of a powerful Republican Party.

d) The Situation in Kansas: 1854–6

Northerners thought that if slavery expanded into Kansas it might expand anywhere. Southerners feared that a free Kansas would be another nail in the slavery coffin. In the Senate Seward threw down the gauntlet to the South: 'We will engage in competition for the virgin soil of Kansas and God give the victory to the side which is stronger in numbers as it is in right'. Senator Atchison of Missouri took up the challenge. 'We are playing for a mighty stake; if we win we carry slavery to the Pacific Ocean; if we fail, we lose Missouri, Arkansas and Texas and all the territories; the game must be played boldly.' A Massachusetts Emigrant Aid Company, set up to encourage Northerners to settle in Kansas, sponsored over 1,500 settlers in 1854–5. However, pro-slavers seemed to be in the strongest position, given the proximity of Kansas to Missouri.

In 1855 Kansas elected its first territorial legislature. Hundreds of pro-slavery Missourians crossed into Kansas to vote and then returned home. This ensured that the legislature which met at Lecompton was dominated by pro-slavers: so much so that the free state candidates were expelled or resigned. The legislature passed a series of tough pro-slavery laws. (It became a capital offence, for example, to give aid to a fugitive slave.) This aroused the anger of Northern public opinion. Meanwhile, 'free state' settlers, denying the validity of the Lecompton legislature, set up their own government at Topeka.

In May 1856 a pro-slavery posse 'sacked' Lawrence, a free-state centre, burning some buildings. This event, blown up out of all proportion by Northern journalists, sparked off more serious violence. The man largely responsible for this was John Brown, a fervent abolitionist. Brown and several of his sons murdered five pro-slavery settlers at Pottawotomie Creek. Northern newspapers, suppressing the facts, claimed that Brown had acted in righteous self-defence. Overnight, he became a Northern hero. In Kansas, his actions led to a worsening of the tension and a series of tit-for-tat killings. The Northern press, exaggerating the situation, described it as civil war. The events, and the distorted reporting of them, helped boost Republican fortunes. 'Bleeding Kansas' became a rallying cry for Northerners opposed to what they perceived to be the Slave Power at work.

e) The Political Situation: 1855–6

The American Party was the main anti-Democrat party in the free states in 1855. Its success spread to the slave states. In 1855 it carried Texas, Kentucky and Maryland and provided strong competition to the Democrats in other Southern states. (It was essentially the Whig Party under a new name.) Ironically this success in the South was to be a major reason for the American Party's undoing. The Know Nothings had won huge support in the North in 1854–5 because they were able to exploit both anti-slavery and nativist issues. However, the American Party, if it was to be a national party, had no option but to drop its anti-slavery position. By so doing, it lost Northern support. Other factors damaged the party. The decline of immigration in the mid-1850s led to a decline of nativism. The fact that Know Nothing-dominated state legislatures failed to make good their promises did not help the nativist cause: critics were able to claim that the Know Nothings did nothing. Events in Congress in 1855–6 also weakened the order. Nativists split North and South. After a great struggle, Banks, an ex-Know Nothing who was now a Republican, became speaker of the House. The speakership contest helped weld the Republicans into a more coherent party.

The Republican Party included abolitionists, ex-Whigs, ex-Democrats and ex-Know Nothings. Not surprisingly historians have different opinions about what the party stood for and why Northerners supported it. It is easier to say what it was against than what it was for. Obviously it was against the Democrat Party. It was also opposed to the Slave Power which was seen as conspiring to re-establish slavery in the North. Republican leaders were not consistent in defining exactly who was conspiring. Was it all or just some planters, all slaveholders or all Southerners? Albeit ambiguous (and mistaken!), the concept of a Slave Power conspiracy was an article of faith for all Republicans. Historians disagree about precisely what the Republican position was on slavery and how central that stand was to the party's appeal. Moral antipathy to slavery was certainly a moving force behind the party. But while almost all Republicans were opposed to slavery expansion, many did not support immediate abolition. They disliked the prospect of thousands of emancipated slaves pouring north and relatively few believed in black equality. Historian Eric Foner has claimed that the concept of 'free labour' lay at the heart of Republican ideology. Republicans, he thought, shared a desire to protect the free labour system by blocking the expansion of slavery. However, most Northern Democrats held similar views. It is thus difficult to claim that free labour was the cornerstone of Republican ideology. In the early twentieth century Charles Beard thought that the party represented the forces of capitalism and that its main concern was the promotion of industrialisation. Few now accept this thesis. Industrialisation does not seem to have been a major concern of most Republican voters in the 1850s, the majority of whom were farmers.

In state elections in early 1856 the American Party had more success than the Republicans. However, events in Kansas ensured that the main Republican issue remained in the public eye. An event in Congress in May also helped Republican fortunes. Following a speech in which Senator Sumner – an abolitionist – attacked Southern Senator Butler, Congressman Preston Brooks entered the Senate, found Sumner at his desk and beat him with his cane. 'Bleeding Sumner' possibly outraged Northerners more than 'bleeding Kansas'. Here was clear evidence of the Slave Power at work, using brute force to silence free speech.

f) The 1856 Presidential Election

The American Party held its national convention in February 1856. After a call to repeal the Kansas–Nebraska Act was defeated, many Northern delegates left the convention. The American Party went on to select ex-President Fillmore as its presidential candidate. Fillmore, more an old-fashioned Whig than a Know Nothing, was known to have pro-Southern sympathies. He thus had limited appeal in the North.

Republican leaders decided that John Frèmont would be the party's best presidential candidate. Born and bred in the South, Frèmont had been a successful Western explorer. Aged 43, he had limited political experience. An ex-Know Nothing, he had been a (Democrat!) Senator for California for just 17 days. A Southern-born, ex-Know Nothing, ex-Democrat was a strange choice for Republican candidate. But the romance surrounding Frèmont's career was likely to make him popular. The Republican platform was radical. Congress, it declared, had 'both the right and the imperative duty … to prohibit in the Territories those twin relics of barbarism – Polygamy and Slavery'. (The polygamy reference was an attack on Mormon practices in Utah.)

The Democrats chose James Buchanan. He had spent four decades in public service and served in the Senate and in cabinet. A Northerner, he was nevertheless acceptable to the South. He came from Pennsylvania – a key 'battleground' state. The Democrat platform endorsed popular sovereignty. The 1856 campaign generated great excitement. In the North, the contest was essentially between Buchanan and Frèmont. In the South, it was between Buchanan and Fillmore. For the first time since 1849–50 there was widespread fear for the safety of the Union. If Frèmont won, it was conceivable that some Southern states would secede. In November Fillmore obtained 871,731 votes (21.6 per cent) and eight electoral college votes. Frèmont got 1,340,537 votes (33.1 per cent) and 114 electoral college votes. Buchanan, with 1,832,955 votes (45.3 per cent) and 174 electoral votes, became president. He won all but one Southern state, plus Pennsylvania, New Jersey, Indiana, Illinois and California. The

THE USA: 1852–6

1854 Kansas–Nebraska Act;
1856 Pro-slavery force sacked Lawrence (May);
Charles Sumner beaten by Preston Brooks (May);
John Brown killed five pro-slavers at Pottawatomie (May);
Democrat James Buchanan won presidential election (November).

ACTIVITY

Brainstorm the points you would make in answering the question: Account for the rise of the Republican Party in the period 1854–6.

Democrats, who also controlled both Houses of Congress, had cause for celebration. However, the Republicans also had some reason for optimism. They had destroyed the Northern Know Nothings. If they had won Pennsylvania and Illinois, Frèmont would have become president.

ISSUE:
To what extent was Buchanan responsible for the outbreak of Civil War?

5 The Presidency of James Buchanan

Ideologically attached to the South and aware that he needed Southern support to ensure a majority in Congress, Buchanan chose a pro-Southern cabinet. From the start, many Northerners feared that he was a tool of the Slave Power. His actions confirmed this fear.

a) The Dred Scott Case

Dred Scott, a slave who had accompanied his master first to Illinois, then to the Wisconsin territory, claimed he was free on the grounds that he had resided both in a free state and a free territory. His case finally came before the Supreme Court, which by 1857 was ready to give judgment. Buchanan referred to the case in his inaugural address in March. Claiming (not quite truthfully) that he knew nothing of the Court's decision, he said he was ready to 'cheerfully submit' to its verdict and urged all good citizens to do likewise. Two days later the Court's decision was made public. Led by pro-Southern Chief Justice Taney, the Court decided that:

▼ Blacks, whether slave or free, did not have the same rights as whites.
▼ Scott's sojourn in a federal territory did not make him free.
▼ The 1820 Missouri Compromise ban on slavery north of 36°30′ was illegal. US citizens had the right to take their 'property' into the territories.

Northerners were horrified. Here was further proof that Buchanan, the Supreme Court and the Democrat Party were all involved in a Slave Power conspiracy against the North. Republicans claimed that whispered conversations between Taney and Buchanan on inauguration day proved that Buchanan had been well aware of the Court's decision when he asked Americans to accept it. Rather than settling the uncertainty about slavery in the territories, the Court's decision helped provoke further sectional antagonism.

THE PANIC OF 1857
In 1857 US industry was hit by depression, resulting in mass Northern unemployment. Buchanan, believing that government should not involve itself in economic matters, did nothing. He was blamed by Northerners for his seeming indifference.

b) Problems in Kansas

In Kansas Buchanan faced a situation which seemed to offer some hope. Although there were still two governments, the official pro-slave at Lecompton and the unofficial free state at Topeka, order had been restored. Given his declared commitment to popular sovereignty, all that Buchanan needed to do was ensure that the will of the majority – the free-staters – prevailed. In March 1857 Robert Walker, an experienced Southern politician who was committed to fair elections, became governor. His first task was to convince free-staters to take part in the election of a constitutional convention. Suspecting that any election organised by Lecompton would be rigged, they refused. Thus the pro-slavers won all the seats in the convention. Walker persuaded the free-staters to participate in elections for a new territorial legislature in October. Attempts by the pro-slavers to fix the election failed. Walker overturned enough fraudulent results to give the free-staters a majority in the legislature.

The Lecompton convention now drafted a pro-slavery constitution. While agreeing to allow a referendum on its proposals, it offered something of a spurious choice: voters had to accept the pro-slavery constitution as it was; or accept another constitution which banned the importation of slaves but still guaranteed the rights of slaveholders already in Kansas. Walker denounced the convention's actions as a 'vile fraud'. Not wanting to alienate Southern Democrats, Buchanan supported the Lecompton convention rather than Walker. In December Walker resigned. That same month Kansas voted on the Lecompton constitution. In fact, most free-staters abstained in protest. The pro-slave returns showed a large majority for the constitution. Buchanan claimed that the question of slavery had been 'fairly and explicitly referred to the people'. This was a huge blunder. By accepting the Lecompton constitution, Buchanan gave the Republicans massive political ammunition. More importantly, he enraged Northern Democrats who were committed to popular sovereignty. Douglas attacked both Buchanan and the Lecompton constitution. A titanic Congressional contest ensured. Some Northern Democrats sided with Buchanan, others sided with Douglas. The House of Representatives refused to pass the Lecompton constitution and Buchanan finally agreed that Kansanians should vote again on the measure. The vote, conducted as fairly as possible in August 1858, resulted in a free state victory: 11,300 voted against the Lecompton constitution while only 1,788 voted for it. Kansas now set about drawing up a free state constitution. It finally joined the Union in 1861 as a free state.

-*Profile*-

1809 born in Kentucky;
1831 moved to Illinois and over the next few years experienced a host of jobs, before becoming a lawyer;
1834 won the first of four terms as a Whig state legislator in Illinois;
1842 married Mary Todd, daughter of a Kentucky slaveholder;
1846 elected to the House of Representatives;
1856 joined the Republican Party;
1858 challenged Douglas for election to Illinois Senate;
1860 elected President;
1864 re-elected President;
1865 assassinated by John Wilkes Booth.

ABRAHAM LINCOLN

Lincoln, a humane and witty man, was also a calculating politician. Historians continue to debate whether he was moderate, radical or conservative. He was certainly cautious, preferring to think over problems slowly and deliberately before reaching a decision. This was true on the slavery issue. He had always been opposed to slavery, believing it to be both immoral and against the Declaration of Independence's assertion that 'all men are created equal'. But realising it was a divisive issue, he had kept quiet on the subject for much of his political career. Given the racist sentiment in Illinois, he knew he was on difficult ground on the race issue in the 1858 election. His opponent, Douglas, stated with brutal frankness that he thought blacks to be inferior to whites. Lincoln, in part, agreed. He said:

> I am not, nor ever have been in favour of bringing about in any way the social and political equality of the white and black races ... I am not nor ever have been in favour of making voters or jurors of negroes, nor of qualifying them to hold office, nor to intermarry with white people ... there is a physical difference between the white and black races which I believe will for ever forbid the two races living together on terms of social and political equality. And inasmuch as they cannot so live, while they do remain together there must be the position of superior and inferior, and I as much as any other man, am in favour of having the superior position assigned to the white man.
>
> *Source A*

However, Lincoln added that to assign 'the superior position to the white race', was not to say 'the negro should be denied everything'. In a debate with Douglas in 1858, Lincoln said:

> The real issue in this controversy ... is the sentiment on the part of one class that looks upon the institution of slavery as a wrong, and another class that does not look upon it as wrong ... The Republican party ... look upon it as being a moral, social and political wrong ... and one of the methods of treating it as a wrong is to make provision that it shall grow no larger.
>
> *Source B*

c) The 1858 Congressional Elections

The 1858 elections came at a bad time for the Northern Democrats, with the party split between those who supported Buchanan and those who supported Douglas. Given that Douglas had to stand for re-election, attention focused on his campaign in Illinois. The Republicans chose Abraham Lincoln to run against Douglas. In his acceptance speech, Lincoln declared:

> A House divided against itself cannot stand. I believe this government cannot endure permanently half slave and half free. I do not expect the Union to be dissolved – I do not expect the house to fall – but I do expect it will cease to be divided. It will become all one thing or all the other. Either the opponents of slavery will arrest the further spread of it, and place it where the public mind shall rest in the belief that it is in the course of ultimate extinction; or its advocates will push it forward till it shall become alike lawful in all the states, old as well as new – north as well as south.

Source C

ACTIVITY

Examine the extract from Lincoln's speech. How might Douglas have responded to the charge that this 'government cannot endure permanently half slave and half free'?

Douglas agreed to meet Lincoln for seven open-air debates. They were confined almost exclusively to three topics – race, slavery and slavery expansion. By today's standards, Lincoln and Douglas do not seem too far apart. This is perhaps not surprising: both men were fighting for the middle ground. But they did differ in one key respect. Douglas never once said in public that slavery was a moral evil. Lincoln may not have believed in racial equality but he did believe that blacks and whites shared a common humanity: 'If slavery is not wrong, then nothing is wrong'. He did not expect slavery to die immediately. He did not suppose that 'the ultimate extinction would occur in less than a hundred years at the least' but he did believe that 'ultimate extinction' should be the goal. Lincoln won some 125,000 votes to Douglas's 121,000. But Douglas's supporters kept control of the Illinois legislature which re-elected Douglas as Senator. Lincoln was disappointed. However, at least he had emerged from the election as a Republican of national stature. Overall, the 1858 elections were a disaster for Northern Democrats. The Republicans, helped by the economic depression and by the fact that the American Party had disappeared in most Northern states, won control of the House. If the 1858 voting pattern was repeated in 1860 the Republicans would win the presidency.

d) John Brown's Raid

John Brown had risen to fame – or infamy – in Kansas. Some thought he was a madman. But many abolitionists believed that he was a man

Figure 4 John Brown.

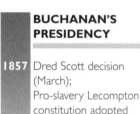

BUCHANAN'S PRESIDENCY

1857	Dred Scott decision (March); Pro-slavery Lecompton constitution adopted (December);
1858	Lincoln–Douglas debates;
1859	John Brown raid.

ISSUES:

Why did Lincoln win in 1860 and why did his victory spark secession?

of moral conviction. The fact that he was able to win financial support from hard-headed businessmen is testimony to both his charismatic personality and the intensity of abolitionist sentiment. In 1859 Brown determined to raid the arsenal at Harper's Ferry, seize weapons, retreat to the Appalachian mountains and from there spark a slave revolt. On 16 October Brown and 18 men succeeded in capturing the arsenal and a number of hostages. But rather than escape, Brown remained in Harper's Ferry. This was irrational. He had no supplies and could hardly spark a slave revolt holed up in the arsenal. His position soon became desperate. Militia units and a detachment of marines, led by Colonel Robert E. Lee, converged on the town. A 36-hour siege followed. On 18 October Lee ordered the arsenal to be stormed. Brown was captured along with six of his men. Seventeen others were killed. Found guilty of treason, Brown was executed in December 1859.

e) Sectional Tension: 1859–60

Brown's raid raised sectional tensions to new heights. Southerners' worst fears had been realised. An abolitionist had tried to stir up a slave revolt. Southerners suspected – wrongly – that most Northerners sympathised with Brown's action. Even leading Republicans condemned Brown's raid as 'utterly repugnant'. Few Southerners were reassured. They saw Republicans and abolitionists as components of an unholy alliance against slavery. Buchanan, who had sought to end sectional tension, had failed. Undoubtedly he faced a difficult situation. The forces driving the nation apart were starting to spin out of control. His policies, however, had helped exacerbate sectional strife. His failure to support fair elections in Kansas had divided his party and aided the Republicans in their claim that an aggressive Slave Power stalked the land.

6 The 1860 Election and Secession

In early 1860 'fire-eaters', who claimed that the South would be better off going its own way, were still a minority. However, the prospect of a Republican president filled Southerners with dread. In the event of a Republican victory, many were ready to consider the possibility of secession. Thus the stakes in the 1860 election were high.

a) The 1860 Presidential Candidates

Douglas, determined to run for president, tried to heal the rifts within the Democrat Party in 1859–60. But his stand against the Lecompton constitution alienated him from most Southerners. Events at the

Democrat convention, which met in April 1860 at Charleston, South Carolina, showed that the party, never mind the country, was a house divided against itself. Although Douglas had the support of most of the delegates, he failed to win the necessary two-thirds majority. After 57 ballots the convention agreed to reconvene at Baltimore in June. When it was clear that the Baltimore convention was likely to select Douglas, there was a mass Southern walk-out. Douglas easily won the nomination of the official convention. But Southern delegates set up their own convention and nominated John Breckinridge of Kentucky. The Democrat split is often seen as ensuring Republican success. However, the fact that Douglas was now able to campaign in the North without the embarrassment of having to try to maintain a united national Democrat Party, probably helped his cause.

The Republican convention met in May at Chicago. Its platform called for higher tariffs, free 160-acre homesteads for western settlers, and government support for a northern trans-continental railway. While opposed to any extension of slavery, the platform promised that the party had no intention of interfering with slavery where it already existed and it condemned John Brown's raid as 'the gravest of crimes'. Seward, Governor of New York for four years and a Senator for 12 years, was favourite to win the party's presidential nomination. But the fact that he had been a major figure in public life for so long meant that he had many enemies. His main opponent turned out to be Lincoln. Lincoln came from the key state of Illinois. Given that it was difficult to attach an ideological label to him, he was able to appear to be all things to all men. Seward won most votes on the first ballot but not enough for victory. By the third ballot there was an irresistible momentum in Lincoln's favour. Amid scenes of great excitement, he won the Republican nomination.

> **THE CONSTITUTIONAL UNIONISTS**
> A new party, the Constitutional Unionists, composed mainly of ex-Southern Whigs, nominated John Bell of Tennessee as presidential candidate. The party denounced the Republicans as abolitionist fanatics and Breckinridge's Democrats as disunionists.

b) The 1860 Election

The election campaign was largely sectional. In the North the main fight was between Lincoln and Douglas. Bell and Breckinridge fought it out in the South. Douglas was the only candidate who actively involved himself in the campaign. The other three opted for the traditional 'mute tribune' role. Arguably Lincoln should have made some effort to reassure Southerners that he was not a threat to their section. But he could hardly go out of his way to appease the South: this would have done his cause no good in the North. Moreover, given that the very existence of his party was offensive to Southerners, it is difficult to see what he could have said to allay anxiety. Although Lincoln, Bell and Breckinridge kept silent, this did not prevent their supporters campaigning for them. Republican propaganda concentrated on the Slave Power conspiracy while

Southern Democrats stereotyped all Northerners as 'Black Republicans' set on abolishing slavery.

In November Bell obtained 593,000 votes, carrying Virginia, Kentucky, and Tennessee. Breckinridge got 843,000 votes and won 11 of the 15 slave states. Douglas won 1,383,000 votes – mainly from the North – but he won only two states. Lincoln won 1,866,000 votes – 40 per cent of the total. He got no votes at all in ten Southern states. However, he won 54 per cent of the Northern vote, carrying all but one of the free states. With a majority of 180 to 123 in the electoral college, he became the new president. If the opposition had united against him in every free state, Lincoln would still have triumphed.

Northerners voted for Lincoln because he seemed to represent their section. A vote for Lincoln was a vote against the Democrats and against the Slave Power, whatever that was. Some Northerners liked the party's economic measures. Nativism, which had not disappeared with the demise of the Know Nothings, may also have been important. Although the Republicans took an ambiguous stand on nativist issues, anti-Catholic Northerners had little option but to vote Republican, if only because the Democrat Party remained the home of Irish and German Catholics.

c) Secession

Rationally, there were excellent reasons why the Southern states should not secede from the Union. Lincoln had promised he would not interfere with slavery in those states where it existed. Even if he had secret ambitions to do away with slavery, there was little he could do: his party did not control Congress or the Supreme Court. Secession would mean abandoning an enforceable Fugitive Slave Act. Finally, it could well lead to Civil War which would threaten slavery far more than Lincoln's election. But few Southerners regarded things so calmly. Lincoln was depicted as a rabid abolitionist who would encourage slave insurrections. Southerners felt wronged. For more than a generation they had seen themselves as the aggrieved innocents in an unequal sectional struggle. They believed they had been denied their share of the Western territories and unfairly taxed through high tariffs to subsidise Northern industry. Honour demanded that a stand be taken against the latest outrage, the election of a Republican president.

Despite fierce anti-Yankee feeling, secession was not inevitable. There was still much Unionist sympathy in the South. Southerners were far from united. There was not even unity on the best political strategy to adopt. While some Southerners believed that Lincoln's election was grounds enough for secession, others thought it best to wait until he committed a hostile act against the South. 'Immediate' secessionists knew that if they forced the issue, they might destroy the unity that they hoped to create; but if they waited for unity, they might never act. How to force the issue was another problem. If individual states acted alone, there was the danger that they would receive no support from other states, as South Carolina had found in the 1832 Nullification Crisis. Yet trying to organise a mass move for secession, might ensure nothing happened – as had been the case in 1849–50. However, events now moved with a rapidity which few had foreseen. On 10 November the South Carolina state legislature called for elections to a convention to meet on 17 December to decide whether to secede. This sparked off a chain reaction. Alabama, Mississippi, Georgia, Louisiana and Florida put similar convention procedures underway. In Texas Governor Houston, who opposed disunion, delayed matters but only by a few weeks. While the states took individual action, they were also committed to joint action. Congressmen from nine Southern states declared in December: 'We are satisfied the honour, safety and independence of the Southern people are to be found only in a Southern Confederacy – a result to be obtained only by separate state secession'. On 20 December the South Carolina convention voted 169–0 for secession. It defended its action in a Declaration of Causes of Secession.

In the election of delegates for conventions that would decide on

Source D

And now the State of South Carolina having resumed her separate and equal place among nations, deems it due to herself, to the remaining United States of America, and to the nations of the world, that she should declare the immediate causes which have led to this act ... We affirm that these ends for which this Government was instituted have been defeated, and the Government itself has been destructive of them by the action of the nonslaveholding States. Those States have assumed the right of deciding upon the propriety of our domestic institutions; and have denied the rights of property established in fifteen of the States and recognized by the Constitution; they have denounced as sinful the institution of Slavery; they have permitted the open establishment among them of societies, whose avowed object is to disturb the peace of and eloin the property of the citizens of other States. They have encouraged and assisted thousands of our slaves to leave their homes; and those who remain, have been incited ... to servile insurrection.

ACTIVITY

Read the extract and answer the following questions:

a) Comment on the statement that South Carolina had now 'resumed her separate and equal place among nations'.

b) Some of the points raised in the Declaration are incorrect. But this source is still essential to historians. Why?

secession, voters usually had a choice between 'immediate secessionists' and 'cooperationists'. While the standpoint of the immediate secessionists was clear, the cooperationists represented a wide spectrum of opinion. Some were secessionists but believed the time was not yet right: others were unionists, opposed to secession. It is difficult for historians to decide the exact distribution of voters along this spectrum. The situation is even more confused because some candidates committed themselves to no position: they ran as local leaders who would make up their minds as events developed. It is thus hard to evaluate the exact meaning of the election results. In Mississippi 12,218 voted for cooperationist candidates. 16,800 voted for immediate secession. On 9 January 1861 the Mississippi convention voted by 85 votes to 15 for secession. On 10 January a Florida convention voted 62 to 7 for secession. On 11 January Alabama voted to secede by 61 votes to 39. In Georgia secessionist candidates won 44,152 votes, cooperationists 41,632. The Georgia convention voted to secede on 19 January by 208 votes to 89. On 26 January the Louisiana convention voted to secede by 113 votes to 17. On 1 February the Texan convention voted for secession by 166 votes to 8. Texas then had a referendum to ratify the convention's action. Secession was approved by 44,317 votes to 13,020.

A Slave Power Conspiracy?

Republicans saw the events in the South as a continuation of the Slave Power conspiracy. They claimed that a small number of planters had conned the electorate into voting for secession, to which most were not really committed. The debate about whether secession was led by a small aristocratic clique or was a genuinely democratic act has continued. Slaveholders certainly dominated politics in many Southern states. Areas with few slaves tended to vote against disunion. Conversely, secession sentiment was strongest wherever the percentage of slaves was highest. According to David Potter, 'To a much greater degree than the slaveholders desired, secession had become a slaveowners' movement'. Potter believed that a secessionist minority, with a clear purpose, seized the momentum and at a time of passion, won mass support. However, he conceded that the secessionists acted democratically and in an 'open and straightforward' manner. Given that there was huge support for secession throughout the lower South, it is hard to claim that there was a conspiracy to thwart the expressed will of the majority.

Had the South the right to secede?

7 The Outbreak of Civil War

Few Americans expected war in early 1861. Most Northerners believed that the seceded states were bluffing or thought that an extremist minority had seized power against the wishes of the majority. Either way, the seceded states would soon be back in the Union: the Southern bluff would be called; or the Unionist majority would asssert itself. In contrast, most Southerners thought that the North would not fight to preserve the Union. Border state Americans were confident that a compromise could be arranged. These hopes and expectations were not to be realised. By April 1861 the United States were no longer united: they were at war. Was this the fault of blundering politicians?

a) The Confederacy

On 4 February 1861 50 delegates of the seceded states met at Montgomery to launch the Confederacy. They comprised a broad cross-section of the South's traditional political leadership. Anxious to win foreign recognition and the support of the **upper South**, the delegates tried to project a moderate image. The Confederate Constitution was closely modelled on the 1787 Constitution. The main differences were features that more closely protected slavery and guaranteed state rights. On 9 February Jefferson Davis of Mississippi was elected provisional president. He had long been a champion of Southern rights but was by no means a fire-eater.

b) The Search for Compromise

Lincoln did not take over until March 1861. In the meantime, Buchanan continued as president. He believed that secession was unconstitutional but his main concern was not to provoke war. He thus took no action as federal institutions across the South – forts, custom houses, post offices – were taken over by the Confederate states. Historians have criticised Buchanan, not so much for not using force, but more for his failure to seek a compromise. In fairness, it is difficult to see what he could have done. Most Republicans did not trust him and the lower South was set upon leaving the Union. In Buchanan's view, Congress had more responsibility for finding a solution to the crisis than himself. Both houses set up committees to explore plans of conciliation. The Senate Committee, headed by Crittenden, recommended a package of compromise proposals. The main idea was to extend the 36°30′ Missouri Compomise line to the Pacific, giving the South some hope of slavery expansion. It also recommended a constitutional amendment guaranteeing that

THE UPPER SOUTH AND SECESSION

The upper South had a much smaller stake in slavery than the lower South. Many non-slaveholders questioned how well their interests would be served in a planter-dominated Confederacy. The upper South, which had close ties with the North, also had more reason to fear the economic consequences of secession. But although the upper South states continued to remain within the Union, their support for that Union was tenuous. There was a deep distrust of Lincoln. If it came to the crunch, many in the upper South would put their Southern before their Union affiliations.

there would be no interference with slavery in those states where it already existed. Republicans rejected these proposals which seemed to smack more of surrender than compromise. In February a Peace Convention, attended by some of the most famous names in American politics, met in Washington. After three weeks deliberation, the Convention supported proposals similar to those of Crittenden. Presented to Congress, they had little impact.

c) Lincoln and the Republicans

Up until 1860 slavery expansion had been the main issue dividing North from South. That had now been replaced by secession. There were some Northerners who thought that the 'erring' Confederate states should be allowed to 'go in peace'. But most were not willing to accept the dismemberment of the USA. They feared this would create a fatal precedent to be invoked by disaffected minorities in the future, until the USA dissolved into a host of petty, squabbling nations. The great experiment in republican self-government would thus collapse. However, few Northerners demanded the swift despatch of troops to suppress the 'rebellion'. There was a fear that precipitous action might have a disastrous impact on the upper South. The best bet seemed to be to avoid needless provocation, hoping that the disunion fever would run its course and that the lower South would see sense and return to the Union. Lincoln thought it best to maintain a strict silence until his inauguration. While he was ready to make some concessions, he refused to budge on the territorial question. He believed that he had won the 1860 election on principles fairly stated and was determined not to concede too much to the slaveholders. Even with hindsight, it is difficult to see what Lincoln could have said or done which would have dramatically changed matters.

On 4 March 1861 Lincoln was finally inaugurated president. His inaugural speech was conciliatory but firm. He made it clear that he would not interfere with slavery where it already existed. But he also made it clear that he regarded the Union as indissoluble and secession as illegal. He thus intended to 'hold, occupy and possess' federal property in the South. His speech ended with the following words:

ACTIVITY

Read Source E. What did Lincoln mean when he spoke of the 'mystic cords of memory'?

> We are not enemies, but friends. We must not be enemies. Though passion may have strained, it must not break, our bonds of affection. The mystic cords of memory, stretching from every battlefield and patriot grave to every living heart and hearthstone all over this broad land, will yet swell the chorus of the Union when again touched, as surely they will be, by the better angels of our nature.

Source E

Most Republicans liked Lincoln's firm tone. Border state Unionists and many Northern Democrats were also pleased at his attempts at conciliation. The speech, however, had no effect at all on the Confederate states.

d) Fort Sumter

Lincoln hoped that time might allow passions to cool. But time was not on his side. The situation at Fort Sumter called for a speedy decision. Over the winter of 1860–61 the Confederacy had taken over all but two forts in the South: Fort Pickens and Fort Sumter. Both were on islands. Fort Pickens, off Pensacola, Florida, was well out of range of shore batteries and could easily be reinforced by the federal navy. Fort Sumter, in the middle of Charleston harbour, was a far more serious problem. By March 1861 it had become the symbol of national sovereignty for both sides. The Confederacy felt it could hardly allow a 'foreign' fort in the middle of Charleston harbour. Lincoln's inauguration speech had made it clear that he was determined to hold on to what remained of federal property in the South. Retention of Sumter was thus a test of his credibility. The day after his speech, he received a dispatch from Major Anderson, the Sumter commander, informing him that the garrison would run out of food in under six weeks. Lincoln knew that any attempt to supply Sumter might lead to war. He sought the advice of his general-in-chief Winfield Scott. Sumter's evacuation, Scott told Lincoln, was 'almost inevitable': it could not be held without a large fleet and 25,000 soldiers, neither of which the Union possessed. On 15 March Lincoln brought the matter before his cabinet. Most favoured withdrawal. Lincoln put off making a decision.

In late March, Lincoln called another cabinet meeting to discuss the crisis. Northern newspapers were now pressing for firm action. Heedful of this clamour, most of the cabinet now spoke in favour of re-supplying Sumter. On 4 April Lincoln informed Anderson that a relief expedition would soon be coming and that he should try to hold out. Two days later he sent a letter to the Governor of South Carolina telling him that he intended to re-supply Sumter. A small naval expedition finally left for Charleston on 9 April. Some historians think that Lincoln deliberately manoeuvred the Confederacy into firing the first shots. In reality, he was probably trying to keep as many options open as possible. He hoped to preserve peace, but was willing to risk, and possibly expected, war. By re-supplying Sumter, he was lobbing the ball into Davis's court. The Confederate leader had to decide what to do next.

On 9 April Davis called a cabinet meeting. Most members thought that the time had come to lance the Sumter boil. Moreover, a crisis

Figure 5 Fort Sumter.

might bring the upper South into the Confederacy. Thus Davis issued orders that Sumter must be taken before it was re-supplied. On 11 April General Beauregard, the Confederate commander in Charleston, demanded the fort's surrender. Anderson refused. And so, at 4.30 am on 12 April, the opening shots of the Civil War were fired. For 33 hours Sumter's defenders exchanged artillery fire with Confederate land batteries. Extraordinarily there were no deaths. On 13 April, with fires raging through the fort, Anderson surrendered. The attack on Sumter electrified the North. 'There can be no neutrals in this war, only patriots or traitors', declared Senator Douglas.

e) Secession: the Second Wave

Lincoln now called on all Union states to send men to put down the 'rebellion'. This meant that the upper South states had to commit themselves. Virginia's decision was crucial. Its industrial capacity was as great as the seven original Confederate states combined. Most Virginians sympathised with the Confederacy and a state convention voted by 88 votes to 55 to support its Southern 'brothers'. A referendum ratified this decision, with Virginians voting 128,884 votes to 32,134 to secede. Richmond, Virginia's capital, now became the Confederate capital. In May Arkansas and North Carolina joined the Confederacy. In June Tennessee voted by 104,913 votes to 47,238 to secede. Support for the Confederacy in the upper South was far from total. Even more important, four slave states – Delaware, Maryland, Missouri, and Kentucky – decided to remain within the Union.

Figure 6 Union v. Confederacy.

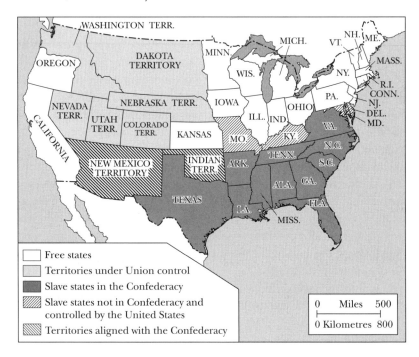

Free states

Territories under Union control

Slave states in the Confederacy

Slave states not in Confederacy and controlled by the United States

Territories aligned with the Confederacy

0   Miles   500

0 Kilometres 800

8 The Causes of the Civil War: Conclusion

In March 1865 Lincoln, in his second inaugural address, presented a succinct explanation of how and why the war came:

> On the occasion corresponding this four years ago all thoughts were anxiously directed to an impending civil war ... One eighth of the whole population was coloured slaves, not distributed generally over the Union, but localised in the southern part of it. These slaves constituted a peculiar and powerful interest. All knew that this interest was somehow the cause of the war.

1860 Lincoln elected President (November); South Carolina seceded (December);

1861 Mississippi, Florida, Alabama, Georgia and Louisiana seceded (January); Texas seceded: establishment of the Confederacy (February); Lincoln inaugurated President (March); Confederate forces opened fire on Fort Sumter (April); Virginia seceded (April); Arkansas and North; Carolina seceded (May); Tennessee seceded (June).

For 50 years after the war, few Northern historians dissented from this view. However, Jefferson Davis insisted in his memoirs, written in the 1870s, that the Southern states had fought solely 'for the defence of an inherent, unalienable right ... to withdraw from a Union which they had, as sovereign communities, voluntarily entered ... The existence of African servitude was in no wise the cause of the conflict, but only an incident'. This explanation was accepted by many Southerners who continued to view the conflict as a war of Northern aggression. 'Progressive' historians in the 1920s claimed that the war was a contest, not between slavery and freedom, but between plantation agriculture and industrialising capitalism. In the 1940s revisionist historians denied that sectional conflicts were genuinely divisive. They pointed out that Northerners and Southerners shared the same language, political culture, religious values, and racist views. Revisionists insisted that the differences separating North and South could have been accommodated peacefully. Far from being irrepressible, the Civil War was brought on by extremists – abolitionists and fire-eaters – who whipped up emotions and hatreds. The passions they aroused got out of hand because politicians failed to find a compromise. The result, claimed revisionists, was a tragic, unnecessary war.

Historiography has now come full circle. The state rights, progressive, and revisionist schools are dormant if not dead. The view that slavery was 'somehow' the cause of the war is now almost universally accepted. Slavery was the sole institution not shared by North and South. It defined the South, permeating almost every aspect of its life. The rise of militant abolitionism in the North exacerbated tension between the sections. But it was the issue of slavery expansion, rather than the mere existence of slavery, that polarised the nation. Most of the crises that threatened the bonds of Union arose over this matter. Convinced that a Slave Power conspiracy was at work, Northerners came to support the Republican Party, which was pledged to stop slavery expansion. For many Southerners the election of a Republican president in 1860 was the last straw – an affront to their honour. So, the lower South seceded.

In 1861 Lincoln was not pledged to end slavery: he was pledged to preserve the Union. The Confederate states were fighting for the right to self-determination. Thus nationalism became the central issue of the struggle. Secession by the Confederate states need not have led to war. The North could have let the Southern states go. But most Northerners were prepared to fight to save the Union. The fire-eaters, who wanted to create a Southern nation, were a distinct minority pre-1860. Most Southerners saw themselves as loyal Americans. The establishment of the Confederacy was a refuge to which many Southerners felt driven, not a national destiny that they eagerly embraced. The Civil War did more to produce Southern nationalism than Southern nationalism did to produce war. In so far as there was a sense of Southern nationalism in 1860–61, it had arisen because of slavery. Slavery set the South apart from the rest of the nation. Differences arising from the slavery issue impelled the Southern states to secede. While the Confederacy might claim its justification to be the protection of state rights, it was primarily one state right, the right to preserve slavery, that impelled secession.

With the benefit of hindsight, it is clear that Southerners got things wrong. Slavery was not in immediate peril in 1860–61. Some Southerners realised the enormity of the mistake. Governor Houston of Texas observed: 'Our people are going to war to perpetuate slavery and the first gun fired in the war will be the knell of slavery'. The North, so much stronger in terms of both men and industrial strength, was always likely to win a Civil War. The fact that this was not obvious to most Southerners is symptomatic of the hysteria that swept the South in 1860–61. Southerners picked the quarrel. They fired the first shots. As a result, one in four white male Southerners of military age died and slavery – the institution which the South had gone to war to defend – ended.

▼ Working on The Causes of the American Civil War

In trying to work out what caused anything in history, it is always useful to consider:

▼ What were the main long-term causes (preconditions)?
▼ What were the main medium-term causes (precipitants)?
▼ What were the main short-term causes (triggers)?

Try and work out what you think were the main preconditions, precipitants and triggers which led to the Civil War. Did any of the preconditions mean that war was inevitable?

Answering Extended Writing and Essay Questions on The Causes of the American Civil War

Consider the following question: To what extent were blundering politicians to blame for the Civil War?

In our view, slavery was always likely to spark a sectional crisis. Perhaps that absolves the politicians in 1860–61. However, a strong case can be made for blundering politicians being to blame for the war. Had the South acted rationally in 1860–61 war would not have occurred. Given that the Confederate states were unwilling to accept any compromise in 1860–61, it seems unfair to blame Lincoln. In our view, Southern leaders were far more to blame for the crisis. Note that you don't have to agree with this view! Have the confidence to formulate your own judgements. Draw up a rough plan for the question. Write down your introduction and conclusion.

Answering Source-based Questions on The Causes of the American Civil War

We have entered upon the career of independence, and it must be inflexibly pursued. Through many years of controversy with our late associates of the Northern states, we have vainly endeavored to secure tranquillity and obtain respect for the rights to which we were entitled. As a necessity, not a choice, we have resorted to the remedy of separation and henceforth our energies must be directed to the conduct of our own affairs, and the perpetuity of the Confederacy which we have formed. If a just perception of mutual interest shall permit us peaceably to pursue our separate political career, my most earnest desire will have been fulfilled. But if this be denied to us, and the integrity of our territory and jurisdiction be assailed, it will but remain for us with firm resolve to appeal to arms and invoke the blessing of Providence on a just cause.

Source F Jefferson Davis's inaugural speech, 18 February 1861.

I hold that, in contemplation of universal law and of the Constitution, the Union of these States is perpetual. Perpetuity is implied, if not expressed, in the fundamental law of all national governments ... It follows from these views that no State, upon its own mere motion, can lawfully get out of the Union – that resolves and ordinances to that effect are legally void; and that acts of violence, within any State or States, against the authority of the United States, are insurrectionary or revolutionary, according to circumstances. ... In your hands, my dissatisfied fellow countrymen, and not in mine, is the momentous issue of civil war. The government will not assail you. You can have no conflict without being yourselves the aggressors. You have no oath registered in heaven to destroy the government, while I shall have the most solemn one to 'preserve, protect, and defend' it.

Source G Lincoln's inaugural speech, March 1861.

▼ QUESTIONS ON SOURCES

1. Comment on Davis's remark: 'As a necessity, not a choice, we have resorted to the remedy of separation'. **[3 marks]**
2. How useful are the sources in informing us about opinion in both North and South in February–March 1861? **[7 marks]**
3. Using both sources and your own knowledge, explain why war broke out in April 1861. **[15 marks]**

Further Reading

Books in the Access to History *series*
The key text is *The Origins of the American Civil War* by Alan Farmer.

General
The best book (by far) is *Battle Cry of Freedom* by J.M. McPherson (Penguin, 1988). *The Impending Crisis* by D.M. Potter (Harper and Row, 1976) remains an essential text. *A House Divided: Sectionalism and Civil War, 1848–1865* by R.M. Sewell (Johns Hopkins University Press, 1988) is more succinct. On slavery the best place to start is *Slavery: History and Historians* by P.J. Parish (Icon Editions, 1989).

THE AMERICAN CIVIL WAR AND RECONSTRUCTION

CHAPTER 2

POINTS TO CONSIDER

620,000 men died in the Civil War – more than died in all America's subsequent wars (to date) put together. Why was it so bloody? Why did it last so long? Why did the North eventually win? The war was essentially about reconstructing the Union. How successful were Reconstruction policies, particularly with regard to ex-slaves?

ISSUES:
Why and how did the North win the war? How successful was Reconstruction?

1 The Nature of the War

Thousands of Americans flocked to the colours in 1861, anticipating one glorious battle. Instead the war turned into a four year 'slog'. This was largely because both sides had strengths and weaknesses which offset those of the other side.

a) Union Advantages in 1861

▼ There were 22,000,000 people in the North compared with only 9,000,000 in the South (of whom only 5,500,000 were whites).

▼ The North had a much greater industrial capacity (see Table 1). In 1860 Northern states produced 97 per cent of the USA's firearms, 93 per cent of its cloth, and 94 per cent of its pig iron. The North had twice as many miles of railway track.

▼ The North enjoyed naval supremacy.

▼ Most men in the US regular army remained loyal to the Union. So did two-thirds of the officers. Thus the Union had a stronger pool of military experience to call on.

▼ Four slave states (Maryland, Kentucky, Delaware and Missouri) remained loyal to the Union. These states would have added 45 per cent to the Confederacy's white population and 80 per cent to its manufacturing capacity.

▼ Not all the people within the Confederacy were committed to its cause. Pockets of Unionism existed, especially in the Appalachian Mountains. The Confederacy suffered a major setback when West Virginia seceded from Virginia in 1861.

CIVIL WAR?
Since 1861 Americans have argued over a name for the war fought between the Union and the Confederacy. The conflict was indeed a civil war in states like Missouri where brother sometimes did fight brother. However, this was not the norm. The reality was that the war was waged by two separate regions: most Northerners were on the Union side and most Southerners were on the Confederate side. Moreover, the term 'civil war' implies that two sides were fighting for control of a nation when in fact the Confederacy wanted independence. But attempts to give the conflict a different name – for example, 'The War between the States' – have failed. By far the most popular name today is 'The Civil War'.

Why did the War last so long?

The Border States

▼ There was never any likelihood that Delaware would secede. Less than 2 per cent of its population were slaves and its economic ties were with the North.

▼ Many Marylanders were pro-Confederate. In April 1861 a riot in Baltimore led to the death of four soldiers and 12 civilians – the first fatalities of the war. Lincoln took strong action, sending in Union troops and suspending the writ of habeas corpus (allowing the arrest of suspected trouble-makers). Unionist candidates won the June 1861 elections and the Maryland state legislature voted against secession.

▼ Kentucky was deeply divided. Its attempt to remain neutral was short-lived. When Confederate forces occupied Columbus in September 1861, the state legislature voted to adhere to the Union.

▼ The Missouri state governor, like many Missourians, was pro-Confederate. But Unionists, despite early setbacks, kept control of most of the state.

b) Confederate Advantages

▼ The Confederacy's size made it difficult to blockade and conquer.

▼ It did not have to invade the North or capture Washington to win. It simply needed to wear down the Northern will to fight.

▼ The South had interior lines of communication. In theory this meant that it should be able to concentrate its forces against dispersed Union armies.

▼ Although Maryland, Missouri and Kentucky did not secede, large elements in all three states were pro-Confederate and thousands served in the Confederate army.

▼ Most of the war was fought in the South. Southerners were thus defending their own land and homes. This may have encouraged them to fight harder.

▼ Southerners were confident that, man for man, they were better soldiers than Northerners. Most military experts assumed that farmers, who knew how to ride and shoot, were better soldiers than industrial workers.

▼ Cotton was assumed to be the Confederacy's great economic weapon. At the very least cotton sales should enable it to purchase military supplies from Europe.

▼ The outcome of the American War of Independence and the Texan–Mexican war in 1836 suggested that a determined 'David' could defeat 'Goliath'.

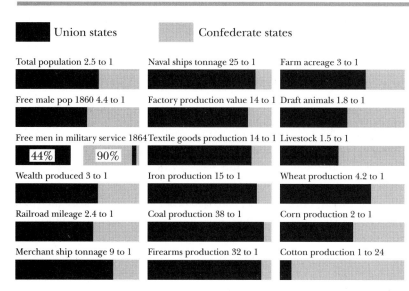

■ Union states   ▧ Confederate states

Table 1 Comparative resources in Union and Confederate states.

Total population 2.5 to 1	Naval ships tonnage 25 to 1	Farm acreage 3 to 1
Free male pop 1860 4.4 to 1	Factory production value 14 to 1	Draft animals 1.8 to 1
Free men in military service 1864 44% 90%	Textile goods production 14 to 1	Livestock 1.5 to 1
Wealth produced 3 to 1	Iron production 15 to 1	Wheat production 4.2 to 1
Railroad mileage 2.4 to 1	Coal production 38 to 1	Corn production 2 to 1
Merchant ship tonnage 9 to 1	Firearms production 32 to 1	Cotton production 1 to 24

ACTIVITY

Examine the statistics in Table 1. Why might its greater railway mileage be an advantage for the Union?

c) The Situation in 1861

Neither side was prepared for war. The Union had only a 16,000-strong regular army, most of which was scattered in frontier posts out West. The War Department totalled 90 men. Lincoln had no military experience. General Winfield Scott, the leading Union general, was 74 years old and suffered from ill health. In April 1861 Lincoln asked for 75,000 volunteers to serve for three months. It was soon obvious that this was insufficient. In July Congress agreed to raise 500,000 men who would serve for three years.

The Confederacy had to start its military organisation from scratch. President Davis at least had some military experience. Trained at West Point, he had fought in the Mexican War and been Secretary of War. The 300 Southern officers who resigned from the regular army provided a useful pool of talent. In February 1861 the Confederate Congress had authorised the raising of 100,000 volunteers for up to a year's service. In May 1861 it authorised an additional 400,000 troops, this time for three years' service.

Both sides were similarly unprepared at sea. The Union, on paper, had some 90 ships but most were obsolete sailing vessels and few were ready for action. The South had no navy at all in 1861. Although some 300 naval officers resigned their commissions and joined the Confederacy, the likelihood of them finding ships to command seemed minimal. Nearly all the American shipbuilding capacity was in the North.

In 1861 both armies were amateurish, from the top down. Neither side had a recognisable high command structure. Taking whatever advice seemed appropriate, both Lincoln and Davis had the job of appointing the chief officers. Political criteria, not just military con-

MASS ARMIES

In 1861 the problem for the authorities was not to obtain men but to hold volunteers to manageable numbers. However, by 1862 the flood of recruits had become a trickle. In March 1862 Davis had no option but to introduce conscription. Every white male aged 18 to 35 (soon raised to 45 and later to 50) became liable for military service. In the North most states adopted a carrot and stick approach. The carrot was bounties – large sums of money offered to men who enlisted. The stick, initially, was the Militia Law (July 1862) which empowered Lincoln to call state militias into federal service. In March 1863 the Union adopted a system of conscription for all men aged 20 to 45. As in the Confederacy, this act was bitterly criticised, particularly the fact that it was possible to avoid the draft by hiring a substitute or paying $300 (half a year's wages for working men). By 1865 some 900,000 men had fought for the Confederacy: the Union enlisted about 2.1 million men.

cerns, played a role in these appointments. A few 'political' generals became first rate soldiers: many were incompetent. Only a few junior officers on either side had any military qualifications. Many were elected by the men under their command.

d) Strategy and Tactics

Americans assumed the war would be similar to the Mexican War (1846–8). This had been a war where offensive tactics had usually won the day. However, by 1861 the smoothbore musket, which had an effective range of under 100 yards, had been supplanted by the rifle-musket. Rifle-muskets, while still muzzle-loading and single-shot (skilled men could fire three shots a minute), were accurate at up to 600 yards. This meant that battle tactics now favoured the defending force which could fire several rounds at the attackers before they could get close enough to thrust bayonets. Indeed bayonets soon became redundant. Less than 1 per cent of battle-wounds were caused by bayonets: 90 per cent were caused by bullets. Infantry attacks were even more likely to fail if the defenders had dug trenches. By 1864 almost every position was entrenched.

By 1862 attacking infantry often approached the enemy in one, two or three lines, of two ranks each, perhaps a thousand men long. The second line followed about 250 yards behind the first while the third line was usually held in reserve. The attack usually broke down into an 'advance by rushes', elements of the first line working forward, from one bit of cover to the next, with pauses to build up enough fire to cover the next rush. If the first line stalled, the second line would be fed in to restore the attack's momentum, followed, if necessary, by the third line. The assaulting force, at the moment of collision with the enemy, would thus usually consist of one disordered mass, making it difficult for officers to retain control and follow up any success that might be achieved. Usually the beaten army retreated a few miles to lick its wounds; the winners stayed in place to lick theirs. Politicians on both sides denounced their generals for not pursuing a beaten foe. They did not realise how hard it was for a victorious army to gather exhausted men for a new attack.

The accuracy of the rifle meant that cavalry were no longer a major force on the battlefield. The main role of cavalry was now to scout, make raids against supply lines, guard an army's flanks, screen its movements, obtain supplies, cover retreats, and, very occasionally, to chase a broken enemy. In battle cavalrymen often dismounted and fought as infantry rather than charging with sabres.

Artillery had proved itself in the Mexican War, with horse batteries firing solid shot, grape shot, shell or cannister into the enemy ranks. However, the rifle-musket forced artillerymen to retire to safer,

---

THE IMPORTANCE OF COMMUNICATIONS

▼ The Civil War was the first great railway war. Both sides made use of railways to move masses of men and to keep them supplied.

▼ On the Mississippi and its major tributaries, steamboats played a vital supply role.

▼ The telegraph enabled commanders to communicate directly with units on widely separated fronts, thus ensuring co-ordinated advances.

but less effective, ranges. Artillery also had limited impact against an entrenched enemy.

e) The War's Main Theatres

▼ North Virginia was seen as the crucial area. Richmond, the Confederate capital, was the principal target of Union forces. It was only a hundred miles or so from Washington. The fighting area between the Appalachian Mountains and the sea was small. Geographical factors – dense forests, swampy areas and a half-dozen major rivers running west to east – favoured the defender.

▼ Between the Appalachians and the Mississippi lay a vast region of plains and hills. The sheer size of the 'West', its lack of natural lines of defence, and the fact that its main rivers flowed into the heart of the Confederacy, meant it was the South's 'soft underbelly'. Both sides had difficulty organising their Western forces. Confederate armies were split into various departments, commanded by different generals who found it hard to coordinate strategy. Union forces had to hold down the areas they occupied and also guard their extensive supply lines.

▼ West of the Mississippi was a massive, but thinly populated area. The fighting here was small scale and none of the campaigns had a major effect on the war's outcome.

f) The Naval War

As soon as the war began the Union bought scores of merchant ships, armed them, and sent them to do blockade duty. By December 1861 the Union navy had over 260 warships and a hundred more were under construction. Much of this expansion was due to the dynamism of Navy Secretary Gideon Welles. He was helped by several factors: first, most naval officers remained loyal to the Union; second, the North had a proud naval tradition; and third, it had the industrial capacity to build a huge fleet. The blockade of the South was crucial. If the Confederacy could sell its cotton in Europe and purchase weapons in return, the war might continue indefinitely. Given the 3,500 miles of Southern coastline, the blockade was easier to declare than to enforce. But as the months went by it grew tighter, hindering the South's war effort. The Union was also able to use its naval supremacy to transport its troops and to strike at coastal targets. In 1862 river gunboats helped Union troops capture a number of key fortresses on the Western rivers. By August 1862 all of the Mississippi, except a 150-mile stretch from Vicksburg to Port Hudson, was in Union hands. Without its 'inland navy', the Union could not have established or maintained control in the West.

A MODERN WAR?
Factories and machines transformed warfare. Outproducing was as important as outfighting the enemy. Given the industrial dimension, railways, the telegraph, the rifle-musket, and iron, steam-driven ships, the Civil War can be seen as the first 'modern' war, more akin to the First World War than the Napoleonic Wars. However, it is possible to exaggerate its 'modernness'. There was no battle in the entire war when there were more than 100,000 men on each side. The strategy and tactics of the armies would have been familiar to Napoleon. Horse-drawn transport remained the norm. Experiments with machine guns, submarines and underwater mines were rudimentary and made little impact on the war's outcome. There was also little of the cruelty that characterised twentieth-century wars. Civilians were generally safe. Women were rarely, if ever, raped.

The Confederacy started the war with a dearth of men and ships, and few facilities for building a navy. Secretary of the Confederate Navy Mallory believed that the South's best chance to break the Union blockade was to build ironclad warships. The Confederacy's greatest moment in the naval war came on 8 March 1862 when the ironclad *Virginia* sank two blockading ships. Unfortunately for Mallory, the Union now had its own ironclad, the *Monitor*, and on 9 March the first ironclad encounter in history occurred. Neither ship was able to sink the other but the *Virginia* was so damaged it had to return to port and was later abandoned. While the South stretched its resources to build other ironclads, the North was able to mass produce them. Confederate agents purchased a number of fast raiders from Britain. While they had some success against Union merchant ships, they were eventually hunted down. Torpedoes (underwater mines) were the most successful Confederate naval weapon, sinking or seriously damaging more than 40 Union ships.

g) The Soldiers' Experience

Was the Civil War a 'total war'?

Historian Bell Wiley believed that the similarities between 'Johnny Reb' and 'Billy Yank' far outweighed the differences. But he accepted that there were some differences. Although the Union army was mainly composed of native-born Americans, some 20 per cent of its troops had been born overseas, mainly in Ireland or Germany. By 1865 10 per cent of Union troops were African Americans. In contrast, 95 per cent of 'rebel' soldiers were native-born Southerners. According to Wiley, Union soldiers were better educated than Southerners, less religious, and held a less romantic view of the war: Southern troops were reputed to be more independent and less likely to take military discipline seriously. Union soldiers were certainly better equipped and better supplied than the rebels. By 1862 most Union troops wore a blue uniform. Confederate soldiers wore assorted colours.

Military units usually consisted of men from the same neighbourhoods. The closeness of the soldiers to their home community was a strong impetus. Soldiers were aware that any cowardice or misdoing was reported home. So too was bravery, which earned a soldier respect both at home and among his comrades. Ethnic affinity was also important. Irish and German troops usually fought in their own regiments. African Americans always did. For most men the novelty of army life was short-lived. In its place came homesickness. At least one in ten men deserted. They did so for a variety of reasons: boredom; fear; concern for families at home; and lack of commitment. Actual fighting took up only a small part of a soldier's time. In battle, most men fought well: indeed their ability to absorb punishment astounded European observers. Several historians, including Bell

Wiley, think that most soldiers had little idea of what they were fighting for. Certainly many fought bravely simply because they did not want to let down their close comrades. However, James McPherson believes that men on both sides were aware of the issues at stake and passionately concerned about them.

2 The War 1861–3

ISSUE:
Why did the war not end in 1861, 1862 or 1863?

a) First Manassas (or Bull Run)

The main Confederate army of 22,000 men was at Manassas. On 16 July McDowell marched south with a 30,000-strong Union army. His attack on 21 July came close to victory. However, Southern forces were saved by the arrival of troops from the Shenandoah Valley. Union troops panicked and fled. The Southern army, as disorganised as the routed Union army, was unable to follow up its victory by marching on Washington. For the next few months Confederate troops held the line along the Potomac river. There was little fighting.

b) General McClellan and the Peninsula Campaign

After Manassas McDowell was replaced by General McClellan. Credited with some minor victories in West Virginia, he exuded an air of optimism and soon replaced Scott as General-in-Chief. McClellan is one of the most controversial figures of the war. An able administrator, he restored the morale of the Union army. Anxious not to create scars that might take a generation to heal, his hope of winning the war by manoeuvre and bringing it to an end without too much gore made (humane) sense. However, even McClellan's supporters concede that he was an arrogant egotist. He failed to work collaboratively with his political masters whom he constantly derided. (He described Lincoln as 'a well-meaning baboon'.) The main charge levied against him is that, having built a fine army, he was too reluctant to use it. Indecisive and over-cautious, he tended to exaggerate the odds against him. This was apparent over the winter of 1861–2. Lincoln and Republican politicians grew increasingly impatient as McClellan refused to move.

In April 1862 McClellan's 121,000-strong Army of the Potomac was transported to Fortress Monroe, planning to attack Richmond up the peninsula between the York and James rivers. McClellan advanced slowly, not reaching the outskirts of Richmond until May. Although he had twice as many men as the Confederates, he believed he was outnumbered, and awaited reinforcements. Stonewall Jackson ensured that they never arrived. With just 18,000 men, Jackson

UNION PLANS IN 1861
General Winfield Scott thought it would take many months to train and equip the armies needed to crush the insurrection. He supported the Anaconda Plan, the aim of which was to put pressure on the South by naval blockade and by winning control of the Mississippi river. But Lincoln looked for a quick victory, urging General McDowell, commander of the Union army, to march on Richmond. 'You are green, it is true', he wrote, 'but they are green; you are all green alike'.

CONFEDERATE PLANS IN 1861

President Davis pledged himself to defend every part of the Confederacy. He realised that lost territory would result in a depletion of resources and a decline in Southern morale. Rather than fight a guerrilla war, he thus supported the raising of conventional armies.

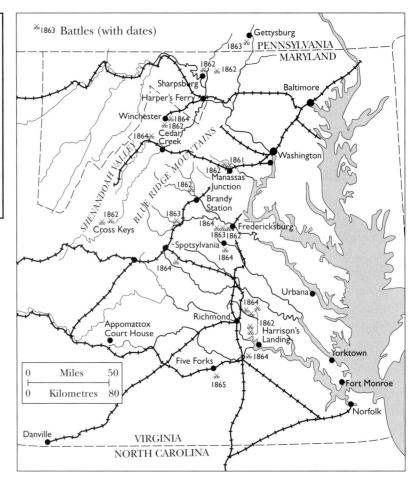

Figure 7 The Virginia Theatre.

How good a commander was McClellan?

fought a brilliant campaign in the Shenandoah Valley. Lincoln, worried at the threat that Jackson might pose to Washington, reversed his decision to send men to help McClellan. Instead it was Jackson who marched south to take part in the fighting around Richmond.

c) Lee and the Army of North Virginia

On 31 May General Joe Johnston attacked McClellan's forces outside Richmond. The battle of Fair Oaks was a costly draw. Its most important outcome was the fact that Johnston was wounded and replaced by Robert E. Lee. Lee, a 55-year-old Virginian, had served with distinction in the Mexican War. Lincoln had offered him high command in the Union army but Lee had remained loyal to his state. Now he had a chance to display his skill. Renaming his army the Army of Northern Virginia, he determined to seize the initiative. In the last week in June he hurled his outnumbered men against the enemy. The week of battles which followed is known as 'The Seven Days'. The Confederacy lost more men (20,614) than the Union (15,849) but a demoralised McClellan retreated down the peninsula.

Lincoln now appointed General Pope to command the Union forces around Washington. McClellan was ordered to evacuate the peninsula and join Pope who would then have enough men to advance on Richmond. Lee decided to strike first. Although some historians have been critical of this 'offensive–defensive' strategy, it is hard to imagine a better one. A war fought purely on the defensive would allow the Union to pick off the South at will. By going on the offensive, Lee hoped to win a decisive victory. Dividing his army, he sent Jackson on a long sweep west and north of Pope. The Second Battle of Bull Run (or Second Manassas), fought on 29–30 August, was a Union disaster. Failing to appreciate that the rest of Lee's army was marching to Jackson's aid, Pope was defeated when Longstreet's corps attacked his left flank. Pope's poor generalship had cost the Union 16,000 men (Lee lost only 9,000). Reluctantly Lincoln re-appointed McClellan as commander-in-chief.

Figure 8 Robert E. Lee.

In September, Lee sent Jackson to capture Harper's Ferry while he himself invaded Maryland. His aims were many: to take the fight to the North; protect Virginia's harvest; gain Maryland volunteers; demoralise the North; and persuade Britain to recognise the Confederacy. However, his invasion not did go to plan. He lost more soldiers by desertion than he gained from Maryland. He also lost a copy of his operational orders which mysteriously fell into McClellan's hands. Aware that Lee's army was divided, McClellan was now in a superb position to defeat him. Lee took up a position behind Antietam Creek. Given that he was outnumbered, that he failed to entrench, and that he had the Potomac behind him, Lee's decision to offer battle seems incredible. If McClellan had attacked on 15 or 16 September Lee must surely have been defeated. But McClellan did not attack. On 16 September Jackson's corps rejoined Lee's army which reduced the odds. Even so McClellan still had a two-to-one advantage when he finally attacked on 17 September. Antietam was really three separate battles. All three Union attacks were no more than partially successful and Lee managed to hang on. Antietam was the bloodiest single-day battle of the Civil War. The Confederacy lost 10,000 casualties, the Union 14,000. McClellan was able to claim a victory because Lee retreated into Virginia. But McClellan failed to follow up his 'victory'. Lincoln, exasperated with McClellan's excuses for inactivity, finally relieved him of command in November, replacing him with General Burnside.

Figure 9 The Western Theatre.

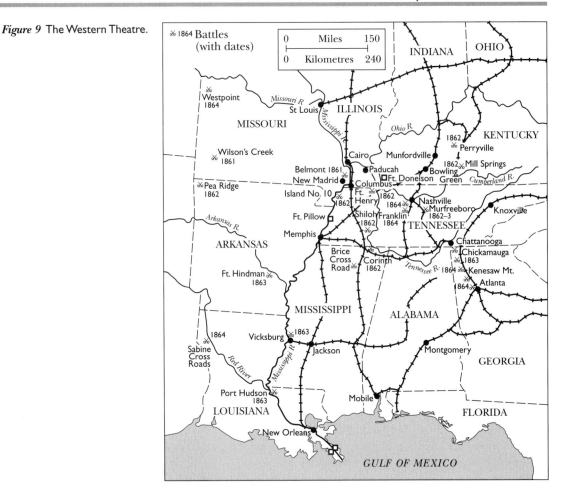

Figure 10 Ulysses S. Grant.

d) The War in the West: 1861–2

General Albert Johnston, the Confederate Western commander, hoped that a number of strategically built forts would hold up any Union advance. In February 1862 Union forces under General Ulysses S. Grant captured the key river forts of Fort Henry and Fort Donelson, forcing Johnston to abandon Kentucky and most of Tennessee. In March 1862 Grant pushed into south-west Tennessee. On 6 April Johnston launched a surprise attack on Grant's army, encamped at Shiloh, and came close to victory. Johnson's death seemed to make little difference. Beauregard, who took over Confederate command, telegraphed to Davis that he had won a 'complete victory'. But Grant remained calm and with good reason. That night, 25,000 troops from General Buell's army arrived. The next day, the Confederates were forced to retreat. They had suffered 10,600 (to the Union's 13,000) casualties. Although Shiloh was not Grant's best-fought battle, its outcome was of great importance. The

Union had turned back the Confederate bid to regain the initiative. Davis now replaced Beauregard with Bragg. On the Union side, General Halleck's appointment as General-in-Chief, to coordinate strategy from Washington, enhanced Grant's position.

e) The East: 1862–3

On 13 December 1862 Burnside, the new commander of the 100,000 strong Army of the Potomac, launched a series of suicidal attacks on Lee's 75,000 men, well-positioned at Fredericksburg. Union losses amounted to 11,000. Lee's army lost less than half that number. Lincoln now replaced Burnside by 'Fighting' Joe Hooker. By April 1863 he was ready to try his luck against Lee. While General Sedgewick threatened Lee at Fredericksburg, the bulk of Hooker's army moved against Lee's left flank. Lee now showed himself at his most brilliant. Leaving 10,000 men to hold Sedgewick, he led 50,000 men to meet Hooker at Chancellorsville. On 2 May, he further divided his army, sending Jackson to attack Hooker's right flank. Union troops fell back in confusion. Nightfall brought an end to the fighting and to Jackson, mistakenly shot by one of his own men. Hooker retreated. Lee had achieved what many see as his most impressive victory. With far fewer men, he had inflicted greater casualties (17,000 compared with 13,000) on the Union army.

How good a commander was Robert E. Lee?

Davis's advisers were now split on how best to use Lee's army. Some favoured sending forces to relieve Vicksburg. Others wanted to advance through Tennessee and Kentucky. Convinced that only victories on Northern soil would force Union leaders to accept Southern independence, Lee favoured an invasion of Pennsylvania. Such a move would relieve pressure in Virginia and would ensure that his men could live at Union expense. Lee got his way and in mid-June began his advance northwards. Meade, who replaced Hooker, had little time to get to grips with his new command. On 30 June Confederate soldiers stumbled across Union forces at Gettysburg. Both Lee and Meade ordered all their forces to converge on the small town. Thus began the greatest battle fought on the American continent. The first day of the battle – 1 July – belonged to the Confederacy. Union troops were pushed back, taking up a strong position on a range of hills. On 2 July Confederate forces came close, but not close enough, to victory. On 3 July Lee launched his main attack on the Union centre. Led by General Pickett, 15,000 men charged up Cemetery Ridge. In under one hour the Confederates suffered 6,500 casualties. Lee had been beaten. In three days he had lost 28,000 men, a third of his command. (The Union had lost 23,000 men.) Lee retreated back to Virginia. He accepted full responsibilty for Gettysburg: 'The army did all it could', he said. 'I fear I required of it impossibilities.' He offered his resignation. Davis refused to accept it.

Gettysburg was a serious Confederate defeat. But it was probably not the major turning point of the war. If Lee had won, it seems unlikely that Union morale would have collapsed. Nor did Gettysburg make Confederate defeat inevitable. Meade was unable to follow up his victory and Lee's army continued to hold North Virginia.

Figure 11 Union forces attack Vicksburg, 1863: a twentieth century artist's view.

Figure 12 Atlanta 1864: a post-1865 lithograph.

Figure 13 A battery of 12-pounder cannon prepares to fire against Confederate lines outside Petersburg, 1864.

ACTIVITY

Examine Figures 11, 12 and 13. What do they suggest about the nature of the Civil War?

f) The West: 1862–3

i) Vicksburg

From August 1862 Union forces under Grant tried to take Vicksburg, which prevented Union control of the Mississippi. As the threat to Vicksburg grew, Davis appointed Joe Johnston to oversee military operations in the West but Bragg (in Tennessee) and Pemberton (at Vicksburg) continued to exercise independent command. The hope that Johnston would bring a unified vision to the West was not realised.

Over the winter of 1862–3 Grant probed unsuccessfully for a crossing which would enable him to get his forces east of the town. Finally he determined to gamble. Moving his army down the west side of the Mississippi, he relied upon a Union fleet sailing past Vicksburg. This was achieved in mid-April 1863. Two weeks later Grant's army was ferried across the Mississippi. Grant now cut inland, defeating Johnston and Pemberton, and forcing the latter to retreat into Vicksburg. Grant lay siege to the town. On 4 July it surrendered. Some 30,000 Confederates were taken prisoner. The capture of Port Hudson five days later meant that the Mississippi was now a Union highway and the Confederacy was cut in two.

ii) Tennessee

In October 1862 Confederate forces led by Bragg blundered into a Union army at Perryville in Kentucky. Bragg won a tactical victory but had to retreat. Union forces led by Rosecrans now tried to drive Bragg's army out of Tennessee. On 31 December the two armies mauled each other at Murfreesboro. Bragg renewed the battle two

THE WAR: 1861–3

1861 First battle of Manassas (July);

1862 Union capture of Fort Henry and Fort Donelson (February);
Battle of Shiloh (March);
Seven Day battles (June–July);
Second Manassas (August);
Battle of Antietam (September);
Battle of Fredericksburg (December);

1863 Battle of Chancellorsville (May);
Battle of Gettysburg (July);
Fall of Vicksburg (July);
Battle of Chickamauga (September);
Battles of Lookout Mountain and Missionary Ridge (November).

days later but his attack was beaten back and he had to withdraw. Tennessee remained quiet for six months. Rosecrans finally advanced in June 1863, forcing Bragg to retreat. On 19–20 September Bragg came close to winning a major victory at Chickamauga but the Union army managed to retreat to Chattanooga. Bragg besieged the town but failed to cut its supply line. Lincoln now gave Grant command of all the Union's western forces. Grant acted swiftly to re-supply Chattanooga. Then on 24 November Union troops stormed Lookout Mountain. The next day Grant's men seized Missionary Ridge. Confederate forces retreated in disarray into Georgia.

The defeats at Gettysburg, Vicksburg and Chattanooga were severe blows to Southern morale. Nevertheless, the Confederacy was far from beaten. Out west the Union faced the problem of long supply lines. In the east the Confederacy still had Lee and the Army of Northern Virginia. If Lee could continue to inflict heavy casualties on the Union, there was every chance that the Northern electorate might oust Lincoln in the 1864 election.

ISSUE:
How well did the Confederacy wage war on the domestic front?

3 The Confederate War Effort

a) President Jefferson Davis

Davis remains a controversial figure. His vice-president Stephens thought him 'weak, timid, petulant, peevish, obstinate' and blamed him for practically everything that went wrong in the war. Historian David Potter saw Davis's performance as the most important reason why the Confederacy lost the war. Yet it is also possible to claim that his leadership qualities ensured that the Confederacy held out for as long as it did. Lee said he could think of no one who could have done a better job than Davis.

The Case against Davis

▼ He was unable to establish good working relationships with many of his colleagues. In the course of the war he appointed six Secretaries of War.
▼ Some of his military appointments were disastrous.
▼ He is blamed for meddling in the affairs of subordinates.
▼ Finding it hard to prioritise and to delegate, he got bogged down in detail.
▼ While some contemporaries attacked Davis for having despotic tendencies, historians have criticised him for exercising his executive powers too sparingly.

▼ He has been charged with failing to mobilise public opinion and to build a sense of Confederate nationalism.

The Case for Davis

▼ He showed a good overall appreciation of the war. Despite later accusations, he did not over-command his forces. To generals he trusted, he gave considerable freedom. The fact that he appointed Lee says much for his military good sense.

▼ He supported tough measures when necessary, even when these ran contrary to concerns about state rights and individual liberty.

▼ For the most part he left his Secretaries to get on with running their departments, involving himself only in the detailed decision making of the War Department.

▼ During the war, he made several tours of the South to try to rekindle flagging faith.

▼ Few have questioned his dedication to the Confederate cause or the intense work he put into a difficult job.

b) Davis's Cabinet

In all, Davis made 16 appointments to head the six departments. Benjamin accounted for three of these as he was appointed, in succession, to Justice, War and State. He owed his survival to his ability and to his close relationship with Davis. Benjamin, Mallory (Navy) and Reagan (Postmaster General) served in the cabinet from start to finish. But there was a high turnover in the War and State Departments. This resulted, not from feuds between Davis and his Secretaries, but from Congressional criticisms which sometimes forced Davis to accept resignations. Most of the Secretaries were capable men and government operations functioned reasonably smoothly for most of the war.

c) States and State Rights

To wage a successful war, the Confederacy had to have the full co-operation of all its states. It also needed a strong central government. But some state leaders were not keen to concede too much power to Richmond. Governors Joseph Brown of Georgia and Zebulon Vance of North Carolina are often blamed for not working for the common cause. Brown, for example, opposed conscription and exempted thousands of Georgians from the draft. In reality, however, most states cooperated effectively with Davis. All the 28 men who served as state governors, including Brown and Vance, were committed to the Confederacy.

THE CONFEDERATE CONGRESS

Congressmen in the Provisional Congress (which met in 1861–2) were selected by their state legislatures. After this, there were two popularly elected Congresses, the first from 1862 to 1864, the second from 1864 to 1865. Politicians who had once been enemies tried to present a united front. Many historians believe that the absence of a two-party system and the lack of an 'official' opposition resulted in less channelling of political activity and more squabbling. Davis, moreover, had no party organisation to mobilise support or to help him guide bills through Congress. In 1861–2 most Congressmen rallied round Davis. However, as morale on the home front deteriorated under the impact of military setbacks, inflation, conscription and impressment, opposition grew. The anti-Davis faction defies easy categorisation. Some held extreme state rights views: others simply disagreed with the way the war was being waged.

VOLUNTARY ASSOCIATION

Much of what was achieved in the Confederacy was due more to local initiative than to government order. Southern clergymen played an important role, preaching and writing in defence of the new nation. Church buildings often became centres for women's groups who made clothing and other items for the troops. Women also helped found hospitals and organised societies to feed the poor.

d) 'Died of Democracy'?

Historian David Donald has claimed that concern for individual liberties cost the South the war. Unwilling to take tough action against internal dissent, the Confederacy 'died of democracy'. Donald's argument is not convincing. His supposition that the Confederacy allowed total individual freedom is mistaken. In 1862 Congress authorised Davis to declare martial law in areas threatened by the enemy. He immediately placed front-line towns under military rule. Given the opposition to conscription, he also suspended the right of habeas corpus for a total of 16 months. Nor was there total freedom of speech. In lieu of specific legislation, public pressures generally succeeded in imposing loyalty to the Confederacy.

e) Financing the War

Arguably the Confederacy's greatest failure was in the area of finance. Memminger, Treasury Secretary from 1861 to 1864, has often been singled out for blame. In his defence, the Confederacy was always likely to find it hard to finance a long war. It had few gold reserves and the Union blockade made it hard to raise money from tariffs. Raising taxes by other means was not easy. Taxes on income, profits and property, levied in 1863, were unpopular and difficult to administer. In 1863, in an effort to feed Southern troops, Congress passed the Impressment Act, allowing the seizure of goods to support front-line armies, and the Taxation-in-kind Act, authorising government agents to collect 10 per cent of produce from all farmers. Davis accepted the unfairness of these measures but thought them justified by 'absolute necessity'. Only 8 per cent of the Confederacy's income was derived from taxes. The less it taxed, the more it had to borrow. But as the tide of battle turned against the South, European financiers were reluctant to loan money. It also grew harder to sell war bonds in the South. Given that the Confederacy only raised about one-third of its war costs through taxes, bonds and loans, Memminger was forced to print vast amounts of Treasury paper notes. (States, towns, and banks all did the same.) The result was serious inflation. Shortages of basic goods, resulting from the breakdown of the railway system and from the blockade, also helped push up prices. By 1865 the general price index in the eastern Confederacy was over 5,000 times the 1861 level. This led to widespread suffering which helped erode Southern will.

f) The Confederate Economy

In many respects Davis's government acted forcefully to place the South's economy on a war footing and to expand its industrial base. Officials soon intruded into almost every aspect of economic life, managing conscription, manufacturing and transportation. The Ordnance Bureau, ably led by Josiah Gorgas, played a crucial role. By 1863 there were enough factories and gunpowder works in the South to keep its armies supplied with munitions. Steps were also taken to regulate foreign trade. In 1863 a law required all blockade runners to carry, as at least one-third of their cargo, cotton out and war supplies in. However, not all historians are convinced that the Confederacy did as well as it might have done. Short of trained personnel, Richmond was simply not up to the task of carrying out many of its ambitious schemes. More could and should have been done to supervise the railway system which, handicapped by shortages of materials and labour, slowly collapsed. The Confederacy might also have used cotton to better effect. The 'informal' embargo on cotton exports in 1861, supported if not officially sanctioned by Richmond, had two aims: to ensure that planters turned to food production; and to create a cotton scarcity which might lead to foreign recognition. More food was produced but the embargo failed to have much impact on Britain or France. Had cotton been exported in 1861, when the Union blockade was weak, the money from the sales could have been used to buy vital war supplies.

By 1865 the Southern economy was near collapse. Machinery and spare parts were wearing out and could not be replaced. Raw materials had been lost as Union forces took over large areas of the South. The breakdown of the railway system, much of which was destroyed by advancing Union armies, proved decisive in the Confederacy's final demise.

g) The Social Impact of the War

▼ The Confederacy succeeded in mobilising about 900,000 men – over 40 per cent of its white males of fighting age. This had important implications for all aspects of life, particularly the role of women. Wives of ordinary farmers had to work even longer hours to provide enough food for their families. Wives of planters had to manage large plantations. In towns women took over some jobs which had been done by men.

▼ Shortages of basic items, inflation and impressment had a demoralising effect on all parts of the South. Some areas were also devastated by Union troops. Refugees flooded the South as slaves fled their owners and whites fled contesting armies. In an effort to tackle the problem of refugees – and poverty in general – Confederate and state governments, town authorities, private charities and wealthy individuals became involved in unprecedented relief efforts. Yet by the winter of 1864–5 the scale of the problem was so great that it overwhelmed the relief activities. Elsewhere the social order collapsed as Union raiders, guerrilla bands, deserters and fugitive slaves roamed the countryside, looting and wantonly destroying.

h) Opposition to the War

Opposition grew as the war progressed. The introduction of conscription in 1862 was a major cause. Lukewarm Southerners now faced a choice of military service or overt opposition. In the mountain regions of North Carolina and Alabama, armed men joined together to fight off enrolment officers. Ordinary farmers resented the fact that rich men could avoid military service by hiring substitutes or exempting themselves if they were in a managerial role on a plantation with over 20 slaves. The perception of a 'rich man's war and a poor man's fight' grew. (In reality few rich men did exempt themselves: indeed they were more likely to fight and die than poor Southerners.) However, opposition to the war was not essentially 'class'-based. It was strongest in upland areas where it was hard to grow cotton and thus where there were few slaves. Many people in these areas had opposed secession from the start.

i) Conclusion

Morale was as crucial on the home front as on the battlefield. Southern morale seems to have been high in 1861–2, helped by a good harvest in 1861 and battlefield success. However, military reverses, and growing hardship on the domestic front, damaged morale. There was an understandable, if not necessarily justified, loss of faith in the Confederate leadership. Certainly Davis's government made mistakes. But, arguably, it was no more mistake-prone than Lincoln's government. Nor were Southerners less dedicated than Yankees. Most fought hard and long, enduring far greater suffering than Northerners. Although ultimately not equal to the challenge, the Confederacy's efforts on the home front were, in most respects, better than might have been expected. The bitter truth was that most of its domestic problems were essentially insurmountable.

ACTIVITY

What points might you make to claim that the Confederacy lost the war, not on the battlefield, but on the home front?

4   The Northern Home Front

ISSUE:
How well did the Union wage war on the domestic front?

a) President Abraham Lincoln

Lincoln is often regarded as the USA's greatest president. Contemporaries would have been staggered by this opinion. He was so unpopular in 1864 it seemed unlikely he would be re-elected.

The Case against Lincoln

▼ His choice of army commanders between 1861 and 1863 did not inspire confidence.

▼ He can be seen as just a devious politician.

▼ He deserves little credit for foreign policy (handled by Seward), financial measures (handled by Chase) or economic matters (which were left to Congress).

▼ Democrats accused him of acting tyrannically and abusing the constitution. In 1862 he suspended the writ of habeas corpus: anyone could be imprisoned by military authority for impeding conscription, or affording aid or comfort to the enemy. Some 40,000 people were subject to arbitrary arrest.

▼ In 1861–2 he moved hesitantly on the slavery issue and seems to have been driven more by practical concerns than conscience.

▼ He had an easier task than Davis. The North was always favourite to win the Civil War.

▼ Arguably it was his murder, rather than his war leadership which assured his reputation.

The Case for Lincoln

▼ He selected able men and delegated well. Ultimately he appointed the winning military team of Grant and Sherman.

▼ One of his great strengths was his ability to articulate the Union's war aims.

▼ He shaped the strategy of unconditional surrender, vital to the war's outcome.

▼ He handled the slavery issue with great skill (see section 6).

▼ He was a consummate politician, keeping in touch with public opinion and devoting much time and energy to matters of patronage and party organisation. This ensured there were many men within both his party and the government who were loyal to himself, a fact which served him well in 1864. His views tended to represent the middle ground but he kept open lines of communication with both the radical and conservative wings of the Republican Party. Sensitive to the pulse of public opinion, he was always a pragmatist, concerned more with what might be achieved than with what should be achieved.

▼ Although he stretched the authority of his office beyond any previous practice, overall, he remained faithful to the spirit of the Constitution. Military, not political, goals were foremost in his mind when he allowed the restriction of civil liberties. Most of those imprisoned without trial came from the South or from states like Missouri which had many Southern sympathisers. Given the grim reality of guerrilla war in Missouri, martial law was essential. Elsewhere moderation was usually the norm. Arrests rarely involved Democrat politicians or newspaper editors.

▼ For four years he stuck at his job. He worked hard – from 7am to 11pm most days. His good health gave him an edge over Davis who suffered from stress-related illnesses.

Figure 14 Lincoln and his cabinet.

b) Lincoln's Cabinet

Lincoln's cabinet was far more stable than that of Davis. Most of the Secretaries remained at their posts for most of the war. Secretary of State Seward was regarded as Lincoln's right-hand man. Treasury Secretary Chase was the main spokesman for the radical wing of the Republican Party. Lincoln's first War Secretary Cameron had a reputation for corruption before the war and this reputation quickly grew.

In 1862 he was replaced by Stanton, who proved himself energetic, efficient and incorruptible. Welles, Secretary of the Navy, served the Union well throughout the war. Lincoln held few formal cabinet meetings, using those that did meet to get approval for actions he was about to take.

c) State Government and Voluntary Associations

Throughout the war, most state governments provided invaluable assistance to Lincoln, especially in raising troops. Most states were Republican-controlled. Those that did fall under Democrat control did little to hinder the Union war effort. Neither the federal nor state governments had the apparatus to manage all aspects of the war. Voluntary organisations helped fill the gaps. For example, the United States Sanitary Commission created in 1861 did much to help the Army Medical Bureau. Sanitary Commissioners prowled Union camps and hospitals, insisting on better food and conditions.

d) Financing the War

In 1861 the Union had an established Treasury, gold reserves, land assets and an assured source of revenue from tariffs. Nevertheless, financial problems threatened to overwhelm the Union cause over the winter of 1861–2. Secretary Chase kept the Treasury afloat by raising loans and issuing bonds. Two-thirds of the Union's revenue was raised in this way. One-fifth was raised by taxes. An income tax, the first in US history, imposed a 3 per cent tax on annual incomes over $800. Far more important was the Internal Revenue Act of 1862 which basically taxed everything. Congress approved an inflationary monetary policy. In 1862 the Legal Tender Act authorised the issuing of $150 million in paper currency. Ultimately 'greenback' notes to the value of $431 million were issued. During the war the North experienced inflation of 80 per cent.

e) The Northern Economy

Before the war Republicans had pressed for the use of federal funds to advance enterprise and develop America's resources. After 1861 they were able to pass major economic legislation, previously held up by Democrat obstructionism. Some of the measures were designed to stimulate agriculture. The 1862 Homestead Act, for example, offered 160-acre farms out west, free of charge, to settlers who worked on them for five years. Other measures aimed to help industry. Higher tariffs not only provided the government with extra revenue but also protected industry from foreign competition. The

CONGRESS

Lacking its Southern members, Congress was controlled by the Republicans. In 1861 the House of Representatives had 105 Republicans, 43 Democrats and 28 'Unionists'. Of the 48 Senators, 31 were Republican. The Republicans retained control after the 1862 mid-term elections. Given the Republican dominance, Congress generally cooperated with Lincoln. Radical Republicans often blamed Lincoln for failing to prosecute the war more vigorously or to move against slavery more rapidly. However, the radicals were not a disciplined group. Nor were they inveterate enemies of Lincoln. When he wanted their support, he usually got it.

most important railway development was the decision to build a transcontinental line from Omaha to San Francisco. By twentieth-century standards, there was little assertion of federal power in the management of the wartime economy. There was no rationing, no attempt to control prices, wages and profits, and no central control of railways.

The Northern economy was able to ensure that Union armies were well-equipped and that civilians did not go short of basic items. The war is often seen as stimulating economic growth. Production gains were notable in war-related industries such as the boot and shoe industry, shipbuilding, and munitions. Railways made great profits. Farmers also benefited from the war. Union forces had to be fed and there was an increased demand from abroad. Not all historians accept that the war had a positive effect: arguably Northern economic growth in the 1860s was slower than in any other decade in the nineteenth century. Some industries, especially New England cotton mills, suffered hard times. Nevertheless the economy grew in spite, if not because, of the war. Historian Peter Parish claims: 'The abiding impression [of the Northern economy] is one of energy and enterprise, resilience and resource … The war was not the soil in which industrial growth took root, nor a blight which stunted it, but a very effective fertiliser'.

f) The Impact of the War on Northern Society

▼ In many ways life for most Northerners went on as usual. However, given that Union regiments were often made up of men from a single town or county, high casualties in battle could mean sudden calamity for a neighbourhood.

▼ There were more opportunities for women, who worked as teachers, in industry and in government. However, the war did not bring women much closer to political or economic equality. They were not given the vote and after the war returned to their old roles.

▼ The war initially led to a fall in immigrant numbers: 92,000 in 1861–2 compared with 154,000 in 1860. But by 1863 there were over 176,000 immigrants and by 1865 nearly 250,000 – proof of the North's booming war economy. Many immigrants fought in the Union army. This may have aided the process of assimilation and help tame the anti-immigrant feeling of the 1850s.

g) Opposition to the War

Lincoln, aware of the need to maintain Northern unity, promoted ex-Democrats to his cabinet and gave military command to men whom he knew were political opponents. So-called War Democrats threw in their lot totally with Lincoln. But as the war went on, opposition grew. Democrats criticised the way the war was being handled, condemned Republican economic policies, attacked Lincoln's arbitary measures, and opposed all measures that proposed an end to slavery. Reflecting and exploiting Northern racist views and capitalising on war weariness, the Democrats had some success in the 1862 mid-term elections. Worried at the growing opposition, Republicans branded some Democrats as traitors. In the west, Republicans labelled their Democratic opponents 'Copperheads' (after a poisonous snake) and claimed that they belonged to pro-Southern secret societies which planned to set up a Northwest Confederacy.

Democrat dissent probably reached its height in early 1863 when Union military failures fostered a sense of defeatism. Some Democrats suggested that the time had come to make peace. One of the leading peace Democrats was Vallandigham. Campaigning to become governor of Ohio, he denounced the war and called upon soldiers to desert. On the orders of General Burnside, Vallandigham was tried by a military court, found guilty of treason and sentenced to imprisonment for the rest of the war. This led to a chorus of protest from outraged Democrats. Lincoln, while not liking what Burnside had done, saw no alternative but to support him. Anxious to avoid making Vallandigham a martyr, Lincoln decided to banish him to the Confederacy for the duration of the war. The upturn in Union military fortunes after July 1863 undermined the hopes of peace Democrat candidates, most of whom lost election contests in 1863.

The most serious internal violence in the North came in New York in July 1863. The New York riots followed the enforcement of the 1863 Conscription Act. Denouncing it as an unconstitutional measure to achieve an unconstitutional end (the freeing of the slaves), Democrats in Congress had voted against it. New York's Democrat Governor Horatio Seymour whipped up opposition to the draft. When the names of the first draftees were drawn, a mob of mostly Irish workers attacked the recruiting station. The mob then went on the rampage, venting its fury on blacks, some of whom had recently been used as strike-breakers. For a few days New York was in chaos. Economic, racial and religious factors all played a part in the riots. Whatever the main cause, the situation posed a major challenge to Lincoln's authority. He moved quickly, sending in 20,000 troops who shot more than a hundred rioters and restored order.

5 Britain and the Civil War

In 1861 most Southerners were convinced that Britain would join the war on their side. Had Britain done so, this might have changed the

---

ACTIVITY

Historian David Potter claimed that 'If the Union and Confederacy had exchanged presidents with one another, the Confederacy might have won its independence'. What points might you make a) to support and b) to attack Potter's claim?

ISSUE:
Why did Britain not get involved in the Civil War?

war's outcome. Palmerston, the British Prime Minister, realised that Britain's long-term self-interest might well be served by the break-up of the USA – a potential rival in the near future. There was also a matter of more immediate concern. In order to prevent economic hardship at home, it might be necessary for Britain to break the Northern blockade to acquire Southern cotton. Palmerston was aware, however, that war with the Union might result in the loss of Canada. It would certainly result in the loss of valuable Northern markets and investments. Moreover, British public opinion was divided. While many sympathised with the South, others, aware that slavery lay at the heart of the war, supported the North. For Palmerston the best solution seemed to be to avoid entanglement.

One immediate problem was whether Britain should recognise the Confederacy as a sovereign state. Lincoln's administration made it clear that it viewed the conflict as a domestic insurrection. Thus, recognition of the Confederacy was tantamount to a declaration of war against the Union. In May 1861 Britain adopted a compromise position. While not recognising the Confederacy as a sovereign state, Britain recognised its belligerent status. Under international law belligerents had the right to contract loans and purchase arms. Although denied British recognition, the Confederacy received valuable assistance from Britain.

The main difficulty between Britain and the Union was the issue of neutral rights at sea. The most serious crisis was the *Trent* affair. In November 1861 Mason and Slidell, Confederate commissioners to Britain and France respectively, left Cuba for Europe in the *Trent*, a British steamer. The *Trent* was stopped by Captain Wilkes, commander of the *San Jacinto*, who forcibly removed Mason and Slidell. This action, a violation of international law, angered Palmerston who demanded a public apology and the release of the two men. To back up the threat, soldiers were sent to Canada. A compromise was eventually found. The US government, while not apologising for Wilkes's action, admitted that he had committed an illegal act and freed Mason and Slidell.

FRENCH POLICY
Napoleon III hoped for a Confederate victory. He had ambitions in Mexico and knew he stood a better chance of realising them if the USA splintered. But he was not prepared to take on the Union without British support, which he could not get.

The closest the Confederacy came to getting British recognition was in August–September 1862. Napoleon III's proposal that Britain and France should mediate in the conflict was seriously considered by Palmerston. But the failure of Lee's Maryland invasion convinced him that it would be unwise to intervene. After Lincoln's Emancipation Proclamation, it was even more unlikely that Britain would risk war against the Union. Given that the British economy was generally prospering, there was limited pressure on the government to take action. The last serious crisis between the Union and Britain came in 1863. Charles Adams, the US minister in London, aware that Laird Brothers were building two ironclad 'rams', threatened war if the boats were sold to the Confederacy. Palmerston, as Adams was aware, had no intention of allowing the 'rams' to be sold and the crisis quickly fizzled out.

Union politicians (like Seward) and diplomats (like Adams) are often praised for their dealings with Britain. But given that Palmerston had no desire for war, the claims for Union diplomatic skill should not be pushed too far. Nor should Confederate diplomacy be heavily criticised. The South did its best to win British support. Its agents established useful contacts with British MPs. In an attempt to influence public opinion, it even set up a British newspaper. It is hard to see what more it could have done.

6 The Destruction of Slavery

ISSUE:
How well did Lincoln handle the slavery issue?

In September 1862 Lincoln proclaimed: 'If I could save the Union without freeing any slave I would do it, and if I could save it by freeing all the slaves, I would do it, and if I could save it by freeing some and leaving others alone I would also do that'. Lincoln was articulating the view of most Northerners. From start to finish most Northern Democrats fought simply to restore the Union. They opposed freeing slaves. In 1861 most Republicans were also reluctant to support a pro-emancipation policy, realising this would leave no possibility of a compromise peace. It would also alienate the four slave states which remained within the Union. Thus both Congress and Lincoln tackled the slavery issue with great caution. Lincoln said in April 1861 that 'I have no purpose, directly or indirectly, to interfere with the institution of slavery in the States where it exists. I believe I have no lawful right to do so, and I have no inclination to do so.' In July 1861 Congress adopted the Crittenden resolutions disclaiming any intention of meddling with 'the established institutions' of the South.

However, a set of forces placed pressure on the federal government to take some action. One problem was what to do with refugee slaves who fled to the camps of Union armies occupying areas of the South. By the letter of the Fugitive Slave Law, the slaves should have been returned to their owners. Some Union generals did just that. Others, on both humane and pragmatic grounds – the slaves would be punished and could also help the Southern war effort – opposed such action. In May 1861 General Butler hit upon a practical solution. He declared that slaves who came to his camp would be confiscated as 'contraband of war'. Butler's action was supported by the terms of the Confiscation Act (August 1861) which threatened any property used 'for insurrectionary purposes' with confiscation. It left unsettled the issue of whether or not 'confiscated' slaves became free.

As it became clear that there was little likelihood of the Southern states being enticed back into the Union, radical Republicans began to make their influence felt. To many radicals, it seemed that to fight slaveholders without fighting slavery, was (in Frederick Douglas's words) a 'half-hearted business'. Most radicals were genuinely concerned for blacks. All had a loathing of slaveholders whom they blamed for causing the war. All believed that if the Union was restored without slavery being abolished, nothing would have been solved. Most thought that freeing the slaves would weaken the Confederate war effort. Slaves would become a fifth column in the South. Moreover, if emancipation became a war aim there was little chance that Britain would support the Confederacy. 'It is often said that war will make an end of Slavery,' declared Charles Sumner in 1861. 'This is probable. But it is surer still that the overthrow of Slavery will make an end of the war.' By 1862 many Republicans supported a tougher stand against slavery. Month by month Congress passed anti-slavery measures. In April slavery in the District of Columbia was abolished. In July Congress enacted a more sweeping Confiscation Act, allowing the seizure of all enemy 'property'.

Lincoln was still reluctant to act. He feared that if emancipation became a Union war aim half the officers in his army 'would fling down their arms and three more states would rise'. In July 1862, the abolitionist Garrison described Lincoln's policy as 'stumbling, halting, prevaricating, irresolute, weak, besotted'. However, by mid-1862, Lincoln was convinced that a bold step was necessary. On 22 July he presented an Emancipation Proclamation to his cabinet. It met with general approval. However, Seward recommended that it should only be issued after a military success; otherwise it would seem like an act of desperation born of weakness. Lincoln accepted the logic of this and waited patiently.

The Emancipation Proclamation was finally issued on 22 September 1862, after the battle of Antietam. Justified as 'a fit and necessary war measure', it seemed, on the surface, to be cautious. Slavery was to be left untouched in states that returned to the Union before 1 January 1863. Thereafter all slaves in enemy territory conquered by Union armies would be 'forever free'. Thus the Proclamation had no effect whatsoever on slavery in the North: it did not even affect slavery in those areas already brought back under Union control. Nevertheless, most radicals, appreciating that he had gone as far as his powers allowed, were delighted at Lincoln's action. They recognised that the Proclamation added a moral dimension to the conflict. As Union forces advanced, slavery in the Confederacy would end – and once it ended there it could not survive in the border states. According to historian Richard Ransom, 'With the stroke of a pen, the president had turned the war into a revolution'.

Northern Democrats saw it this way and disliked what they saw. Democrat politicians denounced the Proclamation and made it a central issue in the 1862 mid-term elections. Historians once claimed that these elections were a triumph for the Democrats, and thus proof that most Northerners were opposed to emancipation. However, Democrat success should not be exaggerated. The Republicans lost 35 seats in – but still kept control of – the House: they gained five seats in the Senate.

On 1 January 1863 Lincoln proclaimed that the freedom of all slaves in rebellious regions was now a Union war aim. In the short term, this may well have helped to stiffen Southern resistance. However, in the long term, it weakened the Confederacy. By encouraging slaves to flee to Union lines, it worsened the South's manpower shortage.

Lincoln faced conflicting pressure on the question of whether or not to enlist blacks in the Union army. Black leaders were anxious that blacks should fight in a war that was likely to destroy slavery. But initially most Northerners, hating the notion of blacks fighting against whites, opposed black recruitment. So did Lincoln in 1861–2. But after the Emancipation Proclamation, and with casualty lists mounting, his resistance abated and after 1863 large numbers of black troops – 33,000 free blacks, 100,000 Southern slaves and 42,000 slaves from the border states – joined the Union army. There may have been a tendency recently to exaggerate the impact black troops had on the outcome of the war. Of the 37,000 black soldiers who died in the war, only 3,000 died in combat. However, black troops did help the Union war effort at a critical time. By 1865 there were nearly as many blacks in arms against the Confederacy as there were white soldiers defending it.

Given that Lincoln's Proclamation would have questionable force once the war ended, the Republicans determined to pass a constitutional amendment to end slavery. The Senate passed the amendment in 1864 but it failed to get the necessary two-thirds support in the House. After his election success in November, Lincoln applied patronage pressure to a number of Democrats to good effect. On 31 January 1865 the House approved (with three votes to spare) the Thirteenth Amendment for ratification by the states. Lincoln said it was 'a King's cure for all the evils. It winds the whole thing up.' It hardly did that. The problem of race relations after the war was likely to be difficult. Few whites, North or South, accepted that blacks were their equal. For most of the war slavery continued to exist in the border states: it remained legal in Kentucky until December 1865.

From 1863 the North fought for a new Union without slavery. Many – but by no means all – Northerners came to accept this. Lincoln's policies reflected and influenced the change in Northern opinion. He moved cautiously. His main aim throughout was to pre-

THE SITUATION IN THE SOUTH

Most blacks remained slaves throughout the Civil War. Comprising more than a third of the Confederacy's population, they made a major contribution to its war effort. They worked in factories and mines, maintained the railways, and helped grow crops. Many states passed laws requiring slave owners to furnish their bondsmen for military labour. As the war intensified, there were fewer white men to supervise slave labour. Many slaves took advantage of the situation, becoming more insubordinate and working less diligently. But there was no slave rebellion. Aware that freedom was coming, slaves bided their time. When a chance came to escape, most took it. In the course of the war some 500,000 slaves fled to join Union armies. This had a devastating effect on the Southern economy.

ACTIVITY

Debate the motion: Abraham Lincoln deserves the accolade 'The Great Emancipator'.

ISSUE:
Why did the Confederacy accept defeat in 1865?

serve the Union, not to free the slaves. But by 1862 he believed that the two issues had become nearly one and the same. By freeing the slaves he could help preserve the Union. His Emancipation Proclamation was a vital step forward. Frederick Douglass said: 'Viewed from the genuine abolition ground, Mr Lincoln seemed tardy, cold, dull and indifferent; but measuring him by the sentiment of his country, a sentiment he was bound as a statesman to consult, he was swift, zealous, radical and determined'.

7 Union Victory

a) 'Simultaneous movement all along the line'

In March 1864 Lincoln appointed Grant General-in-chief. Grant immediately came east to supervise the effort to destroy Lee. Determined to make use of the Union's greater manpower, he called for a 'simultaneous movement all along the line'. Grant himself would attack Lee. In the West Sherman would capture Atlanta and then 'get into the interior of the enemy's country ... inflicting all the damage you can'. The 30,000 men in Louisiana under Banks were to capture Mobile and push north. Butler's 30,000 men at Yorktown were to advance on Richmond. Sigel's 26,000 men were to march up the Shenandoah Valley. Grant's strategy did not go entirely to plan. Banks and Butler's operations failed and Sigel was ineffective in the Shenandoah Valley. Indeed in July 1864 a small Confederate force pushed up the Valley and reached the suburbs of Washington, forcing Grant to send reinforcements to defend the capital.

Grant himself had mixed success. In May 1864, with a two-to-one superiority, he tried to slip round Lee's flank. On 5–6 May Confederate and Union forces met in the Wilderness. The Union army suffered 18,000 casualties, twice the losses sustained by Lee. But Grant continued to edge southwards, trying to get between Lee and Richmond. For the next month the two armies were never out of contact. Grant's probings were foiled by Lee's skilful defence. On 3 June at Cold Harbour Grant lost 7,000 men in just over one hour: Lee lost 1,500. In the first month of his offensive, Grant lost 50,000 men, twice as many as Lee. But his doggedness paid off. By mid-June Union forces had crossed the James river and threatened Petersburg, a crucial railway junction. Lee, aware that the loss of Petersburg would result in the loss of Richmond, was forced to defend the town. He was thus unable to fight a war of manoeuvre. In spite of the huge casualties sustained in May and June, Grant had more men at the end of his campaign than he had at the start. Lee had fewer men. In the autumn the Confederacy also suffered setbacks in the Shenandoah.

Sheridan, the new Union commander, won victories at Winchester and at Cedar Creek.

In May 1864 Sherman, with 100,000 men, left Chattanooga and headed towards Atlanta. His Confederate opponent, General Johnston, commanded some 70,000 men. Although Johnston had done a creditable job restoring the Army of Tennessee's morale, he had also spent much of 1863–4 bickering with Davis. Rather than going on the offensive, as Davis wanted, Johnston retreated, taking up strong positions and hoping Sherman would attack. Instead Sherman repeatedly turned his flank, forcing him back. By July Union forces had reached the outskirts of Atlanta. Davis now replaced Johnston with John Bell Hood. A series of attacks on Union lines resulted in the loss of 20,000 Confederates. At the end of August Hood was forced to abandon Atlanta. Its capture was an important boost to Northern morale.

b) The 1864 Election

The South's last (and best) hope was that Lincoln would be defeated in the 1864 election. This hope was a realistic one. In August, with the war going badly, Lincoln wrote: 'I am going to be beaten and unless some great change takes place, badly beaten'. The Democrat convention, hoping to capitalise on Northern war weariness, called for a negotiated peace. However, General McClellan, the Democrat presidential candidate, would not agree to the peace platform which meant that his party was in something of a muddle. Its strongest card was accusing Lincoln of plotting 'miscegenation' – the blending of the white and black races.

It had not been certain that Lincoln would win the Republican nomination. Many Republicans would like to have nominated General Grant but he made it clear he would not stand. Treasury Secretary Chase had presidential ambitions but failed to mount a challenge. In the event, Lincoln was easily renominated, with Andrew Johnson, a War Democrat, as his running mate. The Republican platform endorsed a policy of unconditional surrender. In September the war turned in Lincoln's favour. Atlanta fell; Sheridan was successful in the Shenandoah; and there was a sharp drop in Grant's casualty rate. Republicans were able to depict the Democrats as at best unpatriotic defeatists and at worst traitors. In November Lincoln won 55 per cent of the popular vote (212 electoral college votes) to McClellan's 45 per cent (21 electoral college votes). Native-born Protestant Americans remained loyal to Lincoln. He also won 80 per cent of the soldier vote. The election had been a referendum on whether the North should continue fighting. Lincoln's success was the death-knell of the Confederacy.

GEORGIA AND TENNESSEE
In the autumn of 1864 Sherman divided his army. Leaving General Thomas to watch Hood, Sherman set off from Atlanta on a march through Georgia: his aim was to destroy the South's capacity and will to fight. Leaving a swathe of destruction, his army reached Savannah in mid-December. Instead of trying to stop Sherman, Hood invaded Tennessee. In mid-December he was defeated by Thomas at Nashville. Hood resigned what little was left of his command.

c) The End of the Confederacy

In his December 1864 address to Congress Lincoln spoke confidently of victory. Union resources, he said, were unexhausted and inexhaustible: its military forces were larger than ever; and its economy was prospering. The Confederacy's situation, by contrast, was desperate: its Western armies were in tatters and there were mass desertions from Lee's army. Lee was now given command of all that was left of the Confederate armies. There was little he could do. The Confederacy was falling apart. In February Sherman began to march north towards Richmond. In March 1865 the Confederate Congress, with Lee's support, agreed to arm 300,000 slaves. The measure came too late to have any effect. By March 1865 Lee had fewer than 50,000 troops. Grant had 125,000 men, not counting Sheridan approaching from the north and Sherman approaching from the south. On 2 April Grant broke through Lee's lines, forcing him to abandon Petersburg and Richmond. Davis fled. Lee retreated westwards. Surrounded by Union forces, he realised, 'There is nothing left for me to do but to go and see General Grant and I would rather die a thousand deaths'. Lee and Grant met at Appomattox Court House on 10 April. Grant was generous: Confederate troops were allowed to keep their side arms and horses; they were also given Union army rations. Lee's surrender was the effective end of the war. Most Southerners showed no interest in a guerrilla war. On 16 April Johnston surrendered to Sherman. Davis was captured in May.

Military Debates

1. Did Davis and Lee focus too much on Virginia at the expense of the West?
It may be that the Confederacy lost the war because it lost the West. However, it could not have won the war by concentrating its resources in the West. Virginia, the South's economic heartland, had to be defended. In Virginia geographical conditions favoured the defender. It made sense to give most resources to the best army (the Army of Northern Virginia) and the best General (Lee).

2. Was the Confederacy too attack-minded?
It has been claimed that the Confederacy bled itself to death in the first years of the war by making costly attacks. Lee is seen as a main culprit. This argument is not convincing. Lee, while recognising the advantage of fighting on the defensive, realised that a purely defensive strategy would result in the South being picked off at will. The only hope, in Lee's view, was to retain the initiative and to make use of the *élan* and spirit of his men. On several occasions his offensive strategy almost won him the decisive victory he was seeking.

3. How inept were the Confederacy's Western commanders?

The under-resourced Western Confederate armies did suffer from inept generalship. The first Western commander, Albert Johnston, let Union forces break through his river defence line. Beauregard made plans not based on realities. Bragg quarrelled with everyone. Joe Johnston refused to take chances. Hood was responsible for a series of defeats in 1864. However, the sheer size of the West and the poor state of communications were major problems. So too was the fact that in the West the Confederates faced some good Northern commanders – Grant, Sherman and Thomas.

4. Should the Confederacy have relied more on guerrilla warfare?

In many parts of the Confederacy there was guerrilla warfare. It was particularly nasty in Missouri where Quantrill's 'bushwhackers' fought against Union 'jayhawkers'.

5. Does skilful Union military leadership explain the outcome of the Civil War?

Grant is often regarded as the greatest soldier of the war. His supporters claim that he had a concept of the total war strategy necessary to win the conflict, and the determination to carry it out. Sherman has also been praised. His marches through Georgia and the Carolinas weakened the South logistically and psychologically.

d) The Historiographical Debates

Efforts to explain the war's outcome have generated a great deal of controversy. Perhaps the most basic argument is – did the Confederacy lose or did the Union win?

Some historians have explained the Confederacy's defeat by claiming it was badly led by its political leaders (especially Davis) and its generals (including Lee). However, it is probably fairer to praise Southern leaders than to blame them. It is hard to think of a Southerner who could have done a better job than Davis. Lee, despite being outnumbered in every battle in which he fought, won victories that gave Southerners hope.

Other historians have explained Confederate defeat by focusing on divisions within the South. There are several variations on this theme. Some think that the notion of state rights crippled the efforts of Davis's government to wage war. Individual states are seen as putting their own interests before those of the Confederacy. But recent scholarship has shown that the negative effects of state rights sentiment have been much exaggerated.

THE WAR: 1864–5

1864 Capture of Atlanta (September);
Lincoln re-elected President (November);
Sherman captured Savannah (December);
Battle of Nashville (December);

1865 Fall of Petersburg and Richmond (April);
Lee surrendered at Appomattox (April);
Assassination of Lincoln (April).

Another major explanation for Confederate defeat is the claim that Southerners lacked the will to make the sacrifices necessary for victory. One lack-of-will argument is that the Confederacy did not generate a strong sense of nationalism: thus when the going got tough Southerners found it tough to keep going. This argument is not convincing. The strength of patriotic feeling in 1861 produced 500,000 volunteers for military service. The war, by creating both a unifying hatred of the enemy and a new set of heroes, strengthened Confederate nationalism. Far from explaining Confederate defeat, nationalism helps explain why Southerners fought as long as they did. A second lack-of-will view – the notion that many Southerners felt moral qualms about slavery, which undermined their will to fight to preserve it – is even less convincing. Most Southerners went to war to preserve slavery and remained committed to it to the end. A related lack-of-will interpretation focuses on religion. As the Confederacy's suffering increased, some Southerners began to wonder if God was on their side. Did these doubts corrode Confederate morale? It seems unlikely. In 1863–4 a great religious revival movement swept through the Confederate army. Rather than explaining Confederate defeat, religion played a vital role in sustaining Southern will. A final lack-of-will argument emphasises the South's dire economic situation. Misery on the home front led, it is claimed, to a growth of defeatism which was conveyed by letters to the troops. Women wanted their sons and husbands home and told them to put family before national loyalty. In 1864–5 Confederate soldiers responded by deserting. While there is some truth in this argument, there is a major difference between loss and lack of will. A people whose armies are beaten, railways wrecked, cities burned and crops laid waste, lose their will to continue fighting because they have lost the means to do so. By 1865 Southern will had collapsed. But it was military defeat which caused the loss of will, not lack of will which caused military defeat.

The reason for Confederate defeat lies in the North. To win, the South had to wear down Northern will. A long, bloody war was the best way to do this. The war was long and bloody but Northern will endured. Union success in battle helped sustain morale. That success was largely due to the fact that the North had more men and resources. Historian Richard Current, reviewing the statistics of Northern strength – two and a half times the South's population, nine times its industrial production, overwhelming naval supremacy – concluded that 'surely in view of the disparity of resources, it would have taken a miracle to enable the South to win. As usual, God was on the side of the heaviest battalions.'

ACTIVITY

Consider the following question: To what extent was poor leadership to blame for Confederate defeat?

Which aspects of leadership – military, political, economic, diplomatic – are you going to focus on? Was poor leadership to blame for the Confederacy's defeat? Or was it so well led that, against all the odds, it succeeded in fighting a four year war?

8 The Problem of Reconstruction

In 1865 the federal government faced the problem of restoring the 11 Confederate states to the Union. Virtually every aspect of the Reconstruction process has been the subject of controversy.

a) Reconstruction During the War

From 1861 Lincoln faced the problem of how to restore loyal governments in the South. In fact, there were a series of interrelated problems. On what terms should the defeated states be reunited to the Union? How should Southerners be treated? What should happen to the ex-slaves? And who should decide Reconstruction policy: Congress or the president?

Lincoln was convinced that Reconstruction was a presidential concern. The Constitution gave him the power of pardon: he was also commander-in-chief. Lincoln's strategic aim was consistent throughout the war: he wanted to restore the Union as quickly as possible. His usual policy in those areas which had been partially reconquered was to install military governors. He hoped that military government would only last until enough loyal citizens could form a new state government. In 1863 he offered pardon to Southerners who would take an oath of allegiance to the Union. When 10 per cent of the electorate had taken this oath, a new state government could be established. Provided the state then accepted the abolition of slavery, Lincoln agreed to recognise its government. In 1864 Tennessee, Louisiana and Arkansas used this '10 per cent plan' to set up new governments.

Not all Republicans agreed with Lincoln's actions. During the war, radical Republicans tended to be the president's most vocal opponents. Although the radicals did not work in close harmony, most held similar views with regard to Reconstruction. They wanted to impose a harsh settlement on the South, punishing the main rebels by confiscating their land. They were also concerned about the plight of ex-slaves and believed they should have the same rights as white Americans. It has been claimed that radical concern for black rights, particularly black suffrage, was triggered by shabby political motives rather than idealism. Certainly radicals feared that once the Southern states were back within the Union, the Democrat Party must triumph. There seemed two ways to prevent this: first ensure that ex-slaves could vote (they would surely vote Republican); and second disfranchise large numbers of rebels. Many radicals did not separate idealism and political pragmatism: they believed that blacks should be entitled to vote and were not ashamed to assert that such a policy would ensure Republican ascendancy. Whatever their motives, most radicals were convinced that the Southern states, by seceding, had reverted to the condition of territories and should be subject to Congress's authority. Congress, not the president, should thus control the Reconstruction process.

Radical dissatisfaction with Lincoln's 10 per cent plan was soon apparent. In April 1864 a Louisiana convention had drawn up a constitution banning slavery but not giving blacks the vote. Over 10 per cent of Louisiana's electorate voted in favour of the constitution and Lincoln treated the state as if it had been restored to the Union. However, Congress rejected Louisiana's new constitution and refused admission to its two Senators. Two radicals, Davis and Wade, introduced a bill requiring 50 per cent of the electorate to take a loyalty oath before the rebel states could return into the Union. Moreover, anyone who had held political office during the Confederacy or had voluntarily borne arms against the Union was to be excluded from the political process. The Wade–Davis bill passed both houses of Congress. Lincoln vetoed the bill. This caused a short but bitter political storm. It was clear that Lincoln's hopes of devising a definitive method by which rebel states would be allowed back into the Union, had failed.

This was by no means the only Reconstruction problem. As Union forces reconquered parts of the South, Lincoln's administration faced the problem of what to do with tens of thousands of ex-slaves. Fearing that blacks and whites could not live peacefully together, Lincoln had supported the idea of colonising ex-slaves in West Africa or the Caribbean. But attempts to put colonisation schemes into effect had floundered, largely because most blacks refused to participate. Given that the Union found itself in control of huge tracts of land either abandoned by Southerners or confiscated from them, one solution was to redistribute the land to ex-slaves. Lincoln, fearing that such action would undermine his efforts to win the support of Southern whites, had little enthusiasm for confiscation. Given no firm presidential or Congressional guidance, the situation in the reoccupied areas of the Confederacy was chaotic, varying from place to place and from time to time. Federal agents, especially army officers, instituted their own remedies. On the South Carolina Sea Islands blacks were able to buy small amounts of land. More often, abandoned plantations were administered by government agents or leased to Northern investors. Some plantations were still controlled by Southerners who had taken an oath of allegiance to the Union. In these circumstances, life for most ex-slaves did not change much. They continued to work on the same plantations (for low wages) and were usually closely supervised by white managers.

In January 1865 General Sherman declared that coastal territory from Charleston to Florida should be set aside for freed slaves, with black families receiving 40 acres and an army mule. Sherman's motives were far from humanitarian: his main concern was to 'dump' the thousands of blacks following his army. Some 40,000 blacks were given land. While Sherman's actions raised black expectations, federal policy remained uncertain. A few Republicans were opposed to giving blacks any land (or help), convinced that they must learn to stand on their own feet. Most favoured confiscating plantation land and redistributing it among ex-slaves. However, they were unable to agree on a precise measure. In March 1865 Congress did set up the Freedman Bureau. Its aim was to help relieve the suffering of Southern blacks and poor whites by providing food, clothes, and medical care.

b) The Situation in 1865

In 1865 Lincoln's position on many Reconstruction issues was unclear. Generally he had no wish to punish the South. In his second inauguration speech in March 1865, he had talked of 'malice towards none' and the need for a 'just and lasting peace'. However, he seems to have been moving cautiously towards accepting that blacks should have equality before the law and talked of giving some blacks the vote. Precisely what he would have done will remain a mystery. On 14 April he was murdered by the actor John Wilkes Booth. Booth had long wanted to strike a blow for the Southern cause. Lincoln's murder did little to help that cause.

Vice-President Andrew Johnson, an ex-Democrat and ex-slave owner from Tennessee, now became president. He had been the only Senator from any of the Confederate states to stay loyal to the Union. A few radicals were (privately) pleased that Johnson had replaced Lincoln. They hoped he would take a tougher stance against the rebel leaders. However, the Johnson–radical honeymoon was short-lived. Differences over Reconstruction policies were soon to lead to bitter separation.

Johnson, who kept Lincoln's cabinet, claimed his intention was to continue Lincoln's policy. Viewing Reconstruction as an executive, not a legislative, function, he hoped to restore the Southern states to the Union before Congress met in December 1865. Keen that the USA should return to its normal functioning as soon as possible, Johnson saw no alternative but to work with ex-Confederates. He thus favoured leniency. Committed to state rights, he believed it was not the federal government's responsibility to decide suffrage issues or to involve itself in economic and social matters. Nor had he any wish to promote the position of ex-slaves. He did not consider blacks to be equal to whites and was opposed to black suffrage.

THE SITUATION IN THE NORTH

Segregation and discrimination were still the norm in many Northern states. In 1865 only five states allowed blacks to vote on equal terms with whites.

The emancipation of the slaves meant that the South had lost over $2 billion of capital. It also meant the end of a whole way of life. Developing new social relations between blacks and whites was unlikely to be easy. The fact that many blacks had great expectations (which might be difficult to realise) was one problem. The attitude of Southern whites was another. Few considered blacks to be their equals. Resentful and fearful of emancipated slaves, many were appalled at what they saw as black insolence and insubordination.

Presidential Reconstruction: 1865

▼ Johnson recognised the Southern governments created under Lincoln's administration.
▼ He issued a general amnesty to Southerners who were willing to swear an oath of allegiance. While major Confederate office holders were exempted, they could apply for a presidential pardon. Over the summer of 1865 Johnson granted thousands of pardons.
▼ Confiscated land was returned to pardoned Southerners.
▼ Southern state conventions were to be elected (by whites only) to draw up new constitutions which accepted that slavery was illegal. Once this was done the states would be readmitted to the Union.

---

c) 'Reconstruction Confederate Style'

White Southerners set about implementing Johnson's terms. State conventions repudiated secession and acknowledged the end of slavery. The South then proceeded to elect legislatures, governors and members of Congress. Many men who had held high office in the Confederacy were elected. The new Southern governments then searched for means of keeping the freedmen under control. No state enfranchised blacks. All introduced 'black codes', designed to ensure that blacks remained second-class citizens. Most states required blacks to possess contracts which provided evidence of employment. Those who were unemployed or who broke the contracts could be forcibly set to work. The codes also prevented blacks from buying land, marrying whites or serving on juries.

By the time Congress met in December 1865, there were misgivings about Johnson's leniency. The fact that Southern Congressmen included Stephens (the Confederate vice-president), four Confederate generals and 58 Confederate Congress members, did not reassure Northerners of the South's good intent. Nor did the black codes. Most Republican Congressmen were moderates – not radicals. They had no wish to bring about social revolution in the South. Many were not enthusiastic about black suffrage: nor did they wish greatly to expand federal authority. But most thought that Confederate leaders should be barred from holding office and that the basic rights of ex-slaves should be protected. Thus the Republican-dominated Congress refused to admit the Southern Congressmen or to recognise the new regimes in the South. A Committee on Reconstruction was set up to recommend a new policy.

Instead of working with the moderate Republicans, Johnson chose to side with the Democrats. When Congress tried to enlarge the powers of the Freedman's Bureau, he vetoed it claiming that it was an unwarranted continuation of war power. Moderate Republicans now joined forces with radicals to introduce a Civil Rights Bill which aimed to guarantee minimal rights to blacks. Johnson, arguing that civil rights were a state matter, vetoed the measure. Congress struck back. In April 1866 a two-thirds majority ensured that Johnson's veto was overridden and the Civil Rights Bill became law. A few weeks later Congress passed a second Freedman's Bureau Bill, over Johnson's veto. Then, to ensure that civil rights could not be changed in future, both Houses of Congress adopted the 14th Amendment. This guaranteed all citizens equality before the law. It also banned from office Confederates who before the war had taken an oath of allegiance to the Union. The Amendment was rejected by all the ex-Confederate states (except Tennessee) and thus failed to get the approval of 75 per cent of the states that was necessary for it to become law.

In the 1866 mid-term elections Johnson supported – and was supported by – the National Union Convention, which hoped to unite Democrats and conservative Republicans. This strategy was a disaster for Johnson: his Republican enemies triumphed. They now had a two-thirds majority in both Houses, ensuring they could override any presidential veto.

d) Radical Reconstruction

In the spring of 1867 Congress passed a Military Reconstruction Bill. This stated that no legal government as yet existed in any Southern state (except Tennessee). The ten unreconstructed states were divided into five military districts, each placed under a federal commander. To get back into the Union, Southern states had to elect constitutional conventions which would accept black suffrage and ratify the 14th Amendment. The bill was passed despite Johnson's veto. Congress then moved to weaken Johnson's power. A Command of the Army Act reduced his military powers. The Tenure of Office Act barred him from removing a host of office-holders. It was designed to protect Secretary of War Stanton, a fierce critic of Johnson, who had still not resigned from his cabinet. Johnson, unwilling to accept this muzzling without a fight, dismissed Stanton. Republicans now

determined to impeach Johnson for 'high crimes and misde-
meanours'. The impeachment proceedings took place in the Senate
in 1868. Johnson faced a mixed bag of charges but essentially they
narrowed down to the removal of Stanton from office and non-
cooperation with Congress. After a two month trial, 35 Senators
voted against Johnson and 19 for him. This was one vote short of the
two-thirds majority needed to impeach him.

In 1868 the Republicans chose General Grant as their presidential candidate. His Democrat opponent was Horatio Seymour who
opposed Republican reconstruction and campaigned against black
equality. Although Grant easily won the electoral college vote, he
won only 52 per cent of the popular vote. His popular majority was
the result of Southern black support. Given the 1868 election
result, Republicans had even better cause to support black suffrage.
In 1869 the 15th Amendment was introduced. (It was ratified in
1870.) This stated that, 'The right to vote should not be denied …
on account of race, colour or previous conditions of servitude'.
With civil and political equality seemingly assured, most
Republicans believed that blacks no longer possessed a claim upon
the federal government. Their status in society would now depend
upon themselves.

e) Reconstruction in the South 1867–77

Following the Military Reconstruction Act, all the ex-Confederate
states, except Tennessee, were under military rule. The extent to
which the South was under the heel of a 'military despotism' should
not be exaggerated. There were never more than 20,000 troops in
the whole of the South. Military rule was also short-lived. From the
autumn of 1867 onwards Southern Republicans produced the necessary constitutions. In every state, except Virginia, they also took over
the first restored state governments. By June 1868 Republican governments in Alabama, Arkansas, Florida, Louisiana, North Carolina
and South Carolina had ratified the 14th Amendment and been
received back into the Union. Texas, Virginia, Georgia and
Mississippi were re-admitted in 1870.

Professor Dunning in the early twentieth century referred to the
period of Republican rule as 'Black Reconstruction'. He thought the
new governments were essentially undemocratic, ruling against the
will of the white majority and representing the worst elements in
Southern society – illiterate blacks, self-seeking Northerners ('car-
petbaggers') and renegade whites ('scalawags'). He also accused the
new governments of corruption on a grand scale. However, most of
Dunning's views have been challenged, including the very term
'Black Reconstruction'. Blacks certainly wielded some political

power. In South Carolina and Mississippi, they constituted a real majority of the electorate. In three other states (in 1867) black voters outnumbered whites because so many rebels were disenfranchised. Thus two black Senators and 20 black Representatives were elected to Congress. Large numbers of blacks were elected to state legislatures. But while this was a revolutionary break with the past, black political influence never reflected black numbers. The lack of black experience and education, and divisions within the black community, particularly between free-born blacks and ex-slaves, help explain why black office-holders did not equate with black voters. But perhaps the main reason was the fact that blacks were a minority in most states. Assured of black support, the Republican party often put forward white candidates for office hoping to attract more white voters.

Without winning support from Southern whites, few Republican governments would have been elected. 'Scalawags' voted Republican for a variety of motives. Many had opposed the Confederacy during the war. 'Carpetbagger' influence has been much exaggerated. In no state did Northerners constitute even 2 per cent of the population. Nor were they set on fleecing the South economically. They voted Republican, not for selfish gain, but simply because they believed that Republican policies were best for the country. Most white Republicans did not support full racial equality. But they knew that if they were to maintain political control, they must retain the black vote.

Many Republican politicians were undoubtedly corrupt, using their powers of patronage to benefit their own supporters. Bribery, especially by railway companies, was commonplace. Some administrations were also incompetent. Southern state debts multiplied and taxes sharply increased. However, the late 1860s and 1870s saw corruption, bribery and inefficiency everywhere in the USA. Moreover, there had been massive corruption in Southern state governments pre-1861 and also similar corruption after the states had been 'redeemed'. Republican governments had little option but to raise and spend large sums of money. Much of the Southern transportation system had been destroyed during the war. Public buildings needed to be repaired. Schools, hospitals, and orphanages had to be built for blacks as well as whites. The fact that new schools (etc) were built indicates that the money spent was not always wasted.

f) Economic Reconstruction

From 1867 to 1873 the South benefited from general US prosperity and from high cotton prices. Railways were rebuilt and there was an increase in textile manufacturing. But promising as this was, it did not keep pace with industrial progress elsewhere and the South became the poorest section in the USA. By 1870 the average white Southern income had fallen to less than two-fifths that of Northerners. Short of cash and credit, the South remained essentially an agricultural region, heavily dependent upon cotton. In many parts of the South the old plantations remained, sometimes with new owners, sometimes not. Blacks continued to do most of the hard labour. During the 1870s most became sharecroppers. White landowners provided the land, seed and tools: black tenants supplied the labour. Whatever crop was produced was divided in a fixed ratio – often half to the landowner and half to the tenant. Sharecropping provided black farmers with freedom from day-to-day white supervision and some incentive to work hard. But neither the freedom nor the incentive should be exaggerated. In the early 1870s, a world-wide glut of cotton led to a disastrous fall in prices which resulted in most sharecroppers being in a perpetual state of indebtness to landowners and local storekeepers.

This is an institution of chivalry, humanity, mercy and patriotism; embodying in its genius and its principles all that is chivalric in conduct, noble in sentiment, generous in manhood, and patriotic in purpose; its peculiar objectives being ... to protect the weak, the innocent, and the defenseless from the indignities, wrongs, and outrages of the lawless, the violent, and the brutal...to succor the suffering and unfortunate, and especially the widows and orphans of Confederate soldiers.

Source A From the Klan's *Organization and Principles*, 1868.

White Resistance: the Ku Klux Klan

Republican rule sparked a vigorous backlash as Southern whites tried to recover political ascendancy. In 1866 paramilitary groups formed in most Southern states to fight for white rights. The most notorious was the Ku Klux Klan. The Klan, led for a time by the war hero Nathan Bedford Forrest, spread rapidly, drawing support from all sections of the white community. Its terrorist activities reached their peak in the years 1869–71. Blacks who held public office were particular targets. So were black schools and churches. In most states Republican governments found it hard to enforce the law. When Klan suspects were arrested, witnesses were reluctant to testify and Klansmen were ready to perjure themselves to provide one another with alibis. If there was a Klansman on a jury, it was impossible to convict. In 1870–71 Congress passed three Force Acts, authorising Grant to use the army to break up the Klan. Hundreds of suspected Klansmen were imprisoned. While this reduced Klan terrorism, violence and intimidation still remained.

Figure 15 The White League and the Klan.

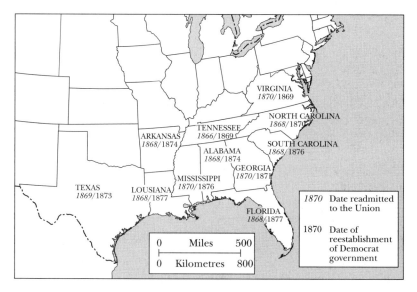

Figure 16 The Southern states redeemed.

g) The South 'Redeemed'

In many Southern states Radical Reconstruction was over almost before it began. Tennessee was under Democrat control by 1869; Virginia and North Carolina were redeemed in 1870; Georgia in 1871; Texas in 1873; Arkansas and Alabama in 1874; and Mississippi in 1875. By 1876 only Louisiana, Florida and South Carolina were still under Republican control. Several factors played a part in Republican defeat. While most historians have emphasised the importance of white intimidation and terror, others have stressed the destructive effect of factionalism within Republican parties at state level. Racism was a major cause of the in-fighting: scalawags were reluctant allies of the blacks. But there was also rivalry between different groups of scalawags and between different groups of blacks. Some historians claim that Southern Republicans were betrayed by the Northern wing of the party. After 1867 radical influence declined as old leaders died or retired. Most Northern Republicans had little sympathy for the plight of Southern blacks and felt that it was not the federal government's job to intervene too much in state affairs. Two actions in 1872 symbolised the desire to build bridges to white Southerners: an Amnesty Act resulted in 150,000 ex-Confederates having their rights returned; and the Freedmen's Bureau collapsed. In the 1874 mid-term elections the Democrats won control in the House. Thereafter there was little that Grant could do in terms of embarking on new initiatives to help Southern Republicans. The 1875 Civil Rights Act, the last measure to help Southern blacks, was little more than a broad assertion of principle and had virtually no impact in the South.

In truth, the end of Radical Reconstruction was almost inevitable given that whites were the majority in most Southern states. The Democrat Party was the white party: the Republican Party the black party. Those who think that a strong Republican Party might have been founded upon policies that appealed to poor whites and blacks are probably deluding themselves. The reality was that few poor whites identified with poor blacks. Given that race was the dominant issue, many of the election campaigns in the South in the 1870s were ugly. While Democrats tried to prevent blacks from voting, Republicans tried to ensure that they did vote – often several times! Events in Louisiana are typical of events throughout the Deep South. Every election in the state between 1868 and 1876 was marred by violence and fraud. After 1872 two governments claimed legitimacy. A Republican regime, elected by blacks and protected by the federal army, was the legitimate government. But a Democrat government, elected by whites and aided by its own militia unit, the 'White League', controlled the countryside.

h) The End of Reconstruction

Even though most states had been redeemed well before, the 1876 presidential election is often seen as the end of Radical Reconstruction. The Republican candidate was Rutherford Hayes. The Democrats chose Samuel Tilden. Tilden clearly won the popular vote, gaining 4,284,000 votes to Hayes' 4,037,000. But US presidential elections are determined by the electoral college, not by the popular vote. While Tilden had 184 electoral college votes to Hayes' 165, the voting returns from Oregon, South Carolina, Louisiana, and Florida were contested. These four states had 20 electoral college votes. If all 20 went to Hayes he would win. If just one state went to Tilden, he would become president. There was never much doubt that Oregon's votes would go to Hayes. The real problem lay in the South. It was – and is – impossible to know how the people in the contested states voted or how far Democrat intimidation offset Republican fraud. The dispute lingered on over the winter. Eventually Congress established a Commission to review the election returns. Eight commissioners were Republicans: seven were Democrats. By votes of eight to seven the Commission awarded all the disputed elections to Hayes.

The 1877 Compromise ended the crisis. The Compromise seems to have been as follows: the Democrats would accept Hayes as president: he, in return, agreed to withdraw all troops from the South and recognise Democrat governments in the three disputed states. Whether Hayes agreed to this is debatable. He claimed that he made no concessions to the South. Whatever had – or had not – been agreed, Hayes did withdraw troops from the South with the result that South Carolina, Louisiana and Florida fell under Democrat control. Thus, by 1877 all the ex-Confederate states had returned to white Democratic rule.

i) Did Reconstruction Succeed or Fail?

In the early twentieth century, white Southern historians, such as Professor Dunning, saw Reconstruction as 'The Tragic Era' – a dreadful time when Southerners suffered the indignity of military occupation, and when the South was ruled by incompetent and corrupt governments. In Dunning's view the heroes were President Johnson who tried to continue the aims of Lincoln, and Democrats who waged a forceful campaign to redeem the South. The villains were the vindictive radical Republicans. In the 1950s and 1960s, historians such as Kenneth Stampp and John Hope Franklin depicted Reconstruction very differently. 'Rarely in history', said Stampp, 'have participants in an unsuccessful rebellion endured so mild penalties as those Congress imposed upon the people of the South and particularly upon their leaders'. In Stampp's opinion the villains were Johnson and the Klan. The heroes were the radical Republicans who fought for the rights of ex-slaves. In this view, black, not white, Southerners were the real losers of Reconstruction.

Given the scale of the Civil War, the North was remarkably generous to Southern whites. Only one man, the commandant of the notorious Andersonville prison camp, was executed for war crimes. Jefferson Davis spent two years in prison but was then freed. Slavery apart, there was no major confiscation of property. For decades to come, the Democrat Party, the political agency of white supremacy, controlled the South. However, white Southerners had not escaped from the war scot-free. Control had been wrested away from them for at least a few years. Moreover, after 1865 there was a major reduction of Southern political influence in the USA. Between 1788 and 1860 Southerners had held the presidency for 50 years and dominated the Supreme Court. Between 1864 and 1914, there was just one (elected) Southern president and only seven of the 31 Supreme Court justices were Southerners.

The main debate about Reconstruction has been the effect it had on the ex-slaves. One major criticism is that blacks came out of slavery with little or no land. However, major land redistribution was never really a viable option. Property in America was sacrosanct. Confiscation of land would have left white Southerners even more embittered. Recently, historians have pointed out that after 1865 blacks had far more control over their own lives than they had had under slavery. In the decades after 1865 they steadily increased the amount of land they farmed. Living standards improved and did so despite the adverse economic conditions of the 1870s.

A second major criticism of Reconstruction is that it failed to guarantee civil rights. Blacks were regarded and treated by most whites in the South as second-class citizens. In the late nineteenth century, every Southern state introduced segregation – 'Jim Crow' – laws. The Supreme Court, in the 1896 *Plessy* v. *Ferguson* case, accepted segregation provided that blacks and whites had equal facilities. (They rarely did.) White-controlled state governments introduced a variety of measures, like literacy tests, to ensure that blacks were unable to vote. Blacks were also taught to know their place. Savage punishments were meted out to blacks who committed petty crime. Lynchings of those suspected of more serious crimes were a common feature of Southern life in the late nineteenth and early twentieth centuries.

However, recent historians have stressed that Southern blacks were not just objects to be manipulated: they were important participants in the Reconstruction process. Segregation was not something which was always imposed on blacks by whites. Many blacks had no wish to mix socially with whites. Segregation was often a statement of black community identity. Many blacks viewed the situation in a similar way to that of the Supreme Court in 1896. The Court did not approve of segregation. It simply thought there was little it could do to end it. The real issue was not segregation as such but equal treatment. Separate schools were infinitely superior to no schools at all. The fact that there were black institutions, paralleling those of whites, meant

RECONSTRUCTION: 1865–77

1865 Lincoln assassinated: Andrew Johnson became president (April); 13th Amendment (December);
1866 Civil Rights Act;
1867 Military Reconstruction Act;
1868 14th Amendment (July); Ulysses S. Grant elected president (November);
1870 15th Amendment;
1876 Rutherford Hayes won disputed presidential election;
1877 'Compromise'.

there were opportunities for blacks to lead and manage. A small but growing number of men became doctors, lawyers, businessmen and teachers. Black education was one of the successes of Reconstruction.

In the context of the 1860s and 1870s Reconstruction should probably be seen as revolutionary. The essential fact was that blacks were no longer slaves. Although they did not emerge from Reconstruction as equal citizens, at least the 14th and 15th Amendments were enshrined in the constitution and could be invoked by later generations of Civil Rights activists.

Effects of the Civil War

1. Was the Civil War 'the Second American Revolution'?
Some historians are convinced that the Civil War was America's second revolution. (The first was the War of Independence.) Others remain sceptical.

2. Did the war change the whole emphasis of the Constitution?
Arguably the war shifted the balance in a national direction at the expense of state rights. One thing was clear: states did not have the right to secede. The war had also resulted in the federal government asserting its power in ways unimaginable in 1861. It had mobilised hundreds of thousands of men, levied new sources of revenue and issued a national paper currency. However, many of the functions assumed by the federal government during the war were clearly exceptional and justified only by the unique circumstances of the war. Individual states continued to play a crucial role after 1865.

3. Did the war stimulate the growth of big business?
Some think the war encouraged new methods of production and organisation. However, others claim the war brought about few economic changes which would not otherwise have occurred.

4. Did the war transfer economic and political power into the hands of big business?
It was once thought it did and that industrial capitalists had deliberately planned such an outcome. However, such views are simplistic. Even if big manufacturers were the chief economic beneficiaries of the war (and this is debatable), their victory was an incidental rather a planned result of the conflict.

5. Did the war transform the position of African Americans?
Some four million slaves were freed. However, their lot did not improve very much.

> Had the South won, the Civil War would indeed have been one of the great turning points in modern history. But Union victory meant that the status quo – slavery apart – was preserved. If the war was revolutionary, it was only because it resulted in slaves being freed.

▼ Working on The American Civil War and Reconstruction

As a result of reading this chapter, you should appreciate that historians have a host of different opinions about why the North won/South lost. Our view is that the North was always favourite to win and that, in the circumstances, the South fought rather well. You should not meekly accept this view. Your notes should provide you with ammunition to challenge it.

Answering Extended Writing and Essay Questions on Reconstruction

Consider the question: To what extent was Reconstruction 'A tragedy for the nation'?

The question requires you to construct a two-part answer. One part argues 'Yes … Reconstruction was a tragedy … in these ways/to this extent'. The other part argues 'No … Reconstruction was not a tragedy…in these ways/to this extent. Try a 'brainstorming' session to pinpoint the arguments you could put forward. When you have sorted out your views, try to work out a paragraph-by-paragraph plan.

Answering Source-based Questions on The American Civil War and Reconstruction

> I admit that slavery is the root of the rebellion … I would also concede that emancipation would help us in Europe … And then unquestionably it would weaken the rebels by drawing off their labourers … But I am not sure we could do much with the blacks. If we were to arm them, I fear that in a few weeks the arms would be in the hands of the rebels … I will mention another thing … There are fifty thou-

sand bayonets in the Union armies from the Border Slave States. It would be a serious matter if, in consequence of a proclamation such as you desire, they should go over to the rebels ... I think you should admit that we already have an important principle to rally and unite the people in the fact that constitutional government is at stake. This is a fundamental idea, going down about as deep as anything.

Source B Lincoln in debate with some Chicago ministers, September 1862.

Any different policy in regard to the coloured man [than black recruitment] deprives us of his help and this is more than we can bear ... This is not a question of sentiment or taste, but one of physical force which can be measured and estimated as [can] horse power and steampower ... Keep it up and you can save the Union. Throw it away and the Union goes with it.

Source C Lincoln, writing in September 1864.

▼ QUESTIONS ON SOURCES

1. What, in Lincoln's view, was the 'fundamental idea' of the war? **[5 marks]**

2. Using your own knowledge as well as the information in the two sources, explain and account for the difference of opinion expressed in Sources B and C. **[15 marks]**

Further Reading

Books in the Access to History series

The key texts are *The American Civil War* and *Reconstruction and the Results of the American Civil War*, both by Alan Farmer.

General

Battle Cry of Freedom by J.M. McPherson (Penguin, 1988) remains the best one-volume survey of the course of the Civil War. *The American Civil War* by P.J. Parish (Holmes and Meier, 1975) is still an essential text. Try also *Why the North won the Civil War*, edited by D. Donald (Collier, 1960). The best book on Reconstruction is *Reconstruction: America's Unfinished Revolution 1863–1877* by E. Foner (Harper and Row, 1988).

3

THE USA:
1900–41

POINTS TO CONSIDER

This chapter examines the domestic history of the USA from 1900 to 1941. After considering the nature of the so-called progressive decades (1900–20), it goes on to examine the 'Twenties'. Was the decade a golden age when the USA came close to realising the fulfilment of the American dream? Or was it a rotten age – a decade of irresponsibility and materialism which aptly ended with the Great Depression? What were the main causes and consequences of the Depression? And how successful were President Franklin D. Roosevelt's New Deal measures in coping with the Depression?

ISSUE:
What was the nature of progressivism?

1 Progressivism

Historians often refer to the first two decades of the twentieth century as the 'progressive era'. Unfortunately, they do not agree about what caused progressivism, what it actually was, which groups supported it, or how successful it was. There is not even agreement about when the progressive era started or ended. Indeed some historians challenge the whole notion of a progressive era or movement. They think it more sensible to talk about a series of movements with quite distinct aims rather than one united movement.

a) What Was Progressivism?

Presidents Theodore Roosevelt (1901–9) and Woodrow Wilson (1913–21) are usually seen (and saw themselves) as progressives. But arguably Presidents McKinley (1897–1901) and Taft (1909–13) were also progressives. Neither the Republican nor the Democrat Party had a monopoly of progressivism. McKinley, Roosevelt and Taft were Republicans: Wilson was a Democrat. In 1912 there was even a short-lived Progressive Party. A great number of progressive reforms were introduced at state rather than federal level. Historians also see progressive reformers at work in various professions – the media, education, and law. The fact that so many people and groups were involved at so many levels and for so long a time is one reason why historians find it difficult to agree about the meaning of progressivism. De Witt, one of the first historians of progressivism, thought that progressives were concerned with regulation of big business, political reform and social reform. However, not all progressives agreed about all aspects of reform. Moreover, all the problems De Witte highlighted had existed throughout the nineteenth century and attempts, not usually seen as being part of progressivism, had been made to tackle them. More recently Chambers has defined progressivism as 'a new inter-ventionism' – a belief that intelligent, direct effort could manipulate the environment for the improvement of society. The progressives, in Chambers' view, were not socialists. They accepted capitalism, had faith in democracy, and believed in moderate change.

Why Was the USA So Economically Successful After 1865?

▼ With huge natural resources, the USA was virtually self-sufficient in every commodity.

▼ The great railway development – in 1865 there were 35,000 miles of track; by 1900 there were 193,000 – opened up the country's natural resources.

▼ Capital, especially from Britain, helped the USA develop its economy.

▼ Vast numbers of east and southern Europeans poured into the USA in the late nineteenth and early twentieth centuies. They provided cheap labour and a growing home market.

▼ Given that workers were paid high wages (by European stan-dards), employers had to make goods more productively than their competitors if they were to compete in the world markets. Mass production of interchangeable parts became the 'American way'. By 1900 the USA produced 30 per cent of the world's man-ufactured goods.

▼ Government policy pre-1900 had generally been one of laissez-faire – leave alone. Most politicians believed that government should not involve itself in economic matters. But in certain ways government action may have encouraged economic development. High tariffs, for example, protected US producers from foreign competition.

▼ Farming remained a huge business. In 1900 only one in three Americans was a city dweller.

---

b) What Caused Progressivism?

i) The Need to Regulate Big Business

In the late nineteenth century some large businesses, known as trusts, became so powerful that they threatened to establish monopolies in particular industries. This meant they could fix prices without there being any competition. They were seen as the 'baddies' acting against the interests of the people and a threat to free enterprise. While virtually all progressives wanted to regulate or to 'bust' the power of trusts, they did not agree about how trusts should be brought under control.

ii) The Need for Political Reform

Progressives were opposed to corrupt party machines and big business domination of the political process. They wanted government to be more responsive to the people. Many favoured the use of referenda (for introducing or repealing legislation), direct primaries (so that voters, not party machines, chose candidates for elections), direct election of Senators (in 1900 most Senators were chosen by state legislatures), and female suffrage (only four states allowed women to vote in 1900). But not all progressives agreed about the extent of democratic reforms. Some, for example, were reluctant to give women the vote.

iii) The Need for Social Justice/Welfare Reform

Many Americans lived in desperate poverty. Progressives wanted government action to help the 'have nots'. They tended to support compensation for injury at work, old age pensions, an end to child labour, factory inspection, and education reform. Many also supported direct taxation to pay for the welfare costs and to ensure a more equitable distribution of income. Not all progressives agreed on 'social' solutions. For example, while some thought Prohibition (of alcohol) was the solution to all America's problems, others were totally opposed to it.

iv) The Influence of the Middle Classes

Progressivism is usually seen as a middle-class movement. Certainly, progressive leaders were usually middle-class professionals – lawyers, doctors, and academics. Many of them passionately wanted to bring efficiency and stability to society. Most were confident that scientific methods, especially data gathering and analysis, should ensure that social and economic problems were overcome in an ordered way.

v) Religious Influences

For most of the nineteenth century, American Protestants had stressed the need for individual enterprise and hard work. God, it was usually claimed, had intended that the wealthy should be wealthy. Because of this, most Churches had shown relatively little interest in helping those in need. However, in the late nineteenth century, many Protestant clergy accepted that adverse social conditions could lead to people becoming evil. They argued that Christians should promote social and economic reform. The so-called Social Gospel movement is often seen as an important factor in progressivism.

IMMIGRATION

Between 1900 and 1910 over 8 million immigrants, mainly from southern and eastern Europe, came to the USA. This was the largest number in any decade before or since. Many native-born Protestant Americans saw Catholic and Jewish immigrants as a threat to traditional American values and there was pressure to restrict immigration.

BIG BUSINESS REFORM

Not all big business leaders were uncaring of their workers' interests. Many supported reform, both generally and within their own corporations (partly because such reform might well lead to more efficiency). In general the lot of industrial workers did improve in the early twentieth century. Real wages rose and the length of the working week was cut.

vi) The Influence of the Media

In the early twentieth century there was a huge increase in newspaper and magazine circulation. In 1902 *McClure's Magazine* hit on a winning formula when it exposed political and business corruption in most of America's main cities. Other editors rushed to follow *McClure's* lead. The spate of 'muckraking' articles had several effects. Public opinion became more 'progressive', progressive legislation was passed (often at state level) and many corrupt politicians suffered defeat at the hands of 'clean' opponents.

vii) The Left-wing Threat

Socialist organisations, particularly trade unions, grew in strength in the early twentieth century, and this despite the fact that many firms fought all forms of unionism. By 1904 the moderate American Federation of Labour (AFL) had over 1.5 million members. Some US workers supported more militant unions. Violent strikes became common. Union troubles reinforced the suspicion that all was not well with America. It seemed that something had to be done to improve the lot of the working class or the USA might face violent class struggle. This fear was probably exaggerated. Under 6 per cent of the total US labour force was unionised by 1910. Moreover, AFL leaders were hostile to socialism. They were only concerned with promoting the interests of skilled workers.

> ### THE ROLE OF WOMEN
>
> Two issues particularly concerned women who involved themselves in public affairs: women's suffrage and Prohibition. Between 1900 and 1917 several states gave women the vote. Once it was recognised that women were likely to support Prohibition, liquor interests campaigned against giving women the vote.

c) How Progressive was President Theodore Roosevelt (TR)?

TR became president in 1901 after McKinley's assassination. He was aged 42 and was a man with many interests and colossal energy. His career was as chequered as his character. He had been a writer, a western rancher, Assistant Secretary of the Navy and he had led the Rough Riders in the war against Spain in Cuba, after which he returned to the USA a war hero. He was elected governor of New York in 1898 and became Republican vice-presidential candidate in 1900. He had a vigorous conception of the presidency and supported a number of progressive reforms.

▼ A Bureau of Corporations, set up in 1903 with the power to investigate and publicise but not to enforce, carried out a number of useful studies into several major industries.

▼ TR took action against the Northern Securities Company. After a long battle, the Supreme Court decided in 1904 that the Company was illegal and it was dissolved. After this successful assertion of power, many business leaders were prepared to work out 'gentlemen's agreements' with TR.

▼ In 1902 TR supported striking miners who were demanding a pay increase, an eight-hour day and recognition of their union.

▼ TR added millions of acres to federal forest reserves and also set up several national parks. By supporting conservation, he seemed to be supporting the 'people' against mining, timber and oil 'interests'.

TR was a great self-publicist and his relative youth and young family helped his image. Despite the suspicions of the 'old guard', he had no difficulty winning his party's nomination in 1904 and easily defeated his Democrat opponent Alton Parker, winning over 57 per cent of the vote. His second term saw more progressive legislation.

▼ The 1906 Hepburn Act gave a federal government commission the power to inspect the books of railway companies and to lay down the maximum rates they could charge. The reason for doing this was to protect the public from exploitation.

▼ A 1906 act led to a federal programme of meat inspection.

▼ The 1906 Pure Food and Drug Act forbade the manufacture and sale of fraudulently labelled products.

Figure 17 Theodore Roosevelt (TR) speaking.

TR continued to take action against some big business practices. He also continued to support conservation measures: some 120 million acres were taken into the public domain between 1905 and 1909. However, TR was unable to persuade Congress to pass more in the way of progressive reform. He was not helped by the fact that there was a growing divide in the Republican Party between conservatives and progressives.

It is possible to claim that TR's commitment to reform was all 'noise and smoke'. Some historians see him as a reactionary who supported reform in order to stave off revolution. He was not against big business: he believed that very large corporations were essential to America's economic well-being. His main concern was to persuade big business to reform itself. However, most historians think that he helped dramatise progressive concerns and gave them respectability. He also seems to have had a genuine concern for the underdog. The fact that conservatives viewed him with suspicion is testimony to his progressive credentials. His popularity was not in doubt. Had he been prepared to stand again in 1908 he would almost certainly have won. But he respected the two term tradition, established by George Washington, and refused to run for a third term as president.

d) President William Howard Taft

TR's successor was William Taft. He seemed to have similar aims to TR. His presidency saw more trustbreaking than had occurred under TR and he continued TR's conservation policies. However, Taft lacked TR's political skills and failed to handle the progressive–conservative divisions among Republicans. To many progressives, it soon appeared as though he lined up with the conservatives. When TR returned to the USA after an African safari in 1910, he tried to heal the wounds within the party. But privately he soon gave up on Taft and sided with the progressives. In 1910 TR made an important speech at Osawatomie in which he attacked the 'lawbreakers of great wealth', urged the need for more social reform, and supported the need for the expansion of federal power. In 1911 he determined to run against Taft for the Republican presidential nomination. He won the support of the states which held primary elections. But Taft controlled the party machine and was able to dominate the convention. TR, claiming that 'special interests' were operating against the wishes of the 'People', quit the convention and formed his own Progressive Party.

e) The 1912 Election

The four presidential candidates – Taft (Republican), Woodrow Wilson (Democrat), TR (Progressive) and Eugene Debs (Socialist) – while recognising that it was the duty of government to concern itself with the general welfare of people, disagreed about the extent to which it should involve itself in social and economic matters.

While some historians believe there were major differences between **New Nationalism** and **New Freedom**, others stress the similiarities. In truth, most voters seem to have seen little difference between the two platforms. Even so, the campaign was keenly fought.

> **WOODROW WILSON**
> Born in 1856, Wilson had been an academic for most of his life – a political philosopher with an interest in history. (He remains the only president with a PhD.) Between 1902 and 1910 he was president of Princeton University. In 1910, he became governor of New Jersey (the first time he had run for public office) and set about introducing progressive reforms.

NEW NATIONALISM

TR attacked the evils of 'class government' and 'greedy, short-sighted materialism'. He claimed that trusts should be regulated but not 'busted'. 'Conduct not size' was what mattered. He advocated inheritance and income taxes, the end of child labour, pensions and worker insurance, a minimum wage for women, female suffrage, government aid to agriculture, national party primaries, and the introduction of the referendum.

NEW FREEDOM

Wilson attacked the great corporations and supported trustbusting rather than regulatory commissions. He favoured tariff reduction. He also tended to oppose federal government involvement in social/welfare matters on the grounds that these matters should usually be left to state governments.

The main battle was between TR and Wilson. Wilson triumphed, winning 435 electoral college votes – 6,283,019 votes – 41.9 per cent of the total. TR won 88 electoral college votes: 4,119,507 votes— 27.4 per cent. Taft won 8 electoral college votes: 3,484,956 votes – 23.2 per cent. Debs won some 900,000 votes – 6 per cent, the largest share ever won by a Socialist candidate in the USA. Wilson thus became the first Democrat president since 1897. The Democrats also won majorities in both Houses of Congress. Perhaps the most surprising thing about the election result was that there were few surprises. Wilson kept the Democrat vote while the Republican vote was split between Taft and TR.

f) How Progressive was President Woodrow Wilson?

Wilson admired the British system of government and saw himself as filling a role similar to that filled by a British prime minister. He would formulate legislation, manage Congress, and lead the nation. In April 1913 he addressed a special session of Congress at which he revealed his plans. This had not happened since 1801. Thereafter, he followed the government-sponsored bills closely, persuading and cajoling to ensure his measures passed. Aloof and austere, Wilson was not on close or even good terms with many of his colleagues, some of whom disliked his moralising tone. But he proved himself to be a skilful leader. His measures in 1913–14 were unprecedented in scope and extent.

▼ The Underwood–Simmons Tariff reduced tariffs.

▼ Wilson introduced the first permanent income tax law in US history.

▼ The Federal Reserve Act gave the USA a central banking system for the first time since the 1830s.

▼ The Federal Trade Commmission replaced the Bureau of Corporations. It had more power over trusts.

▼ The Clayton Anti-Trust Act made a number of restrictive business practices illegal. Big businessmen could now be held individually responsible when found guilty of violating anti-trust laws.

By 1914 Wilson was satisfied with his achievement. But many Americans thought he had not gone far enough. Little had been done on the welfare front, largely because Wilson thought this was the responsibility of individual states rather than of the federal government. Nor was there any real attack on big business. In 1916 Wilson introduced a second wave of reform. Historians have questioned his motives. Some think he may genuinely have become a convert to measures which in many respects were similar to New Nationalism. Others believe that political motives were uppermost in his mind. A presidential election was coming up. Wilson had won in 1912 because the Republicans had split. By 1916 TR had rejoined the Republican Party. If Wilson was to win in 1916 he needed to win ex-

Progressive support. Whatever his motivation, a spate of measures was pushed through Congress.

▼ The Farm Loan Act provided low-cost loans to farmers.

▼ A Child Labour Act barred goods made by child labour from inter-state commerce.

▼ A Workmen's Compensation Act ensured that federal employees who were absent from work because of injury or illness received financial assistance.

▼ The Adamson Act laid down a maximum eight-hour day for railroad workers.

▼ Wilson now declared his full support for female suffrage.

g) What Impact Did the First World War Have on Progressivism?

Wilson's victory in 1916 had been helped by the fact that he had kept the USA out of war. It was thus somewhat ironic that in April 1917 he took the USA into the First World War. While some historians think this marked the end of progressivism, others see the war as the high-water mark of progressivism. They point to the facts that:

▼ The ideals which the USA brought to the war ('the war to end war', 'the war to save democracy') can be seen as progressivism applied to foreign policy.

▼ During the war, the federal government involved itself in a host of economic and social concerns. For example, it took over the running of railways and telephone lines.

▼ There was an increase in income, inheritance and corporate taxes.

▼ Nationwide female suffrage, a major aim of many progressives, came after the war.

▼ The 18th Amendment, which introduced Prohibition in 1919, became law after the war.

h) The Triumph of Conservatism?

Left-wing historians see the progressive decades as 'The Triumph of Conservatism', claiming that tit-bits of reform were introduced to keep the masses happy. They are critical of the fact that there was no basic reorganisation of society. Big business survived and prospered. So did corrupt political bosses. Much of the emphasis on democracy proved illusory. Progressivism also seems to have had a darker side of racism, intolerance and repression. Southern progressives were often racists and the early years of the twentieth century saw a solidifying of racial discrimination and segregation in the south. Right-wing historians are also critical of progressivism. Some hold the view that the real achievements of the progressive decades – wage increases, work-

---

> **THE 1916 ELECTION**
>
> Wilson campaigned on his record of 'Peace, Progress, Prosperity'. He was helped by the fact that the First World War provided a great boost to the US economy. His Republican opponent Charles Hughes won 254 electoral college votes – 8,500,000 popular votes – 46 per cent. Wilson won 277 electoral college votes – 9,100,000 votes – 49 per cent. The North-east and Mid-West voted for Hughes. The South and West voted for Wilson.

THE USA: 1900–20

1901 assassination of President McKinley: TR became president;

1904 TR re-elected;

1908 President Taft elected;

1912 Woodrow Wilson became president;

1916 Wilson was re-elected;

1917 the USA entered the First World War.

Which president was most progressive – Theodore Roosevelt or Woodrow Wilson? Suggested line of response:
▼ What was progressivism?
▼ What did TR do between 1901 and 1909?
▼ What were the differences between Wilson and TR in 1912?
▼ What did Wilson do between 1913 and 1921?

ISSUE:
Were the twenties the best of times or the worst of times?

THE SACCO–VANZETTI CASE

In 1920, two immigrant Italians, Sacco and Vanzetti, admitted anarchists, were arrested for armed robbery and murder. After a trial conducted in a hostile atmosphere by a conservative judge, they were sentenced to death. An array of writers, as biased in the two men's favour as the judge had been prejudiced against them, demanded a retrial. But the verdict was upheld on appeal and Sacco and Vanzetti were executed in 1927. Modern ballistics tests suggest that the murders had indeed been committed with Sacco's gun.

ers' welfare, pension and profit-sharing schemes – resulted from the voluntary actions of big business. However, a case can be made to support progressive reformers.
▼ Some action had been taken against corporations to ensure they did not operate to the disadvantage of the public interest.
▼ Progressive reforms reduced the harshness of industrialisation and made government more responsive to the people.
▼ The progressive presidents had paved the way for the later twentieth century 'imperial' presidents – activist, reform-minded, and mobilisers of public opinion.

2 The Twenties

a) 1919–21

The First World War did not leave the USA impoverished and in turmoil, as it did much of Europe. Yet it does seem to have resulted in a mood of disillusionment. This affected attitudes to foreign policy (see Chapter 4). It also influenced many aspects of social and political life. Many Americans, weary of radicalism and frightened by class and racial strife, longed for stability and order.

i) The Red Scare 1919
The Bolshevik Revolution in Russia aroused fears of a new alien threat. Many Americans were alarmed at the pro-Soviet leanings of some Socialists and at the emergence of an American Communist movement, largely foreign-born in membership. A wave of industrial unrest in 1919 was widely, though wrongly, interpreted as revolutionary. Public opinion became strongly anti-union, especially after the Boston police strike of September 1919 had led to an outbreak of rioting and looting. Fear of revolution increased when home-made bombs were posted to leading politicians and industrialists. On Wall Street an anarchist bomb killed 38 people. A wave of repression followed. Congress expelled Socialist members. Thirty-two states passed laws making membership of syndicalist organisations a criminal offence. Attorney-General Mitchell Palmer launched a series of raids against left-wing organisations. Nine thousand people were arrested and held without trial; over 500 aliens were deported.

ii) Racial Strife
During the First World War a labour shortage in the North had led to an influx of Southern blacks. By 1920 New York had 152,000 blacks (an increase of 66.3 per cent during the decade) and Chicago 109,000 (148.2 per cent up). When a post-war **recession** set in, white workers felt that blacks threatened their jobs. In July 1919 there

were race riots in 20 cities. In Chicago 23 blacks and 15 whites were killed.

iii) Reaction

By 1920 Wilsonian zeal, whether for domestic reform or a new world order, was out of fashion. Incapacitated by a stroke, Wilson proposed no further reform measures during his last two years in office. Wartime controls were abandoned and the railroads were returned to private ownership. Sympathy for big business was evident also in the lack of vigour in prosecuting anti-trust suits. Further evidence of the revival of laissez-faire was the withdrawal of price guarantees to farmers.

iv) The 1920 Election

Confident that the tide was running in their favour, Republican bosses chose Warren Harding – a conservative and tractable candidate. The Democrats nominated James Cox. Cox tried to make membership of the League of Nations the main campaign issue, but voters were more concerned about rising prices, industrial strife, and the post-war recession, all of which they blamed on the party in power. Harding said little about anything. (Senator Penrose said: 'Keep Warren at home. Don't let him make any speeches. If he goes out on a tour, somebody's sure to ask him questions and Warren's just the sort of damned fool that will try to answer them.') In a typically bland speech he declared that 'America's present need is not heroics but healing, not nostrums but normalcy'. Whatever 'normalcy' was supposed to mean, it was apparently what Americans wanted. Harding won by a greater margin (61 per cent) than any previous presidential candidate.

b) Republican Dominance: 1921–9

i) Warren Harding

Harding was an amiable and outgoing man. He enjoyed the trappings of office but often found complex issues beyond him. Nevertheless, he appointed a number of able men to key posts. Ex-governor of New York, Charles Hughes, became Secretary of State; Herbert Hoover, director of wartime relief to Belgium, became Secretary of Commerce; and millionaire banker Andrew Mellon became Secretary of the Treasury. Unfortunately, Harding gave other posts to some of his cronies – his 'Ohio Gang'. Sympathetic to big business, Harding believed that government intervention in the economy should be kept to a minimum. He declared, 'We want less government in business and more business in government'. His administration repealed the high wartime taxes, returned to the traditional Republican policy of high tariffs, did not enforce the

> **RECESSION**
> The USA suffered a short but severe recession between 1919 and 1921. By 1919 some 4 million Americans were unemployed. Many blamed Wilson and the Democrats.

Figure 18 President Warren G. Harding (left) and Vice-President Calvin Coolidge.

anti-trust laws, and supported employers in industrial disputes. The Supreme Court also dealt trade unionism a series of blows, ruling that trade unions were not immune from prosecution in respect of practices such as mass picketing: they were also liable for damages caused by a strike.

In 1923 it emerged that there was extensive corruption within Harding's administration. The head of the Veterans' Bureau had mis-appropriated or wasted $250 million while the Alien Property Custodian had accepted bribes. Both men were imprisoned. Jesse Smith, a member of Harding's 'Ohio Gang' and a friend of Attorney General Daugherty, was implicated in various corrupt practices, including selling pardons to lawbreakers. When the facts came out, he committed suicide. The most sensational scandal involved the lease to private interests of government lands earlier set aside for naval use. Secretary of the Interior, Albert Fall, having secured the transfer of these lands to his own department, then secretly leased those at Elk Hills, California, and Teapot Dome, Wyoming, to two oil magnates, receiving in return large 'loans'. Fall was convicted of receiving a bribe and was sentenced to a year in prison. (He became the first cabinet member in US history to go to jail for crimes committed in office.)

Harding, who was not personally implicated in any of the corrupt activities, unexpectedly died in 1923.

ii) Calvin Coolidge

Vice-President Calvin Coolidge now became president. He was honest and incorruptible. Unlike Harding, he did not smoke, drink, play cards or chase women. As governor of Massachusetts, he was credited with having broken the Boston police strike and, therefore, had come to symbolise law and order. He had a conservative, laissez-faire philosophy. 'The business of America', he said, 'is business'. Liberal intellectuals criticised Coolidge for sleeping a lot and for saying little. (When he died in 1933, writer Dorothy Parker quipped: 'How can they tell?') But, to most Americans, Coolidge's presence in the White House was reassuring; he became a symbol of traditional values threatened by the forces of change.

The social, sectional, and religious antagonisms reflected in the controversies over immigration, the Klan, and Prohibition (see below) divided the Democrat Party. In 1924 rural and 'dry' Democrats favoured William McAdoo for the presidential nomination. Urban and 'wet' Democrats backed Governor Alfred Smith of New York. With the two men evenly matched, the Democrat convention was deadlocked for 16 days. Finally McAdoo and Smith both agreed to withdraw and John Davis, a corporation lawyer, was chosen as a compromise candidate.

Since the Republicans renominated Coolidge, there were now two conservative candidates with very similar platforms. A genuine alternative appeared when a coalition of Western farmers, trade union leaders, and ex-progressives nominated Robert La Follette as candidate of a new Progressive Party. Its platform, denounced by Republicans and Democrats alike as dangerously radical, condemned monopoly, called for railway nationalisation, and proposed tariff reduction and aid to farmers. La Follette waged a vigorous campaign, Davis a colourless one, while Coolidge hardly campaigned at all. Even so the voters 'kept cool with Coolidge': he won 15 million votes to Davis's 8 million. La Follette won a respectable 4.8 million votes. After the election the Progressive Party fell apart, disappearing altogether after La Follette's death in 1925.

iii) Prosperity

Coolidge's victory in 1924 led to an extension of Republican pro-business policies – low taxation, low interest rates, and frugal government expenditure. For most of the 1920s, the support of business seemed to be spectacularly vindicated. Once the brief depression of 1919–21 was over the USA entered an era of unparalleled prosperity. Business made huge profits, there was little unemployment, and standards of living rose. The key to the boom was a great increase in productivity resulting from technological innovation. While the population increased by 16 per cent during the 1920s, industrial production almost doubled. The US chemicals industry did well, particularly in the manufacture of synthetic textiles and plastics. The electricity industry did even better. Electricity consumption more than doubled during the decade. Electrical household appliances – cookers, irons, fridges – came into general use. Another important new industry was radio. In 1920, the first broadcasting station in the USA, KDKA in Pittsburgh, began regular services. Unlike Britain, which granted a

ADVERTISING

Newspapers, magazines, billboards, radio and cinema were all used by advertisers in an effort to sell products to consumers.

monopoly to the BBC, the US allowed private enterprise to develop 'wireless'. The earliest stations were set up by the manufacturers of radio equipment, but commercial broadcasting companies, financed by advertisers, soon dominated the field. In 1927 the number of radio stations had grown to 732. By 1930, nearly half of all American families possessed radio.

Figure 19 Traffic St. Louis, 1920.

What contributed most to the business boom was the automobile revolution. Its architect was Henry Ford. By adapting assembly-line techniques and concentrating on a single, standardized model, the famous Model T, Ford brought the car to the masses. By 1925 he was producing a car every ten seconds. There was competition from other manufacturers, notably General Motors and Chrysler, who offered more stylish models. In 1920 9 million cars were registered in the USA; by 1929 there were nearly 27 million – one car for every five Americans. In 1929 the USA produced about 5 million motor vehicles (about ten times the total produced by Britain, France and Germany combined) and its car industry employed 447,000 workers, 7 per cent of all manufacturing wage-earners. The automobile industry (and the spread of motoring) stimulated other industries – steel, rubber, leather, oil, and road building.

There was a huge increase in house building as people moved from the countryside to the towns and from towns to suburbs. Industrial and commercial construction also went on apace. By 1929 the USA had some 400 skyscrapers – buildings over 20 storeys high. The 102-storey Empire State Building in New York, completed in 1931 and providing office space for 25,000 people, become the tallest building in the world – 1,250 feet high.

To most industrial workers prosperity brought substantial gains. Hours of work declined, real wages increased by 30 per cent, and unemployment fell from 12 per cent in 1921 to 3.2 per cent in 1929. Many employers, in an effort to prevent labour unrest, improved working conditions, extended recreational facilities, and introduced profit-sharing, life insurance, and pension plans. Employers also sought to suppress unionism by using strike-breakers and spies. These tactics, together with the anti-union bias of the courts – and of public opinion – weakened the unions. Union membership fell from 5 million in 1920 to 3.5 million in 1929.

Some groups, particularly textile workers and coal miners, did not enjoy prosperity. Farmers also suffered. A decline in foreign demand and the withdrawal of government price supports after 1920 led to a drastic fall in farm prices. Although dairy farmers and fruit and vegetable growers profited as city markets grew, most farmers – still one in five of the population – remained depressed, especially those in the South and Midwest. The farm crisis prompted Congress to propose a complicated price-support scheme – the McNary–Haugen bill – in 1927–8. But Coolidge vetoed it on the grounds that it would encourage overproduction and create a vast bureaucracy.

iv) The Election of 1928
Coolidge refused to stand in 1928. (He had some health concerns.) In his place the Republicans selected Herbert Hoover. Hoover epitomised the self-made man. An orphaned farm-boy, he became a successful mining engineer and was a millionaire before he was 40. Hero of Belgium relief and then head of the Food Administration in the First World War, he was Secretary of Commerce between 1921 and 1928. Efficient and humanitarian, he was nicknamed 'the wonder boy'. The Republican platform called for continued high tariffs, tax cuts, help for farmers, and upheld Prohibition. Hoover promised 'a chicken in every pot and two cars in every garage'. 'We shall soon with the help of God', he said, 'be in sight of the day when poverty will be banished from this nation.'

The Democrat candidate was New York governor Al Smith, a Catholic of Irish descent. An economic conservative who was sympathetic to business, Smith's platform differed only in detail from the Republican one. However, by calling for an end to Prohibition, Smith created a campaign issue. Moreover, his religion revived fears of popery. Not surprisingly, given the prevailing prosperity, Hoover won 58 per cent of the popular vote – 444 electoral college votes to Smith's 87. The Republicans also won large majorities in Congress. The Democrats' only solace was that Smith carried the nation's 12 largest cities – cities which the Republicans had won in 1924.

c) American Society in the Jazz Age

In spite of the general prosperity many Americans feared that new ideas and customs were undermining society. They yearned to put the clock back.

i) Immigration Restriction

The Red Scare and the post-war economic recession gave new strength to demands for immigration restriction. Politicians, newspaper editors and popular writers warned that America's old 'Anglo-Saxon' stock was in danger of being swamped by hordes of 'new' immigrants and raised fears of racial degeneration and national decline. Congress, in response to the clamour, imposed restrictions on immigration in 1921. There was to be a limit of 357,000 immigrants a year and quotas for each eligible national group based on the number of foreign-born residents in the USA in 1910. A 1924 act tilted the balance still further against 'new' immigrants. Immigration was limited to 150,000 a year and a quota was allocated to each nationality according to the 1890 census. In practice, over 80 per cent of the quotas were allocated to the countries of north-western Europe. The Act prohibited immigration from most Asian countries – a move deeply resented in Japan.

ii) The Ku Klux Klan

Like the Reconstruction organisation from which it took its name (see page 80), the new Klan originated as a Southern, white supremacist movement. It was founded in Georgia in 1915 by an insurance salesman, William Simmons, who had been influenced by D.W. Griffith's film, *The Birth of a Nation*, which glorified the earlier Klan. The new Klan, which soon became national rather than sectional, professed to stand for Americanism, Christianity, and morality. Klan hostility was directed, not so much against blacks, as against Catholics, Jews, and foreigners – who, along with drink, dancing, and short skirts, were seen as undermining American values.

The Klan quickly expanded, and by 1925 had over 2 million members and great political influence in several states in the Mid- and South-West. In the South, Klansmen did resort to beatings and even murder, in order to terrorise black people. But elsewhere Klan members were more likely to be the victims as the perpetrators of violence. Known Klansmen were assaulted, Klan property was set on fire, and Klan gatherings were broken up by armed mobs. The introduction of immigration restriction took much steam out of the Klan's efforts to mobilise white Protestant opinion and after 1925 the Klan's political influence declined.

iii) The 'Monkey Trial'

Protestant fundamentalists, who believed in the literal truth of the Bible, were angered by the growing acceptance of evolution. Fundamentalism was strongest in the rural South and Midwest. In 1925 Tennessee introduced a law forbidding the teaching in public schools of any evolutionary theory that denied the Old Testament version of the creation. Biology teacher John Scopes was soon arrested, convicted and fined for breaking the law. His so-called ' monkey trial' attracted huge publicity.

iv) Prohibition

In 1919 the 18th Amendment prohibited the sale and manufacture of alcohol. Prohibition was fairly well observed in small towns and rural areas. But in large cities the law proved hard to enforce. 'Bootleggers' smuggled in liquor from the West Indies, Canada and Mexico. Industrial alcohol was redistilled and converted into synthetic gin and whisky. Many Americans brewed their own beer or made 'bathtub gin'. 'Speakeasies' (illicit saloons) flourished. In 1929 there were 32,000 speakeasies in New York – twice the number of its saloons before Prohibition.

Poorly paid enforcement agents were susceptible to bribery from organised crime. Attracted by huge profits, underworld gangs set out to control the liquor business. They established their own breweries, distilleries, and distribution networks and surrounded themselves with private armies, murdered competitors, and blackmailed speakeasy proprietors into paying for 'protection'. Corrupt alliances with politicians, policemen, and judges enabled them to dominate some city governments. Al Capone, whose illicit earnings brought in $60 million annually by 1927, had huge influence in Chicago, where gangland wars were commonplace. More than 500 gang murders occurred in Chicago between 1927 and 1930. The most infamous was the Valentine Day Massacre in 1929 which ended the 'war' between the Irish O'Bannions and the Italian Capone–Tomo gang, establishing the latter as the dominant power in Chicago.

The evident failure of the 18th Amendment produced a growing demand for repeal. But the 'dry' forces, particularly strong among fundamentalists, remained devoted to what Hoover described in 1928 as 'a great social and economic experiment'. The struggle over repeal was not a simple matter of rural fundamentalist bigotry against urban liberalism. 'Drys' included many social workers concerned about the damaging effects of alcoholism. 'Wets' numbered not only brewers but also millionaire businessmen who claimed that a restored tax on alcohol would mean income-tax reductions.

v) Moral Conformity

Prohibition and anti-evolution were part of a wider movement to enforce moral conformity by law. Some states outlawed gambling, made 'petting' a crime (along with extra-marital sexual intercourse), and forbade the sale of contraceptive devices. There was strict local censorship of books, plays, and films. The motion-picture industry, reacting to adverse publicity about Hollywood sex scandals, set up its own censorship board in 1922.

vi) A Vibrant Society?

In the twenties Americans worked less, produced more, were paid more, were healthier and had more leisure time than ever before. The car meant greater mobility and freedom. Before 1914 the USA had tended to follow European trends. In the twenties it set the trends. Hollywood was particularly influential. Cinema-going became a national habit. The appearance in 1927 of the first full-length talking picture, *The Jazz Singer*, swelled cinema audiences still further. Increased leisure led to a variety of crazes like dance marathons and flagpole sitting, and to a boom in spectator sports. Baseball star Babe Ruth and world heavyweight boxing champion Jack Dempsey became national celebrities.

If materialism and pleasure-seeking were features of the decade so, too, were rebellion and protest. Repelled by the prevailing conformity, a new generation of writers, among whom were Sinclair Lewis and F. Scott Fitzgerald, launched scathing indictments of modern civilisation in general and of America in particular. Leaders of the younger generation were critical of traditional codes of behaviour. There was a widespread obsession with sex which magazines, newspapers and Hollywood were quick to exploit. Youthful restlessness also explained the growing popularity of jazz, which many older people denounced as crude, even degenerate. They were particularly alarmed by the new dance forms it inspired. The Charleston and the 'Black Bottom' seemed proof to conservatives of collapsing standards of sexual morality. In fact there were probably fewer changes in sexual behaviour than contemporaries believed. Although they thought of themselves as daring, the young of the 1920s were fairly conventional.

THE TWENTIES

1919 Red Scare, recession and racial strife;
1920 Harding won presidential election;
1923 death of Harding: Coolidge became president;
1924 Coolidge won the presidential election;
1928 Hoover won the presidential election.

To What Extent Did Women's Role Change in the 1920s?

Women wore shorter skirts, discarded corsets, bobbed their hair, and used more cosmetics. The more daring drank and smoked in public and claimed the same sexual freedom as men. However, beneath the appearance of change there was an underlying continuity in women's status.

▼ Although the 19th Amendment had nominally granted them political equality, women still played an insignificant role in politics. Few held political office.

▼ Women did not make much progress toward economic equality. Few married women worked. Most working women had menial jobs. Women earned much less than men even for comparable work, were rarely given managerial positions, and few worked in business or as lawyers or doctors.

▼ Women's primary responsibility was still seen as being in the home. Within the domestic sphere women did become more independent as electrical appliances and processed foods freed them from much drudgery. They also bore fewer children. Birth control, increasingly practised despite statutory obstacles, brought down the birth rate and gave women more control over their lives.

ACTIVITY

Consider the question: Were the twenties the 'best of times' or the 'worst of times'?

Brainstorm the main points you would make a) defending and b) criticising the twenties.

3 The Great Depression: 1929–33

ISSUES:
What were a) the main causes and b) the main effects of the Great Depression?

a) The Wall Street Crash

'I have no fears for the future of our country', said Hoover in March 1929. 'It is bright with hope.' However, there were signs that all was not well with the economy. Since 1927 house building had slowed down, the demand for cars had fallen, and exports had declined. But the illusion of health was preserved by the rise of share values on the stock-market. From mid-1927 to mid-1929, the average price of stocks increased by nearly 300 per cent. (Most of the investment in shares came from corporations and banks, not individuals.) However, the rise in share prices did not reflect the performance of the companies concerned. By September 1929 the market had clearly lost touch with reality and some speculators began selling their holdings. On 24

Company	3 March 1928	3 Sept. 1929	13 Nov. 1929
American Can	c77	c182	c86
Anaconda Copper	c54	c162	c70
Electric Bond and Share	c90	c204	c50
General Electric	c129	c396	c168
General Motors	c140	c182	c36
New York Central	c160	c256	c160
Radio	c94	c505	c28
United States Steel	c138	c279	c150
Westinghouse E & M	c92	c313	c102
Woolworth	c181	c251	c52

Table 2 Some US share prices, 1928–9.

October (Black Thursday) 13 million shares were sold and prices plummeted. On 29 October (Black Tuesday) 16.5 million shares were sold. The gains of months vanished in a few hours, ruining hundreds of investors. By November 1929 the value of stocks and shares had fallen by a third.

b) The Onset of Depression

The Wall Street Crash was followed by the most devastating economic collapse in US history. Business confidence evaporated as bankruptcies and bank failures multiplied. US trade fell from $10 billion in 1929 to $3 billion in 1932. By mid-1932 industrial output had dropped to half the 1929 level. In early 1929 some 1.5 million were unemployed – 3 per cent of the work-force. By December 1930 unemployment had risen to 7 million. By December 1932 it was over 12 million – a quarter of the work-force. There was no dole. Thus, unemployment brought real fear and despair. Private charity was unable to cope with the scale of the emergency. Millions of people roamed the countryside, stealing rides on freight trains and looking for work. Others congregated on the outskirts of cities in shanty towns known as Hoovervilles. It was not just the unemployed who suffered.

▼ Those lucky enough to be in full time work saw their average weekly earnings fall by a third. Many were only employed part time.

▼ Farmers, badly off to begin with, suffered more than anyone as farm prices collapsed. In 1929 wheat was $1.05 a bushel: by 1932 it was 39 cents a bushel. Cotton fell from 17 cents a pound in 1929 to 6 cents a pound in 1932. Farmers' income plummeted from $6 billion in 1929 to $2 billion in 1932.

The Great Depression affected every industrialised country (except the USSR). But the US collapse was more complete than elsewhere (except Germany), and more damaging psychologically, if only because it was in such contrast to the prosperity of the 1920s.

c) What Caused the Great Depression?

Scholars today, like politicians at the time, disagree about the Depression's causes.

▼ Some think it was caused by the Wall Street Crash. The Crash took money out of the system and led – by a vicious circle – to Depression. However, the USA actually weathered the Crash. Business activity did not begin to decline significantly until mid-1930. Fewer than 5 per cent of Americans owned stock so most were not directly affected. By April 1930 share prices had actually regained a fifth of the losses of the previous autumn. The really disastrous falls came in 1931–2. Arguably the Crash was more a symptom than a cause of the Depression.

AFRICAN AMERICANS

The Depression had a catastrophic effect upon African Americans. In northern cities, where they were the last to be hired and the first to be fired, unemployment among African Americans was about twice that among whites. In the South, where 75 per cent of them lived, many African Americans were still dependent upon cotton, the crop hardest hit by the Depression.

▼ At the time, many economists thought that the economic downturn was just part of the normal business cycle. They believed there would be an inevitable natural recovery.

▼ Some think the USA economy was fundamentally unsound. The main charge is that income was not fairly distributed. By 1929 the richest 5 per cent of the population owned a third of the income, while 71 per cent had incomes of less than $2,500 a year, the minimum thought necessary for decent comfort. Unable to afford to buy their share of consumer goods, ordinary Americans could not sustain the level of mass production.

▼ The USA was unable to sell its surplus products overseas. Its high tariff policies had resulted in many countries placing similarly high tariffs on American goods.

▼ Many think that the banking system was the weakest link in the US economic system. Historian David Kennedy claims that 'American banks were rotten even in good times'. One major problem was the lack of regulation. Although the president appointed members to it, the Federal Reserve Board which supervised the banking system was largely independent. Moreover, the Board had only limited control over the larger banks and less control over the smaller banks, many of which were far too small. The vast majority were solitary institutions: they were not part of a chain. Thus they could only look to their own resources. This meant they were vulnerable if depositors withdrew funds – as they did in the early 1930s. Troubled banks were then forced to sell their stocks in order to get cash: this drove down share prices. Banks also called in loans and refused to make new ones: there was therefore little investment. The Federal Reserve Board did not do enough to aid those banks which got into difficulties. Its failure to support the New York City Bank which closed its doors in December 1930 is often seen as a crucial event. A banking panic set in. By 1933 over 5,500 banks had failed with losses in excess of $3 billion.

While many scholars believe the Depression arose from problems within the US economy, others point out that there was a world depression. World factors, over which the USA had little control, might have been the major cause of the US Depression (rather than the Wall Street Crash being the cause of world slump). Different historians have stressed different aspects of the world economy which possibly led (in 1931) to a depression becoming the Great Depression.

▼ Some stress the world over-production of food which led to a fall in prices for farmers.

▼ Some stress the chaotic financial situation after 1918. In the 1920s the USA provided Germany with massive amounts of short-term loans. Germany used these to pay reparations to Britain and France. They, in turn, used the money to pay the interest on US war debts. This money was then returned to Germany in loans. Once US bankers stopped investing in Germany and called in their short-term loans, the German economy was bound to be in difficulty. This had a knock-on effect across Europe.

▼ Some think a serious bank collapse, first in Austria and then in Germany in early 1931, at a time when it seemed that the USA was pulling out of depression, was an important factor. This produced a world financial crisis which had a devastating effect on the US banking system. (US banks held a large stake in Austrian and German banks.)

▼ Some point a finger at Britain, which went off the gold standard in September 1931. This caused ructions in the world's money markets and to world trade. Over 500 US banks collapsed in the month after Britain abandoned gold.

d) President Hoover and the Depression

It is also possible to blame the Depression on the actions – or inaction – of Hoover. The main charges against Hoover are as follows:

▼ A supporter of 'rugged individualism', he believed that too much government interference in economic and social matters would destroy individuals and ultimately the nation. Therefore, he did not take much action. Most of his measures depended for success on the voluntary action of others – of state governments in maintaining spending, of farmers in reducing production, of employers in sustaining wages, of bankers in extending credit. Hoover saw unemployment relief as a matter for private charity and state and local – and not federal – government. He thought that a federal relief programme would unbalance the budget, create a permanent class of dependants, deprive individuals of a sense of responsibility, and destroy the nation's moral fibre. Private charity and local authorities proved incapable of handling a relief problem of such dimensions. But Hoover still adamantly opposed direct federal relief to individuals.

▼ He believed in balancing the budget. The government had less money because it obtained less in taxation as a result of falling personal and corporate income. Therefore, Hoover reduced government spending in 1931 and supported a sharp increase in taxes in 1932 as he tried to control the budget deficit. This only made things worse.

▼ The Federal Reserve Board did not increase the quantity of money in circulation.

▼ After 1931 Hoover claimed that the Depression's causes lay mainly outside the USA and were therefore outside the USA's control.

▼ He chose not to leave the gold standard.

▼ He can be charged with agreeing to sign the 1930 Hawley–Smoot Tariff Act which raised import duties to the highest levels in US history. Foreign countries took similar action against the USA. This had a disastrous effect on world trade.

However, Hoover may have been too much maligned. In his defence:

▽ Although his sombre manner conveyed an impression of indifference, he did very much care about people's suffering and worked tirelessly to try to improve the situation.

▽ He assumed government responsibility and intervened in the economy more energetically than any of his predecessors. In 1930 he secured a pledge from employers to maintain wage rates and avoid lay-offs in order to prevent a shrinkage of purchasing power, urged state governments to increase spending, stepped up federal spending on roads, bridges, and public buildings, cut taxes to try to increase the consumers' spending power, favoured lower interest rates, and attempted through a newly created Federal Farm Board to bolster grain, cotton, and other farm prices. His efforts to break the deflationary spiral before it gathered momentum seemed to have some success in 1930. The depression seemed to be under control in early 1931. However, as things deteriorated in 1931–2, he was prepared to experiment and take direct government action. In 1932 he set up the Reconstruction Finance Corporation (RFC) to lend money to ailing banks, railroads and insurance companies. Other measures included the Glass–Steagall Banking Act, which expanded credit facilities, a Home Loan Bank Act, which gave loans to building societies, and the Relief and Construction Act which empowered the RFC to lend state governments $1.5 billion for public works. He nearly doubled federal public works expenditure in three years. The 1932 federal budget ended up $2.7 billion in the red – the largest peacetime deficit in US history: no New Deal deficit would be proportionately larger. Hoover's measures thus paved the way for the New Deal.

▽ Few politicians advocated more radical measures than those Hoover supported. Congress, Democrat-controlled after 1930, advocated a balanced budget. It had no real programme, except to obstruct Hoover.

▽ The federal government at the time was a flimsy edifice. There was little in the way of a federal bureaucracy. This severely limited the scope of the federal government's action, whatever the ideology of the president.

> **MALNUTRITION**
> Grim though American sufferings were during the Depression, they were not comparable to those of, say, the USSR in 1920–21 when famine claimed millions of lives. The total reported number of deaths from starvation was 110. Even so there was a dramatic rise in cases of malnutrition. As late as 1935, it was estimated that 20 million people were not getting enough to eat.

e) The Situation in 1932

By the summer of 1932 despair and bitterness were almost universal. Hoover was condemned for his supposed coldheartedness. The destitute found it hard to understand how it could be right to use federal funds to save banks and corporations but wrong to do so to feed the hungry. Astonishingly, in view of the amount of suffering, there was little violent protest. In some places people looted food shops; in others demonstrations by strikers or the jobless led to clashes with the police. Some Western farmers blocked roads to prevent farm produce from getting to market. But the only large-scale organised protest move-

Figure 20 New York, December 1931. A 'breadline' of unemployed men waiting for free food.

ment was the march of 22,000 unemployed ex-servicemen on Washington in June 1932. The marchers threatened to stay there until Congress passed a bill authorising immediate payment of a bonus due to First World War veterans in 1945. Hoover had no sympathy with the proposal. Aware that communists had helped organise the march and believing that it was a threat to democracy, he ordered General MacArthur to evict the veterans from the government buildings they had occupied. Troops equipped with machine-guns, tanks, and tear gas drove the marchers out of Washington and burned down their shanties. Many Americans sympathised with the bonus marchers and believed the government had over-reacted. The episode was a symbol of Hoover's supposed insensitivity to the plight of the unemployed.

f) The 1932 Election

The Republicans renominated Hoover as their presidential candidate in 1932. The Democrats chose Franklin D. Roosevelt (FDR), a man acceptable to all factions within the party. As governor of New York, FDR had won a reputation as a moderate reformer who tried to help those in need. But there had been little in his career to suggest his future greatness: indeed, some contemporaries thought him a lightweight. In his acceptance speech in July 1932, FDR pledged himself to a 'new deal for the American people' and promised 'bold, persistent experimentation'. But neither then nor during the campaign

did he define exactly what he intended to do. The Democrat platform differed little from the Republican, except that it called for an
end to Prohibition. FDR's campaign, while lacking in revolutionary
promise and consistency (he spoke both of cutting the federal budget and spending more on the jobless) was upbeat: his theme tune
was 'Happy Days Are Here Again'. Republicans cast doubts about his
health and stamina but he travelled 13,000 miles on the campaign
trail. His zest and self-assurance contrasted strongly with Hoover's

FRANKLIN D. ROOSEVELT (FDR)

-Profile-

Inaugurated in 1933, FDR was
to remain president for the
rest of his life. He had to
deal with two great
crises – the Depression
and the Second World
War. Virtually every-
thing he tried to do
sparked intense contro-
versy. He was both the
most loved and the most
hated president in modern times.
His political career is a paradox. Conservative in dispo-
sition, he never feared experimentation. Genuinely
committed to certain moral principles, he was the most
pragmatic of leaders. Raised in affluent surroundings,
he was loved by the common people but seen as the
betrayer of his class by many rich Americans. The com-
plexities of his character baffled contemporaries and
still baffle historians. On one hand, he projected
extraordinary charm and warmth. But he also possessed
a remote quality. Secretary of Labour Frances Perkins
said he was 'the most complicated human being I have
ever known'. FDR once told his close friend Henry
Morgenthau, 'You know I am a juggler, and I never let
my right hand know what my left hand does'. Historian
Ted Morgan has described FDR as 'part lion, part fox'.
He could be evasive and devious. 'He was the kind of
man to whom those who wanted him convinced of
something could talk and argue and insist, and come
away believing they had succeeded, when all that happened was that he had been pleasantly present', said
FDR's adviser Rexford Tugwell.

1882 born to wealthy parents in New York
(30 January);
1900 went to Harvard University;
1905 married Eleanor Roosevelt, a distant
cousin and niece of Theodore
Roosevelt;
1910 elected to New York state assembly as a
Democrat;
1913 accepted post of under-secretary of
the Navy in Woodrow Wilson's administration;
1920 Democrat vice-presidential candidate;
1921 stricken with polio: despite years of
physical therapy he never regained the
use of his legs. He could stand only with
the use of heavy steel braces and when
he could lean on something. Remaining
cheerful and optimistic, he refused to
let his disability end his political career
(and took care to hide the extent of
his disability). His wife Eleanor worked
tirelessly to keep his political career alive
throughout the 1920s;
1928 became governor of New York,
America's largest state. Re-elected in
1930, he showed more resource in
dealing with the Depression than most
governors;
1932 won presidential election;
1936 won presidential election for the second
time;
1940 won presidential election for a third
time;
1941 the USA entered the Second World
War;
1944 won fourth presidential election;
1945 died (12 April).

gloom. On election day, FDR obtained 22.8 million popular and 472 electoral college votes to Hoover's 15.8 million popular and 59 electoral college votes. The Democrats also won large majorities in both houses of Congress. The Socialist candidate won 882,000 votes, the Communist 103,000 votes. The election seemed to confirm the faith of Americans in capitalism and democracy.

Hoover remained as a 'lame duck' president until March 1933. Over the winter of 1932–3, the economy took a further nosedive. Many blamed the length of the interregnum, a view which led to the adoption later in 1933 of the 20th Amendment, which reduced the interval between election and inauguration to two and a half months. FDR's intentions remained a secret. In his inaugural address in March 1933, he proclaimed: 'the only thing we have to fear is fear itself'. He said that he would ask Congress for broad executive powers to wage war against the emergency. Historian William Leuchtenburg believed that his inaugural address 'had made his greatest single contribution to the politics of the 1930s: the installation of hope and courage in the people'.

ACTIVITY

Examine the share prices in Table 2 on page 105. To what extent do the share prices suggest that the Wall Street Crash was a major economic disaster?

ISSUES:
What were the aims of FDR? How successful was he in achieving them?

4 Franklin D. Roosevelt: 1933–6

a) Who Made the New Deal?

▼ FDR took advice from an unofficial group of academics, lawyers and journalists. Key members of this 'Brain Trust' were Samuel Rosenman, Rexford Tugwell, and Raymond Moley. The 'Brain Trust' – a novelty – attracted a lot of attention but had less influence than many thought.

▼ FDR's cabinet played a crucial role, for example, Frances Perkins, Secretary of Labour and Harold Ickes, Secretary of the Interior.

▼ Congressmen had plenty of proposals for recovery. Democrat leaders in Congress influenced FDR's thinking and played a pivotal role in shaping the New Deal legislation. FDR was fortunate that the Democrats controlled both houses. While many Democrat congressmen were conservative who favoured state rights and a balanced budget, the fact that the crisis was of such magnitude meant that FDR could count on an extraordinary amount of cooperation.

▼ Many of the 1933 measures were very similar to those Hoover's administration had been planning or had already adopted.

▼ Although FDR was not a great legislator, there seems little doubt that he led and shaped the recovery package – more so than Congress in 1933. He was responsible for choosing his advisers and officials. He chose well. Historian Michael Heale has written: 'It may be doubted whether any other US administration of the twentieth century has been staffed at all levels with such a wealth of ability and skill'. Another of

FDR's strengths was the fact that he was receptive to new ideas: 'It is common sense to take a method and try it. If it fails, admit it frankly and try another. But above all try something', he said in 1932. He was also able to 'sell' his ideas to both Congress and the public. His radio 'fireside chats' were very effective. He projected a sense of utter self-confidence and emanated optimism: 'He knew how to make half a loaf sound like a feast', says Ted Morgan. He was also on good terms with journalists. Reporters liked him and the light banter of his frequent press conferences was translated in newspapers into a president in easy command of his job. He had faults. He was loath to admit mistakes; he was a poor administrator; and he often prevaricated. But he was a masterly politician. His main function – by no means an easy one – was to reconcile the sharply conflicting views of his reform-minded supporters.

b) What Were FDR's Aims?

Rex Tugwell described FDR's aims in 1933 as 'a better life for all Americans and a better America to live it in'. His main concern was to get the USA out of the Depression and on the road to recovery. However, he was also aware that the Depression provided an unmatched opportunity to effect major social reforms which would help the 'have nots' in the future. While he and his advisers argued over the shape of the New Deal, they did at least agree that the main causes of the Depression were internal and not international. Thus, the government was in a position to solve the crisis. If FDR's specific policies were ill-defined in 1933, his general intentions were clear. He meant to preside over an administration which was more interventionist and directive than Hoover's. Ordinary Americans, he believed, should have some measure of economic security. His programme soon involved an unprecedented amount of national economic planning. However, contemporary allegations that he sought to introduce socialism are absurd. Many of his aims were conservative. He intended to save, not destroy, US capitalism. He hoped – eventually – to balance the budget and believed that the dole was demoralising – 'a narcotic: a subtle destroyer of the human spirit'.

c) The Hundred Days

i) The Banking Crisis

Over the winter of 1932–3 a sudden epidemic of bank failures prompted panic-stricken withdrawals all over the country. By the time FDR took office on 4 March 1933, 75 per cent of banks had closed their doors and 38 states had proclaimed indefinite 'bank holidays'. The entire banking structure seemed in danger of collapse. On his

FDR'S SOCIAL PHILOSOPHY

Addressing Congress in 1938 FDR summed up his social philosophy:

> Government has a final responsibility for the well-being of its citizenship. If private co-operative endeavour fails to provide work for willing hands and relief for the unfortunate, those suffering hardship from no fault of their own have a right to call upon the government for aid; and a government worthy of its name must make fitting response.

Source A

THE NATURE OF THE HUNDRED DAYS

In his first Hundred Days FDR peppered Congress with proposals and draft bills. Congressmen, glad to be given a lead, responded by passing 15 major bills affecting unemployment relief, industry, agriculture, labour, transport, banking, and the currency. This body of legislation, as unparalleled in scope and volume as in the speed with which it was enacted, was full of contradiction, duplication, and overlap. There were some well-considered moves but much was knee-jerk reaction and experimentation. As historian Michael Parrish says, it 'bore the stamp of many authors, arose from no master plan, and did not fit neatly into a single ideological box'.

first full day in office, FDR moved swiftly to deal with the crisis, proclaiming a nationwide bank holiday and calling Congress into special session. His Emergency Banking Relief Bill, sent to Congress on 9 March, was essentially a product of Hoover's administration. It reinstated rather than reformed the existing system. Passed in only ten hours, it placed all banks under federal control and arranged for the reopening under licence of those found to be solvent. On 12 March FDR delivered the first of his radio 'fireside chats'. He told Americans it was safe to bank their savings. They believed him. Deposits flowed back into the banks and the crisis was over. FDR had pulled off his first coup: by speedy, dramatic action, he had restored confidence in US banks. 'Capitalism was saved in eight days', said Moley. FDR's critics argued that if he had cooperated with Hoover over the winter, he could have saved many of the 1,100 banks which never reopened.

ii) The Agricultural Adjustment Act (AAA)

FDR gave farming problems his top priority. (Farmers still comprised 30 per cent of the work-force.) By 1932 total farm income was a third of what it had been in 1929. Things were starting to turn nasty in the countryside and there was fear of revolution. The AAA tried to raise farm prices by cutting output. In return for reducing production, farmers received government subsidies. The AAA programme required the partnership of farmers to help set quotas and administer production controls. This worked to the advantage of richer farmers who dominated the local committees.

The Results of the AAA

▼ Under the AAA programme farmers ploughed up a quarter of the cotton crop and slaughtered 8.5 million pigs.

▼ By 1936 gross farm income was up by 50 per cent and farm prices had risen by 66 per cent. However, the rise in prices was in part accounted for by drought and dust storms and the devaluation of the dollar rather than as a result of production controls.

▼ AAA payments only benefited farmers who owned their own land.

▼ Given that AAA programmes reduced the acreage farmed, there was less need for farm labourers who often lost their jobs. Many tenant farmers were evicted.

▼ The credit made available to farmers by other New Deal measures was often more helpful to farmers than the AAA. The Commodity Credit Corporation, set up in late 1933, provided loans on stored crops like cotton and corn: only if prices rose above a given level would the loans have to be repaid. This was the start of a price-support system which would provide stability for farmers for the next half century.

iii) The National Industrial Recovery Act (NIRA)

NIRA created the National Recovery Administration (NRA). The act, often seen as the centrepiece of the first Hundred Days, was an attempt at joint economic planning by government and industry. It aimed at regulating prices and wages with the goal of keeping both high enough to ensure fair profits and decent wages. Manufacturers were virtually invited to set prices that might give them a reasonable return, thus avoiding over-production and bankruptcies. They were also encouraged to draw up codes of fair competition that would become legally binding on all in a given industry. Codes forbade or restricted a broad range of practices, for example, the use of child labour. Section 7a of the law guaranteed the right of collective bargaining. FDR appointed Hugh Johnson to supervise the NRA. Thanks to Johnson's flair for publicity, the NRA generated great enthusiasm. By the autumn of 1933 most major companies had signed codes endorsing wages and hours agreements and enabling them to display the NRA's Blue Eagle symbol.

NRA probably helped to prop up US industry at a time when it needed support. But the experiment soon turned sour. Small firms resented the fact that big business dominated the code-writing process, often taking the opportunity to strengthen monopolistic practices. Many big companies looked with suspicion on the Blue Eagle (Henry Ford said he wouldn't have 'that Rossevelt buzzard on my cars') and hated the encouragement given to trade unions by Section 7a. Labour leaders, by contrast, were dissatisfied because Section 7a proved largely ineffectual. The government was disillusioned by NRA's failure to create new jobs or to stop prices rising faster than wages. FDR's adviser Moley described NIRA as 'a thorough hodge-podge of provision', 'a confused two-headed experiment – a mistake'. Most historians think NRA created a muddled bureaucracy (at a time when there was no corps of skilled bureaucrats) – and little more.

iv) The Public Works Administration (PWA)

The PWA was set up (as part of the NRA) with an appropriation of $3.3 billion. Under the prudent direction of Secretary of the Interior Harold Ickes (rather than the energetic but erratic Hugh Johnson), it built schools, hospitals, dams, and roads. Ickes, determined to give the taxpayer value for money, insisted on rigorous appraisals before approving projects. Thus the money was invested too slowly to give immediate relief. However, the PWA was ultimately responsible for some 34,000 projects, including the building of the Golden Gate Bridge and the Grand Coulee Dam.

v) The Federal Emergency Relief Act (FERA)

Unlike Hoover, FDR accepted that unemployment relief was a federal responsibility. In 1933 $500 million was given to FERA to provide direct relief. Administration of the programme was entrusted to Harry Hopkins, who believed that the self-respect of the jobless required that the government should provide them with paid jobs instead of putting them on the dole. With a skeletal Washington staff, FERA necessarily relied on state and local governments to propose and oversee public projects, sometimes on a matching funds basis (which meant that relief payments varied enormously from state to state). By the time it closed in 1935, FERA had spent some $4 billion on all kinds of work-relief projects: road repairs, improvements to schools, parks and playgrounds.

vi) The Civilian Conservation Corps (CCC)

The CCC recruited unemployed young men for work on conservation projects including planting millions of trees, fighting forest fires, reseeding grazing lands, constructing roads, bridges etc. By the summer of 1933 300,000 men had been enlisted.

vii) The Tennessee Valley Authority (TVA)

The TVA became the most widely admired New Deal achievement. Ever since 1916, when the federal government had built a dam and two munitions plants at Muscle Shoals on the Tennessee River, progressives urged the government – unsuccessfully – to use the facilities to develop power resources. Progressive proposals now became the basis of a much broader plan to develop the Tennessee River basin, a region covering 40,000 square miles and reaching into seven states. The people who lived there – mainly farmers – earned less than half the national average wage. The whole area was placed under the control of the TVA which built dams and hydro-electric plants to provide cheap electricity. It also embarked on a programme of flood control, afforestation, and re-housing. Though cheap electricity did not attract industry on the scale that had been hoped, the TVA dramatically raised living standards throughout the region.

d) The Situation in 1934

Historian David Kennedy says that 'Taken together the accomplishments of the Hundred Days constituted a masterpiece of presidential leadership unexampled then and unmatched since (unless in the "second Hundred Days")'. FDR had halted the banking panic, created new institutions to reconstruct industry and farming, authorised the largest public works programme in US history, set up the TVA, and set aside millions of dollars for relief to the unemployed. The main economic indicators ceased to turn down and looked stronger by 1934. Average earnings for workers and corporate receipts were moving up. Farm-mortgage debts were declining: so were the number of business failures. But real economic recovery still proved elu-

MONETARY EXPERIMENTS

▼ In April 1933 the USA went off the gold standard. This lowered the exchange rate of the dollar by about 40 per cent. It made US goods more competitive abroad.

▼ To strengthen the banking structure, the Glass–Steagall Banking Act extended the Federal Reserve System and created the Federal Bank Deposit Insurance Corporation to guarantee individual deposits under $5,000.

▼ The Home Owners' Loan Corporation aimed to help those with mortgages in towns.

▼ The Farm Credit Act helped farmers who were having difficulty repaying their mortgages.

▼ The Federal Securities Act brought some regulation to the stock market. In 1934 a Securities and Exchange Commission was set up curb speculation of the pre-1929 variety.

sive. As the 1933–4 winter loomed, FDR secured another emergency measure, the Civil Works Administration (CWA) to provide work relief for the needy. Better funded during its short life (it only lasted until March 1934) than FERA, it found work for 4 million people. By 1934 the various relief agencies – FERA, CCC and CWA – were reaching over 20 per cent of the population.

e) Critics of the New Deal

In 1933–4 FDR still enjoyed huge support. The 1934 mid-term elections were a triumph for the Democrats. The Republicans won only a quarter of the seats in the House and only a third of Senate seats. However, criticism of the New Deal was growing.

i) Right-wing Criticism

▽ Conservatives had watched with growing distaste the New Deal's intervention in the economy, the huge cost of its relief measures, and the consequent budget deficits. Their hostility found open expression in the American Liberty League, set up in 1934 with the financial backing of a number of wealthy businessmen and the support of two ex-Democrat presidential candidates, Al Smith and John Davis. The League attacked the New Deal for trying to 'regimentalise' and 'Sovietise' America.

▽ By 1935 FDR's attempt to work with the business community was breaking down.

▽ More seriously, FDR encountered opposition from the Supreme Court. In 1935–6, the Court, chosen for the most part by Republican presidents, ruled that many of the New Deal measures were unconstitutional.

ii) 'The Thunder on the Left'

'The thunder on the Left' is the term historians have used to describe the clamour of visionaries and demagogues who claimed to speak for the less well off. It was not surprising that a radical outcry should have developed. Eleven million people – one-fifth of the work-force – were still jobless in mid-1934. The New Deal had often benefited big business and big agriculture – well-organised groups on whose fate an upturn, it was believed, depended – rather than the disadvantaged. The 'have-nots', while not much attracted to either socialism or Communism, were ready to turn to leaders whose ideas seemed to offer an end to the prevailing misery.

▽ Minnesota Governor Floyd Olson called for state ownership of mines, transport and public utilities.

▽ Dr Francis Townsend, a retired Californian medical practitioner, proposed that everyone over 60 should be granted a federal monthly pension of $200 on condition that they spent it within 30 days. He claimed this would end the Depression. His proposal (which was economic madness) struck a responsive chord among the elderly who

---

THE END OF PROHIBITION

In 1933 Congress passed the 21st Amendment, repealing the 18th. By December 1933, the repeal amendment had been ratified and control over drinking reverted to the states. Only seven of them voted to retain Prohibition.

THE DUST BOWL

In the mid-1930s drought, over-planting, and over-grazing combined to create a huge dust bowl in Oklahoma, Arkansas, and neighbouring states. The acreage reductions prescribed by the AAA and the increasing use of tractors also forced large numbers of farm workers off the land. Tens of thousands of farm families piled their belongings into ramshackle cars and headed west for California to become migrant labourers. The plight of such people was highlighted in John Steinbeck's novel *The Grapes of Wrath* (1939).

THE INDIAN RE-ORGANISATION ACT (1934)

This act – the so-called Indian New Deal – ended the 50-year-old policy of forced assimilation of Native Americans into white society. It encouraged Native American tribes to establish their own self-governing bodies and to look back to their ancestral traditions.

Figure 21 Huey Long.

A COHERENT PATTERN?

The 1933–4 measures reflected FDR's penchant for action: there was little coherent pattern. Rex Tugwell wrote later: 'It simply has to be admitted that Roosevelt was not yet certain which direction he ought to take and was in fact going both ways at once.'

THE RURAL ELECTRIFICATION ADMINISTRATION

In May 1935 FDR established the Rural Electrification Administration. At this point less than 20 per cent of American farms had electricity. By 1945 electrification of farms had risen to 90 per cent. 'Probably no other single measure of the New Deal was as responsible for transforming life in the American South', writes Michael Heale.

flocked to join Townsend Clubs. By 1935 the movement claimed 5 million members.

▼ Father Charles Coughlin, a Catholic priest, was a radio star. His weekly broadcasts reached an audience of some 30 million listeners. In 1934 he created his own political movement, the National Union for Social Justice, advocating such measures as the nationalisation of the banks. His hatred of international bankers grew more anti-Semitic, while his political programme increasingly resembled that of Mussolini's Italy.

▼ The most formidable of FDR's opponents was the flamboyant Huey Long of Louisiana. A shrewd, ambitious, ruthless politician and an effective popular orator, Long became Governor of Louisiana in 1928 by stirring up poor-white resentment toward the strong business interests which had long dominated the state. He brought some reform to Louisiana, building roads, improving education, and introducing a fairer tax system. In the process he set up a near-dictatorship, disregarding legal processes when it suited him. He entered the Senate in 1931. After initially supporting FDR, he became a fierce critic, viewing the New Deal as too conservative. In 1934 Long came out with a reform plan under the slogan 'Share Our Wealth'. Essentially, he proposed a guaranteed minimum wage to be achieved through taxing the wealthy and limiting personal fortunes. By 1935 Long claimed a membership of 8 million in Share-Our-Wealth clubs and was planning to run against FDR in 1936 as a third-party candidate. It seemed he might win over 10 per cent of the vote, which would weaken FDR rather than his Republican opponent. Fortunately for FDR, Long was assassinated in 1935.

f) The Second New Deal?

In 1935 FDR demanded that Congress enact five major measures. Over a three-month period, he used all his political skills to ensure his proposals passed through Congress. The result was, in the opinion of journalist Walter Lippman, 'The most comprehensive program of reform ever achieved in this country in any administration'. 'The Hundred Days may have saved capitalism but 88 days in 1935 literally changed the face of America for the next half century', says historian Michael Parrish. FDR's motives for introducing what some see as a 'Second New Deal' have been much debated.

▼ The 1936 election was in the offing and FDR needed to impress the electorate.

▼ The 'thunder on the Left' may explain FDR's tactical shift. To counter criticism from Long and Townsend, he incorporated aspects of their programmes into his own agenda. However, he had been considering introducing many of the measures long before 1935.

▼ In 1935 the Supreme Court struck down some key New Deal measures.

▼ Big business seemed opposed to the New Deal. 'As large numbers of businessmen jumped off the right side of FDR's ship', writes Michael Parrish, 'it began to tilt inevitably to the left, even without encourage-ment from Huey Long and others.' Politically, FDR had little to lose by alienating the right: the real danger was restive forces on the left.

i) The Works Progress Administration (WPA)

In April 1935 Congress set up the WPA. While direct relief was in future to be left to local authorities, the WPA aimed to provide work relief. During its eight-year history it employed a total of 8.5 million people and spent about $11 billion. The WPA (and its associated projects) had its critics from all parts of the political spectrum. The left were disappointed that it reached only about a third of the job-less at any one time, that it paid less than the average wage, and that it did nothing for those who were unable to work. The right thought that many of its projects created work for the sake of cre-ating work. Some of the WPA's projects were of doubtful value (writ-er John Steinbeck, for example, was assigned the task of taking a census of dogs) and there was much waste and political favouritism. But under Hopkins's energetic direction, the WPA was responsible for over 250,000 projects, building roads, schools, sports stadiums and hospitals.

▼ The National Youth Administration gave part-time employment to mil-lions of college and high school students, thus enabling them to con-tinue their education.

▼ The Federal Writers' Project helped unemployed writers. It prepared a series of regional guidebooks, catalogued historical records, and pub-lished local histories.

▼ The Federal Arts Project gave out-of-work artists the chance to adorn schools, libraries, and other public buildings with murals.

▼ The Federal Theatre Project's travelling companies brought drama, ballet, and puppet-shows to rural communities.

In accepting government responsibility for providing public work and relief, the WPA went far beyond anything imagined by Hoover and FDR in 1932.

ii) The Social Security Act

The USA was virtually alone among modern industrial countries in that it had no national system in place to help the unemployed and the old. In 1935 only 27 of the 48 states had introduced (limited) old-age pensions and only one (Wisconsin) had an unemployment insurance scheme. The Social Security Act created a compulsory national system of old-age pensions and a joint federal-state system of unemployment insurance. The Act had major defects. The system it introduced was to be financed exclusively out of current contri-butions rather than out of general tax revenues; hence no payments

THE EMERGENCY RELIEF APPROPRIATION ACT
This authorised the single largest expenditure to date in US history – $4.8 billion, authorising more spending than the sum of all federal revenues in 1934. The act breathed new life into exist-ing agencies like the CCC and PWA: it also helped fund new bodies.

could be made until 1942. Benefits were low and were proportionate to previous income rather than being based on minimum subsistence needs. Many millions of people were exempted, including some groups most in need of protection, like farm labourers and domestic servants. The extent of the coverage, the methods of finance, the level of benefit, and the structure of administrative control varied from state to state, creating a welfare system of bewildering complexity and inequality. Although the act fell far short of FDR's grandest design, Labour Secretary Perkins (who played a major role in passing the act) claimed that the final bill was 'the only plan that could have been put through Congress'. Despite its limitations, it provided a foundation on which all subsequent administrations have built. FDR regarded it as 'the cornerstone of his administration'.

iii) The Wealth Tax

If the Social Security Act spiked the guns of the Townsend Movement, FDR's Wealth Tax was calculated to do the same to Long's 'Share-Our-Wealth' scheme. FDR asked Congress to impose high taxes on inherited wealth, corporate profits and 'very great individual incomes'. In its final form, the Wealth Tax Act did not set rates at the level FDR proposed. Nevertheless, the act identified him with the 'have-nots' and provoked an outcry from conservatives who termed it 'soak the successful' tax. In truth, the measure was designed more to gain votes than to gain revenue from the rich.

iv) The National Labor Relations Act

The National Labor Relations Act was the brainchild of Senator Wagner. FDR, who remained uneasy about organised labour, supported it only after the Supreme Court had invalidated the National Industrial Recovery Act, whose Section 7a had tried to guarantee collective bargaining. The Wagner Act, as the new measure was known, threw the government's influence behind the right of workers to join trade unions. It created a National Labor Relations Board, empowered to bargain on behalf of workers and also to restrain management from using 'unfair labour practices' such as blacklists and company unions. The Act opened the way to a growth of union membership and power. Wagner's hope was that this would keep up wage rates so that there was more consumer purchasing power in the economy as a whole.

OTHER 1935 MEASURES

▼ The Banking Act gave the USA something akin to a central banking system.
▼ The Public Utilities Holding Company Act helped provide cheap power.
▼ The Resettlement Administration provided some aid to displaced tenant farmers.

---

g) Were There Two New Deals?

Some historians have argued that there were two distinct New Deals with different goals. Most believe that FDR moved left in 1935: they claim that the first New Deal had been concerned primarily with relief and recovery while the second was concerned with social reform. They see FDR giving up the attempt to work with big business and instead seeking allies in the labour movement and among the less well off. But it is probably a mistake to exaggerate the sharpness of the break. Most of the measures of the first Hundred Days days were necessarily emergency measures. Those of 1935 tended to be products of longer-term planning. They do not necessarily represent a change of heart on FDR's part. Reform elements were built into the early recovery policies and recovery policies remained integral to the 1935 reform phase. In any case it is futile to search for neat patterns in the New Deal: FDR's administration was never governed by a single political ideology and many of its components pulled in different directions. Thus, the New Deal is probably best seen as a whole.

h) The 1936 Election

At the Democratic convention in 1936 FDR was renominated on a platform praising the achievements of the New Deal and promising more liberal reform. The Republicans chose Kansas Governor Alfred Landon. Landon promised more aid to farmers, denounced the centralising tendencies of the New Deal and emphasised the Republican commitment to reduce federal spending and to balance the budget. He had the support of big business, the American Liberty League, and most of the main newspapers, some of which denounced FDR as an unprincipled demagogue. The campaign was bitterly fought. FDR seemed to go out of his way to stir up class hatreds – something that was almost unprecedented for a major party candidate. Roosevelt's strategy worked. He won 27,750,000 votes – 60.8 per cent of the total – and carried every state in the Union except two, winning 523 and losing only eight electoral college votes. The Democrats won three-quarters of the seats in the Senate and almost four-fifths of those in the House. Landon won 16,679,000 votes. The National Union Party, Socialist and Communist candidates won 880,000, 180,000 and 80,000 votes respectively.

> **THE DEMOCRAT COALITION**
> Democrat supporters now included middle-class liberals, Catholics, Jews, African Americans, small farmers in the West, the working man in the cities, and the South.

FDR's Advantages

▼ A third party threat did not materialise. The National Union Party, set up by supporters of Coughlin, Townsend and Long, had little support once Long was dead.

▼ The Republican Party was in a bad shape. The party was divided between its conservative and progressive wings. It was still associated with the Depression.

AFRICAN AMERICANS AND THE NEW DEAL

Black Americans lost and gained from the New Deal. The AAA displaced many black farmers. The NRA excluded them from most skilled jobs and adopted discriminatory wage rates; the CCC operated segregated camps. FDR, unwilling to antagonise Southern Democrats, was unresponsive to demands for black civil rights. Nevertheless, blacks did benefit from the New Deal. By 1935 nearly 30 per cent of all black families were on relief – three times the proportion of whites. FDR also made some gestures which pleased civil rights activists. Black leaders were given posts in the administration and FDR's wife, Eleanor, had a well-deserved reputation as a champion of racial equality. This helps to explain FDR's popularity with blacks. In 1932 nearly 75 per cent of blacks had voted Republican (the party of Lincoln); in 1936 over 75 per cent voted Democrat.

ACTIVITY

Examine Table 3. Do the statistics suggest that the New Deal was failing or succeeding? Explain your answer.

▼ FDR's standing was high. Millions of Americans had benefited from New Deal programmes. The 1935 legislation was fresh in people's minds. Although some 8 million people were still unemployed, the economy was doing better than at any time since 1930.

▼ Catholics and Jews, the two fastest growing groups in the USA, were solidly Democrat.

▼ FDR was seen as a champion of labour. Trade unions gave support and generous funds to the Democrats.

Table 3 Unemployment figures, 1929–44.

Year	Unemployed (in millions)	Unemployed (% of workforce)
1929	1.5	3.2
1930	4.3	8.7
1931	8.0	15.9
1932	12.1	23.6
1933	12.8	24.9
1934	11.3	21.7
1935	10.6	20.1
1936	9.0	16.9
1937	7.7	14.3
1938	10.4	19.0
1939	9.5	17.2
1940	8.1	14.6
1941	5.6	9.9
1942	2.6	4.7
1943	1.8	2.3
1944	1.0	1.2

(Presidential election years are indicated by the use of italics.)

5 FDR's Second Term

ISSUE:
Why was FDR's second term less successful than his first?

After his 1936 election triumph, FDR seemed to have all the authority he needed for more reform. In his second inaugural address in January 1937 he seemed to promise as much for he drew attention to 'one-third of a nation ill-housed, ill-clad, ill-nourished'. He said that he painted this grim picture not in despair but in hope 'because the nation, seeing and understanding the injustice in it, proposes to paint it out'. He declared that the test of a nation's progress was 'whether we provide enough for those who have too little'. But FDR's second term was to prove an anticlimax. There were few major legislative accomplishments and FRD's standing with Congress and within his party declined.

a) The Supreme Court Controversy

Early in 1937 FDR attempted to reform the Supreme Court. This proved to be the single biggest blunder of his political career. Dominated by a group of arch-conservatives, the Court had been hostile to government intervention in economic and social affairs. In 1935 and 1936 it struck down the twin pillars of the early New Deal – the NRA and the AAA – declaring both to be unconstitutional. FDR thought it wrong that the Court majority, appointed by his Republican predecessors and reflecting a laissez-faire attitude which public opinion no longer shared, should render the federal government powerless to deal with pressing problems. Immediately after his victory, he determined to do battle with 'the nine old men' (their average age was 71) and presented to Congress a Court reorganisation plan. It proposed that the president be authorized to appoint one additional judge for every member of the Court who passed the age of 70 without retiring. Since six of the existing justices were above that age, FDR would be able to increase the Court's membership to 15. He claimed that the Court's efficiency would be improved by an influx of younger members. But his real motive was to secure a more sympathetic bench. The storm of protest that his 'Court-packing' plan provoked showed that he had miscalculated. He was accused of seeking to increase his executive powers. Democrat leaders were angry that he had made no effort to consult them on the matter. Nor had it been mentioned in the 1936 election. Even some of those who wished to curb the Court disliked FDR's devious approach. In Congress a long and bitter debate on the Court Bill seriously divided the Democrats, especially North and South. FDR was fighting an unnecessary battle. It should have been evident that all he had to do was bide his time: he would soon be able to make appointments, ensuring

ADMINISTRATIVE REFORM

The New Deal had resulted in the presidency having increased power. However, a lack of staff made it difficult for FDR to exercise those powers effectively. In 1937 he asked Congress for more White House staff and the creation of new departments. However, his proposals reawakened fears of presidential dictatorship and were rejected. A modified bill, passed in 1939, watered down many of the provisions of the original measure.

that a majority of Court members supported his actions.

FDR lost the battle to expand the Court but won the war. A succession of events in 1937 made reform seem less necessary. One conservative justice retired and two others decided to support the administration. In a number of leading decisions between March and May the Court upheld such key measures as the Social Security Act and the National Labor Relations Act. This effectively ended the chances of the Court Bill. FDR abandoned the measure in July 1937 because he was opposed in the Senate by a coalition of Southern Democrats and Republicans. During the next four years deaths and retirements enabled him to fill no fewer than seven vacancies on the Court, thus giving it a strong liberal character. The New Deal measures enacted in 1935 were now constitutionally safe. But FDR's Court plan had shattered Democrat unity. It convinced many Democrats – never mind Republicans – that FDR did indeed have dictatorial tendencies. After 1937 he found it hard to win support in Congress for his measures.

b) Opposition from Southern Democrats

Because they had been uneasy for some time about the New Deal's retreat from laissez-faire, conservative (mainly Southern) Democrats looked with distaste upon the bureaucrats, academics and social workers who surrounded FDR. Many disliked the fact that he seemed more responsive to the urban North than the rural South. Some suspected that he had dictatorial tendencies and feared he intended to revolutionise race relations. Others supported state rights and revered a balanced budget. Thus, in 1937–8 conservative Democrats united with Republicans to oppose a number of reform measures. Nothing of major importance passed in 1937.

c) Industrial Strife

The collective-bargaining guarantees of NIRA and the Wagner Act helped Union membership rise from just over 2 million in 1933 to almost 9 million in 1938. This resulted in bitter conflicts both within the ranks of labour and with the employers. Though the American Federation of Labor (AFL) shared in the expansion, most of its leaders, wedded to the principle of craft unionism, were not greatly interested in organising unskilled workers. In 1935, a frustrated minority of union leaders formed what became the Congress on Industrial Organisation (CIO) with the aim of organising all workers in a given industry into a single union. Over the winter of 1936–7 the USA was hit by a wave of strikes as CIO unions demanded recognition. The Union of Automobile Workers forced General Motors to capitulate. A few weeks later US Steel also gave in to union pressure. In previous eras troops would have been sent in to break the strikes. This did not happen. Conservatives were appalled: here it seemed was further evidence of FDR's socialist leanings. Employers fought back using lock-outs, strike-breakers and private armies; they could also often count on help from the local police. In the Memorial Day Massacre (30 May 1937) the Chicago police clashed with strikers picketing a steel plant, killing ten and injuring 75. Strikers responded by intimidating non-unionists, and adopting a new, effective 'sit-down' technique in order to seize control of factories. By the end of 1937 'sit-down' strikes had enabled the United Automobile Workers to win union recognition from every car manufacturer except Ford. However, middle-class opinion, initially pro-labour, was suspicious of union power, particularly as evidence suggested that some unions were run by racketeers and that many CIO leaders were Communists. Thus, much public support ebbed away from the unions – and from FDR who was blamed for the union activity. Ironically, FDR did not have much sympathy with the strikers but realised that to condemn their action might lose him worker support.

d) The Roosevelt Recession

In June 1937 US output finally surpassed that of 1929. Worried about the mounting national debt, FDR now tried to balance the budget by sharply cutting government spending. This promptly sent the economy into reverse. Indeed, the rate of decline in 1937–8 was sharper than it had been in 1929. Over a ten month period, industrial production fell by a third and national income by a tenth. By 1938 some 11.5 million people were unemployed – one in five of the work-force. For several months FDR let things slide. According to historian Alan Brinkley there was an intense ideological struggle within FDR's administration – 'a struggle to define the soul of the New Deal'. Only in April 1938 when it was apparent that the recession could spell disaster for the Democrats in the mid-term elections did FDR accept the advice of those who favoured additional spending even if this meant creating a larger budget deficit. Therefore, he asked Congress for $3.75 billion for relief and public works. Congress obliged and by the summer the economy had begun a slow upward climb. Even so, unemployment remained high until 1941, when the threat of war, not enlightened New Deal policies, forced government expenditure at levels previously unimagined.

The Third New Deal (1938)?

▼ The Farm Security Administration had the authority to lend money to help small farmers, and to provide camps and medical care for migratory labourers.

▼ The Wagner–Steagall Act set up a Housing Authority to provide aid for slum clearance.

▼ A new Agricultural Adjustment Act, reviving in modified form its 1933 predecessor, tried to stabilise farm prices by fixing marketing quotas and acreage allotments.

▼ A Fair Labour Standards Act set a minimum wage of 25 cents an hour rising to 40 cents within two years, and a maximum working week of 44 hours, to be reduced in the same period to 40 hours. The act also forbade child labour in inter-state commerce. Southern Democrats had opposed the act, fearing that any measure that raised wages across the board would deprive their region of its competitive advantage as a cheap labour market. It also threatened to overturn the prevailing system under which blacks earned less than whites. The bill was finally passed in 1938 but only after it had been amended to exclude domestic workers and farm labourers. Even so the act had greatest impact in the South where 20 per cent of workers earned below the minimum wage, compared with only 3 per cent in the rest of the USA.

THE 1940 ELECTION

FDR stood for an unprecedented third time for the presidency in 1940. There was no obvious Democrat successor and the foreign situation meant there was need for an experienced pair of hands to steer the USA. FDR's opponent was Wendell Wilkie – a Democrat until 1938. Helped by the start of a war boom, FDR won almost 55 per cent of the popular vote – 449 electoral college votes to Wilkie's 82.

e) The End of the New Deal

FDR had to fight hard for the 1938 measures. Other presidential recommendations were either ignored or rejected. Smarting under these reverses, FDR set out to purge his party of anti-New Dealers, intervening directly in Democratic primaries, especially in the South, and appealing to voters to replace conservatives with liberals. His strategy failed. Almost all the candidates he campaigned against were re-elected and now had even less reason to support him. The 1938 elections were a serious setback. Although the Democrats retained control of both houses of Congress, the Republicans made striking gains. The new Congress was more conservative than any FDR had so far faced. It was clear that the New Deal had run out of steam. FDR acknowledged the fact in his annual message in 1939. For the first time since coming to office, he proposed no new reforms. As he became preoccupied with world affairs, he became more reluctant to press for reform. He did not want to alienate Congress, given that he needed its support for foreign policy initiatives.

After 1940 FDR continued to advocate an enhanced role for government in making a better life for ordinary Americans. In his 1941 State of the Union message, he included 'freedom from want' on his list of the 'Four Freedoms' (along with speech, religion and freedom from fear) and reiterated his belief in equality of opportunity, 'jobs for those who can work' and 'security for those who need it'. In 1944 he called for an 'Economic Bill of Rights' which guaranteed Americans employment, decent housing, a good education, and protection from the hazards of old age, sickness and accident. However, as historian John Morton Blum has observed, 'he made no convincing effort to give substance to his oratory'. After 1941 winning the Second World War was his chief priority. But, if he was willing to abandon his liberal agenda, it was largely because significant portions of it were being realised. The war accomplished what the New Deal had not – the rescue of the US economy from depression. Rarely has an economy catapulted from slump to boom so rapidly. By 1944 unemployment was down to 670,000 – 1.2 per cent. The personal income of farmers more than doubled between 1940 and 1945. Business profits rose from $6 billion in 1939 to $10.5 billion in 1945. The war led to cooperation between the government and big business. Business accepted that the government had a role to play in managing the economy. The government, in turn, accepted that it needed business to come up with the goods – which it did on a huge scale. Between 1940 and 1945 American industry produced over 100,000 tanks, 300,000 aircraft, and 93,000 ships. By 1944 the USA was producing twice as much as Germany, Japan and Italy combined.

> **WOMEN AND THE NEW DEAL**
> The New Deal agencies were riddled with sex discrimination. Many NRA codes allowed employers to pay women less than men, even when they did the same job. Married women were not considered a priority. The Social Security Act made no provision for domestic servants or housewives.

f) Was the New Deal New?

In Richard Hofstadter's view the New Deal was a 'drastic new departure … in the history of American reformism … different from anything that had yet happened'. David Kennedy agrees: 'the country was, in measurable degree, remade'. Those historians who think the New Deal was 'the third American Revolution' argue as follows:

▼ FDR founded the modern American welfare state based on the concept that the federal government has a responsibility to guarantee a minimum standard of living and to intervene in a variety of economic and social matters.

▼ The federal government's assertion of power reduced the autonomy of individual states. Americans now looked to Washington not their state capitals for solution to problems.

▼ In expanding the authority of the federal government, FDR had transformed the institution of the presidency, becoming in William Leuchtenburg's view, 'the first modern president'. He expanded the president's lawmaking functions. He also introduced and skilfully stage-managed the presidential press conference and mastered the technique of communicating directly with a mass audience by means of radio. Future presidents found it hard to escape from his legacy. The presidency became the centre stage of political life, the chief policy-maker and the focus of Americans' hopes and expectations.

However it is also possible to claim that the New Deal was at best a half-way revolution.

▼ FDR's aims were not revolutionary. He wanted to save, not destroy, capitalism.

▼ With very few exceptions (for example the TVA), the New Deal did not challenge the basic tenets of capitalism. In contrast with the pattern in most other industrial societies, no significant state-owned enterprises emerged in New Deal America.

▼ Much of FDR's policy simply echoed that of Hoover and Woodrow Wilson.

▼ Arguably the outcome of the New Deal was far from revolutionary. It failed to redistribute national income. The US income profile in 1940 resembled that of 1930.

▼ FDR was reluctant to engage in massive deficit spending, as the economist Keynes proposed. He hankered after balancing the budget.

g) How Successful was the New Deal?

It is possible to claim that the New Deal was not very successful.

▼ At best, it brought about only partial recovery. The USA was less successful at reducing unemployment than Germany or Britain. In no year after 1933 did the unemployment rate fall below 14 per cent. Some 10 million Americans – 17 per cent of the work-force – were still out of work in 1939. Not until 1941 would full employment and prosperity return, and only then because of the war and rearmament.

▼ The work programmes were inefficient, doing little to enhance skills. (WPA became known as 'We Piddle Around'.)

▼ There was limited social reform. Welfare payments were limited. Many groups were excluded from pensions and from unemployment insurance. The poor remained poor.

▼ Right-wing critics claim that FDR had gone too far in terms of government intervention. By setting up too many overlapping and inefficient agencies, he created something close to administrative anarchy in Washington. The agencies simply got in the way of recovery. Arguably whatever economic success there was, occurred despite New Deal policies, not because of them.

▼ Left-wing critics claim that FDR had not gone far enough. They stress that many New Deal measures benefited privileged groups (like large farmers), not the weak and dispossessed (like sharecroppers). There was little redistribution of wealth. The New Deal left big business intact.

However, most historians stress the achievements of the New Deal.

▼ It brought jobs, electricity and hope to some of America's most depressed areas.

▼ It introduced much-needed controls on banks and stock exchanges. Federal guarantees ensured that Americans' mortgages and bank savings were safe.

▼ It gave the USA new roads, dams, hospitals, sports facilities and public buildings.

▼ It laid the foundations of the American welfare state, giving all Americans a measure of security from the cradle to the grave. While it did not eradicate poverty or economic inequalities, it did begin to deploy the resources of the federal government on behalf of those who had received little help in the past.

▼ Although it is too much to claim that FDR saved America from revolution – there was never any real danger of one – he did restore national morale. FDR gave almost all Americans a stake in the country at a time when despair and alienation led elsewhere to dictatorship. This was no small achievement.

▼ The New Deal was a successful political slogan, helping FDR to win four presidential elections. By constructing a coalition that included the South, organised labour, the intelligentsia, and the poor, he ensured that the Democrats replaced the Republicans as the normal majority party.

▼ While FDR's government did little to redistribute wealth, it did redistribute power between capital and labour. In legitimising and strengthening trade unions, FDR helped them to secure for their members the generous wages and benefits that they were to enjoy for a generation after 1945.

▼ Working on The USA: 1900–41

To help draw your thoughts together, construct a time line of the period showing:

▼ who the presidents were and to which parties they belonged;

▼ what you consider to be the ten main events of the period;

▼ which years (do you think) were years of conservativism and which were years of reform.

Answering Extended Writing and Essay Questions on the Great Depression

Consider the question: What were the main causes of the Great Depression in the USA?

Start by listing all the reasons why the USA experienced an economic Depression after 1929. Then decide the order of importance of the causes you have listed. How important was the Wall Street Crash? Was this a major cause or merely a symptom of the USA's economic problems? To what extent was the Depression US-based? To what extent was it a world phenomenon? To what extent was Hoover to blame?

Answering Source-based Questions on the New Deal

Source B (Figure 22) A cartoon from the Chicago newspaper *Tribune* in September 1935.

THE ILLEGAL ACT.

PRESIDENT ROOSEVELT. "I'M SORRY, BUT THE SUPREME COURT SAYS I MUST CHUCK YOU BACK AGAIN."

Source C (Figure 23) A British cartoon from *Punch* in June 1935 on the quarrel between Roosevelt and the Supreme Court.

Source D (Figure 24) 'The last of a long line': a cartoon from the *Washington Post* (1936).

▼ QUESTIONS ON SOURCES

1. Examine Source B. What point was the cartoonist trying to make?
[3 marks]
2. Compare the three cartoons. Do you think the cartoonist in each case was pro or anti the New Deal? Explain your answer? **[7 marks]**
3. Using the three cartoons and your own knowledge, explain the struggle between FDR and the Supreme Court in the years 1935 to 1937. **[15 marks]**

Further Reading

Books in the Access to History *series*

The Key text is *Prosperity, Depression and the New Deal* by Peter Clements.

General

Try *America in the Era of the Two World Wars, 1910–1945* by P. Rensaw (Longman, 1996) and *State and Society in Twentieth Century America* by R. Harrison (Longman, 1997). *Franklin D. Roosevelt and the New Deal 1932–1940* by W.E. Leuchtenburg (Harper & Row, 1963) remains one of the best books on the New Deal. *Franklin D. Roosevelt: The New Deal and War* by M. Heale (Routledge, 1999) is a good short introduction. *The New Deal: The Depression Years, 1933–1940* by A.J. Badger (Macmillan, 1989) is longer. *The Great Depression, 1929–1941* by R. McElvaine (New York Times Books, 1984) is a vivid account. *Freedom from Fear: The American People in Depression and War 1929–1945* by D. Kennedy (OUP, 1999) and *Anxious Decades: America in Prosperity and Depression, 1920–1941* by M. Parrish (Norton, 1992) are both excellent. *FDR: A Biography* by T. Morgan (Simon & Schuster, 1985) is a good read.

AMERICAN FOREIGN POLICY, 1914–45

POINTS TO CONSIDER

In the nineteenth century the United States was preoccupied with the conquest of North America and generally isolated from world affairs. In the first half of the twentieth century, the United States played a more active role in international relations. Between 1900 and 1945, the United States was involved in two world wars, and contributed to the development of a third great conflict, the Cold War. If you are particularly interested in the Cold War, sections 1–4 give you useful background information to help you to understand the United States. Sections 1–4 examine nineteenth century US foreign policy, US involvement in the First World War, the return to 'isolationism', and how the United States got into the Second World War. Section 5 looks at US diplomacy during the Second World War, seeking the origins of the Cold War therein. Sections 6 and 7 consider the responsibility of Roosevelt and Truman for the **Cold War**.

> **COLD WAR**
> After the Second World War, the relationship between the United States and the USSR became hostile and remained so until the collapse of the USSR nearly half a century later. The two countries never fought each other directly, which is why the conflict is known as a 'cold' war.

1 Introduction: American Foreign Policy before 1914

> **ISSUE:**
> What were the international preoccupations and status of the United States, 1787–1914?

a) US Foreign Policy Preoccupations, 1787–1914

After Americans escaped the clutches of their colonialist British masters in the late eighteenth century, the young New World nation eyed the Old World with suspicion. The United States wanted to trade and maintain friendly relations with other nations, while avoiding 'entangling alliances'. Concern for national security made Americans anxious about Old World ambitions in the **Western Hemisphere**, although ironically Americans proved to be as imperialistic as their European ancestors were. For most of the nineteenth century, Americans were preoccupied with acquiring the North American continent from Native Americans and Mexicans. American expansionism then led to the acquisition of overseas territories.

> **WESTERN HEMISPHERE**
> A term used to describe the North and South American continents.

Americans wanted to acquire extra land and new markets, in order to enhance security. They also sought to export American culture. President McKinley famously told a group of clergyman that he had spent a night kneeling in prayer, asking God whether or not to annex

AMERICAN ACQUISITIONS

Hawaii was acquired in 1897, and what President Theodore Roosevelt called 'a splendid little war' against Spain (1898) left the United States in possession of the islands of Puerto Rico, Cuba, and the Philippines.

the Philippines. God had answered him, 'that there was nothing left for us to do but to take them all, and to educate the Filipinos, and uplift and civilise and Christianise them'. McKinley's failure to recognise that the Filipinos had been Christian since their sixteenth century conquest by Spain illustrates American ignorance of and arrogance towards foreigners. By 1900, around 7,000 American missionaries were trying to spread Christianity in various corners of the globe.

Early twentieth century America had many preoccupations, particularly the safeguarding of the nation, its empire and its trade. American businessmen constituted the nation's best ambassadors, according to President Taft (1901–13), under whom the term 'dollar diplomacy' gained currency. There was also the belief that America had a great deal to offer the world and what the American diplomat George Kennan called the 'urge to make the rest of the world over into the American image'. In 1913, President Woodrow Wilson said he wanted to see Latin America freed from the 'thraldom of foreign [European] interests' and 'to teach the South American republics to elect good men'.

ACTIVITY

Make a list of reasons (a) why and (b) how the United States had been keen and able to make itself a leading world power by 1914.

b) America's International Position in 1914

By 1914 the relatively new American nation had moved into the forefront of world powers. Countries such as Britain and France had larger empires, but size, natural resources, rapid industrialisation and thriving commerce made the United States formidable. Furthermore, the United States was a country with few genuine security fears, with oceans to the east and west, and unthreatening nations (Canada and Mexico) to the north and south.

ISSUES:

Why did the United States enter the First World War? Did it achieve its war aims?

2 The United States and the First World War

a) Why Did the United States Enter the First World War?

When war broke out in Europe, President Wilson thought it another example of the foolish conflicts in which Europeans indulged. He hoped America could safely abide by the old neutrality traditions, whereby neutral ships could carry non-military products to any belligerent (nation at war), and neutral civilians could travel to belligerent nations on the passenger ships of combatants. However, technology had moved on. New submarines such as German U-boats were not going to sail obligingly on the surface in order to accost and search neutral ships. In 1915, Germany warned that her U-boats would simply fire upon and, it was hoped, sink neutral shipping in the war zone around the British Isles. Wilson's complaint that this violated neutral rights was ignored. German U-boats sank the British liner *Lusitania*, which carried American passengers along with weapons purchased by Britain from America. The Germans were more careful during 1916, but the British blockade threatened to starve them of all imports, so Germany began unrestricted submarine warfare again in January 1917.

The loss of American lives and the perceived violation of neutral rights were two reasons why America got involved in the First World War. However, during the 1920s and the 1930s, American revisionist historians such as Harry Elmer Barnes stressed that the most important reasons for US entry into the war were economic. Barnes contended that US entry was due to the influence of American bankers and munitions makers who had made loans and sales to Britain and did not want Britain to be defeated, lest they lose their investment and their business. In the 1930s, popular journalists unforgettably christened those bankers and munitions makers as 'Merchants of Death'.

The sympathies of one particular American ethnic group affected US entry into the war. Those of British ancestry (an ethnic group which has traditionally dominated American politics) favoured joining in the war on the side of Britain. Balance-of-power considerations also affected US entry into the war. Several of Wilson's advisers perceived Germany to be an aggressive, expansionist nation that would threaten US security if it achieved its aim of continental domination. The Americans were also infuriated by the Zimmermann telegram (1917), wherein a junior German minister cabled the German ambassador in Mexico City, telling him to offer some US territory if Mexico would join Germany in the event of American entry into the war.

By April 1917, Wilson had concluded that Germany was a threat to US security and trade, and to morality everywhere. He wanted to join the First World War to transform it into a crusade:

> for democracy, for the right of those who submit to authority to have a voice in their own governments, for the rights and liberties of small nations, for a universal dominion of right by such a concert of free peoples as shall bring peace and safety to all nations and make the world itself at last free.

Source A

> **THE OPPOSING SIDES IN THE FIRST WORLD WAR**
> Britain, France, Russia (dropped out after Revolution in 1917), Italy (joined 1915), USA (joined 1917) v. Germany, Austria-Hungary, Turkey.

b) Historians' Interpretations of Why America Entered the First World War

American involvement in a European war represented a great departure from American traditions. Historians disagree over why Wilson took America to war in 1917. Wilson's official biographer, journalist

Ray Stannard Baker, took Wilson's claims at face value. Baker said America went in to defend neutral rights after Germany's 'barbarous' affront to international law. In the 1930s, the emphasis was on American economic motivation. Bankers and munitions manufacturers were blamed for US involvement. When America again faced Germany in the Second World War, a 'realist' school of writers condemned Woodrow Wilson for his idealism, and his failure to emphasise the threat that German domination of Europe posed to US security. According to Arthur Link (1979) Wilson practised 'missionary diplomacy' and wanted to use American power to create a better world.

c) President Wilson and the Post-war World

There is no doubt that Wilson wanted to create a better world. Unexpectedly, he had a rival in his missionary zeal. In 1917, Communists overturned the old tsarist regime in Russia. Americans interpreted democracy as characterised by a multi-party state in which all men had the vote. As the Communist Party supposedly represented the people, Communists saw less need for a multi-party state. Communists interpreted democracy as characterised by economic equality. Initially this necessitated state-controlled economies. Communism thus represented a great ideological threat to American capitalism, American democracy, and to imperialism. Lenin's writings suggested that subjugated peoples should throw off colonialism. Wilson feared that a Russian-led world Communist movement would be anti-capitalism and anti-democracy (American style). This would threaten US security. He therefore tried to offer an equally if not more attractive ideology in his **Fourteen Points**.

With America's vast resources in men and materials brought into play, exhausted Germany sought peace in October 1918. Wilson then went to the **Paris Peace Conference** to make a 'world safe for democracy'. He believed his Friday 13 December arrival to be a good omen. He was wrong. The French, and to a lesser extent the British, pushed Wilson into a less liberal peace than he had intended. However, Wilson hoped that his new international organisation, the League of Nations, would serve to combat any harshness in the peace treaty. Back home, Wilson worked hard to obtain public and congressional support for his League of Nations. His 22-day, 8,000-mile itinerary, with 36 speeches and 12 parades, led to a near fatal stroke. Partially recovered, he stubbornly refused to accept some relatively minor Republican amendments to his peace settlement. Because the US Senate refused to ratify the Paris peace settlement, the United States never joined the League of Nations.

THE FOURTEEN POINTS – A SUMMARY

▼ 'New Diplomacy' – 'open covenants openly arrived at'.

▼ Self-determination (for white nations only).

▼ Freedom of the seas.

▼ Free trade.

▼ 'Reduction of armaments to the lowest level consistent with national security'.

▼ 'A general association of nations' in which all states mutually guaranteed each other's 'political independence and territorial integrity'.

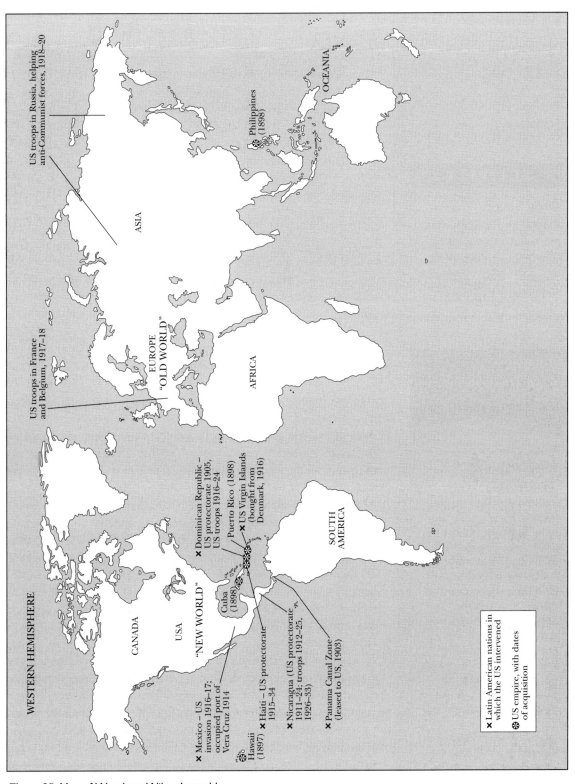

WESTERN HEMISPHERE

CANADA

USA

"NEW WORLD"

✕ Mexico – US
invasion 1916–17;
occupied port of
Vera Cruz 1914

❀ Hawaii
(1897)

✕ Dominican Republic –
US protectorate 1905,
US troops 1916–24

Puerto Rico (1898)

✕ US Virgin Islands
(bought from
Denmark, 1916)

❀ Cuba
(1898)

✕ Haiti – US protectorate
1915–34

✕ Nicaragua (US protectorate
1911–24; troops 1912–25,
1926–33)

✕ Panama Canal Zone
(leased to US, 1903)

SOUTH
AMERICA

US troops in France
and Belgium, 1917–18

EUROPE
"OLD WORLD"

AFRICA

US troops in Russia, helping
anti-Communist forces, 1918–20

ASIA

❀ Philippines
(1898)

OCEANIA

✕ Latin American nations in
which the US intervened

❀ US empire, with dates
of acquisition

Figure 25 Map of Woodrow Wilson's world.

The Paris Peace Conference, 1918–19

The victorious powers made several peace treaties. The most important was the Treaty of Versailles with Germany (June 1919). This treaty included the provision for a League of Nations. Further treaties were signed with Austria, Hungary, Bulgaria and Turkey. Wilson hoped that all independent nations would be members of the League of Nations. He hoped they would discuss and try to avoid threats to international peace and order, and then act (for example, by imposing trade restrictions) against aggressors.

ACTIVITY

Look at the 'Fourteen Points summary'. Think up as many reasons as you can to explain why Wilson thought their adoption would stop future wars.

American entry into the First World War failed to produce a better world shaped and guided by the United States. Americans concluded that this brief period of international involvement was an aberration and drew back into what some contemporaries called 'isolationism'.

ISSUE:
To what extent and why was America isolationist?

3 American 'Isolationism', 1919–33

During the 1920s and early 1930s, Americans were wary of foreigners. Why?

▼ Tales of the 'Merchants of Death' reinforced American suspicions of Europeans. Americans became convinced that the First World War was the result of unsavoury rivalries between corrupt inhabitants of the Old World, who had somehow managed to drag innocent Americans into their nasty war. So, in the 1920s and early 1930s, Americans were determined to keep out of future European quarrels.

▼ Americans perceived the new Communist nation, the USSR, as ideologically, economically and politically threatening (see page 150). Were Communism to spread, it would threaten America's economic well-being. The United States was the last great power to give full diplomatic recognition to the USSR (1933). The main reason for that recognition was shared Soviet-American fear of Japan.

▼ Now that the American navy was virtually unequalled in the world, America wanted to halt the naval arms race. Americans feared Japan as a naval rival and because of Japanese designs upon China. Americans had a sentimental affection for China, which they considered to be a great potential market for American goods. The maintenance of the status quo in the Far East was America's aim when it invited the other great powers to the Washington Conference. Three treaties were signed (1922). The treaties, if adhered to, would limit the growth of Japanese power.

INNOCENTS ABBROAD

Wilson's successor, Warren Harding, 'knew nothing and cared little about foreign affairs', according to the historian David Schulzinger. Some Americans acted like nineteenth century author Mark Twain's *Innocents Abroad*. In 1924, the US vice-consul in Tehran tried to photograph a particularly sacred religious celebration; the offended participants took time out to club him to death. Political commentator Walter Lippmann contended that the American electorate was too ignorant, fickle and emotional to be entrusted with any say in foreign policy.

<table>
<tr><td>

Washington Treaties, 1922

1. America, Britain, Japan, France and Italy, agreed (a) to stop the naval arms race and (b) to respect each other's position in the Pacific.

2. Nine powers with interests in the Pacific agreed to respect Chinese territorial integrity.

</td></tr>
</table>

THE KELLOGG–BRIAND PACT (1928)

The pact was signed by all but five of the world's nations. This pact had its origins in repeated French requests for a formal alliance. US Secretary of State Kellogg felt that the expansion of this proposed alliance into a world-wide alliance for peace would serve to silence the French while demonstrating America's commitment to peace.

Although the United States had opted out of the League of Nations, Americans were still willing to make agreements such as the **Kellogg–Briand Pact,** which demonstrated their interest in world peace. The necessity of international cooperation in economic affairs was demonstrated after the 1929 Wall Street crash precipitated a slump in the economies of many nations.

ACTIVITY

Look up US relations with Germany in the 1920s in *The United States of America and the World, 1917–45* volume in the *Access to History* series. Was America isolationist in relation to Germany?

4 Roosevelt's Foreign Policy, 1933–41

a) The Closet Internationalist and the Neutrality Legislation

ISSUE:
How and why did Roosevelt get America into the Second World War?

In 1933, new President Franklin Roosevelt was preoccupied with the Depression. Roosevelt was a closet internationalist, a Wilsonian, who favoured active US participation in the international community. However, he felt that he dared not 'come out' while American voters were preoccupied with domestic (economic) issues. Roosevelt therefore withdrew America from the 1933 International Economic Conference, saying each nation needed to sort out its own economic problems before further discussions on how to revitalise world trade, stabilise currencies, and settle war debts. However, Roosevelt anxiously watched potentially expansionist nations such as Japan and Nazi Germany. He knew that even if those countries threatened US security, he would be powerless to do anything because of Congress. In 1934 Congress accepted the 'Merchants of Death' interpretation of US involvement in the First World War. Congress concluded that

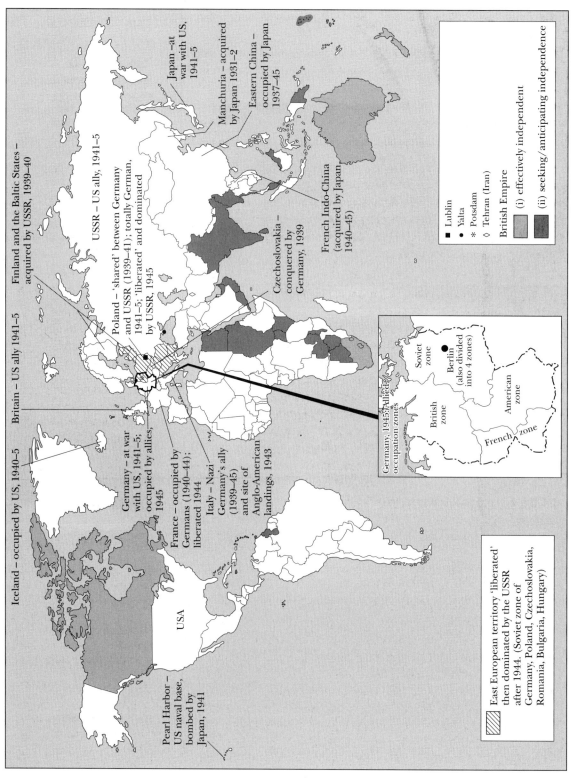

Iceland – occupied by US, 1940–5

Finland and the Baltic States – acquired by USSR, 1939–40

USSR – US ally, 1941–5

Britain – US ally 1941–5

Poland – 'shared' between Germany and USSR (1939–41); totally German, 1941–5; 'liberated' and dominated by USSR, 1945

Japan – at war with US, 1941–5

Manchuria – acquired by Japan 1931–2

Eastern China – occupied by Japan 1937–45

Czechoslovakia – conquered by Germany, 1939

French Indo-China (acquired by Japan 1940–45)

Germany – at war with US, 1941–5; occupied by allies, 1945

France – occupied by Germans (1940–44); liberated 1944

Italy – Nazi Germany's ally (1939–45) and site of Anglo-American landings, 1943

USA

Pearl Harbor – US naval base, bombed by Japan, 1941

Germany, 1945: Allied occupation zones

Soviet zone

Berlin (also divided into 4 zones)

British zone

American zone

French zone

East European territory 'liberated' then dominated by the USSR after 1944. (Soviet zone of Germany, Poland, Czechoslovakia, Romania, Bulgaria, Hungary)

■ Lublin
● Yalta
* Potsdam
◇ Tehran (Iran)

British Empire

(i) effectively independent

(ii) seeking/anticipating independence

Figure 26 Map of Franklin Roosevelt's world.

in order to keep out of future wars, America would have to avoid all dealings with belligerents. In 1935, Congress passed the first Neutrality Act. The act required the President to put an impartial arms embargo on all belligerents. Roosevelt feared that this would prevent Americans selling armaments to innocent victims of aggression. Aggressors could expand unchallenged, until they threatened American security. Roosevelt warned Congress that the act's inflexible provisions might eventually drag America into war rather than keeping it out, so Congress agreed on a six-month limitation on the act's operation.

In 1936 Hitler was openly rearming and had remilitarised the Rhineland. German economic penetration of Latin America seemed to threaten US predominance in the Western Hemisphere. Roosevelt was therefore even more anxious when the second Neutrality Act (1936) extended the 1935 Act until May 1937, and added a ban on loans to belligerents. However, despite his anxieties about American security, Roosevelt knew that when campaigning for re-election (1936) he needed to assure the electorate that he liked the neutrality legislation.

The neutrality legislation came up for renewal in May 1937, by which time some Americans feared that the inability to trade with belligerents would have adverse effects on American exports. A financier friend of Roosevelt suggested a 'cash and carry' policy, which would keep America trading but keep US ships off the seas in war zones. So long as they paid cash and collected the goods themselves, belligerents could buy anything except lethal weapons from America. Roosevelt liked the idea, as it would favour the democracies of Britain and France in any struggle with Germany, which had fewer ships. Thus the **Neutrality Act** of April 1937 added 'cash and carry' (to expire in May 1939) to the previous terms, which were made permanent.

b) Japanese and German Expansion

Japanese actions worried Roosevelt. In 1936, Japan signed the Anti-Comintern Pact with Germany. Although the pact was aimed at the Soviet Union, this Japanese–German fascist combination concerned Roosevelt. He began to feel that there was a worldwide conspiracy threatening American security and interests. When in 1937 Japan attacked and occupied much of eastern China, it confirmed Roosevelt's fears of a world-wide fascist conspiracy. However, few other Americans believed national security to be threatened by fascist expansionism. The press was often isolationist. There was an outcry in some newspapers when Roosevelt ambiguously said in Chicago in October 1937 that aggressors should be 'quarantined'.

> We are not isolationists, except in so far as we seek to isolate ourselves completely from war.

Source B Roosevelt on isolationism, 1936.

THE 1937 NEUTRALITY ACT

The historian Robert Divine described the 1937 Neutrality Act as 'a compromise that reflected the contradictory desire of the American people to remain economically in the world and politically out of it', a compromise which encouraged Hitler and made the United States his 'silent accomplice'.

EARLY SIGNS OF JAPANESE AGGRESSION

When Japan had first invaded then taken over the Chinese province of Manchuria (1931–2), Americans who had long indulged in a sentimentally affectionate policy toward China were unhappy. Japan withdrew from the 1922 Washington Conference agreements (1934) and walked out of the London Naval Conference (1935) when America and Britain rejected her demands for naval equality.

MUNICH (1938)

In 1938 Hitler took over Austria. Britain and France agreed at Munich that he should have the Czech Sudetenland, wherein there was a narrow majority of ethnic Germans.

FOREIGN POLICY AND THE NEW DEAL

Fears that the New Deal had dangerously increased presidential power made Congress anxious to limit presidential initiative in foreign policy.

THE NAZI–SOVIET PACT

In August 1939, Hitler and Stalin had divided part of Eastern Europe into spheres of interest. When war broke out, Stalin took parts of Poland and the Baltic states.

In 1938, Roosevelt congratulated Britain for the morally dubious agreement at **Munich**. He knew, as did the British government, that voters wanted to avoid war. American parents did not want to pay extra taxes to finance war nor to have their sons sent to fight in Europe again. However, believing that a German-dominated Europe and a Japanese-dominated Asia threatened US security, Roosevelt quietly stepped up the pace of American rearmament. He began to work slowly, carefully, and often dishonestly, to prepare the American people for a fight against fascism.

Roosevelt was painfully aware that the US neutrality legislation would stop the democracies purchasing arms from America if they found themselves fighting against Germany. However, even when Hitler took over the rump of Czechoslovakia (March 1939), Congress would not act.

c) The Second World War: 1939

When Hitler attacked Poland in September 1939, Britain and France declared war on Germany, and the Second World War had begun. Roosevelt worked hard and successfully to gain revision of neutrality legislation. The arms embargo was repealed and America could sell armaments (through 'cash and carry') to Britain and France. However, the close struggle over the revision was a warning to Roosevelt that he could not go too far too fast. Privately he was convinced that Germany was a threat to civilisation. He was horrified by the prospect of a German victory and German acquisition of the British and French empires.

In November 1939, Stalin attacked Finland. In this 'Winter War', American sympathies lay with 'little Finland', but Roosevelt worked to avoid any great break with the USSR, hoping that eventually Hitler and Stalin would fall out.

Meanwhile, Japan's continued aggression in China had further alienated the United States, which in summer 1939 had threatened to cut Japanese–American trade. As American oil and steel were fuelling the Japanese war effort, this was a significant threat.

d) The Second World War: 1940

In the spring of 1940, Germany speedily conquered Denmark, Belgium, Holland and France. By summer 1940 only Britain opposed Hitler. The Germans were sinking British ships at an alarming rate in the Atlantic. This meant Britain was not obtaining the supplies necessary to continue fighting. This worried the increasing number of Americans beginning to agree with Roosevelt's contention that Britain was America's first line of Atlantic defence. In May 1940

Prime Minister Winston Churchill begged President Roosevelt for 40–50 over-age US destroyers for **convoy** duty in the Atlantic. Roosevelt hesitated for months. He feared that American voters would dislike the deal. Furthermore, Britain might soon be defeated and thus waste the destroyers. However, Britain agreed to give America bases in British colonies in the Western Hemisphere. With Republican support, and effective campaigning by pro-British organisations, the destroyers-for-bases deal was agreed (September 1940). It could be argued that this marked the end of American neutrality.

The end of American neutrality in the Pacific came in July 1940, when America imposed its first economic sanctions on Japan. Certain strategic exports (such as aviation gasoline) were halted. Japan quickly sought to secure supplies of raw materials. Japan demanded bases in Indo-China from the defeated French (August 1940). US Ambassador Grew in Tokyo warned Washington there could be no compromise with the 'predatory' Japanese. America put further sanctions on Japan. Japan retaliated with the September 1940 Tripartite Pact. This defensive alliance with Germany and Italy was aimed at the United States.

Thus by the end of 1940, Roosevelt's conviction that Germany and Japan had to be stopped had been translated into American acts which Germany and Japan could justifiably claim were hostile.

Roosevelt hoped that a mixture of fascist aggression, anti-fascist campaigning by American interest groups, and his own gentle persuasion, might be enough to keep America on course to protect her interests, whether by helping Britain to do the fighting for her, or by eventually joining in the war. Some contemporaries criticised him for not doing enough. However, the isolationist opposition was strong, so much so that Roosevelt let the FBI use a 'whispering campaign' against an isolationist group that campaigned to put 'America First'. The FBI opened their mail, followed them, and concocted phoney letters that 'proved' they were traitors.

Meanwhile, Churchill warned Roosevelt that Britain lacked the money and materials to continue the fight. Roosevelt told Americans that Britain was their first line of defence, and Britain needed help. When your neighbour's house was on fire, Roosevelt said, you did not sell him your hose. You loaned it. With that homely and effective metaphor, Roosevelt got support for 7 billion dollars worth of **lend-lease** aid to Britain. Secretary of War Stimson described lend-lease as a declaration of economic warfare.

e) The Second World War: 1941

Lend-lease did not solve Britain's problems. German submarine warfare stopped many vital supplies crossing the Atlantic. Roosevelt

> **CONVOYING**
> is when a military vessel escorts an unarmed vessel.

> **THE 1940 ELECTION**
> In order to win the election, Roosevelt assured American mothers, 'Your boys are not going to be sent into any foreign wars'. 'That hypocritical son of a bitch', exclaimed his Republican opponent with some justification. 'This is going to beat me.' He was right.

> **LEND-LEASE**
> Roosevelt invented this phrase to make Americans feel that they would be getting their money and materials back. This was highly unlikely, but it did the trick. Britain got the supplies, just as Roosevelt wanted.

THE SELECTIVE SERVICE ACT

The tremendous difficulties Roosevelt faced as he tried to manoeuvre the United States into a war for national security are illustrated by the struggle over the renewal of the August 1940 Selective Service Act, which ensured that America would have men with which to defend herself should she find herself at war. The Act was renewed in July 1941, by the narrowest possible margin (203–202) in the House of Representatives.

DECLARATIONS OF WAR

On 8 December 1941 Roosevelt sought and obtained a Congressional declaration of war on Japan. On 11 December Germany declared war on America, asserting that America had first violated neutrality then committed open acts of war against Germany.

knew American destroyers had to convoy British merchant shipping across the Atlantic otherwise lend-lease would not work. However, polls showed most Americans opposed the idea. From spring 1941 onward, Roosevelt had a stop-go policy on convoying. He privately admitted that he was 'waiting to be pushed' into fighting.

In June 1941 Britain gained an ally when Hitler invaded the USSR. Despite anti-Communist cries from isolationists, Roosevelt extended lend-lease to the Russians. The isolationist minority were furious when Roosevelt met a leader of a belligerent nation, Churchill, off the coast of Newfoundland. There, Roosevelt and Churchill issued the Atlantic Charter (August 1941). Here the Wilsonian internationalist came out of the closet. The Charter condemned aggression, and called for the rights of self-determination, free speech, free trade, and for an international peacekeeping organisation.

In September 1941, Roosevelt got his opportunity for full transatlantic convoying. German submarines attacked the US destroyer *Greer* that was carrying passengers and mail to American-occupied Iceland. Roosevelt's declaration that this was a deliberate and unprovoked attack by the 'rattlesnakes of the Atlantic' was not quite true. The *Greer* had been trailing the German submarine for three hours, giving radio assistance to a British plane that was dropping depth charges on the submarine! A similar incident occurred in October, when a German submarine torpedoed a US destroyer, *Kearney*, which was protecting British ships. This led Congress to repeal most of the neutrality legislation.

Roosevelt was always convinced that Germany was a greater threat than Japan, but he felt he had to stop fuelling the Japanese war effort against China. Further exports (such as iron and steel products) were stopped in winter 1940–41. American oil was still exported. It was to be the ultimate diplomatic weapon, to be held back as a final sanction which might stop Japan. However, neither Japan nor America would compromise over China. America insisted Japan must get out; Japan insisted she could not. In summer 1941, America finally stopped exporting oil to Japan. Japan was now convinced it needed further expansion to guarantee supplies of raw materials necessary to continue its war against China.

Last-minute talks with Japan proved unprofitable. When Japanese planes bombed the US Pacific fleet at Pearl Harbor, Hawaii (7 December 1941) it brought the United States into the Second World War.

Thus America had got into the Second World War, because of Roosevelt's belief that Germany constituted a dangerous threat to American security, the American tradition of sympathy for China, and actions Roosevelt took against Germany and Japan. Whether

America would have entered the war under a different president is perhaps doubtful.

Historians' Conclusions About Roosevelt and US Entry into the Second World War

Historians differ in their assessments of the wisdom and abilities of Franklin Roosevelt. Some criticise him for standing up to Japan, and for making that country choose its suicidal course. William Carr blamed America for being over emotional and excessively moralistic with regard to the defence of China. A few historians go so far as to blame Roosevelt for Pearl Harbor in the sense that he deliberately ignored warnings and left the Pacific fleet vulnerable in order to encourage a Japanese attack which would get America into war. However, the disaster at Pearl Harbor was more likely due to confusion and incompetence at all levels.

Some historians, for example Robert Divine, consider Roosevelt an isolationist. Others disagree: 'Roosevelt meant to shape the world his way and bided his time' (Michael Simpson). Simpson saw Roosevelt as a Wilsonian internationalist, who wanted a world full of free-trading democracies. Simpson defended Roosevelt's Pacific policy, pointing out that a massive Japanese Empire would damage free trade. Robert Dallek's exhaustively researched book substantiates the argument that Roosevelt was an internationalist, whose ideal world contained many democracies, much free trade, and little imperialism. The leader of that free world would be America, for the security of which no aggressive power such as Germany or Japan could be allowed to expand unchecked. That philosophy was well thought out, if not necessarily right, and it led Roosevelt to cajole and connive so as to ensure America got into war to defend what he perceived to be its national interest. Dallek praises him for carefully and slowly building the popular consensus that enabled America to enter the Second World War with the national unity that the Vietnam War subsequently demonstrated to be so essential.

ACTIVITY

Essay: 'Why was America a participant in the Second World War by December 1941?'

Suggested paragraph headings: (a) Roosevelt's view of US security needs; (b) German actions and US reactions, 1933–41; (c) Japanese actions and US reactions, 1931–41.

ISSUE:
To what extent can the
origins of the Cold
War be found in the
diplomacy and events
of the Second World
War?

5 The Diplomacy of the Second World War and Origins of the Cold War

From December 1941, the United States, the USSR and Great Britain were co-belligerents in the war against Nazi Germany. In 1945, the fascist powers were finally defeated. Within two years, the victorious allies turned into enemies. By late 1947, the acute Soviet–American antagonism known as the Cold War was well under way. The question that most interests historians with regard to US diplomacy in the Second World War is the extent to which the origins of the Cold War lay within these years.

a) The Second World War: the Aims of the 'Big Three'

After Pearl Harbor, America's overriding aim was the defeat of Germany and Japan. As yet, the USSR was only at war with Germany, but America and Britain were also at war with Japan.

The great aims of American diplomacy were to try to keep what Churchill called the 'Grand Alliance' cooperating effectively in the war effort against Germany, and to persuade Stalin to join in the war against Japan. Roosevelt exercised close personal control over American foreign policy. He considered both his knowledge and his personal diplomatic skills to be unrivalled.

The 'Big Three' allies had different preconceptions and preoccupations. Roosevelt hoped for a post-war world in which free governments and free trade flourished, benevolently policed by America. Britain too favoured democratic governments, except in the British Empire, wherein Britain had exclusive trading privileges which America eyed enviously. America and Britain saw post-war security in terms of a restoration of the pre-war status quo, although Roosevelt never gave up hoping that Britain could be persuaded to give up her Empire. On the other hand, Stalin believed Soviet security in the post-war world demanded the acquisition of buffer zones in Eastern Europe, to protect the Soviet Union's western frontiers from further invasions. These difficulties would inevitably cause great tension in the Grand Alliance.

ROOSEVELT, CHURCHILL AND STALIN

American diplomacy became highly personalised in the Second World War. Roosevelt and Churchill met throughout the war. The American, Soviet and British leaders met together at Tehran, Yalta and Potsdam. Roosevelt got on well with both Churchill and Stalin. For much of the war, Roosevelt felt that British imperialism was more likely to disturb the peace of the post-war world than Stalin was.

b) The Second World War: 1942

As the first step in the defeat of Nazi Germany, American and British forces needed to land in German-occupied Europe, while the Soviets fought to get the Germans off Soviet territory. Churchill worked hard and successfully to persuade Roosevelt that Anglo-American landings in Africa and Italy should precede any clash with the Germans in occupied Europe. Naturally, Stalin wanted landings in France as soon as possible, to take the pressure off the Soviets. Although America had given the USSR massive lend-lease aid from autumn 1941, Stalin was very unhappy with his allies in 1942. He believed the USSR was doing more than its fair share to defeat Germany. He resented what he perceived to be crucial Anglo-American failures to provide a 'second front' in Western Europe, to recognise Soviet territorial demands in Eastern Europe, and to get sufficient supplies across the Atlantic to the Soviets.

As far as Roosevelt and Churchill were concerned, these 'failures' were excusable because America and Britain

▼ lacked the landing craft necessary for an invasion of occupied France;

▼ already had their 'second front' in the Pacific;

▼ could not accept Soviet demands for parts of Poland and the Baltic states because those demands were incompatible with the Atlantic Charter and the wishes of Roosevelt's Polish-American voters;

▼ had still to win the battle of the Atlantic against German submarines.

> ### THE SOVIET WAR EFFORT
> Churchill rightly said the Soviets 'tore the guts' out of the German army. One Soviet account bitterly pointed out that 50 Russians died for every one American.

c) The Second World War: 1943

There were further tensions within the Alliance in 1943. Stalin continued to complain about the second front. He resented his exclusion from the negotiations with the Italians, who first surrendered in summer 1943. American administrators found the Soviets to be surly and uncooperative recipients of lend-lease who refused to provide the basic essential information on their resources that the Americans needed to maximise the effectiveness of the aid. Clearly, mutual suspicions made cooperation difficult. There was also tension over the government of post-war Poland. However, it would be Russian troops who would liberate Poland. Therefore, it was hard to dictate to Stalin about any post-war Polish government, particularly after Anglo-American troops had landed in Italy and excluded Stalin from the peace negotiations there.

Soviet–American tensions are further indicated by the history of the development of the **atomic bomb**. Unlike Churchill and some of his own advisers, Roosevelt remained outwardly optimistic about the possibilities of post-war cooperation with the USSR. On the other hand, he kept the atomic bomb secret from his Soviet allies. Perhaps he thought that the fewer who knew, the safer the secret. Perhaps he held some deep-seated distrust of his Communist ally.

When looking for examples of cooperation and non-cooperation during 1941–5, many acts can be interpreted either way. In October 1943, Stalin assured the grateful Americans he would declare war on

> ### THE POLISH GOVERNMENT PROBLEM
> After Hitler's invasion, Polish leaders had fled to London. This Polish government in exile hated the Russians, who traditionally tried to dominate Poland. Churchill sympathised with this Polish government in exile, and Roosevelt had Polish American voters to worry about.

> ### BRITAIN AND THE BOMB
> Churchill persuaded Roosevelt to share atomic secrets with Britain, on the grounds that Britain would need the information to help handle the Soviet Union in the post-war world.

Japan once Germany was beaten. That could be interpreted as the helpfulness of an ally, or simply as a Soviet desire to be in on the peace in order to gain 'pickings' and influence in the Pacific. At this stage, the Americans were certainly desperate to have Stalin's assistance in the Pacific war, as Japan was a formidable opponent.

d) The Second World War: Tehran (1943)

TEHRAN
The 'Big Three' leaders finally met together at Tehran in Iran. The location was significant. This was the only time Stalin travelled outside the USSR to meet his allies. He did not have to travel far. Iran was on the southern border of the Soviet Union. Roosevelt twice travelled outside the Western Hemisphere to places Stalin chose. Churchill made countless journeys to meet the other two.

At Tehran, Roosevelt played Stalin and Churchill off against each other. Privately, Roosevelt told Stalin of his dislike of British imperialism and his hope that America and the Soviet Union could cooperate in the liquidation of the British Empire. While Churchill pointed out to Roosevelt and Stalin that Britain had gone to war for an independent Poland, Roosevelt privately told Stalin that he was currently constrained by his need for Polish-American votes. This implied that once the presidential election was over, Roosevelt would not mind what Stalin did with Poland. This style of diplomacy had the effect of temporarily easing relations, but storing up future problems if, as happened, America decided that a Soviet-dominated Poland was not in American interests after all. In other areas, the meeting went better. Stalin reiterated his promise to join the war against Japan, and the spring 1944 Allied landings in France were planned. All agreed that Germany must never again be in a position to threaten others.

Did Roosevelt handle Stalin well? He knew that Soviet troops would 'liberate' East European countries such as Poland. Consequently, America would not be in a position to do much about those countries. He had no real bargaining leverage with Stalin. If America withdrew lend-lease, Russia would still survive, but defeat of Germany would take longer. That would hurt America. There was always the fear that Stalin might make a separate deal with Hitler, as he had in August 1939. Furthermore, all American experts said American needed Stalin's assistance in Japan. Given all this, it was probably sensible of Roosevelt to try to charm Stalin, and to try to meet his security needs wherever possible, as in Poland. However, pressure from American public opinion soon forced Roosevelt to make a stand on Poland, when 'liberating' Soviet forces set up a Communist Polish government based at Lublin. Sometimes Roosevelt worried about Communist expansionism. In autumn 1944, he went along with Churchill's installation of British forces into Greece to try to undermine the Greek Communist party.

e) The Second World War: 1944

Not surprisingly, the question of what to do with the defeated Germans loomed far larger than questions relating to Eastern Europe. During 1944, the Allies planned the division of Germany into Soviet, American and British zones of occupation. The Soviets, Britain and America would each have a share of Berlin, the German capital, which was over 100 miles inside the Soviet zone of Germany. Although some of Roosevelt's advisers warned that the question of Anglo-American access to their sections of Berlin should be settled in advance, Roosevelt was optimistic that there would be no problems.

Early in 1944, a majority within the Roosevelt administration believed America could continue to get along with Stalin. However, by late 1944, an increasing number disagreed. On the eve of the second Big Three meeting at the Russian Black Sea resort of Yalta (February 1945) Churchill was particularly pessimistic. Roosevelt repeatedly told him that the American public would not want American troops left in Europe after the war, to which Churchill responded that he did not want to be left alone in Europe facing the Russian 'bear'. That fear made Churchill more lenient towards defeated Germany and more anxious to restore France as a great power than was Roosevelt.

f) The Second World War: Yalta (1945)

At Yalta, it was agreed the Germany should be disarmed, demilitarised, and dismembered. At Churchill's urging, it was agreed that France should have a zone in Germany. Stalin seemed to acquiesce in having fewer reparations than he had demanded, although subsequently he simply took what he wanted.

In late 1944, Roosevelt had bluntly told Stalin that his Polish Communist government, based at Lublin, was unrepresentative. At Yalta, the Lublin government was recognised, but it was agreed that it would soon hold democratic elections. An American admiral told Roosevelt the agreement on Poland at Yalta was 'so elastic that the Russians can stretch it all the way from Yalta to Washington without ever technically breaking it'. 'I know', answered Roosevelt, 'but it's the best I can do at this time'. Similarly, the 'Declaration on Liberated Europe' said that the Big Three wanted to help liberated nations form 'democratic' governments. However, each had a different definition of democracy. 'Democracy' meant universal suffrage to Americans. For Soviets, Communism was democratic in that economic rather than political equality was gained. Economic equality negated any need for multi-party elections.

There were promising signs at Yalta. The Soviets seemed coopera-

---

1944 TROOP MOVEMENTS
Anglo-American forces moved across France, Belgium Holland, toward Germany. Soviet forces crossed Poland, Romania, Bulgaria, Hungary and Czechoslovakia, en route to Germany.

YALTA
Significantly, the ailing Roosevelt travelled 6,000 miles to meet Stalin at Yalta. The 70-year-old Churchill travelled 4,000, and groused that ten years of research could not produce a worse place than humid, bug-ridden Yalta.

THE DEBATE OVER YALTA
In Cold War America, 'Yalta' became a byword for Soviet treachery. It was felt that Stalin broke his promises with regard to the establishment of democratic governments in post-war Eastern Europe. Yalta has been much debated. Did the dying president, losing his powers, give too much away? Or did he get the best deal possible in the circumstances?

ROOSEVELT AND BRITAIN

Roosevelt half-jokingly told his cabinet that Britain was causing him more difficulties than Russia, and that:

> the British were perfectly willing for the United States to have a war with Russia at any time and that, in his opinion, to follow the British programme would be to proceed toward that end.

Source C

tive on Roosevelt's revamped League of Nations, the United Nations. Stalin confirmed that he would join the war against Japan. Roosevelt confirmed that Stalin's prize would be territorial and economic concessions in China. When Stalin asked whether America's Chinese ally knew and approved, Roosevelt assured him that he could handle the Chinese.

However, within days of Yalta there were ominous signs of Soviet intent. The Soviets forced a subservient government on Romania, obstructed non-Lublin Poles, and brought mass arrests and intimidation to East European countries they were 'liberating' from Nazi rule.

Roosevelt's ambivalent attitude to the Soviets lasted until the day he died. At one point, Roosevelt said, 'we can't do business with Stalin — he has broken every one of the promises he made at Yalta'. Yet hours before his death (12 April 1945) he cabled Churchill:

> I would minimise the Soviet problem as much as possible, because these problems, in one form or another, seem to arise every day, and most of them straighten out.

Source D

6 To What Extent was Roosevelt Responsible for the Cold War?

When Roosevelt became president (1933) the United States had not yet given diplomatic recognition to the USSR. Roosevelt inherited a tradition of Russo-American suspicion and mistrust.

Russo-American Relations before 1933

When the new American nation was born (1787), Tsarist Russia was sympathetic. Relations remained amicable. In 1867 the Tsar saw no danger in selling Alaska to the United States. However, with the immigration of many Jews who had fled Russian persecution at the end of the nineteenth century, America began to feel ideological antipathy toward Russia. In the early stages of the Russian Revolution (March 1917) Americans thought they liked what they saw. However, Americans became puzzled (it was said the American ambassador would not have known a left Socialist revolutionary from a potato) and hostile during the November Revolution. In 1918, America sent troops into Russia, ostensibly to pre-empt a German seizure of military supplies, but the historian John Lewis Gaddis claims underlying hatred of Communism was America's basic motivation. The last US troops left in 1920, two years after Germany was defeated. Understandably, the Soviet Union found it hard to forgive and forget what they saw as an American attempt to 'strangle Communism in its cradle'. The Wilson, Harding, Coolidge and Hoover administrations did not recognise the USSR, although America gave humanitarian aid in the famine of 1921–2, and American businessmen such as car manufacturer Henry Ford traded profitably with the new nation.

When Roosevelt became president, he quickly recognised the USSR because:

▼ Polls suggested most Americans favoured recognition.

▼ Non-recognition had not achieved anything – it had not brought down the Soviet government.

▼ Problems such as the Depression and Japanese aggression needed Soviet cooperation.

▼ America was the only major nation without full diplomatic representation in the USSR. This had become an embarrassment. When the Americans wanted to discuss Japanese aggression in Manchuria, the Soviets pointed out that as America did not recognise them, discussion could be difficult!

However, relations remained cool. America was virulently anti-Communist, and particularly loathed **Comintern**. From Moscow, the US embassy staff reported Stalin's executions with distaste. They doubted that America could ever cooperate with such a state. However, Roosevelt persevered and sent the highly sympathetic Joseph Davies as ambassador to Moscow. Both Davies and Roosevelt thought the ultimate aim of Communism (the betterment of the human condition) was admirable even if Soviet policies were not. In 1939 Americans found the Nazi–Soviet pact and the Soviet Winter War against Finland distasteful, but again, Roosevelt, with his greater vision, kept the lines of communication open. He hoped that Hitler and Stalin would fall out. They did.

After Hitler invaded the USSR, Roosevelt persuaded Congress to extend lend-lease to the Soviets. From their own viewpoint, the Soviets were cooperative allies. They 'tore the guts' out of the German armies. In June 1944 the Soviets put extra pressure on the Germans in the East to ease the Allied landings in Normandy. They promised to enter the war against Japan as soon as possible, and even Churchill felt that they stuck to the so-called '**percentages agreement**'. On the other hand, as far as the Soviets could see, America and Britain did not always play straight with them, particularly in their slowness in the provision of the second front. Some historians have seen this as the greatest single cause of the Cold War. They

COMINTERN ('COMMUNIST INTERNATIONAL')

Comintern was set up in Moscow (1919) as the world organisation of Communist supporters of the Russian revolutionaries. Non-Communist nations such as America believed Comintern to be a Soviet puppet organisation, through which Moscow controlled and could use Communist citizens of other nations.

THE PERCENTAGES AGREEMENT (1944)

Winston Churchill and Stalin agreed on spheres of interest in south-east Europe: for example, Romania and Bulgaria were to be in the Soviet sphere, Greece in the British. Stalin duly kept out of the struggle between Greek Communists and Greek right-wingers.

blame Roosevelt for delaying it. However, the Americans lacked the required numbers of landing craft and combat aircraft for landing in France before 1944. Furthermore, Stalin 'forgot' Britain and America already had their own 'second front' in the Pacific. 'Suspicion', said the American historian Adam Ulam, 'was built into the Soviet system'. Suspicion was mutual. Roosevelt had no intention of letting the Soviets in on negotiations with Italy or atomic secrets. Just as the Americans wanted sole control over Italy, Stalin wanted to keep Eastern Europe to himself. From his viewpoint, the area constituted a Soviet security zone, which millions of Russians had died to acquire. As he made relatively little fuss about Italy, and never even mentioned the Western Hemisphere, he felt threatened when America attempted to impose its will on countries such as Poland, which bordered the USSR. However, Roosevelt's charm offensive and hints that he sympathised with Stalin but had to make the occasional protest because of the American electorate, combined to keep US–Soviet relations as good as anyone could possibly have hoped them to be. Did he thereby encourage Stalin too much, so that when his successor began to talk tough, a Cold War was inevitable? Roosevelt probably did the best he could in the circumstances. At the time, the defeat of Germany and Japan was what mattered most. He was assured that Stalin's help in defeating Japan was vital. Consequently, it made sense to keep in with Stalin, in the hope that friendly persuasion might modify his actions in East Europe. It seems conceivable that, had Roosevelt lived, the Cold War might have been avoided, or at least postponed. However, his successor was far less experienced in foreign policy, and perhaps culpably 'tough'.

ISSUE:
How well did Truman handle Stalin, April–August 1945?

7 President Truman: the End of the Second World War and the Start of the Cold War

Harry Truman had an inauspicious background for one who had to maintain the increasingly tense alliance with the USSR. Truman's had been a fairly ordinary career in domestic politics until Roosevelt chose him as his vice-presidential running mate in 1944. Roosevelt had not kept Vice-President Truman informed on foreign policy. Initially and not surprisingly, the inexperienced Truman followed Roosevelt's policies and advisers.

There were early signs that Truman would get on with Stalin. The new president rejected Churchill's suggestion that troops should be deployed in order to forestall Soviet domination of post-war Eastern Europe. American troops waited for several days outside Prague and made no effort to reach Berlin first. After Germany's surrender, American troops were quickly withdrawn up to 100 miles westward to the lines of zonal demarcation agreed by Stalin and Roosevelt. Truman made conciliatory moves, sending Roosevelt's friend Harry Hopkins to Moscow, and pro-Soviet Joseph Davies to London. Davies contended that Churchill's attitude 'could and does undoubtedly account for much of the aggressiveness of the Soviets since Yalta.' For his part, Stalin acceded to the UN Charter in June 1945 and accepted a Polish government containing a minority of non-Communist Poles. On the other hand, Truman joined Churchill in protesting when the Soviets set up an Austrian government without consultation. Furthermore, or so Truman subsequently claimed, he gave Soviet foreign minister Molotov a hard time in talks in May 1945.

The last Big Three wartime conference took place in the Berlin suburb of Potsdam (July–August 1945). It gave Stalin and Truman the opportunity to weigh each other up. Privately, Stalin claimed to be unimpressed by Truman, although Truman felt that they could work together. Truman triumphantly informed Stalin of America's amazing new weapon, the newly tested atomic bomb. Thanks to spies, Stalin knew. America had not shared the secret with him, which demonstrated American mistrust. Not surprisingly, Stalin had his own scientists working on a Soviet atomic bomb. While Stalin ignored Truman and Churchill's protests about Poland's frontier disputes, there was relatively amicable agreement on Germany and the '5 Ds'. Stalin confirmed that he would soon join in the war against Japan. In the Potsdam Declaration, America warned Japan that they would face 'prompt and utter destruction' if they did not surrender.

The Japanese ignored America's warning so the Americans dropped the atomic bomb on Hiroshima. The Japanese would not surrender, partly because America had given them no assurance in the Potsdam Declaration that they could keep their emperor. A second bomb was dropped on Nagasaki on 9 August. Between bombs, the USSR had declared war on Japan. Japan's Emperor finally decided on surrender. As in Italy, the Americans strove to keep the Soviets out of the peace settlement.

From Stalin's viewpoint, Truman's America was an economic, military and technological giant, far ahead of the USSR, which was devastated after the Second World War. This imbalance of power, coupled with the long-term and short-term tensions between America and the Soviets, could be argued to have made the Cold War inevitable.

THE 5 DS

These were: demilitarisation; deindustrialisation; decentralisation; democracy; denazification.

WHY DID AMERICA DROP THE BOMB?

▽ Japan was a determined enemy. It only surrendered after two atomic bombs. So, without the bombs the war could have gone on for a very long time.

▽ Enemy life was cheap in wartime.

▽ It quickly ended the war, saving American lives that would have been lost had the fighting continued.

▽ It had cost the Americans a great deal to develop the bomb. Once American taxpayers knew about the new weapon, they would want it used.

▽ America wanted revenge for Pearl Harbor.

▽ Revisionist historians, for example Stephen Ambrose, believe that the bomb was used to warn the Russians of American power.

ACTIVITY

Make a list of US foreign policy aims and actions 1787–1945. In a parallel column, assess whether the actions were an effective approach to achieving the aims.

Create a table with columns headed **Dates**, **US aims**, **US achievements**, and **Who or what impacted upon US foreign policy**.

Answering Source-based Questions on American Foreign Policy, 1914–45

Look at Sources E, F and G. These three cartoons were produced during Wilson's presidency. Cartoons often used the white-bearded figure of 'Uncle Sam' to represent the United States. 'Uncle Sam' always wore the Stars and Stripes.

Source E (Figure 27) Uncle Sam lectures the world on 'how to reform the world' while there are race riots in the United States.

Source F (Figure 28)
Uncle Sam talks of peace
while selling munitions.

OVERWEIGHTED.

President Wilson. "HERE'S YOUR OLIVE BRANCH. NOW GET BUSY."
Dove of Peace. "OF COURSE I WANT TO PLEASE EVERYBODY; BUT ISN'T THIS A
BIT THICK?"

Source G (Figure 29) A dove of
peace usually carries a twig.
President Wilson hands it a
heavy branch.

▼ QUESTIONS ON SOURCES

1. Cartoons E and F have the same attitude towards US foreign policy. What is it? **[5 marks]**

2. Do cartoons E and F get their message across effectively? **[5 marks]**

3. What is cartoon G trying to say? **[5 marks]**

4. Do these cartoons give an accurate picture of Woodrow Wilson's foreign policy? **[10 marks]**

Answering Essay Questions on American Foreign Policy, 1914–45

Working on these brief essays could help revision:

1. Why did the United States enter the First World War?

2. Why did the United States enter the Second World War?

This title requires a longer essay response: 'The study of relations between the United States and the Russians up to the end of 1945 suggests that conflict was inevitable'. Do you agree?

Further Reading

Books in the Access to History *series*

The United States of America and the World, 1917–45 by Peter Brett, and *The United States of America and the Cold War* by Oliver Edwards.

General

Robert Schulzinger's *American Diplomacy in the Twentieth Century* (Oxford, 1994) is excellent – clear, thoughtful and lively. More detailed are the excellent volumes in the John Wiley series *America in Crisis*, including Daniel Smith, *The Great Departure: the United States and World War I* (1979), Robert Divine, *The Reluctant Belligerent: American Entry into World War II* (1979), and Gaddis Smith, *American Diplomacy During the Second World War* (1985). Robert Dallek, *Franklin Roosevelt and American Foreign Policy 1932–45* (Oxford, 1979), is exhaustive, sympathetic and persuasive. Michael Simpson's *Franklin D. Roosevelt* (Oxford, 1989), gives a briefer, simpler and equally sympathetic introduction to Roosevelt's policy, while William Carr, *Poland to Pearl Harbor* (London, 1989), is critical and complex.

TWENTIETH CENTURY RACE RELATIONS

At the start of the twentieth century, African Americans, Native Americans, Hispanic Americans and Asian Americans were for the most part legally, socially and economically inferior to other US citizens. During the twentieth century, blacks in particular worked hard to try to improve their situation, culminating in the great civil rights movement of the mid-twentieth century. You need to familiarise yourself with the situation of these ethnic minorities at the start of the twentieth century, and to clarify for yourself how, why and to what extent their situation had improved by the end of the twentieth century.

1 Race Relations in the United States in 1900

ISSUE:
What was the situation of ethnic minorities in the United States of America in 1900?

a) Who Were the 'Ethnic Minorities'?

When an early twentieth century American writer described the United States as a 'melting pot', he implied that different national backgrounds and racial characteristics had somehow merged into a homogeneous 'American' group. This was not the case. By 1900, descendants of European emigrants were generally considered to be 'acceptable' Americans. However, even amongst them, there was still an often unspoken hierarchy of acceptability. For example, those of British and Dutch ancestry whose ancestors had been amongst the first white settlers in North America were 'ranked' above the more recent immigrants from south European countries such as Italy. However, although there were economic and social differences between those of European descent, their position was for the most part superior to the United States' 'inferior' ethnic minorities, the African Americans, Asian Americans, Native Americans, and Hispanic Americans.

The African Americans were the descendants of slaves who had been brought to North America from Africa. The Hispanic Americans were the Spanish-speaking descendants of the predominantly Native American peoples of Mexico (which had been conquered by Spain in the sixteenth century). Native Americans had

> ### Negro, Black or African American?
>
> Up to and including the 1960s, Americans of African descent living in the United States were generally referred to as (and called themselves) 'Negroes'. Hostile whites also used the term 'nigger'. The term 'black' was also used throughout the twentieth century. In the 1960s some blacks called themselves 'Afro-American' and in the late 1980s 'African American' became and has remained popular. A recent survey published by the Joint Center for Political and Economic Studies (a black research think tank based in Washington DC) said the term 'black' is the most preferred self-description.

THE LEGAL POSITION OF BLACKS IN THE LATE NINETEENTH CENTURY

1865 13th Amendment abolished slavery;

1868 14th Amendment conferred US citizenship on freed blacks and authorised federal government intervention if any state abridged citizens' rights;

1870 15th Amendment said no one was to be denied the vote because of his race;

1875 Civil Rights Act tried but failed to prevent discrimination in public places in the South;

1883 Supreme Court ruled (*US v. Harris*) that neither the 14th nor the 15th Amendments were designed to deprive states of their control over elections;

1890s Southern states disfranchised black voters and upheld 'Jim Crow' segregation laws;

1895 Supreme Court ruled (*Plessy v. Ferguson*) that states had to provide 'separate but equal' facilities for blacks, thereby giving its approval to segregation.

been the original inhabitants of the North American continent. In what became the United States of America, European whites took Native American land. By 1900, most of the Native Americans in the United States were confined to reservations, mostly on land for which white Americans had no use or desire. Native American culture was despised. Reservation life was usually hard and short. Hispanic Americans in states such as California and Texas were only slightly better off. Asian Americans were mostly concentrated in the West, particularly California. The fear, resentment and racism they aroused were well demonstrated in 1882, when Congress had prohibited further Chinese immigration.

White Americans of European ancestry considered all these ethnic minorities to be inferior and undesirable, particularly the largest ethnic minority, the African Americans, most of whom lived in the South.

b) What Was the Situation of Black People in America by 1900?

In 1900, over 90 per cent of blacks lived in the South. Despite the legislation that supposedly granted them equality after the Civil War, blacks in the South remained economically, legally, socially and politically inferior. Most former slaves and their descendants were sharecroppers. They rented farmland from white landlords. High rents kept sharecroppers impoverished. Blacks' daily lives were subject to the discriminatory 'Jim Crow' laws. Blacks could not eat, play, or get educated alongside whites. Less than 1 per cent of eligible black children attended high school. By 1900, only 5 per cent of eligible blacks voted in the South. Southern whites used a variety of means to keep blacks from voting. Blacks had to pay an expensive poll tax, or pass a difficult literacy test, or prove their grandfathers had voted. Blacks therefore lacked the political power that would gain them representation, which in turn could gain them legislation to improve their situation. Whites had to be addressed as 'sir', 'master', or 'miss', while grown black men were called 'boy' by whites. If a black met a white on a sidewalk, the black had to step into the gutter to let the white pass. Blacks lacked legal protection. Any 'uppity' (assertive) black might find himself the victim of **lynching**. Not surprisingly, desperate blacks left the South hoping to find a better life in the North, West or Midwest.

In the last decades of the nineteenth century, tens of thousands of blacks went North in search of work, for example, in the meatpacking factories of Chicago. Northern whites frequently responded with hostility. Blacks soon found themselves excluded from hotels, restaurants, theatres, and stores in Northern cities.

Thus blacks constituted an American underclass in all parts of the United States in 1900. Relations between the races were not good. In the first half of the twentieth century individuals and groups from both sides sought for a solution, in a variety of ways.

ACTIVITY

Look at the extract from Theodore Roosevelt:

(a) Which phrases indicate that Roosevelt was a racist?
(b) Can you suggest any reasons, other than racism, why Roosevelt said this?

LYNCHING

Lynchings were unlawful hangings of blacks. Between 1885 and 1917, 2,734 blacks were lynched. The perpetrators were never punished, indicating that their actions had a great deal of support from other whites. As more blacks migrated northward, more lynchings took place in the North.

As a race ... the [blacks] are altogether inferior to the whites ... A perfectly stupid race can never rise to a very high place ... I do not believe that the average Negro ... is as yet in any way fit to take care of himself and others ... If he were, there would be no Negro race problem.

Source A Theodore Roosevelt on race, before he became president.

---

2 Tensions between Blacks and Whites: the Search for a Solution in the First Half of the Twentieth Century

ISSUES:
What were the aims, methods and achievements of those that suggested solutions for tensions between blacks and whites in the first half of the twentieth century?

There were several suggested solutions to American race relations problems. Many whites wanted to maintain the status quo, whether through violence, political manipulation, or simply tacit acceptance. A few whites were willing to make a more liberal stand, usually through association with black individuals and/or organisations.

Most blacks thought the way to improve American race relations was to improve the black position, although many whites disagreed. Sometimes black attempts to improve the black position caused a white backlash.

Some blacks favoured integration and thought the best way forward was to concentrate upon economic improvement. Others wanted to use the law courts to try to obtain rights (such as those enshrined in the 1875 Civil Rights Act) which had been granted in theory but not yet attained in practice. Some emphasised black pride and indicated that separation of the races was probably more desirable than integration.

Several suggested solutions are dealt with in this section, usually with particular reference to the most famous individuals or organisations that favoured them.

Suggested Solutions to Race Problems, 1900–50

Solution	Some famous supporters
Accommodationism	Booker T. Washington
Economic advancement	Booker T. Washington
Legal activity	W.E.B. Du Bois and NAACP
Publicity	Washington, Du Bois, NAACP, Marcus Garvey
Migration	
Black pride	Marcus Garvey
White violence	Ku Klux Klan
Trade unionism	A. Philip Randolph
Socialism and/or Communism	A. Philip Randolph
Political participation and political pressure	Washington, Randolph, NAACP, Adam Clayton Powell
Federal intervention	McKinley, Roosevelt, Truman
Black violence	
Peaceful protest	James Farmer and CORE

---

a) Booker T. Washington and 'Accommodationism'

Booker T. Washington was born into slavery on a Virginia tobacco plantation in 1856. He attended a vocational training college, which had been established to help freed slaves. He became a teacher and was the first head of Tuskegee, a college of higher education for blacks, in Alabama.

i) Aims

Booker T. Washington aimed to help blacks to improve their economic position. His solution to the problems facing black Americans was vocational education. This was not surprising, given his own career and enthusiasm for education. He (and Tuskegee) emphasised vocational training for Southern blacks, for example, agricultural techniques for males and 'keeping house' for females.

As an articulate and a successful teacher, Washington inevitably became the leading spokesman for blacks after the death of the equally articulate and successful ex-slave Frederick Douglass in 1895. It was hard for the majority of blacks to escape the cycle of poverty, deprivation, and lack of educational opportunities. Blacks who managed to escape that cycle frequently aimed to help others do likewise. As yet, few escaped. Those that did were almost guaranteed fame if they had practical aims designed to help solve the problems of American blacks. Fame gave Washington the opportunity to pursue his aims in a national context. In 1900 Washington established the National Negro Business League, which supported black enterprises. In 1911 he was important in establishing the National Urban League, which aimed to help blacks adjust to urban life. Booker T. Washington saw economic advancement as the first great necessary step for blacks. His eventual aim was equality and desegregation. However, while blacks concentrated upon improving their economic position, he felt that peaceful race relations required blacks to accept social segregation.

ii) Methods

Booker T. Washington used several methods by which he hoped to achieve his aims. We have seen that he promoted vocational education at Tuskegee and established two national organisations to help urban blacks. He also generated publicity for the disadvantages facing blacks through his speeches and writings, and through maximum possible association with white leaders, particularly presidents. In his talks with a succession of presidents, Booker T. Washington worked for an end to lynchings and a softening of the Jim Crow laws in the South, wherein blacks suffered segregation and disfranchisement.

iii) Achievements

Washington's Tuskegee gave many blacks vocational education. This increased their self-confidence and economic opportunities. In the ghettos of the North, Washington's National Urban League helped blacks to find jobs, promoted better health care and education, and tried to prevent delinquency.

Booker T. Washington's achievements are controversial. Some blacks thought him an 'Uncle Tom', humiliatingly begging for aid from influential whites, and keeping blacks 'down' by his emphasis on vocational training and by his refusal to demand a speedy end to segregation and disfranchisement. One black journalist called him 'the greatest white man's nigger in the world'. However, Booker T. Washington's 'accommodationist' philosophy was probably realistic. When President McKinley appointed many blacks to governmental positions, it probably contributed to the increased incidence of race riots across America. While on the one hand President Theodore Roosevelt had Washington to dine at the White House in 1901,

AMERICAN PRESIDENTS, 1897–1953

1897 –1901	William McKinley;
1901 –9	Theodore Roosevelt;
1909 –13	William Howard Taft;
1913 –21	Woodrow Wilson;
1921 –3	Warren Harding;
1923 –9	Calvin Coolidge;
1929 –33	Herbert Hoover;
1933 –45	Franklin Delano Roosevelt;
1945 –53	Harry Truman.

The action of President Roosevelt entertaining that nigger will necessitate our killing a thousand niggers in the South before they will learn their place.

Source B South Carolina Senator Ben Tillman on President Theodore Roosevelt's invitation to Booker T. Washington to dine at the White House.

Figure 30 White families cheering, outside a black Chicago home that has just been fire-bombed (1919).

Roosevelt also told Congress that the lynching of blacks was a lesser crime than the black raping of white women which 'caused' lynchings. President Woodrow Wilson (a Southerner) segregated federal institutions such as the Post Office to 'reduce friction'. Booker T. Washington knew that change would have to be a gradual process. Educational improvement and opportunities of the kind offered at Tuskegee were an uncontroversial way forward. His association with presidents contributed to greater awareness of the black plight, and helped to boost black morale. Without Washington's prominence, it is likely that presidents would have avoided greater black representation within federal government service. Although he claimed that he accepted segregation, Washington began to work quietly against it. He was important in the organisation of a conference to discuss black voting rights in the South (New York, 1904). However, by the time Washington died (1915), most articulate blacks preferred the aims and methods of his great rival, W.E.B. Du Bois.

b) W.E.B. Du Bois and NAACP

The backgrounds of Booker T. Washington and W.E.B. Du Bois were very different. Du Bois was born a free man in the North. He was educated at top universities in America and Europe, and lectured in an academic discipline at Atlanta University, Georgia. Du Bois was one of what he called 'the talented tenth', the black intellectual elite whom he considered to be the most appropriate leaders of the race.

i) W.E.B. Du Bois' Aims

Whereas Washington aimed primarily to effect greater economic equality, Du Bois not only aimed at equal educational and economic opportunities, but also at legal and political equality for blacks. While Washington initially aimed for 'separate but equal', Du Bois initially aimed at rapid racial integration. Their disagreements helped propel Du Bois into the foundation of the NAACP (National Association for the Advancement of Colored People) in 1909.

ii) W.E.B. Du Bois' Methods

Du Bois' methods differed from those of Washington. Du Bois worked to raise awareness among blacks by establishing a national organisation (NAACP) and publicising its ideas through a newspaper, *The Crisis*. In that paper, Du Bois wrote emotional accounts of lynchings and riots, and articles which asserted that blacks were God's chosen people. Du Bois' NAACP tried to promote black equality and desegregation through the law courts. In 1934, disagreements over methods within NAACP caused Du Bois to leave the organisation he had founded. Du Bois wanted to put a new emphasis on black nationalism and self-help. He talked about a black economic 'nation within the nation'. His advocacy of separatism infuriated integrationists within NAACP.

iii) W.E.B. Du Bois' Achievements

Du Bois never attained the fame and respect of Booker T. Washington. Possibly Du Bois sought too much too soon. However, he helped to increase black awareness and pride in black culture. The establishment of NAACP was his greatest achievement. Although he left NAACP in 1934, that organisation went on to achieve a great deal in the struggle for a better life for black Americans. The anti-lynching campaign that Du Bois initiated at NAACP helped decrease the numbers of lynchings by publicising their horrors. Du Bois' NAACP won its first great court victory in 1915, against the '**grandfather clause**'. In its early decades, NAACP did not attract many members. The Southern black middle class usually followed Booker T. Washington's accommodationism. However, some Northern middle-class blacks joined NAACP. The organisation worked quietly away, eroding segregation through the law courts, raising black (and white) awareness, and gaining the gravitas and acceptability that come with age.

iv) NAACP's Aims

After 1934, Du Bois' successor as NAACP leader was Walter White. White aimed to achieve social, legal and political equality for blacks.

v) NAACP's Methods

White used a variety of methods, some of which were new. He orchestrated a publicity campaign to stop an opponent of black voting

---

NATIVE AMERICAN PRIDE

While Du Bois encouraged black pride in black culture, a Native American called Carlos Montezuma urged Native Americans to have pride in their cultural traditions. He despised Native Americans who were dependent upon the white man, calling them 'papooses' (the Native American word for baby). Like Booker T. Washington, Montezuma urged his people to be self-reliant.

GRANDFATHER CLAUSE

The grandfather clause was used in some Southern states. It said a black person could not vote unless he could prove that his grandfather voted. It was of course impossible to have voted under slavery.

BLACKS AND THE SECOND WORLD WAR

Between 1941 and 1945 over 2 million blacks migrated North for work, and met white resentment there. In the summer of 1943 there were around 250 race riots in nearly 50 Northern cities. The worst riots were in Detroit and Harlem. There were frequent riots on military bases, particularly in the South. In some ways, blacks clearly benefited from the Second World War. The war generated jobs. Around one million blacks served in the (segregated) armed forces, which helped to raise black self-esteem and consciousness. NAACP membership increased. A new and more militant organisation, CORE, was established in 1942. NAACP said the war gave blacks the opportunity to 'compel and shame a nation… into a more enlightened attitude toward one-tenth of its people'. Articulate blacks lost no opportunity to point out that the evils of the Nazism against which America fought were in many ways replicated in the racist South. Many black veterans took advantage of the GI Bill to go to college or learn a skilled trade. These educated black professionals and technicians became part of the growing black middle class that would be so important in the civil rights movement of the mid-twentieth century.

becoming a Supreme Court judge. White worked with trade unionists, churches, and white liberals, to forge a civil rights coalition to persuade the House of Representatives to promote anti-lynching bills. White's NAACP mobilised Southern black city dwellers, to campaign for voter registration and abolition of the poll tax. NAACP promoted black exploitation of purchasing power to effect change. In New Orleans in 1947 NAACP activists picketed stores that refused to allow black women to try on hats. White's NAACP continued Du Bois' method of working through the law courts. After 1931, NAACP used black lawyers such as Thurgood Marshall.

vi) NAACP's Achievements

NAACP achieved a great deal in its first half-century of existence. It raised the black profile and increased black awareness, especially in the South. Its effectiveness in galvanising black activism could be seen by its rise in membership – from 50,000 in 1940, to 450,000 in 1945. It was helped by the Second World War, when the US fight against fascism inspired more blacks to campaign against their own lack of freedom and equality. White's NAACP legal campaign achieved several triumphs. Marshall worked to pressurise the Supreme Court into ruling that unequal expenditure on black and white higher education was against the 14th Amendment. That opened the way for a similar ruling on pre-18 education. Another Supreme Court decision (*Smith v. Allwright*, 1944) made it easier for blacks to vote in the South. In 1950, three further important Supreme Court decisions resulted from NAACP activity. The Supreme Court ruled that segregation on railway dining cars was illegal, that a black student could not be physically separated from white students in the University of Oklahoma, and that a black student could attend a white Texan law school that was superior to the local black one. NAACP was developing into an effective pressure group, demonstrating that it was possible for a black organisation to influence Congress. In 1937 and 1940, the House of Representatives accepted anti-lynching bills, although Southern Democrats ensured that the bills made no progress in the Senate.

NAACP thus successfully used a variety of different methods and a variety of different allies. NAACP's breadth of vision and range of activities and membership had set an important example and precedent for the plethora of civil rights organisations that developed during the great mid-twentieth century civil rights movement.

c) Migration

i) Aims

Well-educated and articulate blacks such as Booker T. Washington and W.E.B. Du Bois acted as spokesmen for their race. Other educated and successful blacks could join their organisations, such as the National Urban League and NAACP. However, educational opportunities for blacks were limited. In the North, blacks usually attended all-black schools in the poor areas in which blacks lived. While the North had *de facto* (in fact) segregation, the South had *de jure* (in law) segregation, and Southern blacks had no choice but to attend poor, all-black schools. Not surprisingly, many poorly educated Southern blacks aimed to get a better life, through a better job, in a place where there was less discrimination. The method by which they hoped to achieve these improvements was migration northwards.

ii) Method

Between 1910 and 1970 over 6 million blacks emigrated from the rural South, which was one of the poorest parts of the United States. The migrants went to cities of the North, Midwest and West such as Chicago, Detroit, Los Angeles, New York, and Philadelphia. In 1910, 89 per cent of American blacks lived in the South; by 1970 it was 53 per cent. The industrialised North offered more and better paid jobs, for example, in the Ford car factories of Detroit. The First World War (1914–18) stimulated US manufacturing, and offered more economic opportunities for blacks in the North.

iii) Achievements

The extent to which these blacks achieved their aims is uncertain. The influx of blacks caused deterioration in race relations in the North. Northern cities began to pass residential segregation laws. Working-class whites resented black competition for jobs and housing, and were alarmed by the increasing black political influence in local elections. Riots frequently resulted, especially after soldiers returned from the First World War and job competition was particularly fierce. In 1919 there were race riots in most major American cities. The Ku Klux Klan had a great revival in the 1920s in the North and the South. Migration did not end the problems of racial tension and discrimination, nor did it necessarily promote better living conditions. Blacks congregated in the poorest parts of the great cities of the North and West, in what became widely known as 'ghettos'. Discrimination and limited educational and employment opportunities made it hard to get out of the ghetto. Thus many Southern blacks exchanged a disadvantaged rural life for a disadvantaged urban life.

d) Marcus Garvey (1887–1940) and Black Pride

i) Aims

Garvey was born in British Jamaica. He felt that blacks had been unfairly treated and oppressed by 'corrupt' whites throughout histo-

HISPANIC AMERICANS
In the twentieth century, many Mexicans migrated to the South-west of the United States. An estimated 3–400,000 migrated to cities such as Los Angeles (California) and San Antonio (Texas). Like blacks, they faced residential segregation, and therefore crowded into low-rent inner-city districts. Similarly, poor agricultural workers from Puerto Rico moved to New York City. These Hispanic Americans worked for low wages and lived in primitive conditions. However, as with blacks, some established businesses and became middle class.

OSCAR DE PRIEST
De Priest was the first black Congressman elected in the twentieth century (1928). He represented a Chicago district.

NORTHERN BLACK ACTIVISM
NAACP did not gain many followers from amongst Northern ghetto blacks. Booker T. Washington's National Urban League was more useful, giving Southern blacks practical help as they adjusted to city life. Black Christian churches, which played an important part in the South, were never quite as appealing to blacks when they moved to or lived in the North. The first urban black movement that had mass appeal was that which grew up around Marcus Garvey.

Figure 31 Marcus Garvey in a UNIA parade.

HARLEM
Due to the Great Migration from the South and to immigration from the British West Indies, New York City's black population rocketed from 70,000 in 1890 to 200,000 in 1920. During those years, Harlem changed from an all-white, fashionable upper-class area into a densely populated black ghetto.

...boastful, egotistic, tyrannical, intolerant... gifted at self-advertisement... promising ever, but never fulfilling... a lover of pomp, tawdry, finery, and garish display... a sheer opportunist and a demagogic charlatan.

Source D A. Philip Randolph's magazine *The Messenger* on Marcus Garvey.

ry. He aimed to make blacks proud of themselves and their culture. 'Black is beautiful', he said. A second and more ambitious aim was somehow to unite blacks throughout the world, in order to weld the race into a powerful force:

> I asked, 'Where is the black man's government? Where is his King and his Kingdom? Where is his President, his country, and his ambassador, his army, his navy, his men of big affairs?' I could not find them; and then I declared, 'I will help to make them'.
>
> *Source C*

In 1914 Garvey founded the Universal Negro Improvement Association (UNIA), which aimed to get blacks to 'take Africa, organise it, develop it, arm it, and make it the defender of Negroes the world over'. In 1916, the 29-year-old Garvey visited the United States. He aimed to make Harlem the headquarters of UNIA. Garvey aimed to elevate the blackest of blacks above the light-skinned blacks who traditionally dominated black American movements. He also aimed at separatism and a return to Africa, all of which antagonised W.E.B. Du Bois and NAACP.

ii) Methods
Garvey's main method was the publicising of his ideas. He was an inspiring speaker, with a gift for memorable phrases, such as 'Africa for the Africans'. He spoke at rallies and also spread his ideas through his editing of the *Negro World*, which soon had a circulation over 100,000, making it the most popular black weekly. It was the only black publication to refuse advertisements for products such as skin bleaches that promised to make the user look white. Perhaps Garvey's most controversial method was to set himself up as leader-come-role-model in an especially grandiose fashion. He had himself elected 'President-General' of UNIA, and wore the elaborate uniform of a head of state as he led a massive parade to celebrate his International Convention of the Negro People of the World in New York City in 1920. When Garvey was declared 'provisional President of Africa', there was some ridicule, for example, from Du Bois. However, many blacks said that Marcus Garvey made them feel proud. After an ill-judged meeting with a Ku Klux Klan leader, and an equally ill-judged venture into business, Garvey was increasingly discredited and the United States government ensured his deportation in 1927. UNIA did not long survive his departure.

iii) Achievements
Initially, Garvey seemed to be very successful in America. Within a few months of his arrival, UNIA had 2,000 members. However, it

could be argued that his movement achieved little that was concrete. Once a person joined UNIA, there was little to do, other than attend its morale-boosting meetings and invest in its business schemes. On the other hand, he had achieved a commendable increase in black American pride. He had reminded blacks that Africa had been culturally more sophisticated than Europe in past centuries: 'Black men, you were once great; you shall be great again'. It was perhaps no coincidence that the **Harlem Renaissance** occurred soon after Garvey achieved fame in America. Historians generally agree that UNIA was the first protest movement that gained real popularity among American blacks. Subsequently, influential black Americans such as Congressman Adam Clayton Powell and the Black Muslim, Black Power, and Black Panther activists of the 1960s and 1970s, recognised their debt to Garvey.

e) White Violence and the Ku Klux Klan

i) Aims

The Ku Klux Klan was a white racist organisation that had grown up in the South in the aftermath of the Civil War. The Ku Klux Klan aimed to maintain white supremacy. In 1871 President Grant ordered the Ku Klux Klan to disband. Thousands of Klansmen were arrested. White racists responded by forming White Leagues throughout the South. The white racists were frequently lower-class workers who aimed to decrease the threat of competition from free black labour. The Ku Klux Klan was re-founded in 1915 by William J. Simmons. He said he aimed to purge Southern culture of corrupting influences. He also aimed to assert Protestant supremacy over Catholics, Jews and Communists.

ii) Methods

The favourite and traditional Ku Klux Klan methods for dealing with black were threats and mob violence. In the late 1860s and early 1870s hooded Ku Klux Klansmen had frightened black voters into staying away from election polls by threats, flogging, and torture. The most 'uppity' blacks were lynched. Mob violence and lynchings (over 2,000 in the last 20 years of the nineteenth century) were a daily fact of life in the South.

iii) Achievements

The new Ku Klux Klan had far more members than the old, and its membership was national rather than simply Southern. The re-founded Klan became particularly successful in the Midwest and North, where there was white resentment at the Great Migration of blacks from the South. By 1925 the Klan had 5 million members and

GARVEY AND 'BLACK IS BEAUTIFUL'
Garvey urged black children to play only with black dolls, demanded a Black House in Washington, and asked black Christians to think of a black God and Jesus.

THE HARLEM RENAISSANCE
The Harlem Renaissance produced great black cultural figures in the fields of literature, art and music. Black writer Langston Hughes declared, 'We younger Negro artists who create now intend to express our individual dark-skinned selves without fear or shame... We know we are beautiful.' This new black cultural awareness spread to other cities.

Today, there are a lot of people who think Garvey's still alive ... I was conducting radio interviews with some young Rastafarians, who look to Garvey as their prophet ... and realised they were quietly laughing behind me. One of them said, 'That man think Marcus Garvey dead.' They felt pity for me. I was uninformed. In black folk culture, there is no death for the righteous.

Source E Extract from a *New Yorker* article on the Marcus Garvey Centennial Exhibition in Harlem (1987).

Figure 32 Ku Klux Klan members marching in Washington DC in 1926.

HOLLYWOOD AND RACISM

One of the most popular of the early movies to come out of Hollywood was *The Birth of a Nation*. The movie glorified the Ku Klux Klan as defenders of white civilisation against a post-Civil War black regime of terror. Klan recruitment dramatically increased after the movie was released (1915).

---

dominated state legislatures in Colorado, Kansas, Louisiana, Maine, Oklahoma, and Texas. Klansmen felt particularly threatened by black soldiers returning from more racially tolerant Europe after the First World War: 78 black veterans were lynched in the South in 1919. Ku Klux Klan membership increased during the Depression, when competition for jobs exacerbated racism in the South. The number of lynchings tripled between 1932 and 1933. Thus the white supremacists achieved much that they set out to achieve. They successfully terrorised and repressed blacks throughout America, but particularly in the South, where lynching persisted into the 1960s.

f) A. Philip Randolph and Trade Unionism

i) Aims

A. Philip Randolph aimed to improve the living standards and raise the political awareness of black people.

ii) Methods

Randolph's main method was the organisation of black workers into powerful trade unions that could negotiate better wages and working conditions. He advocated collaboration with white trade unionists. He knew that economic power was one of the few advantages that blacks had. He used that power in a militant fashion during the Second World War and the Cold War, when he threatened the withdrawal of black labour in time of crisis in order to gain concessions for blacks. Randolph used his prominence as a leading trade unionist as a platform from which he spoke for black rights. Randolph was elected president of the Communist-dominated National Negro Congress, which aimed to promote civil rights and economic equality for blacks. He publicised socialist ideas in his magazine, *The Messenger*.

iii) Achievements

Randolph established the first really successful black trade union (for railroad porters, in 1925). However, a large proportion of black workers were not unionised until the Great Depression encouraged desperate workers of all colours to join unions. The achievements of his National Negro Congress were limited because of the suspicion with which black churches and NAACP (along with most other Americans) regarded Communism. Randolph's militancy was sometimes highly effective. When he threatened to bring Washington DC to a standstill during the Second World War unless there was equality within the armed forces and the workplace, it forced President Franklin Roosevelt into action. Roosevelt set up a federal agency (the Committee on Fair Employment Practices – FEPC) to promote equal employment opportunities in defence industries. During the Cold War, Randolph's call for black draft resistance helped force President Truman into the desegregation of the armed forces. However, such militancy often alienated others, particularly during wartime emergencies. It was not the Communist ideology but the Christian ideology (which afforded greater moral status) that proved most productive for black civil rights activists such as Martin Luther King. Randolph, however, had brought about greater black pride and awareness, and he had shown the importance and potential of organised black activity and pressure.

g) Moderate Whites and the Political Solution

In the first half of the twentieth century a few white politicians, particularly presidents, made attempts to ameliorate racial tensions by improving the lot of blacks. However, the extent of white hostility toward blacks meant that attempts at amelioration frequently resulted in a white backlash.

The methods used by moderate white politicians usually consisted of association with black leaders and greater employment of blacks by the federal government. Presidents such as Cleveland,

BLACKS AND COMMUNISM

The 1930s saw many black intellectuals attracted by the inter-racial American Communist Party (CPUSA). CPUSA provided the legal help for the nine 'Scottsboro boys' accused of raping two white women on an Alabama freight train in 1931. CPUSA targeted black industrial and agricultural workers in the early 1930s. CPUSA persuaded workers such as Southern black agricultural labourers to unionise, for example, in Lowndes County, Alabama. Significantly, that county became a hotbed of civil rights activism in the 1960s. Thus it could be seen that American Communism made significant efforts to win over blacks and gave them a considerable amount of concrete assistance. However, Communism was always unpopular amongst most Americans, and even more so once the Cold War was under way. Therefore, association with Communism did a great deal of harm to the black cause. Significantly, the FBI accused Martin Luther King of being a Communist when they were trying to discredit him.

BLACK VOTING PATTERNS

Traditionally, blacks had voted for the Republican Party, the party of their emancipator, Abraham Lincoln. After Franklin Roosevelt, most of the blacks who voted, voted Democrat.

ROOSEVELT AND NATIVE AMERICANS

The Roosevelt administration used sympathetic methods when dealing with Native Americans, who had been hard hit by the Depression. The administration worked to restore tribal control over reservation land and to restore opportunities for traditional Native American culture to be transmitted. For example, Native American children were no longer forced to attend Christian services. Federal intervention gave the Native Americans more government money, more land, and better medical services. Nevertheless, during the Second World War, many Native Americans left the reservations (to work in the cities) and never returned.

McKinley, Theodore Roosevelt and Taft consulted Booker T. Washington. However, when McKinley appointed a significant number of blacks to governmental positions, this contributed to race riots in some American cities. The first twentieth century presidents to give really significant assistance to blacks were Franklin Roosevelt and Harry Truman. Both were Democrats.

i) President Franklin D. Roosevelt's Aims (1933–45)

It is difficult to ascertain Roosevelt's aims with regard to blacks. He was heavily dependent upon his fellow Democrats from the South in Congress, so he dared not articulate any great desire to help blacks. However, whether inadvertently or deliberately, he helped blacks so much that it changed **black voting patterns**.

ii) Roosevelt's Methods

As president, Roosevelt's greatest preoccupation was to get the American economy out of the Depression. He initiated an unprecedented programme of government intervention to stimulate the economy and help the poor. As a disproportionate number of the poor were black, Roosevelt's New Deal affected them greatly. Roosevelt also used the traditional method of making significant black appointments. There were nearly 50 blacks in senior positions in the federal bureaucracy, and they were nicknamed Roosevelt's 'Black Cabinet'.

Roosevelt and Lynching

Roosevelt's New Deal measures depended on the support of his fellow Democrats from the South. White Southern politicians were diametrically opposed to measures directly aimed at improving the black lot. Southern Democrats therefore stopped Roosevelt using the legislative method to help blacks. He never fully supported anti-lynching bills (1934, 1935, 1938).

A favourite method used by moderate white politicians was a 'token gesture' that made the politician look caring, might gain him black votes in the North, but did not cost much and was relatively easy to perform. Roosevelt used his wife to perform this function. Eleanor Roosevelt had a genuine social conscience and was more than willing to use her prestige to help the black cause. She played a pivotal role in the organisation of a bi-racial meeting which she attended in exceptionally racist Birmingham, in Alabama (1938). She tried to persuade New Deal officials to give non-discriminatory aid to blacks, and flew with a trainee black pilot in Tuskegee,

Alabama, to make the point that blacks could serve their country as well as whites.

iii) Roosevelt's Achievements

The New Deal helped alleviate black poverty. One million blacks obtained jobs through the New Deal. The 'Black Cabinet' served to raise black morale. Eleanor Roosevelt achieved small but concrete victories that also helped to raise black morale. For example, she helped to ensure that the US Army used black pilots in the Second World War. The Roosevelt administration successfully established an important precedent when it demonstrated that federal government intervention was the method most likely to succeed in helping ethnic minorities.

Figure 33 Black children lining up for food from a religious charity in Harlem during the Depression.

> The most important contribution of the Roosevelt Administration to the age-old colour-line problem in America has been its doctrine that Negroes are a part of the country and must be considered in any programme for the country as a whole… For the first time in their lives, government has taken on meaning and substance for the Negro masses.

Source F Assessment of Roosevelt, from *Crisis* (the NAACP newspaper), 1940.

ROOSEVELT AND HISPANIC AMERICANS

1.2 million Mexican Americans lived in the South-western United States in 1930. They had little political influence, and many received no help from the New Deal. There was only one significant politician of Hispanic descent in the United States, Senator Dennis Chavez of New Mexico, whom Roosevelt treated as the spokesman of Hispanic Americans. The 1940 census recorded 2.7 million Hispanic Americans. This predominantly rural population suffered poverty, discrimination and segregation. In Los Angeles, young Mexican Americans joined neighbourhood gangs. They signalled their rejection of 'Anglo' culture by wearing 'zoot suits' (baggy trousers flared at the knee) along with wide-brimmed felt hats. In 1943 Anglo servicemen on leave in Los Angeles attacked Mexican Americans and tore off their zoot suits. Local policemen did nothing to stop the attacks, until Roosevelt intervened. However, like blacks, Hispanic Americans emerged from the war with a greater sense of self-esteem. Many took advantage of the GI Bill and joined the Hispanic American middle class.

We will resist to the bitter end, whatever the consequences, any measure or any movement that would have a tendency to bring about social equality and intermingling and amalgamation of the races.

Source G Racist Senator Richard Russell of Georgia (Democrat), speaking in 1946.

ASIAN AMERICANS AND THE SECOND WORLD WAR

120,000 Japanese Americans, two-thirds of whom were native-born American citizens, were put in internment camps in the USA in 1942. They were considered to constitute a security threat in the United States' war against Japan, but there was no proof of any disloyalty. The United States had a history of anti-Japanese racism. There had been anti-Japanese assaults and agitation on the West Coast for half a century. The interned Japanese lost property worth $400 million. After the war, Japanese Americans quietly rebuilt their lives to become one of the most prosperous of ethnic minorities. Black historian Thomas Sowell controversially uses this information to conclude that persecution and deprivation can be overcome, thereby implying that his fellow blacks ought to be able to do likewise.

iv) President Harry Truman's Aims (1945–53)

President Truman continued many of Roosevelt's policies. Although quite openly racist in his youth, Truman developed an ever-increasing sense of responsibility towards blacks as a politician and particularly as president. He aimed to make the United States live up to its ideals of freedom and equality, partly because he wanted to set a good example to the Cold War world. He aimed to eliminate the greatest abuses from American life, such as lynching, the poll tax, black disfranchisement and inequality before the law.

v) Truman's Methods

Like Roosevelt, Truman's methods were sometimes simply reactive. A. Philip Randolph's threat to urge black draft resistance during the Cold War helped force Truman to use executive authority to end discrimination in the armed forces and civil service.

Blacks and the Cold War

In the Cold War, the United States told the world that it stood for freedom, democracy and equality, in contrast to the USSR. The US criticised the USSR for being a one-party state, wherein Soviet citizens lacked the opportunity to vote for a political party of their choice. Naturally, the Soviets pointed out that Southern blacks could not vote, and lacked real freedom and equality in the United States.

However, unlike Roosevelt, Truman sometimes took the initiative. In 1946 he deliberately appointed liberals to a committee to investigate increasing violence against blacks. Naturally, their report endorsed and publicised Truman's aims. He used the prestige of the presidential office when he made speeches about these aims, for example in his 1947 and 1948 State of the Union addresses. He used presidential powers to issue executive orders to end discrimination in the armed forces and to give equal employment opportunities in the federal bureaucracy. He appointed blacks to significant posts, for example a black federal judge. He used federal purchasing power to try to coax businessman into equal employment policies.

vi) Truman's Achievements

Truman's attempt to end segregation in the armed forces was successfully resisted by his 'top brass' for two years. However, discrimination slowly decreased. His attempt to use federal employment and purchasing power to help minorities also had rather limited success. Truman's greatest achievement was probably to increase the awareness of the need for racial change in America. He put race relations at the centre of the US political agenda. There could be no turning back.

h) Blacks and Political Solutions

i) Aims

We have seen that while blacks usually shared the same aim of a better life, they differed on the methods needed to achieve that aim. Booker T. Washington emphasised economic advancement, while W.E.B. Du Bois stressed the need for civic equality. Marcus Garvey emphasised black pride, while A. Philip Randolph urged working-class unity. All were aware of the importance of the vote. The aim when using the vote was to elect sympathetic politicians to represent blacks. Those politicians could pursue policies to give blacks equal political, economic and social opportunities. However, not all blacks had the vote. In 1904 Washington and Du Bois worked together on a New York conference to discuss black voting rights in the South where many blacks were disfranchised by Jim Crow laws.

Figure 34 Brooklyn Dodgers player Jackie Robinson signing autographs. In 1947, Robinson became the first black baseball player to play in the major league (equivalent to the Premier League in English football).

ii) Methods

White Democrats dominated Southern politics. Many Southern blacks therefore 'voted with their feet' when they migrated North, where they could vote if they chose to do so. The black vote in Northern states such as Illinois and New York became crucial in local and national elections during the first half of the twentieth century. Northern blacks increasingly voted Democrat after benefiting from Roosevelt's New Deal, and this was one reason why the Democrat Truman raised the profile of civil rights issues.

Increasing numbers of black newspapers, such as the *Baltimore Afro-American* and *Pittsburgh Courier* raised black political awareness. It was not easy to do so, as blacks had inevitably been preoccupied with earning a living. Traditionally, blacks lacked political consciousness. Black-dominated trade unions, such as Randolph's union of railroad porters and the Communist-dominated (and 75 per cent black) Food, Tobacco, Agricultural and Allied Workers Union, promoted mass meetings in the 1930s and 1940s to discuss voter registration and black citizenship. NAACP campaigned increasingly in the 1930s to get Southern black members interested in voter registration and abolition of the poll tax. NAACP even cooperated with Randolph's Communist-dominated National Negro Congress in 1941 to establish a National Committee to Abolish the Poll Tax.

iii) Achievements

All this agitation about and emphasis on voting rights paid off. Between 1940 and 1947, the number of black registered voters in the

---

YOUNG LYNDON BAINES JOHNSON AND ETHNIC MINORITIES

Although the president of the United States clearly had the most opportunities to help alleviate American racial problems, other individual whites contributed. Future President Lyndon Johnson worked as a teacher in a school for poor Hispanic Americans in Texas in the late 1920s. Johnson's aim was to give the children the education that would enable them to get out of the poverty trap. In the 1930s, Johnson aimed to raise black employment levels in Texas when he worked for a New Deal agency.

South rose from 3 per cent to 12 per cent. NAACP's tactic of working for change through the law courts led to the 1944 Supreme Court decision (*Smith* v. *Allwright*) that the exclusion of blacks from primaries was unconstitutional under the 15th Amendment. Under Truman, the federal government itself took up the call for the universal right to exercise the vote.

A few black politicians made a local and, in the case of **Adam Clayton Powell**, a national impact. In 1944, Reverend Adam Clayton Powell of Abyssinian Baptist Church in Harlem was elected to Congress. Powell was very popular with his Harlem constituents, although his flamboyant lifestyle attracted much criticism from whites. Re-election for 11 consecutive terms gave him the seniority that enabled him to chair important congressional committees. Powell ensured that civil rights were far more of an issue in Washington than they had been before his arrival.

i) Black Violence

In the early 1940s Swedish sociologist Gunnar Myrdal and black Professor Ralph Bunche of Howard University travelled the South interviewing people for their study of prejudice, *An American Dilemma* (1944). Bunche said,

Source H

> There are Negroes … who, fed up with frustration of their life here, see no hope and express an angry desire 'to shoot their way out of it'. I have on many occasions heard Negroes exclaim, 'Just give us machine guns and we'll blow the lid off the whole damn business'.

However, blacks were so downtrodden that they rarely dared to use violent methods of protest, especially when the federal government and the state governments had far more potential physical power. Although blacks became increasingly assertive during the first half of the twentieth century, they rejected the violent solution to racial problems that had been accepted by a minority of whites, such as Ku Klux Klansmen. As yet, the favoured militant black activist solutions were peaceful protest and publicity, as with James Farmer and CORE.

j) James Farmer, CORE and Non-violent Protest

i) Aims
James Farmer was a Christian socialist who aimed to achieve black equality in an integrated American society. In 1942 he established the Congress of Racial Equality (CORE) to achieve those aims.

ii) Methods

CORE's methods were more militant than those of NAACP, which was still concentrating upon working away in the law courts. During the Second World War, CORE organised sit-ins at segregated Chicago restaurants, and in 1947 organised 'Freedom Rides' in North/South border states to try to ensure the enforcement of Supreme Court rulings on desegregation in interstate transport. Farmer's methods owed much to Gandhi's non-violent tactics against British imperialism in India.

iii) Achievements

As yet, Farmer's methods had achieved little, but when civil rights activists took them up in the 1950s and 1960s, they proved to be the most effective method of all for the achievement of black equality.

3 The Mid-Twentieth Century Turning Point

It was in the 1950s that the great American civil rights movement really burst into life. Much was owed to pioneers such as Garvey, A. Philip Randolph, and NAACP. However, they had failed to grab the nation's attention in the way that events in the 1950s did. President Eisenhower (1953–61) was unsympathetic to the black cause; the federal government was led rather than leading in the 1950s. Where, then, lay the responsibility for kick-starting the civil rights movement? It lay with the media, the Supreme Court, white racist bigots, and exceptional individuals such as Martin Luther King.

a) The Situation of Blacks in 1950

In the South, agricultural mechanisation had led most blacks to move to cities and towns by 1950. They usually lived in all-black, run-down neighbourhoods, frequently plagued by loan sharks and narcotics dealers. Black children attended all-black and mostly inferior schools. Most reputable further education institutions were closed to blacks. Blacks could not go to movie theatres, hotels, restaurants, swimming pools and parks frequented by whites. Blacks had to use separate drinking fountains and rest-rooms. Many employers rejected black applicants on grounds of colour, so most blacks found themselves confined to occupations considered 'menial' by whites. Blacks were often street cleaners, garbage collectors, rest-room attendants, or domestic servants. Southern blacks for the most part were not allowed to vote, and were routinely harassed by white law enforce-

ACTIVITY

Look at the photographs on pages 162 and 173. What do they suggest about American race relations in the first half of the twentieth century?

ISSUE:
Why did the American civil rights movement spring to life in the mid-twentieth century?

KU KLUX KLAN
Ku Klux Klan membership shot up in Alabama, Florida, Georgia and South Carolina as a result of the prospect of school desegregation. There were increased numbers of cross burnings, torch-light rallies, bombings and beatings.

ment officials. In the North, blacks lived in poor housing and attended poor schools in ghettos. There was *de facto* segregation. Although blacks could vote, they were economically and socially disadvantaged.

b) The Supreme Court, *Brown*, and Little Rock, Arkansas

Despite Eisenhower's own right-wing leanings, he promoted several more liberal members of his Republican party to the Supreme Court, including Chief Justice Earl Warren. Thanks to NAACP-initiated litigation, the Supreme Court said in *Brown* v. *Board of Education, Topeka* (1954) that schools should be desegregated. Despite resistance by White Citizens Councils, desegregation began to be introduced in border states such as Arkansas.

In 1957, nine black students attempted to attend Central High School in Little Rock, Arkansas. The students had support and encouragement from NAACP. When white racists tried to stop them entering the school building, President Eisenhower was forced to intervene in their support. Eisenhower acted because of fears for law and order, respect for the decisions of the Supreme Court, and concern for America's image during the Cold War. The increase of media coverage of Southern white racism was important. Pictures on television and in the press of whites spitting on and jostling black children as they tried to attend Central High School helped to swing moderate opinion in the North toward an anti-Southern posture. Desegregation was slow. By 1964, only 6 per cent of black American children attended desegregated schools – but it was a start.

The civil rights movement had gained momentum. NAACP's litigation tactics and the bravery of individuals such as the High School students of Little Rock had forced a reluctant federal government to follow the path set out by Roosevelt and Truman and to intervene again. Thus pressure from black activists, violent opposition from white racists, and federal government intervention to halt violence, all combined to put civil rights at the centre of US politics.

c) Martin Luther King and the Montgomery (Alabama) Bus Boycott

In Montgomery, as in Little Rock, several black traditions of solution-seeking coalesced to great effect. The trigger event in Montgomery was what was probably a premeditated act in 1955 by NAACP activist Rosa Parks. She challenged Montgomery's city bus segregation policy, was arrested, and put on trial. Her arrest electrified the local black community. The local black college helped publicise her case.

THE SIGNIFICANCE OF EMMETT TILL

Fourteen-year-old Emmett Till lived in Chicago. When visiting relations in Mississippi, the young black boy wanted to impress his cowed Southern cousins. During a visit to a store, he asked a married white woman for a date. His terrified cousins pulled him out of the store. As he left, Till wolf-whistled at the woman. Her husband and brother beat Till so that when his body was found in the river, he was unrecognisable apart from the distinctive ring on his finger. An all-white jury found his murderers not guilty. The resulting publicity made many Americans, particularly in the North, re-think their attitude to the Southern way of life.

MONTGOMERY BUSES BEFORE THE BOYCOTT

Although it was mostly blacks who used the buses, half the seating was reserved for whites. If the black section was full and the white section had spare seats, blacks still could not sit in the 'whites-only' seats.

NAACP enlisted local black church leaders to help organise, inspire and finance a black bus boycott in protest at her arrest.

Boycotts were not a new method: blacks in the South had used them since 1900, with varying degrees of success. So why did this one have such an impact? Perhaps it was that the black church in Montgomery was so committed and provided such an inspirational leader in Martin Luther King, or perhaps it was the media attention.

Black churches pre-dated NAACP as the most influential organisation available to blacks. The church had given black people the experience of meeting together, and had given them hope and inspiration for decades. White Americans were predominantly Christian in name if not in fact. It was therefore harder for them to persecute and/or ignore a black Christian institution than any other kind of black organisation. Now, with Martin Luther King, the church gave black people a truly exceptional preacher, whose speeches on civil rights were like sermons. In Martin Luther King the black Christian sermon tradition combined with the political sermonising inherent in the American Declaration of Independence and Constitution. That combination created a powerful and unanswerable moral justification for change to put before white Christian America. Martin Luther King asked white Christians how they could reject the teaching of love and brotherhood put forward by the founder of their faith. Did not love and brotherhood mean that black and white should live together as equals? Martin Luther King also asked white Americans how they could ignore the ideals of freedom put forth by the Founding Fathers, for whom, supposedly, 'all men' were 'created equal':

> If we are wrong, the Supreme Court of this nation is wrong. If we are wrong, the Constitution of the United States is wrong. If we are wrong, Jesus of Nazareth was merely a … dreamer.

Source I

Initially, the black protesters in Montgomery only demanded courtesy, 'first-come first-served' seating, and the employment of some black bus drivers. When the white city commissioners refused these demands, the bus boycott (which hit white business interests) was extended and the aims were altered. Montgomery blacks now demanded desegregation on the buses. The two methods of direct action and NAACP litigation now effectively coalesced. NAACP got the courts to rule in favour of desegregated buses, and after one year of the black boycott of the buses, that was achieved in Montgomery, in December 1956.

Q Many history books (particularly those for younger children) inaccurately portray 42-year-old Rosa Parks as a tired old lady who simply wanted to sit down on the bus on the way home after a hard day's work. Why do you suppose they do this?

The Montgomery Bus Boycott was highly significant. It inspired Northern bi-racial support and further black action. In particular, it inspired Martin Luther King to establish a new organisation, the Southern Christian Leadership Conference (SCLC). SCLC was to prove exceptionally effective in the South at a time when NAACP was being persecuted there. It was far harder for whites to persecute a black Christian organisation than to persecute NAACP. Perhaps the most important aspect of the Montgomery Bus Boycott was that, unlike the Little Rock crisis, this was primarily the achievement of black people. True, they had depended upon a Supreme Court ruling against segregated buses. However, in the year before that ruling was given, blacks had shown that they could initiate and sustain successful protests in a dignified and morally justifiable fashion. Furthermore, black protest had developed from a minority black movement, dominated by middle-class organisations such as NAACP, into a mass black movement. At Montgomery the majority of the black population of a city had worked together.

> When in the course of human events it becomes necessary to abolish the Negro race, proper methods should be used. Among these are guns, bows and arrows, sling shots and knives. We hold these truths to be self-evident, that all whites are created equal with certain rights, among these are life, liberty and the pursuit of dead niggers … If we don't stop helping these African flesh eaters, we will soon wake up and find Reverend King in the White House.

ACTIVITY

Find a text of the American Declaration of Independence to compare with Source J. What were the aims of the writers of Source J? How effective is it?

Source J Extract from a White Citizens Council leaflet, printed in Montgomery during the 1955 boycott.

ISSUES:
In what different ways did people approach the problems facing American minorities in the 1960s? Which ways were more successful?

4　Racial Problems: the Search for a Solution in the 1960s

After the Montgomery Bus Boycott, Martin Luther King felt that he had found the solution to the problems facing Southern blacks. In some ways he was right. He worked hard and effectively to end segregation and gain civil rights for blacks in the South. However, he failed to find the solution to black economic inequality, particularly in the North. Malcolm X and other black extremists thought that they had some answers to the problems facing blacks in the ghettos of the North, but ghetto life remains a problem in the twenty-first century.

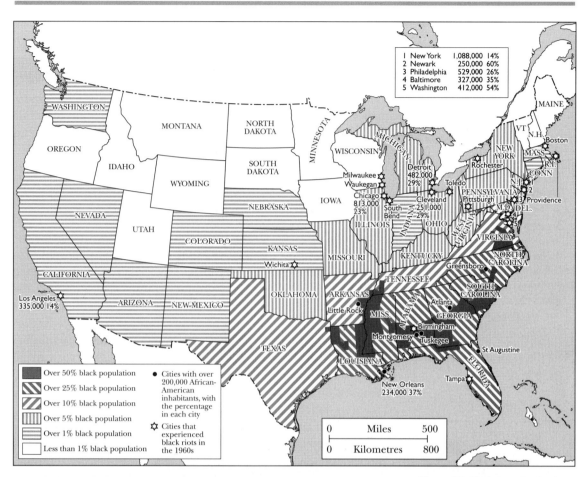

1	New York	1,088,000	14%
2	Newark	250,000	60%
3	Philadelphia	529,000	26%
4	Baltimore	327,000	35%
5	Washington	412,000	54%

Legend:
- Over 50% black population
- Over 25% black population
- Over 10% black population
- Over 5% black population
- Over 1% black population
- Less than 1% black population
- ● Cities with over 200,000 African-American inhabitants, with the percentage in each city
- ✪ Cities that experienced black riots in the 1960s

0	Miles	500
0	Kilometres	800

Figure 35 Black America in the 1960s.

a) Solution 1: Martin Luther King and Direct Non-violent Action in the South

i) Aims

King aimed initially to end segregation and to gain political equality for blacks in the South.

ii) Methods

King's methods were not particularly original: they contained elements adopted and adapted from previous black leaders. Like Booker T. Washington, King wanted blacks to work to help themselves, while taking care to avoid unnecessary alienation of whites. Like NAACP and CORE, King believed in integration and peaceful protest. As a minister of God, King believed that these methods constituted acceptable Christian activities, particularly when infused with the emphasis on loving one's enemy. King's methods were particu-

Christ furnished the spirit and motivation, while Gandhi furnished the method.

Source K Martin Luther King on his methods.

KING'S FIRST PROTEST MARCH

In 1957 Martin Luther King organised a pilgrimage to Washington DC, where he spoke in favour of equality before the Lincoln Memorial. A. Philip Randolph intro- duced Martin Luther King as 'the moral leader of the nation'. The March had long been a dream of Randolph. He had envisaged it as focus- ing upon jobs. It was King who re-directed it toward 'freedom' and civil rights.

Why did Martin Luther King choose to speak at the Lincoln Memorial?

Real men don't put their children on the firing line.

Source L Malcolm X on King's tactics in Birmingham.

larly suited to the South, where blacks had virtually no power and where the Christian church was by far the strongest black institution.

King and SCLC initiated a 'Crusade for Citizenship' in 1958. His crusade aimed to encourage blacks to vote, something which NAACP had been attempting for years. In 1960 some students in Greensboro, North Carolina, used James Farmer's old 'sit-ins' method at an all- white Woolworth's cafe in protest against segregation. King support- ed them. In 1961 Farmer's CORE repeated their 1947 rides on inter- state transport. These 'Freedom Riders' were supported by SCLC and SNCC. SCLC, SNCC, NAACP and the National Urban League then worked together on voter registration in Mississippi.

The Student Non-Violent Co-ordinating Committee (SNCC) had been set up as sit-ins spread throughout the South. Between 1960 and 1963, SNCC mobilised 50,000 students in 100 Southern cities to participate in non-violent demonstrations. When SNCC mobilised students in Albany, Georgia, to protest against segregation and dis- franchisement, Martin Luther King went along to support them (1962). At Albany, he used a protest method that was to become his favourite – peaceful marches. King used marches to draw attention to segregation, lack of economic opportunity and, in Selma, Alabama in 1965, to the problems facing would-be black voters.

When King led a march in Albany in 1962, he got himself arrest- ed. Getting himself arrested was another of his 'favourite' methods, although he hated and feared his spells in Southern jails, from whence 'uppity' blacks frequently failed to emerge. Arrests, usually as a result of marches, were a dramatic way to draw national attention to injustice. King used these situations to make the point that in a 'free' country, which trumpeted its belief in freedom and democracy throughout the Cold War world, a man could get arrested for partic- ipation in a protest march against discrimination and inequality.

Sometimes, King deliberately provoked a violent white reaction in order to publicise his cause. In 1963 he led a black boycott of stores and protest marches in a bastion of Southern racism, Birmingham, Alabama. He knew that Birmingham's hot-headed police chief, Bull Connor, would react violently. Connor made national headlines and prime-time TV viewing when he set his dogs on black marchers. However, the dogs soon became old news. The media lost interest. King therefore brought young black children into the marches. Connor's high-pressure water hoses tore the clothes off the backs of children, many of whom were subsequently jailed. Birmingham ghet- to blacks began to riot in support of the middle-class black protesters. America took notice again.

Another of King's favourite methods was the emotive speech. His greatest speech was made at the Lincoln Memorial at the climax of the 1963 March on Washington. All the leading black organisations and many whites participated in the March on Washington.

Malcolm X on the March on Washington

In 1962 Malcolm had said, 'What is looked upon as an American dream for white people has long been an American nightmare for black people.' When King made his 'I have a dream' speech in the March on Washington, Malcolm made even more use of the dream/nightmare contrast: 'While King was having a dream, the rest of us Negroes are having a nightmare.' Malcolm was scathing when he described the March on Washington: 'The Negroes spent a lot of money, had a good time, and enjoyed a real circus or carnival-type atmosphere. Now that the show is over, the black masses are still without land, without jobs, and without homes. Their Christian churches are still being bombed, their innocent little girls murdered. So what did the March on Washington accomplish? Nothing!' Malcolm described the March on Washington as a 'circus', asking, 'How was a one-day "integrated" picnic going to counter-influence these representatives of prejudice rooted deep in the psyche of the American white man for four hundred years?'

MARTIN LUTHER KING ON THE AMERICAN DREAM

King said the black dream of freedom was 'a dream deeply rooted in the American dream ... I have a dream that one day this nation will rise up and live out the true meaning of its creed, "We hold these truths to be self-evident, that all men are created equal." '

iii) Achievements

The methods espoused by Martin Luther King, frequently in conjunction with others, were often successful. After the Montgomery Bus Boycott, Montgomery buses were desegregated (1956), although some other cities and towns, such as Birmingham, Alabama, were slow to follow. The SNCC sit-ins (1960) speeded up desegregation in some stores and schools, for example, in Atlanta, Georgia. The Freedom Riders (1961) elicited a vicious white racist response, prompting the Kennedy administration to end segregation in interstate travel. The next three great civil rights campaigns were initiated and dominated by King and SCLC, and were successful in helping bring about important legislation from Congress. While marches in Birmingham (1963) did not lead to speedy desegregation there, they surely helped persuade Kennedy to introduce civil rights legislation to Congress. The March on Washington (1963) was a heart warming demonstration of black and white belief in the 'American dream'. The March probably helped bring about the 1964 Civil Rights Act. That act enabled the federal government to end *de jure* segregation in the South. It dismantled the Jim Crow laws, ended discrimination in public places, and provided more equal employment and educational opportunities in the South. However, the act did not solve the problem of black disfranchisement, and it was Martin Luther King who publicised the problem, in Selma, Alabama (1965). King's Selma campaign contributed to the Voting Rights Act (1965), after which the numbers of blacks voting in the South increased dramatically.

Figure 36 Participants in the 1963 March on Washington.

King had failures and setbacks in the South. The Albany Movement (1961–2) with which he became associated did not achieve anything for blacks in Albany in the short term. His involvement in St Augustine, Florida, was similarly unsatisfactory. Furthermore, King sometimes failed to halt inter-organisational tensions with SNCC and NAACP. Those tensions help explain the failure in Albany, although King deserves credit as the most cooperative of the organisational leaders.

Despite some setbacks, there is no doubt that Martin Luther King played a vital role in dismantling Jim Crow in the South. He was highly indebted to others, for example, NAACP, grass-roots activists, and some white idealist and politicians. Nevertheless, his contribution was crucial, because in him the white American Christian and libertarian traditions coalesced. When he spoke of Christian love and equality before God, and the ideals of equality enshrined in the Declaration of Independence and the American Constitution, he made an unanswerable case, particularly to Northern politicians. Northern politicians could vote to end Jim Crow in the South without antagonising their own voters. However, when King turned his attention to the racial problems of the North, the consensus collapsed.

Figure 37 Martin Luther King and Malcolm X met only once. Both were at the Senate when the Civil Rights Bill was discussed in March 1964.

Let us therefore continue our triumphant march to the realisation of the American dream. Let us march on segregated housing until every ghetto of social and economic oppression is dissolved and Negroes and whites live side by side in decent, safe, and sanitary houses. Let us march on segregated schools until every vestige of segregated and inferior education becomes a thing of the past ... Let us march on poverty ... until no starved man walks the streets of our cities and towns, in search of jobs that do not exist. Let us march on poverty until the wrinkled stomachs in Mississippi are filled..., the idle industries of Appalachia are... revitalised, and broken lives in sweltering ghettos are mended and re-moulded.

Source M Martin Luther King speaking after the success at Selma (1965).

b) Solution 2: Martin Luther King and Action in the Northern Ghettos

After playing a vitally important part in gaining the vote and desegregation for blacks in the South, King looked to the black ghettos of the North. Life in the black ghettos was usually miserable. Housing and education were poor and there was chronic unemployment. By the time King visited Los Angeles' Watts ghetto after the black riots in 1965, he was beginning to interpret the word 'freedom' in a different way. As a Southerner, preoccupied with segregation and voting laws, he had thought of democracy in the traditional American manner. To most Americans, 'democracy' and 'freedom' meant the opportunity to vote in a multi-party state and to be a citizen in a state where all were equal in the eyes of the law. For Americans, another essential component of 'freedom' was a capitalist economy, wherein there was a free market, which operated as independently as possible from state control.

King and Watts

'King, and all his talk about non-violence, did not mean much', said a Watts resident. 'Watts had respect for King, but the talk about non-violence made us laugh. Watts wasn't suffering from segregation, or the lack of civil rights. You didn't have two drinking fountains… When Johnson signed the civil rights bill in 64, nobody even thought about it in Watts … It had nothing to do with us.'

'How can you say you won, when 34 Negroes are dead, your community is destroyed, and whites are using the riots as an excuse for inaction?' King asked a group of Watts residents. 'We won because we made them pay attention to us,' they shouted back.

After the Russian Revolution in 1917, a different conception of freedom was offered in the Communist ideology. Communism and socialism had followers in America, but were never strong movements. Communists and socialists defined 'freedom' in terms of greater economic equality. Their desire for a fairer and more equal distribution of wealth was anathema to most Americans, who believed strongly in the capitalist system. Although most Americans might not be millionaires, they relished the possibility that they might become so under capitalism.

The things that Martin Luther King saw in ghettos such as Watts, coupled with his Christian religion, facilitated his conversion from an emphasis upon political freedom to an emphasis upon economic justice. He aimed now to obtain 'a better distribution of the wealth' of America. 'Things are not right in this country,' he said. 'Why are there 40 million poor people in a nation overflowing with such unbelievable affluence?' He thought no genuine professed follower of Jesus Christ ought to be comfortable with the massive differences in wealth in America, when the poorest (invariably ethnic minorities) lived in Third World-style squalor in ghettos. He thought that if he used the methods that had served him so well in his crusade in the South – marches and publicity – he would be able somehow to achieve improvements.

He was wrong. His 1966 sojourn in Chicago's ghetto gained publicity but, while Northern whites and the Northern white churches were often keen supporters of change in the South (which was painless to them), they did not want to pay the extra taxes that would be needed to help improve black ghetto life. Nor did Northern whites want to suffer the drop in housing prices that inevitably occurred if blacks moved into their neighbourhood. Northern whites remained keen to maintain the Northern style of *de facto* segregation whereby blacks remained in the ghettos. Improvement would cost too much. Many Northern whites were as racist and unsympathetic as white Southern civic leaders. Chicago's Mayor Daley resented King's incursion into his city in 1966 and was determined not to give him meaningful and lasting concessions. Most white Chicagoans seemed to agree with Daley. 'I have been in many demonstrations all across the South, but I have never seen in Alabama and Mississippi mobs as hostile and hate-filled as I have seen in Chicago', King said.

In King's 1967 book *Where Do We Go From Here?* he asked a question that he could not successfully answer. In the months before his assassination he was talking about a multi-racial anti-poverty movement, but he admitted his Poor People's Campaign 'just isn't working. People aren't responding'. King sounded increasingly like Malcolm X when he warned his country that unless it started to use its great wealth 'to lift God's children from the dungeons of despair and poverty, then you are writing your own obituary... The judgement of God is on America now.'

In many ways, King the Southerner did wonders for his native region. However, in many ways it was left to Northerners such as Malcolm X to appeal to ghetto dwellers, if not to whites.

c) Solution 3: Black Assertiveness and Violence

As the twentieth century wore on, blacks in both the North and the South became increasingly assertive. Encouraged and stimulated by black role models (such as Marcus Garvey), external events (such as two world wars wherein Americans claimed to fight for freedom), and by the relative slowness in improvement in their condition, increasing numbers of blacks aimed to do something to change their lives.

i) The South

In the early 1960s, young black Southern activists joined CORE or SNCC. They were frequently attacked and hurt in their protests. When SNCC and CORE activists tried to register black voters in the

It's much easier to integrate lunch counters than it is to eradicate slums. It's much easier to guarantee the right to vote than it is to guarantee an annual minimum income and create jobs.

Source N Martin Luther King on the difference between reforming the South and the North.

WHAT EXACTLY WAS 'BLACK POWER'?

The *New York Times* said, 'Nobody knows what the phrase "black power" really means'. CORE director Floyd McKissick said it meant 'political power, economic power, and a new self image for Negroes'. Martin Luther King said, 'I think black power is an attempt to develop black pride... We must never be ashamed of being black... Negroes have to acquire a *share* of power so that they can act in their own interests'. However, King was concerned about the phrase: 'When you put *black* and *power* together, it sounds like you are trying to say black domination. I don't think anything could be more tragic for the civil rights movement than the idea that the black man can solve his problems all by himself.'

Mississippi Summer Project of 1964, thousands of them were beaten up. Not surprisingly, when faced with white violence, blacks began to talk threateningly of 'black power'.

During the Meredith March (1966) Martin Luther King had his first direct clash with fellow activists who rejected his non-violent approach. The aim of the March was to demonstrate support for black student James Meredith. Meredith had been shot when trying to walk that route to demonstrate that blacks now had nothing to fear and should register to vote. By 1966, SNCC and CORE were far more militant. Their participation in the Meredith March caused NAACP and the National Urban League to withdraw. SNCC and CORE had been embittered by the lack of federal protection when their activists tried to encourage voter registration in the Mississippi Freedom Summer of 1964. Now, on the Meredith March, the new SNCC leader Stokely Carmichael demanded 'black power' as SNCC members sang,

Jingle bells, shotgun shells,

Freedom all the way,

Oh what fun it is to blast,

Source O | *A (white) trooper man away.*

Martin Luther King disliked the words 'black power'. He felt they went against the idea of the integrationist America of which he dreamed. He felt that Carmichael had sabotaged an opportunity to use a morally justifiable and peaceful march to expose Mississippi racism and the need for another Civil Rights Act. However, it was Malcolm X more than Stokely Carmichael who had possessed the capacity to inspire support – and violence.

I am black and beautiful.

Source P Martin Luther King on being black.

ii) The North: Malcom X

Malcolm X was the most important voice of 'black power'. While much of King's support came from the black middle class, Malcolm's followers were poor ghetto blacks. In order to understand Malcolm, a great deal of attention must be paid to his background. As he and Martin Luther King represented two different methods for dealing with black problems, it is illuminating to compare them.

Martin Luther King was brought up in a very happy, middle-class, Christian family. He had an excellent education. King had great appeal for other middle-class blacks. The relatively prosperous and successful black middle class favoured integration. Malcolm X's family background was different. Although, like King, Malcolm's father was a Baptist minister, the two fathers had different political

WHO DID BLACKS PREFER – MARTIN OR MALCOLM?

The *New York Times* conducted a survey, asking blacks who they considered did the best work for blacks. Malcolm was disappointed – 75 per cent chose King, and only 6 per cent chose Malcolm.

ideas. 'Daddy' King supported NAACP, while Malcolm's father supported UNIA. While NAACP worked for integration, UNIA emphasised separatism. While NAACP worked through the system (for example in the law courts), UNIA seemed to reject it. UNIA members dreamed of a return to Africa. It was therefore not surprising that Malcolm rejected King's integrationism, and aimed for separatism. It is equally unsurprising that Malcolm rejected King's non-violence teaching. Malcolm contended that non-violence disarmed the oppressed, but King claimed it disarmed the oppressor by working on his conscience and leaving him unsure as to what to do. Given Malcolm's background, however, it was hard for him to accept that. Unlike King, Malcolm claimed he came from a family background characterised by violence. Malcolm's father beat his wife and children, and according to Malcolm, a (surprising) number of his relations were murdered by white racists. When Malcolm's mother was widowed and could not cope, Malcolm and his siblings went hungry and ended up as wards of the state. Malcolm began a pattern of delinquency that led him through drink, drugs, pimping, armed robbery in the Boston and New York City ghettos to a ten year jail sentence.

Jail transformed Malcolm. He converted to the **Nation of Islam**. The Nation of Islam was a black American religion that had been established in Detroit by Wallace Fard in 1930, and then led by **Elijah Muhammad**, a former Baptist preacher from Georgia. Once released from jail, Malcolm quickly became the Nation's best and most famous preacher. The religion stressed the evil nature of the white man. As blacks were good and whites were evil, it made sense for them to live separately. The religion gave black people self-esteem. These beliefs were particularly comforting to Malcolm. They confirmed the rejection of whites and their civilisation that had characterised Malcolm's Garveyite childhood and his criminal phase. Malcolm won recruits for the Nation of Islam in Detroit (1953), then Boston, Philadelphia, and New York City (1954). Malcolm's rally speeches were extreme. He scoffed at the dream of integration. 'Imagine, you'll have a chance to go to the toilet with white folks!' He famously demonstrated his growing power and charisma to frightened white policeman in New York City in 1957. A policeman had beaten up a black Muslim. Malcolm gathered a threatening crowd of 800 blacks who only dispersed when the policemen assured Malcolm that the black Muslim was getting good medical care and that his assailant would be punished. 'No man should have that much power', said one leading policeman. At this stage, Malcolm's aims were to convert blacks to the Nation of Islam, wherein he believed they could be saved from a life of crime such as he had had, and they could regain pride in themselves and their race as he had.

MALCOLM AND MARCUS GARVEY

When Malcolm's father took him to UNIA meetings, the young Malcolm was inspired. He loved chanting Garvey's rallying cry at the meetings: 'Up, you mighty race, you can accomplish what you will'.

> He taught me that I was more than a 'Little Black Sambo' or 'kinky hair' or 'nigger'.

Source Q A Harlem woman on Malcolm X.

THE NATION OF ISLAM AND ISLAM

Elijah Muhammad was the sole authority for defining doctrine and practice in the Nation of Islam. He said his religion was a part of the Islamic movement, but his anti-white doctrines were unique to the Nation of Islam and a distinctive product of the bitter black American experience.

THE TEACHINGS OF ELIJAH MUHAMMAD

▽ Work hard.

▽ Live a puritanical life, for example, reject sex out-side marriage.

▽ Help other blacks.

▽ Keep out of politics.

▽ Carry no weapons; use violence only if attacked.

▽ Keep separate from whites.

Like Malcolm and Martin Luther King, Elijah Muhammad aimed to improve the lives of ghetto blacks. Elijah Muhammad identified whites as the root of blacks' problems. Therefore, to improve their lives, blacks should separate from whites.

MALCOLM X AND CHRISTIANITY

Malcolm disliked what those who called themselves Christians did, rather than Christianity itself. He equat-ed Christianity in contempo-rary America with 'white supremacy', and saw it as a religion 'designed to fill [black] hearts with the desire to be white'. 'A white Jesus. A white virgin. White angels. White everything. But a black Devil of course.'

Martin Luther King and Separatism

Martin Luther King always believed in the desirability of an inte-grated America in which all participated in the American dream. Interestingly, however, like all other black ministers, he made no real effort to integrate his own church. In the last months of his life, King began to articulate the idea that in order to gain ulti-mate integration and equality, blacks needed to remain united and temporarily separate so that their complaints could be heard. Blacks 'don't want to be integrated out of power', he said in 1967. 'There may be periods where segregation may be a temporary way station to an integrated society.' Why did King apparently move from integrationism toward separatism? It was partly the emphasis of people like Malcolm X on separatism and partly a result of King's disappointment in white America's response to his plea for help for the ghettos.

Malcolm and Elijah Muhammad first received nationwide news coverage in a CBS television documentary entitled, *The Hate that Hate Produced*. The TV programme accused Malcolm of 'black racism' and aiming for 'black supremacy'. Malcolm's aims were not always clear to others. He told a reporter that while he and King both aimed to save America from its racism, they had different methods. Malcolm disliked the methods adopted by the more traditional black activists. Malcolm described organisations such as NAACP as white man's organisations, full of 'Uncle Toms'. He criticised CORE and the Freedom Riders, saying they would do better to concentrate upon Northern ghettos. Malcolm criticised Martin Luther King as a white man's Negro. He said only a fool would say love the enemy who had treated blacks so badly. He felt King and Christian teachings here were 'criminal' in that they would encourage white violence against submissive blacks. Whenever whites mistreated black protesters, Malcolm said, 'the Negroes themselves should take whatever steps are necessary to defend themselves'.

Malcolm addressed audiences of thousands at rallies in New York City, Chicago, and Washington, several times a year. Thanks to Malcolm, membership of the Nation of Islam rose from several thou-sands to 40,000. At this stage, Malcolm's aims were those of the Nation of Islam. The Nation of Islam urged blacks to grow their own food, produce their own manufactured goods, have their own stores, and aim at the development of an independent black nation. Muslim schools wherein children learned black history were established in cities such as Detroit and Chicago. Malcolm thought it very important that children should learn black history: 'We are lost people. We don't know our name, language, homeland, God, or religion.' The Nation of Islam worked hard to help drug addicts. 'What is looked upon as an American dream for white people has long been an American nightmare for black people', said Malcolm. He and the Nation of Islam rejected integration and advocated separatism: 'We can establish our own government and become an independent nation.'

In March 1964, Malcolm left the Nation of Islam. He had fallen out with Elijah Muhammad over several issues:

▼ Elijah Muhammad had a weakness for the ladies, and unlike Malcolm, proved unable to stick to the strict moral code of the Nation of Islam.

▼ Malcolm wanted to make political speeches, to which the Nation of Islam was opposed. For example, on hearing of President Kennedy's assassination, Malcolm was critical of him because of Kennedy's failure to do much to help blacks. Elijah Muhammad thought that would make the Nation of Islam unpopular.

▼ Elijah Muhammad was jealous of Malcolm's greater fame and influence. Perhaps the most important division between Malcolm and Elijah Muhammad was the disagreements over methods. Both aimed to improve black lives, but Malcolm had come to the conclusion that political participation, or at least political commentary, was the method most likely to achieve the desired aim. Free at last, Malcolm made political speeches. He said that if the political, economic and social disadvantages of blacks were not removed, 'a bloodbath is on its way in America'. Malcolm began to move closer to the civil rights activists. He began to indicate, privately and apparently happily, that his extremism must be helping Martin Luther King, as it made King a far more acceptable alternative to whites. It now seems that one of Malcolm's aims was to frighten whites into treating blacks better. His aims and methods were evolving and changing.

A 1964 visit to Mecca further changed Malcolm. He saw black and white Muslims cooperating. Ironically, just as he was ready to be more tolerant of whites, whites were blaming him for ghetto riots. While Malcolm said he was willing to work with anyone of any colour so long as they aimed to help American blacks, Harlem erupted with cries of 'Whitey, we gonna get you!' Those were cries that Malcolm had helped inspire. He still urged blacks to defend themselves if necessary, so that he remained hated by whites. He was also unacceptable to the Nation of Islam, which he increasingly attacked in his speeches. He was assassinated in 1965, probably by members of the Nation of Islam.

What had Malcolm X achieved? After his death, 20,000 Harlem blacks filed past his coffin. There were condolences from all the

MALCOLM X ON 'LOVING' THE WHITE ENEMY

White reporters frequently asked Malcolm if he hated whites:

> For the white man to ask the black man if he hates him is just like the rapist asking the raped, or the wolf asking the sheep, 'Do you hate me?' The white man is in no moral position to accuse anyone else of hate!...Mr Muhammad teaches that if the present generation of whites would study their own race in the light of their true history [practising slavery, lynching, etc.], they would be anti-white themselves... History is not hatred.

Source R

> We ain't going nowhere.

Source S Martin Luther King on the dream of returning to Africa.

MALCOLM X ON BEING CALLED A TROUBLE-MAKER

'My hobby is stirring up Negroes'. He liked being called 'the angriest Negro in America'.

I'm black first. My sympathies are black, my allegiance is black, my whole objectives are black... I am not interested in being American, because America has never been interested in me... We're not Americans, we're Africans who happened to be in America. We were kidnapped and brought here against our will from Africa.

Source U Malcolm X on being an American.

I'm not a racist. I believe in human beings.

Source V Malcolm X on being a racist.

Yes, I am an extremist. The black race in North America is in extremely bad condition.

Source W Malcolm X on being an extremist.

Martin Luther King on Malcolm X

Maybe he *does* have some of the answer. I don't know how he feels now, but I know that I have often wished that he would talk less of violence, because violence is not going to solve our problem. And in his litany of articulating the despair of the Negro without offering any positive, creative alternative, I feel that Malcolm has done himself and our people a great disservice. Fiery, demagogic oratory in the black ghettos, urging Negroes to arm themselves and prepare to engage in violence, as he has done, can reap nothing but grief.

Source T

black civil rights organisations and many foreign leaders. He increased black ghetto pride but probably also increased black violence. In 1965 Watts rioters cried, 'Long-live Malcolm X'. Bobby Seale said he and his fellow Black Panthers 'felt ourselves to be the heirs of Malcolm X'. Malcolm was a realistic role model for ghetto blacks. They could relate to him. He had changed himself from pimp, cocaine addict, armed robber and convict, into a world-famous black leader who, once converted, in some ways lived more strictly by the rules of his religion than did Martin Luther King. While King preached chastity but had a string of affairs, Malcolm was a faithful husband. However, history usually records Martin Luther King as a success, and Malcolm X as a failure. History it is often said is written by the 'winners'. White American historians generally subscribe, in varying degrees, to the American dream. They naturally feel more kinship with Martin Luther King than with Malcolm. Furthermore, King set himself concrete and attainable targets in the South. However, King was as much of a failure as Malcolm in the North. Neither of them had the answer to the problems of the Northern ghettos. King's answer was always to try to arouse the conscience of America by publicising ghetto conditions. Initially, Malcolm's solution was separatism, but neither a return to Africa nor a separate black nation within the United States were feasible. Malcolm often seemed to be suggesting violence, or at the very least self-defence, as a possible method whereby separatism could be attained. However, as King knew, given the very limited resources of blacks and the massive military and repressive capacity of the US government, Malcolm's methods, just like his aims, did not always make sense. Towards the end of his life, it seems clear that Malcolm, like Martin Luther King, was aiming to draw attention to ghetto problems. Sadly, neither Malcolm nor Martin found this a very productive method.

iii) The North: Black Power

'Black power' survived the death of Malcolm, and indeed seemed to grow temporarily stronger. By 1966 SNCC had moved away from King to support 'black power'. SNCC and CORE began to exclude whites from membership and activities.

Black Riots

From 1964 to 1968 the black city ghettos of the North, Midwest and West witnessed around 300 riots. The numbers involved and the damage done frightened and alienated white Americans. For example, after Martin Luther King's assassination by a white racist, there were major riots in 100 cities, with 46 dead, 3,000 injured and 27,000 arrested. It took 21,000 federal troops and 34,000 National Guardsmen to restore order. $145 million worth of property was damaged. Black ghettos in cities such as Chicago, Philadelphia and Newark had effectively become no-go areas for whites.

Figure 38 A looted store in Watts, after the 1965 riots.

Some blacks and whites interpreted 'black power' as meaning black violence. However, as King feared, black violence achieved little, other than a white backlash. Blacks working within the system, like King, helped to achieve vital civil rights legislation. However, for militant young radicals like the founders of the Black Panthers in Oakland, California, the legislation was too little too late. Black Panthers such as Huey Newton, Bobby Seale, and Eldridge Cleaver

---

CONTEMPORARY OBITUARIES FOR MALCOLM X

'the spokesman of bitter racism' – *Washington Post*
'an extravagant talker, a demagogue who titillated slum Negroes and frightened whites with his blazing racist attacks on the "white devils"' – *Newsweek*
'an unashamed demagogue whose gospel was hatred and who in life and in death was a disaster to the civil rights movement' – *Time*
'irresponsible demagogue, an extraordinary and twisted man who turned true gifts to evil purpose' – *New York Times*
'a petty punk who pictured himself as a heroic figure' – *Journal American*
'the highly intelligent, courageous leader of one segment of the Negro lunatic fringe' – *Nation*
'If Malcolm were not a Negro, his autobiography would be little more than a journal of abnormal psychology, the story of a burglar, dope pusher, addict and jailbird – with a family history of insanity – who acquires messianic delusions and sets forth to preach an upside-down religion of "brotherly hatred"' – *Saturday Evening Post*
'professional race-baiter' – *Washington Afro-American*
'cowardly hypocritical dog who is worthy of death' – Louis Farrakhan (subsequent leader of the Nation of Islam)
'talented demagogue' – James Farmer of CORE

MARTIN LUTHER KING ON BLACK PRIDE AND VIOLENCE

'We must believe... that [we] are somebody... Too many Negroes... are ashamed of their black and brown skin.'

In 1963 he said he admired the 'magnificent new militancy' in the black community. He said he could 'understand' the 'doctrine of black supremacy', because 'we have been pushed around so long'. However, as a Christian, he stressed that 'God is interested in the freedom of the whole human race'. Violence, he said, would get many blacks killed and give whites an excuse to do nothing but continue repression.

ACTIVITIES

1. Make notes that re-arrange the material on Malcolm X in this section into three categories – aims, methods and achievements.

2. Head two columns 'Martin Luther King' and 'Malcolm X'. Note down as many similarities and differences between the two men as you can think of.

issued the clarion call, 'Power to the People'. At rallies, Panthers chanted, 'The revolution has come – time to pick up the gun'. Black Panthers stockpiled weapons for self-defence against police brutality. They rejected the dominant white culture of America, and sported 'Afro' haircuts. The Black Panthers' practical community action programmes won them support amongst ghetto blacks. Black Panthers served free breakfasts to poor black children, established healthcare clinics, and provided childcare for working mothers. The Black Panthers gained national prominence, with chapters in 33 major American cities.

However, white Americans noted only the 'black power' talk of violence, and equated militant black activists with the annual outbreaks of urban rioting. Black violence might have increased black esteem in the short-term (in 1966 even Mississippi blacks staged a 'black power' march) but there were no long-term gains. The 1968 Civil Rights Act aimed at the elimination of discrimination in housing, and declared violation of civil rights to be a federal crime. However, Southern congressmen tacked on the 'Rap Brown' addition (named after a Black Panther activist) which made it a federal offence to cross state lines 'to further a riot'. The housing provision of the act had little impact on the ghettos, but the Rap Brown rider became a vital tool in the prosecution and destruction of leading black activists by the government. By 1969, the federal government had destroyed the Black Panther leadership through infiltration, intimidation and arrests. Possibly the Black Panthers helped to leave a legacy of greater awareness of black culture and history, which culminated in more black studies in educational institutions. However, as King feared, their most important achievement was probably to return the moral high ground to whites who, while they could be made ashamed of their racism by Martin Luther King and non-violence, could joyfully exploit black ghetto violence to say 'enough is enough' – there should be no more great federal aid programmes for blacks.

d) Solution 4: Federal Government Intervention

During the course of the twentieth century many blacks and whites concluded that the most important factor in bringing about change and improvement for blacks would be the federal government in Washington DC. The actions of the Roosevelt administration during the Depression confirmed this faith in the ability of the federal government to assist disadvantaged Americans. NAACP concentrated for many decades upon using the law courts to try to gain Supreme Court decisions that would bring greater civic equality for blacks. Martin Luther King shared that belief that Washington was the key to progress. It was indeed crucial in bringing about the demise of Jim Crow in the South, with Supreme Court decisions such as *Brown* (1954) and legislation such as the Civil Rights Act of 1964 and the Voting Rights Act of 1965. Winning over the general public was also important, and here the media played a vital role. A CBS-TV spokesman said, 'Certainly the conditions were already there, but no one knew it until 50 million Americans began seeing it on their screens.' Federal government intervention was of course limited by what the white electorate would stand. There came a point in the Johnson administration when the president could no longer rely on Congress (whose members were worried about their white constituents and re-election) to improve the situation of America's racial minorities. The point at which Congress effectively said 'no more' was when black activists focused their attention on the ghettos of the North.

We have seen that Martin Luther King's rhetoric had the ability to engender feelings of guilt and sympathy in white Christian America. Those feelings helped create sufficient national support for the abuses in the South to be resolved by the Civil Rights Act of 1964 and the Voting Rights Act of 1965. However, when King sought to elicit guilt, sympathy and legislation to improve the situation in the black ghettos of the North, he failed. There were some sympathetic whites, among them President Johnson. However, it was not enough. Johnson famously wanted to wage a 'War on Poverty'. The Civil Rights Act of 1964 established the Office of Economic Opportunity (OEO) which gave one billion dollars to local black leaders to try to aid ghetto blacks and to make the new Black Power movement less appealing to them. However, to Johnson's dismay, his attempts to help were deemed by many whites to be encouraging excessively high expectations and riots amongst ghetto blacks. In summer 1965, five days after the Voting Rights Act was passed, 10,000 blacks in the Watts ghetto of Los Angeles rioted for six days, resulting in 34 deaths, 875 injured, 4,000 arrested, and 209 buildings destroyed. Amid cries of 'Burn, baby, burn', white-owned cars and shops were set on fire. Johnson tried again. He launched Head Start, a programme to help black schoolchildren catch up with the more advantaged children. He introduced the Child Nutrition Act which provided free breakfasts for poor children. However, rioting continued and, significantly, Congress refused to pass the 1966 Civil Rights Act. 1967 saw more riots, and Johnson's Advisory Commission reported that the main causes were police racism and repression, black unemployment, and poor housing and education. 'Our nation is moving towards two societies', the Kerner Report concluded, 'one black, one white – separate and unequal'. The 1968 Civil Rights Act did little to help blacks in the ghettos and a lot to help the federal government quash black rad-

THE VOTING RIGHTS ACT, 1965

There had been many previous measures to try to help blacks vote, for example, Eisenhower's Civil Rights Acts. However, it was the 1965 one that really worked. The act gave the federal government the power to send representatives into an area and to put the names of black citizens on the voting rolls.

THE KU KLUX KLAN IN THE 1960S

Johnson asked Congress to investigate the Ku Klux Klan, whom he called a 'hooded society of bigots'. The investigation found the Ku Klux Klan had 381 Klavens (chapters) in the South, and in six Northern states. It found that many members belonged to the local police forces, and that some had plotted to assassinate Johnson.

icals. After a white extremist assassinated Martin Luther King, in April 1968, 125 city ghettos exploded again. Forty-six died, 2,600 were injured, and 21,270 were arrested. Sixty-seven million dollars worth of property was damaged. In Washington DC, the violence nearly reached the White House, and Stokely Carmichael told black crowds, 'Go home and get your guns! When the white man comes he is coming to kill you. I don't want any black blood in the street!' Black Panther leader Rap Brown said, 'We must move from resistance to aggression, from revolt to revolution!'

Johnson's 'War on Poverty' was hit by a white backlash against these riots, and by the ever-increasing costs of the Vietnam War. Welfare payments and food aid were cut. Doctors reported to a 1969 congressional hearing that a considerable number of black children in Mississippi were eating tree bark, laundry starch and clay. The federal intervention solution could not solve the economic problems, either in impoverished rural regions in the South, or in the ghettos of the North.

Hispanic Americans in the Civil Rights Era

By the 1960s, increased mechanisation in agriculture had led around half of the Mexican American population to live in *barrios* (Mexican American communities) in South-western cities such as El Paso, Texas, and Los Angeles, California. These *barrios* were very similar to the black ghettos, but there were no Mexican American riots. Why? Suggested answers include greater ethnic pride (as demonstrated, for example, on Mexican Independence Day), greater family stability, and the ability to enter 'mainstream' American society due to relatively light-coloured skin. Mexican-Americans slowly became more active, for example, trade union leader Cesar Chavez, whom Bobby Kennedy described as 'one of the heroic figures of our time'.

ACTIVITY

Look up some black female activists, and assess their contribution to the civil rights movement. Two famous examples are Ella Baker and Fannie Lou Hamer.

ISSUE:
To what extent had race relations improved by 2000?

5 American Race Relations at the End of the Twentieth Century

In the last quarter of the twentieth century ever-increasing numbers of blacks participated in local and national political life. Major Northern and Southern cities such as Atlanta, Chicago, Detroit, Los Angeles, Newark, New Orleans, and Washington DC elected black mayors. As with all special interest groups, blacks found that participation in politics sometimes brought gains and sometimes brought nothing.

However, many blacks continue to participate in politics. They are the spiritual and political descendants of men like Martin Luther King, who favoured integration into the American dream. The integrationists believe that the solution to America's racial problems is to be found by operating within the American system, wherein political participation and economic success are important.

Much depended on the sympathies and political party of the president. President Richard Nixon worked against **bussing**, which was necessary if schools were to be integrated. However, Nixon also embraced 'affirmative action', whereby blacks were given advantages over whites with regard to employment, in order to offset the disadvantages that frequently resulted from their family background. Nixon's Republican successors Ronald Reagan and George Bush (Senior) had little sympathy for ethnic minorities, and did little to help them. Indeed Reagan and Bush played on white racism to gain white votes. Reagan and Bush appointees on the Supreme Court helped erode affirmative action in decisions in the 1990s.

> **BUSSING**
> Bussing was the transportation of pupils to non-neighbourhood schools in order to ensure that schools were racially mixed.

Race relations remained tense in late twentieth century America. The best examples of this were two Californian legal cases involving black males. In 1991, Rodney King was beaten up by four white policemen. The white jury found the policemen 'not guilty', which led to riots in black areas of Los Angeles. In 1994 black footballer and movie star (in the *Naked Gun* series) O.J. Simpson was tried for the murder of his white wife. A black jury found him innocent, but most white Americans considered him to be guilty.

Thus, as the Kerner report predicted, America is a racially divided society. Although blacks have greater political power, the NAACP still claimed that black voters were effectively disfranchised in Florida in the 2000 presidential election. The Northern, Western and Midwestern ghettos remain a blot on the wealthiest nation in the world. The ghettos are characterised by poverty, fear, unemployment, crime, drugs and one-parent households. They remain as they were (if not worse than) when Martin Luther King went to Chicago in 1966. Housing and schooling remain effectively segregated in many places throughout America. The unpopular bussing experiment did not last. Blacks constitute a disproportionate number of America's poor. On the other hand, there is a growing black American middle class. Some estimate it to be nearly one-third of America's 30 million blacks.

The pattern is similar with Native Americans and Hispanic Americans. Native Americans for the most part prefer the separatist solution. Sixty-eight per cent of them remain on reservations, which one writer described as open-air slums. Inspired by the methods and achievements of the black civil rights movement, they forced the federal government into improving life on Native American reservations. However, for the most part they remain amongst the poorest areas in the United States. Hispanic Americans are the fastest-growing ethnic minority in the United States. The majority of Hispanic Americans live in ghettos in conditions similar to those of black people. However, as with blacks and Native Americans, Hispanic Americans have become more proud of their culture, more assertive and more politically active during the last half-century.

Thus Martin Luther King's American dream has yet to be realised by all. Some still experience Malcolm X's American nightmare.

▼ Working on Twentieth Century Race Relations

Create a chart, with dates down the left side, and headings across the top (suggested headings – North, South, NAACP, CORE, SNCC, SCLC, other black organisations, court cases, legislation, extremism and violence, important individuals, national crises, factors helping progress, factors hindering progress). As you fill in what is happening in each year, you might see patterns emerging that help you to understand when and why there was progress (or not).

Answering Extended Writing and Essay Questions on Twentieth Century Race Relations

This is a structured question of the kind you might answer in Year 12:
(a) What was the situation of American blacks in 1900?
(b) How much had their situation improved by 2000?
The longer essays of Year 13 can often be approached as a combination of two structured questions. The two questions above would become:
To what extent did the situation of American blacks improve in the twentieth century?
It is helpful to try to break down a long essay question into several possible shorter structured questions.

Answering Source-based Questions on Twentieth Century Race Relations

Source i W.E.B. Du Bois, writing in *The Conservation of Races*, 1897.

Here, then, is the dilemma. What, after all, am I? Am I an American or am I a Negro? Can I be both?

Unity as a people, pride in African heritage, the creation of autonomous institutions, and the search for a territory to build a nation were the central ingredients which shaped the early development of the nationalist consciousness… The central claim of all black nationalists, past and present, is that black people are primarily Africans and not Americans… In place of an American dream, nationalists gave the black poor an African dream… In the teaching of Elijah Muhammad (and in Garvey's before him) rejection of white values was expressed in hostility toward integrationism. The solution to the problem of race [according to Elijah Muhammad] is separation, not integration. Black nationalism thrives among poor blacks who have lost all hope in white society and its claims about freedom and justice for all. They know the difference between words about freedom in religious and political documents and their experience of being locked in the ghetto. Unable to see any good whatsoever in whites, black nationalists turn to their own cultural heritage for support of their identity as human beings in a white world that does not recognise black people as persons. Malcolm's experience in the ghetto taught him that the black masses could be neither integrationist nor non-violent. Integration and nonviolence assumed some measure of political order, a moral conscience in the society, and a religious and human sensitivity regarding the dignity and value of all persons. But since the masses in the ghettos saw no evidence of a political order that recognised their humanity or a moral conscience among white people, an appeal to integration and nonviolence sounded like a trick to delude and disarm poor blacks, so whites would not have to worry about the revenge for response to their brutality. Integration was the way of the college-educated, the professional Negro elites whose value system and preoccupation with success was similar to the whites with whom they were seeking to integrate. In the ghetto, where survival was an arduous task and violence was an everyday experience, nonviolence was not a meaningful option and most even regarded the promotion of it as a sign of weakness and lack of courage.

Source ii James Cone, a black professor of theology, in *Martin and Malcolm and America: A Dream or a Nightmare*, New York, 1999.

We are simply seeking to bring into full realisation the American dream – a dream yet unfulfilled. A dream of equality of opportunity, of privilege and property widely distributed; a dream of a land where men no longer argue that the colour of a man's skin determines the content of his character; the dream of a land where every man will respect the dignity and worth of human personality – this is the dream.

Source iii Martin Luther King, in Washington, July 1962.

Source iv Malcolm X, speaking to a black audience, September 1962.

Many of you misunderstand us, and think that we are advocating continued segregation. No! We are as much against segregation as you are. We want separation, but not segregation. Segregation is when your life and liberty is controlled (regulated) by someone else… Segregation is that which is forced upon inferiors by superiors; but *separation is that which is done voluntarily.*

Source v Martin Luther King, speaking in New York, March 1964.

I think it is very unfortunate that Malcolm X continues to predict violence … it would be very tragic… for the Negro to use violence in any form. Many of our opponents would be delighted… if we would take up arms, it would give them an excuse to kill up a lot of us.

Source vi Malcolm X, speaking in Cleveland, Ohio, April 1964.

No, I'm not an American. I'm one of the 22 million black people who are the victims of Americanism. One of the … victims of democracy, nothing but disguised hypocrisy. So, I'm not standing here speaking to you as an American, or a patriot, or a flag-saluter, or a flag-waver – no, not I! I'm speaking as a victim of this American system. And I see America through the eyes of the victim. I don't see any American dream; I see an American nightmare!

Source vii Martin Luther King, speaking in Atlanta, Georgia, December 1967.

In 1963… in Washington, DC … I tried to talk to the nation about a dream that I had had, and I must confess… that not long after talking about that dream I started seeing it turn into a nightmare … just a few weeks after I had talked about it. It was when four beautiful … Negro girls were murdered in a church in Birmingham, Alabama. I watched that dream turn into a nightmare as I moved through the ghettos of the nation and saw black brothers and sisters perishing on a lonely island of poverty in the midst of a vast ocean of material prosperity, and saw the nation doing nothing to grapple with the Negroes' problem of poverty. I saw that dream turn into a nightmare as I watched my black brothers and sisters in the midst of anger and understandable outrage, in the midst of their hurt, in the midst of their disappointment, turn to misguided riots to try to solve that problem. I saw the dream turn into a nightmare as I watched the war in Vietnam escalating… Yes, I am personally the victim of deferred dreams, of blasted hopes.

King's… Proclamation of the 'American dream' was just about inevitable. It was quite easy for him to think of America as a dream [because of his middle-class background] and to be optimistic that it could be realised because he himself was a concrete embodiment of its realisation. He was well-educated, culturally refined, and politically aware … King believed that fear was the primary reason the majority of whites had not advocated the full integration of Negroes into their society … Men often hate each other because they fear each other; they fear each other because they do not know each other; they do not know each other because they cannot communicate; they cannot communicate because they are separated… King's life represented only one side of the African-American experience, the *American* side. The *African* side was represented in the life of Malcolm X. As King's early life shows the bright (American), integrationist side of the African-American struggle, Malcolm X's early life shows its dark (African), nationalist side.

Source viii James Cone, *Martin and Malcolm*, p. 37.

▼ QUESTIONS ON SOURCES

1. Using sources i–viii on pages 196–9, explain the difference between a black nationalist/separatist and a black integrationist. **[5 marks]**
2. Using the sources, suggest reasons why Malcolm X was a nationalist/separatist and King was an integrationist. **[10 marks]**
3. What evidence of differences and similarities between Malcolm and Martin Luther King can you find in the sources? **[10 marks]**
4. Using the sources and your knowledge, explain which methods were the most successful in improving the lives of blacks in the 1960s. **[25 marks]**

Further Reading

Books in the Access to History series
For a more detailed study of twentieth century American race relations, see V. Sanders, *Race Relations in the USA since 1900.*

General
Robert Cook's *Sweet Land of Liberty?* (Longman, 1998), and W.T.M. Riches' *The Civil Rights Movement* (Macmillan, 1997), are good scholarly introductions easily accessible to the British student. James Cone's *Martin and Malcolm and America: A Dream or a Nightmare* (Orbis, 1999), is a brilliant comparative study. Jules Archer, *They Had a Dream* (Puffin, 1993), is an easy read, using the traditional American biographical approach to history. David Garrow's *Bearing the Cross* (Vintage, 1993), is a long but rewarding study of Martin Luther King.

THE COLD WAR (1945–90)

POINTS TO CONSIDER

For roughly half a century, relations between the world's two greatest powers (the United States and the USSR) were exceptionally tense. You need to consider the causes and consequences of the sustained tension, and how attempts were made to improve relations. There are several areas and crises that need particular attention, especially Germany, Korea and Cuba (for Vietnam, see Chapter 7).

ISSUES:
What do we mean by 'Cold War'? When and why was there a Cold War?

1 Introduction

a) What is Meant by 'Cold' War?

The armies of the USA and USSR never met in the way that American forces had faced Germans and Japanese in the Second World War. This was because new (nuclear) weaponry made the prospect of war too terrifying. Although the USA and USSR came close, they never used nuclear weapons against each other. Instead, they expressed their hostility by stockpiling the nuclear weapons, and giving varying degrees of economic and military aid to win over other countries.

How Do Historians Define the Cold War?

a state of extreme tension between the superpowers, stopping short of all-out war but characterised by mutual hostility and involvement in covert warfare and war by proxy as a means of upholding the interests of one against the other. The Cold War remained 'cold' because the development of nuclear weapons had made resort to war a suicidal enterprise …The resulting tensions…ensured that both sides…maintained a high and continuous state of readiness for war.

Source A Michael Dockrill

The Cold War was a traditional contest between two great powers, accentuated by the role of ideology and transformed by the scope of the weapons of mass destruction available.

Source B Peter Lowe

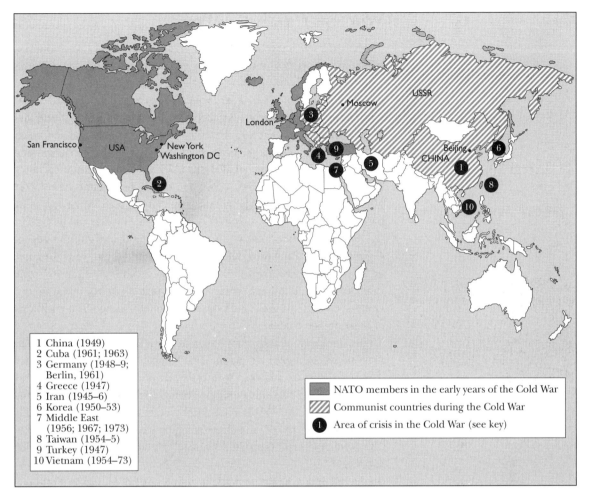

1 China (1949)
2 Cuba (1961; 1963)
3 Germany (1948–9;
  Berlin, 1961)
4 Greece (1947)
5 Iran (1945–6)
6 Korea (1950–53)
7 Middle East
  (1956; 1967; 1973)
8 Taiwan (1954–5)
9 Turkey (1947)
10 Vietnam (1954–73)

⬛ NATO members in the early years of the Cold War
▨ Communist countries during the Cold War
① Area of crisis in the Cold War (see key)

Figure 39 The Cold War world.

b) What Were the Dates of the Cold War?

Historians disagree over when the Cold War started. Did it begin in 1917 with the Russian Revolution? Or during the Second World War? Or, more likely, soon after the Second World War? It is clear that Roosevelt and Stalin were on quite good terms at Yalta in early 1945, but that by 1947 relations were extremely tense. Historians also disagree over whether or not there was more than one Cold War. Some historians say there was a Cold War in Europe, another Cold War in Asia, and one in the Third World. Some contend that a first Cold War lasted from around 1947 to the early 1970s. They say a second Cold War developed during Ronald Reagan's first term as president (1981–5) and ended either with the Reagan–Gorbachev friendship, or with the collapse of the USSR and its empire (1989–91).

WHAT WAS A SUPERPOWER?
The term 'superpower' became popular in the West in the 1950s. It was applied to the United States and the Soviet Union because they were by far the most important military powers in the world.

ACTIVITY

Re-read pages 150–53 on the origins of the Cold War.

c) Why Was There a Cold War?

▼ There had been antagonism between Russia and America since the late nineteenth century. The tension was exacerbated when Russia became Communist and when America intervened in the Russian Revolution.

▼ There were ideological differences between the USSR and USA. Capitalist America wanted free access to the world's markets, and disliked Communist belief in a state-controlled economy and the equal distribution of wealth. America favoured a multi-party democracy while Soviet Communism denied the need for other political parties.

▼ Although the two countries were allied during the Second World War (1941–5) there were disagreements over issues such as the future of Eastern Europe.

▼ By 1945 the US was clearly the most powerful country in the world. Germany and Japan were defeated, Britain and France were exhausted. With Stalin's Red Army in Eastern Europe, some Americans thought the USSR would be the great power most likely to threaten the United States. Thus the Cold War could be interpreted as a traditional great power conflict.

▼ There were misunderstandings over security. The US did not consider itself to be an aggressive power. The Truman administration felt that American security required free trade, democratic governments, and no imperialism. Stalin was convinced that Soviet security required control of Eastern Europe. The US interpreted that control of Eastern Europe as imperialistic, and threatening to free trade and democracy. The Soviets interpreted that American hostility as threatening Soviet security.

▼ Some historians blame important personalities for causing tension. Possibly Roosevelt was too sympathetic to Stalin, after which Truman seemed far more threatening to him. Churchill was always suspicious of Stalin, whom many Westerners considered to be paranoid.

▼ The Soviets were alarmed by American secrecy over the atomic bomb, the awesome power of which was demonstrated in Japan. The bomb demonstrated American technological and military supremacy.

▼ There were problems during 1945–7 over Germany, Greece, Turkey, and Iran, and also belligerent speeches from both sides, any or all of which could be said to have started the Cold War.

2 Events 1945–7

a) Negotiations Over the Atomic Bomb

ISSUE:
Which events/problems between 1945 and 1947 could be said to have started the Cold War?

In July 1945 America tested the world's first atomic bomb. Weeks later, two were dropped on Japan. Were these last acts of the Second World War the first acts of the Cold War? By summer 1945, there is no doubt that the speed of American development and use of the bomb was partly prompted by fears of the USSR. Some Americans were aware of how threatening America's atomic weapon appeared to the Soviets. Consequently, there was a great deal of discussion in Washington of possible international control of atomic weapons. These came to nothing, as the Truman administration did not want to surrender total control over its atomic monopoly.

The new weapon was highly significant. It demonstrated and increased the fear and suspicion felt by the US and the USSR towards each other and was an important cause of the Cold War.

'THE WEST'
During the Cold War, America and its allies frequently referred to themselves as 'the West', as opposed to 'the East', which consisted of the USSR and its satellite (puppet) states in Eastern Europe, and, after 1949, China.

b) Iran (Autumn 1945–Spring 1946)

In the nineteenth century, the great powers recognised northern Iran as part of Russia's sphere of interest, and southern Iran as part of Britain's. In September 1941 Britain and the USSR occupied those spheres of interest to secure oil supplies, and then repeatedly agreed to get their troops out within six months of the end of the Second World War. Roosevelt and Churchill frequently assured Stalin that his interests would be protected in post-war Iran. However, in 1944 Britain negotiated oil extraction privileges with Iran. Under British and American pressure, Iran rejected a similar agreement with the Soviets. The Soviets therefore supported an opposition group in northern Iran, on the southern borders of the USSR. At the end of the war, the British withdrew their troops, but the Soviets did not. The Soviets established an 'independent' Communist government in the north of Iran. Encouraged by the United States, Iran complained to the **United Nations** (January 1946). In March 1946 the Soviets finally agreed to get out, in exchange for oil concessions. In May, Soviet troops finally withdrew. The new northern Communist government and the Soviet-Iranian oil agreement collapsed.

The significance of the Iran crisis was:

▼ These were the first Soviet military actions outside Europe after the Second World War. The West interpreted them as hostile and expansionist.

▼ Stalin felt betrayed. The West had promised to respect his interests in Iran after the war. Stalin felt that as Iran was more vital to his security than to the West's, the West was aggressive.

THE UNITED NATIONS
After much discussion by the Allied powers during the Second World War, the new world peacekeeping organisation was established at San Francisco in June 1945, with 51 members. Within a few years, the UN found a permanent home in New York City. In its early years, the US and its allies dominated the UN. However, the collapse of West European colonialism (decolonisation) resulted in an influx of new Third World member nations. By the 1960s, US domination of the UN had clearly ended.

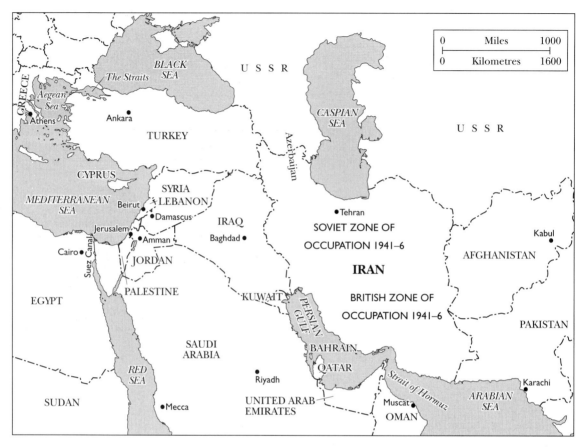

Figure 40 The Iran Crisis
(1945–6).

▼ The crisis confirmed Stalin's suspicions that anti-Soviet interests dominated the UN.

▼ The crisis increased Soviet–American tension.

▼ The crisis was one reason why Churchill made his 'Iron Curtain' speech
(March 1946), which is usually considered to be one of the declarations
of Cold War (see page 208).

c) Germany

Allied troop deployments in Germany at the end of the Second
World War roughly coincided with the planned zones of occupation.
The British and Americans retreated in order to give the Soviets their
agreed zone, then let France have part of their zones. It had been
agreed in the Second World War that the supreme authority for
Germany would be the Allied Control Council (ACC), on which sat
the military governors for the four occupied zones. Subordinated to
ACC, with responsibility for Berlin, was the Allied *Kommandatura*, on
which sat the four military governors of Berlin.

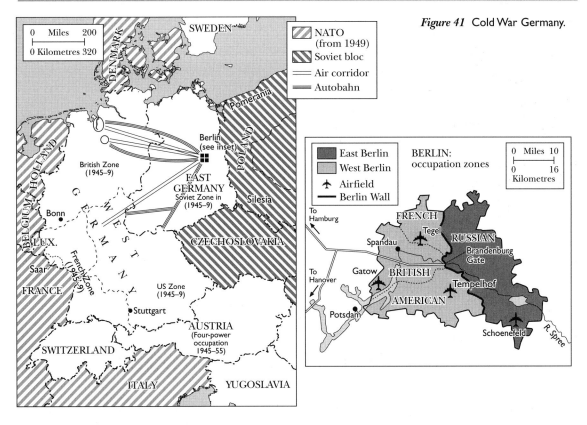

Figure 41 Cold War Germany.

During 1945 France was the most awkward participant in ACC. In early 1946, the problem of German reparations caused the first great West–Soviet Union clash in Germany. During the war the Soviets had agreed to send raw materials from their zone to the other zones, in exchange for reparations from the West's zones. However, in winter 1945–6, Britain and America had to bring in food supplies to prevent starvation in their zones. Meanwhile, the Russians plundered their zone, happily received supplies from the West's zones, and sent nothing in return. After several warnings, the Americans and British stopped deliveries from their zone to the Soviet zone (spring 1946). That led to bitterness in ACC meetings and to an important speech by Secretary of State James Byrnes at Stuttgart (September 1946). He said that American troops would remain in Europe for the foreseeable future, and that the West's zones of Germany should be economically and politically independent. When Britain and America combined their zones in January 1947 (the French joined in 1949) it was clear that the economic and political divisions of Germany were hardening. Within the Soviet zone, the Communist party was dominant, and the local press joined the Soviet press in attacks on the West.

d) Turkey and Greece

The Soviets had been understandably anxious about their access from the Black Sea to the Mediterranean through the Straits. Because Turkey dominated the Straits, Russo-Turkish relations had historically been tense. At Tehran, Churchill had been sympathetic to Russian concerns about the Straits. However, post-war Soviet pressure upon Turkey led Truman to send an American fleet to the Straits (August 1946).

In August 1946 Stalin's Foreign Minister Molotov quite reasonably pointed out that the Soviets only had troops in their 'security zone' whereas imperialist Britain's troops could be found throughout the world. The British had been helping to prop up an oppressive right-wing Greek monarchy since December 1944. There was a great deal of left-wing opposition to that monarchy, including the Greek Communist party. The West (wrongly) believed that Stalin helped those Communists.

In February 1947 severe weather aggravated British post-war economic problems. Britain told America that it could no longer help Greece and Turkey. Within days, Truman announced the 'Truman Doctrine'.

The significance of these eastern Mediterranean crises was great. Both the Soviets and the West felt that the other was guilty of aggression and the crises led to the enunciation of the Truman Doctrine. That Doctrine is generally acknowledged to be one of the declarations (and possibly the start) of the Cold War.

e) The Truman Doctrine

On 12 March 1947 Truman made a speech to Congress, the contents of which became known as the Truman Doctrine. He said Greece and Turkey were threatened by Communist aggression. Truman asked for $250 million to help Greece, and $150 million for Turkey. Congress granted it.

The Truman Doctrine

The very existence of the Greek state is today threatened by…Communists … Greece must have assistance if it is to become a self-supporting and self-respecting democracy. The United States must supply that assistance. There is no other country to which Greece can turn. At the present moment in world history nearly every nation must choose between alternative ways of life. The choice is too often not a free one. One way of life is based upon the will of the majority and is distinguished by free institutions, representative government, free elections, guarantees of individual liberty, freedom of speech and religion and freedom from political oppression. The second way of life is based upon the will of a minority forcibly imposed upon the majority. It relies upon terror and oppression, a controlled press and radio, fixed elections and the suppression of personal freedoms. I believe that it must be the policy of United States to support free peoples who are resisting attempted subjugation by armed minorities or by outside pressures.

Source C Truman's speech, 12 March 1947.

The significance of the Truman Doctrine was tremendous. It affected and dominated US foreign policy for nearly half a century. It was one of the declarations of Cold War, the point at which the Truman administration and Congress made public the decision that Communism was a great threat, which must be opposed. It did not represent a sudden departure in US foreign policy, but the culmination of much anxiety about and discussion of crises such as Iran and Germany. A few contemporaries criticised it. The Republican Senator Taft criticised the simplistic division of the world into two. Diplomat George Kennan said it was too sweeping, and that it failed to ask if a threatened state was (a) worth supporting and (b) within American capabilities to support. Kennan said that Turkey was not threatened by Communism, and that American interest in Turkey was threatening and provocative to the Soviets because of Turkish proximity to the Soviet Union. It demonstrated the drawbacks of conducting foreign policy in a democracy. Truman knew issues had to be painted in black and white, as good versus evil, in order to win over the public. It was tempting for both political parties to note that, as always in time of crisis, the president's popularity was increased.

In short, words as well as deeds were responsible for the intensity of the Cold War, and in the case of the United States, the language employed was designed to intimidate the American people as much as the Soviet leaders.

Source D An assessment by the historian S.R. Ashton of the Truman Doctrine speech.

f) The Marshall Plan (June 1947)

Truman's Secretary of State George Marshall was deeply concerned that the post-war devastation might make Western Europe vulnerable to Communist insurgency and the Red Army. West European countries were important trading partners for the United States. Truman therefore decided to pump $13 billion into the restoration of their economies. When Marshall announced the plan (June 1947) he did not say that the aid would be confined to West European countries. The Soviets and the Eastern European states considered taking the aid. However, the USSR did not want to give full details of their economic devastation to the Americans. In July 1947 they rejected the offer of aid, and ensured that the East Europeans did so too. Had the Soviets accepted the offer, it is doubtful that Congress would have granted the necessary funding for *any* aid.

COUNTRIES THAT RECEIVED MARSHALL AID

Austria, Belgium, Denmark, Holland, Sweden, Iceland, Norway, Luxembourg, Britain, Portugal, Switzerland, Italy, Greece, Turkey, Eire, and the West's zones of Germany.

BIPARTISAN

In the context of the Cold War, this meant that Republicans and Democrats put aside party antagonism on an issue deemed vital to the United States.

ACTIVITY

Make a date list showing increasing Soviet–American tensions, 1945–7.

The significance of the Marshall Plan was great. The aid alienated the Soviets and therefore helped to seal the division of Europe into two antagonistic blocs. In response to US aid to Western Europe, the USSR tightened its hold over Eastern Europe. In the autumn of 1947 the Soviets quickly made bilateral trade agreements with Bulgaria, Czechoslovakia, Hungary, Yugoslavia, Poland, and Romania, and finally established full Communist Party domination in Hungary, Bulgaria, Romania and Poland, and, last of all, Czechoslovakia (spring 1948). The Soviets ordered the West European Communist parties to do all they could to bring down their national governments (autumn 1947).

Marshall Aid demonstrated the **bipartisan** approach to the Cold War in the US. It was quite amazing that the Republican Congress granted Truman the money as a presidential election approached. That grant owed much to the demise of democracy in Czechoslovakia, which ironically owed much to the granting of the Marshall Aid!

WORDS THAT PLAYED AN IMPORTANT PART IN THE START OF THE COLD WAR

1946 Stalin spoke of the incompatibility of capitalism and Communism. The West interpreted this as aggressive, but it was aimed at the domestic rather than the international audience. Stalin was simply spouting the usual Marxist-Leninist line (February);
US Secretary of State James Byrnes indicated that the United States would take a tougher stand against the USSR (February);

1946 At Fulton, Missouri, Winston Churchill condemned the Soviet establishment of an East European 'Iron Curtain' which separated what would become known as the Soviet bloc from the West (March);

1946 At Stuttgart, Byrnes said that American troops would be staying in Germany for the foreseeable future (September);

1946 Ex-Vice-President Henry Wallace called for cooperation with the USSR. He was forced to resign from Truman's cabinet (September);

1947 'Truman Doctrine' speech (March);

1947 The Soviets established Cominform (Communist Information Bureau). The members were the Communist parties of the USSR, Poland, Bulgaria, Czechoslovakia, Romania, Hungary, Yugoslavia, France, Italy, and, later, Holland. The Cominform manifesto said that the world was divided between imperialists and democratic socialists, and that the latter must never compromise with the former. Andrei Zhdanov told the founding members of Cominform that it was time for colonial peoples to expel imperialist aggressors. The West saw this as a Soviet declaration of Cold War (September).

3 The Berlin Blockade (June 1948–May 1949)

ISSUES:
Why did the Berlin Blockade occur? What were the significance and results of the Blockade?

Post-war relations between the West and the Soviets had deteriorated so rapidly that no German peace treaty was signed. Amidst all this tension, it was not surprising that there was a great crisis, and that the crisis took place in Germany. With the Berlin Blockade (see timeline), there could be no doubt that the Cold War was well and truly under way.

Stalin's blockade of Berlin in June 1948 left Truman with three options:

(a) surrender and get out of Berlin; or
(b) send military convoys down the autobahns to West Berlin; or
(c) airlift supplies to the West Berliners.

The feisty Truman rejected (a). It would be humiliating and make America seem an unreliable ally. Truman felt (b) was provocative and might lead to World War III. Furthermore, the Soviets had far more troops in and around Berlin than the West. Truman therefore opted for (c). Millions of tons of supplies were flown into West Berlin until Stalin ended the blockade.

During the blockade, the official Soviet position was that there was no crisis, only 'technical difficulties' of a 'temporary nature'. The Soviets took care to avoid any troop clashes, and to ensure that no planes were brought down because of Soviet interference. Stalin quickly saw that the West was not going to give up, but he could not back down too quickly, lest he looked weak. He ended the blockade in May 1949.

EVENTS LEADING UP TO THE BERLIN BLOCKADE

1948 March – Soviet military governor walked out of ACC and said it had ceased to function;
April – Soviets restricted road and rail links between Berlin and the West's zones;
16 June – Soviets left the Allied Kommandatura;
18 June – West's introduction of new currency (the Deutschmark) in Western zones infuriated Soviets;
24 June – Soviets severed all rail, road and canal links to West Berlin, leaving it stranded 100 miles within Soviet zone.

a) What Was the Significance of the Berlin Blockade?

If the blockade was a Soviet attempt to get the Western allies out of Berlin, it had failed. Although the course of events suggested that neither Stalin nor Truman wanted to risk war, the crisis nevertheless demonstrated Western determination and unity. The blockade precipitated the development of two German states, each tied securely to one Cold War antagonist. In May 1949 a constitution was drawn up for the new West German state. In October 1949, the Soviets set up an East German state. The East Germans began to fence, mine, and patrol their 850-mile frontier with West Germany. The crisis killed off any remaining traces of American isolationism. America massively increased its defence spending, and established NATO.

The historian S.R. Ashton said that the blockade was 'a blunder of incalculable proportions for Stalin'. It alienated world public opin-

WHY DID STALIN BLOCKADE BERLIN?
▼ The Soviets said that their motivation was defensive. They were trying to halt the creation of a militaristic West German state within the Western alliance.
▼ Perhaps Stalin thought the West could/would do nothing about the blockade and he would thereby gain total control of Berlin.

EARLY NATO MEMBERS

USA, Canada, Britain, France, Belgian, Holland, Luxembourg, Italy, Denmark, Norway, Iceland, Portugal (1949); Greece and Turkey (1952); West Germany (1955).

THE NUCLEAR ARMS RACE

The Americans were horrified when they learned the Soviets had exploded an atomic bomb (September 1949). President Truman asked his advisers to consider the advantages and disadvantages of the production of an even more powerful bomb. While some scientists were reluctant, administration members favoured the development of a hydrogen bomb, so Truman gave the go-ahead (January 1950). The first American bomb was tested in November 1952. The first Soviet hydrogen bomb was tested in August 1953. The nuclear arms race had begun.

ion, because the USSR was the power trying to alter the status quo, at the risk of starving the West Berliners. It led to the political and military consequences that Stalin had been trying to avoid – the creation of the West German state, closely tied both politically and militarily to the Western bloc.

b) NATO

As relations with the Soviets deteriorated, the United States and the West Europeans decided that they needed to organise themselves into a defensive association lest the Red Army pour into Western Europe. The fall of Czechoslovakia in spring 1948 inspired Congress to accept participation in a formal military alliance in peacetime. In April 1949, 12 nations signed the North Atlantic Treaty (NATO).

The significance of NATO was great:
▼ It completed the division of Europe. At first the division had been economic and political. Now it was military.
▼ The admission of West Germany to NATO encouraged the Soviets to respond with the Warsaw Pact (1955), a military alliance for the Soviet bloc.
▼ It could be argued that the establishment of NATO stabilised Europe. Both sides now knew where they stood. After the establishment of NATO, Asia became the great Cold War arena.
▼ It demonstrated the extent to which America had become the policeman of the free world. Congress speedily granted funding for NATO, frightened by the explosion of the first Soviet atomic bomb and the fall of China to Communism.

ACTIVITY

Argue for and against the proposition that the USSR was responsible for the deterioration in US–Soviet relations between 1945 and 1949.

4 The Cold War Spreads to Asia

ISSUES:
What was the significance of China becoming Communist? What were the causes, consequences, and significance of the Korean War?

a) The 'Loss' of China

When China became Communist, Truman became a victim of his own Doctrine. Many Americans thought that if Communism were such a threat, Truman should not have allowed China to become Communist. The Republicans blamed the Democrats for the 'loss' of China. It was soon commonly believed that China had been 'lost' because of Roosevelt's 'betrayal' of Chiang Kai-shek at Yalta (see page 149), insufficient American aid to Chiang, and treachery within Truman's State Department, which contained Communist sympathisers. Although many Americans found those accusations persuasive, America could have done nothing short of total war to ensure Mao's defeat. The only 'treachery' of which State Department officials were guilty was a justifiable admiration for Mao's achievements. The 'treachery' and 'loss' theories seemed to be the only way that Americans could reconcile themselves to the fact that 500 million people, for whom they had previously felt a sentimental attachment, had become Communists. The Chinese Nationalist representative at the UN warned that events in China could cause revolts and successes by Communist Parties throughout Asia. Events in Korea in the summer of 1950 caused many Americans to believe that he was right.

b) Course of Events in the Korean War

On 25 June 1950 North Korea attacked South Korea. Both sides had been guilty of cross-border raids, but this was the first large-scale attack by either side. On 26 June, Truman sent American air and naval assistance to South Korea, and the 7th Fleet to the Taiwan Straits. On 27 June, the US-dominated UN agreed that UN forces should be sent to Korea. Meanwhile, with the advantage of preparation and surprise, the North Koreans took the South Korean capital, Seoul (28 June). On 7 July America's General Douglas MacArthur, US Commander-in-Chief in the Far East, was appointed UN commander in Korea. America said its war aims were the restoration of the status quo.

Throughout the summer of 1950, the UN, US and South Korean forces struggled. By September, there were 8,000 US casualties. However, on 15 September, MacArthur made a brilliant amphibious assault on Inchon, which put his forces 200 miles behind enemy lines and only 20 miles from Seoul. UN forces arrived in Seoul on 21 September. There was much excitement over the successes in

SINO-AMERICAN RELATIONS, 1913–50

1913 Many American politicians and businessman felt sympathetic toward the young Chinese Republic;

1937 –45 America gave limited aid to the Chinese Nationalist leader Chiang Kai-shek in his war against Japan but found his corrupt regime exasperating;

1945 After the war, Chiang fought Mao Zedong and his Communist forces for control of China;

1948 America stopped aid to Chiang who clearly had no chance of victory;

1949 Mao proclaimed the People's Republic of China. The Chinese Nationalists fled to Taiwan;

1950 Truman said America would keep out of this Chinese Civil War, had no interest in establishing bases on Taiwan 'at this time', but would give economic aid to the Chinese Nationalists in Taiwan (January).

**THE KOREAN WAR –
BACKGROUND**

**1941
–5** The Allies agreed that the
USSR and the US would
take the Japanese surren-
der in Korea;

1945 Soviet troops entered
northern Korea, then
American troops entered
southern Korea
(August–September);

**1946
–8** Two Korean states devel-
oped, a pro-Soviet
Communist Democratic
People's Republic of Korea
(North Korea, led by Kim Il
Sung) and a pro-American
Republic of Korea (South
Korea, led by Syngman
Rhee);

1948 Soviet forces left North
Korea (December);

1949 American forces left South
Korea (June).

STALIN AND MAO

Most Americans automatic-
ally assumed Mao to be
Stalin's puppet. However,
prior to Mao's success in
1949, the relationship
between Mao and Stalin had
not been particularly good.
When Mao was victorious,
Stalin rightly feared that the
era of Soviet domination of
international Communism
might come to an end.

America, and American war aims began to change. Syngman Rhee and MacArthur wanted to re-unify Korea, and to destroy North Korea's forces. This was no longer a question of the containment of Communism. This was what the Republicans called 'roll back'. Some Americans questioned the wisdom of crossing the 38th parallel (the border between North Korea and South Korea). However, the major-ity favoured 'roll back'. There was a feeling that North Korean aggression must be punished and that it would be bad for South Korean morale if nothing more were done. On the eve of congres-sional elections, it was difficult for Truman to restrain the outburst of national enthusiasm and stop at the 38th parallel. During September, some American pilots foolishly bombed Soviet and Chinese targets. General MacArthur, long an enthusiastic support of Chiang, made no secret of the fact that he wanted to invade China. On 3 October 1950, the Chinese warned the Americans that if they crossed the 38th parallel, China would be forced to intervene in the Korean War. When the Americans showed no signs of stopping, Chinese 'volun-teers' poured into Korea – over a quarter of a million by mid-October. The United States had not anticipated this. MacArthur's troops were forced below the 38th parallel again. However, by April 1951, the UN forces were back in North Korea, thanks to General Matt Ridgeway. He took over from MacArthur, who was dismissed for insubordination in that month. Twelve thousand Chinese troops died on the first day of a great but unsuccessful offensive, so China proposed an armistice (June 1951). After thousands more deaths and many months of difficult negotiations (repatriation of prisoners of war proved problematic) an armistice was signed in July 1953. The pre-war status quo was restored.

c) What Were the Causes of the Korean War?

i) Why Did North Korea Attack South Korea in June 1950?

Owing to Allied decisions about the Japanese surrender and Soviet-American tensions 1945–7, two Koreas were created. Koreans had no say in this. Each Korean leader dreamed of a reunited Korea led by him. Having ensured that North Korea was militarily far superior to South Korea, the Soviets acquiesced in (possibly encouraged) Kim's attack. Stalin probably thought that the Americans would stay out of the conflict. At the very least, a Korean War would distract the Americans from Europe. At best, it would be a triumph for Communism.

   The historian Peter Lowe blames the Americans for an 'unques-tionably foolish' combination of words and deeds in early 1950. The influential chairman of the Senate Foreign Relations Committee

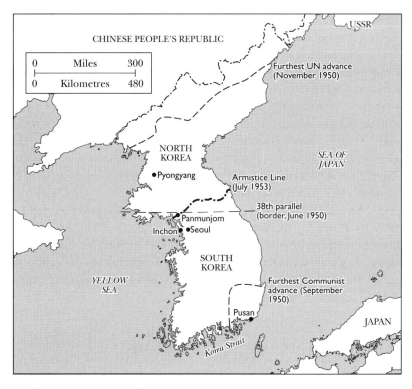

Figure 42 The Korean War, 1950–53.

apparently envisaged a Communist takeover of South Korea with equanimity. Secretary of State Dean Acheson defined America's vital 'defence perimeter' in the Pacific and excluded Korea from it. Congress rejected a bill for aid to Korea in protest against the administration's China policy.

ii) Why Did the United States Get Involved in Korea?
America felt that it had to respond to the North Korean invasion because it seemed as if the world balance of power was tilting in favour of Communism. Less than a year before, the Soviets had exploded their atomic bomb, and China had been 'lost' to Communism. Feeling beleaguered, Truman had commissioned the National Security Council to produce a planning paper (NSC 68) in which the international situation was assessed. NSC 68 (April 1950) described a polarised world divided between the enslaved and the free. NSC 68 said the USSR had a 'fanatic faith' and aimed at total domination of the Eurasian landmass. Two recent crises in Europe, the fall of Czechoslovakia and the Berlin Blockade, led Washington to perceive the Soviets as increasingly and ominously active. All these factors made Truman feel North Korea's attack was highly significant: Communism was entering a new phase, moving from subversion to invasion.

Truman felt that North Korea was testing the UN in the first real challenge to the new post Second World War world order. He did not want the UN to collapse as the League of Nations had after the

DOMESTIC PRESSURES AND KOREA

In the months prior to the North Korean attack, Senator Joseph McCarthy (see page 285) had whipped Americans into an anti-Communist frenzy. McCarthyism made it difficult for Truman to follow his 'loss' of China with the loss of South Korea to Communism.

Abyssinian crisis. He felt that appeasement of the North Korean aggressors would lead to World War III. America had the support of her Western allies in the UN. Britain and France had problems with Communist insurgents in their colonies Malaya and Indo-China. They wanted to see Communism stopped, and also wanted to keep in with the United States. America dominated the UN in its early years, and during the crucial vote for UN action, the USSR was absent from the Security Council (as a protest that Communist China was not in the UN) and therefore could not use its veto. Truman always maintained that Korea was a UN war, as that gave maximum respectability to what was effectively an American war.

Finally, America was very concerned about the safety of Japan, which was within the American defence perimeter. The Americans were developing Japan into a democratic ally, a valuable trading partner, and a bulwark against Communism. South Korea was only 100 miles from Japan. The loss of South Korea to Communism might lead to the loss of Japan.

iii) What Were the American War Aims?

Initially, the Americans wanted to restore the status quo in Korea, to 'contain' Communism. However, after MacArthur's successes in September 1950, American war aims changed. Many Americans now wanted to destroy Communist North Korea, in order to punish aggression, maintain South Korean morale, and prove American dynamism. The Truman administration was confident that the USSR and China would keep out of the war. A few Americans, including General MacArthur, even wanted to attack Communist China. However, President Truman said he did not want to provoke World War III, and it was MacArthur's anti-Chinese statements that led to his dismissal. After the Chinese entered the war, America reverted to the earlier war aim, the restoration of the pre-war status quo.

Why Did MacArthur Have to Go?

MacArthur had become too powerful for the president to control. He had won great prestige as a successful General in the Second World War and at Inchon. He was Commander-in-Chief of the US forces, the UN forces, and the military and civilian supremo in occupied Japan.

Understandably, politicians and other military leaders were afraid of him. The administration's fear of him could and did lead to ambiguous orders, which jeopardised the American strategy in Korea. For example, on 29 October 1950, Secretary of Defence George Marshall gave MacArthur vague orders, which did not seem to confirm Truman's orders that MacArthur was not to use American troops in China. MacArthur frightened and pro-voked Communist China with his pro-Chiang statements. Despite Inchon, he was really too old to be in such a position of respon-sibility. His judgement was failing. He had insisted that the Chinese would never enter the war. When they did, it was General Ridgeway rather than MacArthur who was able to stop the Chinese advance.

iv) Why Did Communist China Enter the Korean War?

The Chinese felt threatened because of the American presence in the contiguous Korean peninsula, MacArthur's declarations that he wanted to invade China, the presence of the US 7th fleet in the Straits of Taiwan, and the September 1950 American bombing of Chinese targets. The new Chinese nation had many internal prob-lems, which desperately needed attention, but American actions made China enter the war for self-defence. China's initial war aim was the restoration of the pre-war status quo. However, when the Chinese began to do well (late 1950) their war aims changed, and they seemed to want to destroy South Korea. When the Chinese were forced to retreat in spring 1951, they reverted to the earlier war aim.

d) Why Did the Korean War Come to an End?

▼ The war was costing Communist China a great deal, in terms of men and money, and the Chinese were keen to concentrate on their domes-tic problems.

▼ In January 1953 America had a new president, Eisenhower, whose impressive military reputation encouraged the American people to give unquestioning support to his decision to end the war.

▼ The American public was tired of the war.

▼ Eisenhower's Secretary of the Treasury stressed that the peace was financially important for America.

▼ Many influential Americans and West Europeans thought it unwise for the United States to be pinned down in Korea, when something might hap-pen in the much more important European arena. The influential General Omar Bradley told Congress in May 1951 that China was not the biggest threat to America, and that if America clashed with them, it was the 'wrong war, at the wrong place, at the wrong time, and with the wrong enemy'.

▼ With the death of Stalin in March 1953, the new Soviet leadership wanted to concentrate upon domestic problems and to try to improve relations with the Americans.

▼ In July 1953, Eisenhower hinted that he might 'unleash' Chiang and also use nuclear weapons. Within days of the latter threat, the armistice was signed on 27 July 1953. A commission containing representatives of all sides involved would continue to meet, to try to arrange a full and meaningful peace treaty.

e) What Were the Results and Significance of the Korean War?

▼ 2.3 million South Koreans, 900,000 Chinese, 520,000 North Koreans, 54,000 Americans and 3,000 UN troops died.

▼ Although no peace treaty was signed, the pre-war status quo was restored – Korea remained divided into North Korea and South Korea.

▼ South Korea (and maybe even Japan) was 'saved' for the United States and the Western alliance.

▼ South Korea prospered economically under American patronage, while North Korea stagnated economically.

▼ Syngman Rhee became even more dictatorial until he was forced to resign in 1960.

▼ It seemed that the Communist dynamic in Asia was slowed down.

▼ It switched American attention from Europe to Asia as the storm centre of the Cold War.

▼ It inspired the Americans to agree to help the French fight Communism in Indo-China. Within a decade, there would be American soldiers in an even more unpopular war in Vietnam. (The Vietnam War is a very important Cold War topic and is dealt with in Chapter 7.)

▼ The US and the USSR dramatically increased their military expenditure.

▼ It made the Western alliance more enthusiastic about NATO. It hastened American rearmament of West Germany which, like Japan, was now seen as a vital American ally.

▼ In its second phase, the war had been in effect a Sino-American war. Sino-American hostility was greatly increased, and the United States gave increased support to Taiwan. Because of the US-dominated UN action, China felt ostracised by and hostile towards the rest of the world. That hostility was reciprocated.

▼ At least in public, American governments continued to see the USSR and China as a monolithic Communist bloc. The war increased Sino-Soviet tension (Mao resented the Soviets charging him for armaments to fight a war that he felt the Soviets had helped to provoke). American policy did not take much advantage of that.

▼ It helped sustain McCarthyism (see page 285) and generally worsened the Cold War antagonism. However, the three leading powers showed they were unwilling to risk World War III. The sacking of MacArthur signalled that the Americans planned to stick to containment. The Chinese had been reluctant to intervene and only did so after several warnings. The Soviets were content to leave North Korea and China to do all the fighting.

ACTIVITY

Think up ideas to back up a Communist Chinese contention that America was an aggressive nation.

5 Eisenhower v. Khrushchev

ISSUES:
Was there a 'new'
USSR after Stalin's
death? What was the
significance of the
Hungarian, Middle East
and Berlin crises?

President Eisenhower and his Secretary of State John Foster Dulles appeared to be real 'Cold Warriors'. They had attacked Truman and the Democrats for being 'soft on Communism' in the presidential election campaign (1952).

Even if he had been so inclined, Eisenhower would have had problems in responding to the new, more moderate Soviet leadership, because America was still in the grip of McCarthyism (see page 285). Instead, Eisenhower and Dulles talked about 'roll back' (of Communism), 'massive retaliation' (they planned to base American defence on nuclear weaponry), and entered into many 'defensive' alliances. From the Soviet viewpoint, these policies and the alliances that encircled them seemed aggressive.

By 1955 it was clear that the new Soviet leader Khrushchev was faced with great problems:
▼ A Cold Warrior administration in United States.
▼ A rival for the leadership of world Communism in Mao.
▼ The West's refusal to recognise the East German state.
▼ The Soviet economy was in difficulty.

Khrushchev's response was a mixture of provocation and conciliation. He tried to stir up the West Europeans to halt West German rearmament and to win friends in the Middle East. In order to tighten the Soviet bloc militarily, he created the Warsaw Pact (May 1955). On the other hand, he returned a naval base to Finland and decreased the Red Army by half a million men. He agreed to talks on agriculture and the peaceful use of atomic energy with the USA and established diplomatic relations with West Germany. In April 1956 Khrushchev dissolved Cominform, while nevertheless retaining as much control as possible over Communists everywhere. In May 1955 he signed the Austrian peace treaty, under which the four occupying powers at last got out of Austria, which became an independent and neutral state. The USSR had thus surrendered territory for the first time since the Second World War. Why? Khrushchev wanted to look reasonable, but also knew that the withdrawal of the West's troops from Austria damaged military communications between the NATO states Italy and West Germany.

The West was not convinced that concessions such as these represented anything other than a new style of leadership but with the same old basic aims. The Soviet response to the Hungarian uprising and the Suez crisis appeared to confirm this.

THE NEW SOVIET LEADERSHIP

Stalin died in 1953. His successors were more moderate. They seemed to favour consumer goods rather than armaments production. They treated the East Europeans better and improved relations with countries with which there had formerly been great tension, such as Turkey and Iran. The Korean armistice negotiations made progress and Soviet anti-Western propaganda become slightly less vitriolic. Why was the new leadership more moderate? They wanted to concentrate upon domestic and bloc problems. The latter seemed particularly urgent. They felt more confident after the explosion of the first Soviet hydrogen bomb in August 1953. They hoped that if the USSR decreased the tension, the Western alliance might disintegrate, as there were disagreements about the wisdom of rearming Germany.

AMERICAN ALLIANCES
NATO – 1949
US/Taiwan – 1954
SEATO – 1955 (see page 263)
CENTO – 1958 (the other members of this Central Treaty Organisation were Britain, Turkey, Iraq, Iran, Pakistan)

a) Hungary (1956)

In February 1956, Khrushchev addressed the Twentieth Congress of the Soviet Communist Party. He rejected some Stalinist ideas. Khrushchev said it was possible to have peaceful coexistence with the West, and that different roads to socialism were acceptable. Khrushchev's denial of Stalin's infallibility shook the East European regimes, which had been closely associated with the late dictator. One result was unrest in Hungary. Because the Hungarians spoke of leaving the Warsaw Pact and establishing a multi-party democracy, Soviet troops brutally put down the Hungarian uprising (November 1956).

The Hungarian crisis of 1956 was significant in that American 'roll back' rhetoric was exposed as a sham. The Hungarian revolutionaries had expected American help but America did nothing. It was clear that the Americans would not liberate Eastern Europe. The Soviets were lucky. They escaped world condemnation of their repressive actions because the rest of the world was distracted by the Suez crisis.

b) The Suez Crisis

i) Background

Figure 43 The Suez Crisis in the Middle East, 1956.

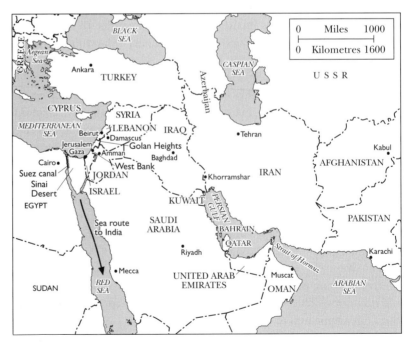

Both the USA and the USSR wanted other nations in the world to be on their side. In 1956 Dulles described neutrality as 'immoral and short-sighted'. By 1956, Western Europe was allied to the United

States through NATO, and Eastern Europe was part of the Soviet bloc. The USA considered Latin American nations to be friendly, although there was great underlying resentment against the 'colossus of the north'. The USSR had a similarly ambivalent relationship with Communist China. The African continent and Asia contained many nations that had struggled or were about to struggle for their independence from colonialism. Contemporaries sometimes referred to these developing nations as the Third World. Both the US and the USSR were keen to 'win' these nations. The Soviets had the advantage of Western unpopularity due to the history of colonialism. The Americans had the advantage of greater material resources with which to 'help' (or bribe) emerging nations.

Owing to its oil resources, the Middle East was a most desirable Third World area to both superpowers. Furthermore, the Suez Canal made the area a strategically important link between the Mediterranean and the Indian Ocean.

After the Second World War, Britain and France withdrew from the Middle East. The USA and the USSR moved into the vacuum. The Americans tried hard to persuade the Arab states that the Soviet Union was their great enemy. However, as far as the Arab states were concerned, Israel was their great enemy. After nearly 2,000 years' absence from the Middle East, Jews had begun to return in ever-increasing numbers in the twentieth century. Their return caused tension with native Palestinians. The UN recommended two separate Palestinian states, one Arab, one Jewish. However, in May 1948 the Jews proclaimed the establishment of the state of Israel, wherein their treatment of the Palestinians soon caused great hostility and tension between Israel and the Arab states. Because of the number and influence of Jewish American voters, Truman welcomed the establishment of the state of Israel.

It is difficult to decide who first brought the Cold War to the Middle East. During the Second World War the British and Americans put pressure on Iran to obtain oil concessions. When the Soviets behaved similarly, Western pressure forced them to retreat (see page 203). From 1951, America tried to organise an anti-Soviet alliance in the Middle East. In 1953 Eisenhower successfully intervened in support of the Shah of Iran, enabling him to defeat his pro-Soviet rival. The Soviets felt that all this threatened their southern borders, and retaliated by establishing a closer relationship with Egypt and Syria. In 1955 Czechoslovakia sent Soviet-supplied weapons to Egypt. In 1956 Egypt recognised Communist China and said that it would obtain arms from there, in defiance of a UN embargo. Both America and Britain felt that Egypt needed to be 'punished'.

WHY DID BRITAIN, FRANCE AND ISRAEL ATTACK EGYPT?

Britain and France had financed the Canal many decades before. They resented the loss of their investments and wanted to ensure continued access to the Suez Canal. Britain resented Nasser's anti-British propaganda, and felt he wanted to dominate the Middle East. France resented Nasser supplying arms to Algerians fighting for independence from France. Israel resented Nasser's organisation of an Arab coalition against Israel, and his sponsorship of terrorists in the Sinai Desert.

ii) Course of Events

The United States had agreed to finance Egypt's Aswan High Dam. However, the US withdrew support (July 1956), to 'punish' the anti-Western Egyptian leader Nasser. Nasser was too friendly with Communist nations and had joined Syria in an anti-Israel alliance, which upset the Jewish American lobby. Southern congressmen opposed giving aid to help Egypt produce more cotton, when the South was a major cotton producer. Convinced the Soviets could not finance the dam, Dulles hoped that influential Egyptians would overthrow Nasser in order to get the money from America.

Nasser retaliated on 26 July 1956. He nationalised the Suez Canal. On 29 October 1956, Israel attacked Egypt and took the Sinai Desert, and on 5 November, Britain and France moved in to safeguard the Canal. World reaction was hostile. The international outcry and American pressure forced Britain and France to withdraw. The British had expected American sympathy for their actions, because the Eisenhower administration disliked Nasser. However, Eisenhower wanted to keep in with the Arab nations, believing the Western world needed their oil and their friendship against the Communist bloc. Furthermore, because of the Cold War, Eisenhower did not want to be associated with neo-colonialism, lest the Third World countries' memories of colonialism made them ally with the Soviet Union. Finally, Eisenhower was furious that Britain, France and Israel had acted without keeping him informed.

iii) The Significance/Results of the Suez Crisis

▼ It demonstrated the new international power realities. British and French power had declined. They were now clearly dominated by and dependent upon the USA.

▼ It showed that the United States would not defend her allies if it did not suit her to do so.

▼ It increased American involvement in the Middle East. In January 1957 Eisenhower asked Congress for military and economic aid for any Middle East country that was threatened by aggression or subversion.

▼ Egypt and Syria turned increasingly to the USSR, as the Anglo-French actions had reminded them of the Western 'colonial' mentality.

▼ Both the USA and the USSR gave and/or sold increasing amounts of armaments to their allies.

▼ Initially, it looked as if the Suez crisis had brought the Cold War to the Middle East. However, in 1958 the Arabs and Israelis made it clear in the UN that they did not want the Cold War in the Middle East, so the region became temporarily less volatile.

c) Arms Race

Eisenhower inherited the hydrogen bomb from Truman. Within a year (1953) the Soviets had caught up. Each superpower wanted more and better atomic weaponry than the other. Atomic bombs could be delivered by long-range bomber aircraft (as at Hiroshima) or by missiles. The first American surface-to-surface ballistic missiles were tested in 1947. When the USSR's long-range Inter-Continental Ballistic Missile (ICBM) was operational a few weeks before the American ICBM, America was humiliated. In 1954 America's first nuclear propelled submarine was operational, and in 1960 America tested a missile fired from a submerged submarine. Soon, America's Polaris missiles had the range to enable an American submarine to hit any target on the globe. As yet, the Soviet Navy was years behind the American Navy.

Both the USA and the USSR frequently tested nuclear weaponry in the 1950s. In 1958, the two countries began nuclear test ban talks at Geneva. This was the first mutual and public recognition that the dangers inherent in nuclear power were so great as to force sworn enemies to moderate their use.

During Eisenhower's presidency the Soviets boasted that they were ahead in the missile race. In the 1960 presidential campaign, John Kennedy used that so-called 'missile gap' to help him win the election. Eisenhower knew (as did Kennedy) that the 'missile gap' was in America's favour. Eisenhower knew this because of American reconnaissance flights over the Soviet Union. Eisenhower kept quiet because the flights were secret (and provocative to the USSR) and also because he did not want to antagonise the Soviets by boasting of the American supremacy of which Khrushchev was aware.

The significance of the arms race was great. It had the potential to affect domestic politics in both the USA and the USSR, as in the presidential election of 1960. The cost dominated and distorted the economies of the USA and the USSR.

d) Berlin

Khrushchev faced problems over Germany. First, the West refused to recognise the legitimacy of the East German state. Secondly, America, Britain and France used West Berlin for espionage and sabotage. Khrushchev tried to force the West to recognise East Germany, by threatening to give East Germany control of the West's access routes to West Berlin. Then he gave the West an ultimatum: they must do something about West Berlin within six months, or face dire consequences (November 1958) (see page 149). However, when it was clear that the West would stand firm, Khrushchev backed down in March 1959.

Khrushchev and Eisenhower had the first ever Soviet–American summit meeting in September 1959. Although the atmosphere was surprisingly relaxed, they made no progress on Berlin. Khrushchev hoped for a Berlin agreement at the Paris summit in May 1960. He wanted to have some great success in foreign policy to confound his critics within the Soviet Union and in China, who thought it impossible to have 'peaceful coexistence' with the Americans. However, the Paris summit failed because of tension over a US spy plane (a U2) which had been shot down over the USSR.

ACTIVITY

Who 'won'? Eisenhower or Khrushchev? Make a list of their successes and failures, for example, with regard to the bloc, the arms race, Suez, Berlin.

ISSUE:
Why and with what results did Khrushchev and Kennedy clash over Cuba and Berlin?

WHY AMERICANS THOUGHT THEY WERE LOSING THE COLD WAR IN 1961
Too much of the world was Communist: the USSR, Eastern Europe, China, North Korea, North Vietnam, and soon, possibly, Cuba. There had been no 'roll back', and there was apparently a 'missile gap' in the Soviets' favour.

6 Khrushchev v. Kennedy

Khrushchev and Kennedy both believed their side was losing the Cold War. Foreign policy problems contributed to Khrushchev's increasing difficulties in maintaining his leadership within the USSR. Therefore Khrushchev desperately needed a foreign policy success. Similarly, Kennedy felt he had something to prove, as many people perceived him to be young and inexperienced. Furthermore, his militant Cold War campaign rhetoric led people to expect some Cold War success. Kennedy was preoccupied by the Third World, wherein he believed the Soviets were doing better than the Americans. Kennedy was wrong but, in the Cold War, it was often perception rather than reality that mattered. Because of all these factors, the relationship between Khrushchev and Kennedy was obviously going to be tense.

a) The Bay of Pigs

Americans dreaded the thought of a Communist state in the Western Hemisphere. Under the domination of the dictator General Batista, Cuba was politically and economically (as well as literally) close to the US. Fidel Castro, an idealistic young lawyer, rebelled against Batista in 1953. By 1959 Castro dominated Cuba and had redistributed the landed wealth of Cuba. US-owned sugar plantations and mills were confiscated. The Eisenhower administration therefore broke off relations with Castro, in January 1961. As yet, Castro's government was not Communist.

UNITED
STATES

GULF OF
MEXICO

Florida

Miami

BAHAMAS

Havana
★★★★★ CUBA
(1961)

Bay of
Pigs
Guantanamo
(US naval base) HAITI

ATLANTIC
OCEAN

DOMINICAN
REPUBLIC
(1965)

PUERTO
RICO (US)

0   Miles   500
0 Kilometres 800

MEXICO

BELIZE
HONDURAS

JAMAICA

CARIBBEAN
SEA

GRENADA
(1983)

EL
SALVADOR
GUATEMALA
(1954)

Managua
NICARAGUA
(1979–90)

COSTA
RICA

Canal
Zone

PACIFIC
OCEAN

PANAMA
(1989)

COLUMBIA

Caracas
VENEZUELA

Country under severe
US diplomatic and
economic pressure

Countries in which the
CIA backed invasions

Countries in which the
US intervened militarily

★ Soviet missile base

Figure 44 Cuba in the Cold War.

WHY THE SOVIETS THOUGHT THEY WERE LOSING THE COLD WAR IN 1961

There was a missile gap in America's favour. A network of American alliances surrounded the USSR. Berlin was a problem and the Chinese were challenging Soviet leadership of world Communism.

We shall pay any price, bear any burden, meet any hardship, support any friend, oppose any foe to assure the survival and success of liberty.

Source E From Kennedy's inauguration speech.

In the 1960 presidential election, the Democratic candidate John Kennedy called for the overthrow of Castro. The Republican candidate, Vice-President Richard Nixon, knew the Eisenhower administration was secretly planning the overthrow, so he could not publicly call for it. Ironically, Kennedy's call for something that Eisenhower and Nixon were already planning to do, was probably a factor in Kennedy's victory.

As president, Kennedy inherited the **CIA**-supported plan for Cuban exiles to invade Cuba in April 1961. Kennedy supported the plan because:

▼ It was inherited from President Eisenhower, whose military reputation was unchallenged. Kennedy therefore assumed that the idea was good.

▼ The prestigious CIA supported the plan.

▼ Within the administration, critics of the plan kept quiet. Secretary of State Dean Rusk felt that as he was no longer a soldier, he should not speak! The Chiefs of Staff thought it was a CIA affair, so they kept quiet.

▼ The CIA chief had taught several leading members of the administration at Yale, so they deferred to him.

▼ Kennedy had promised to support Cuban freedom fighters during the presidential election.

▼ It seemed to be a chance to overthrow a nearby Communist regime at little cost.

THE CIA

The Central Intelligence Agency was set up under Truman (1947) to collect and analyse intelligence and 'perform... other functions', such as the overthrow of a radical Iranian government (1953) and the plans for the Bay of Pigs operation (1961).

The April 1961 invasion was a disaster, because:

▼ The Cuban exiles were supposed to flee to nearby mountains if necessary after landing on the Bay of Pigs. However, they could not reach the mountains.

▼ The local population did not rise up in support of the exiles. Castro had frequently holidayed in the Bay of Pigs, and was particularly popular there.

▼ The promised US air support never materialised because of bad weather and Castro's air force.

▼ The plan was leaked, and Castro was forewarned.

The Bay of Pigs invasion was highly significant. It was a humiliating fiasco that damaged America's reputation throughout the world. It increased Castro's popularity at home (as the champion of Cuban nationalism against US imperialism) and won him respect abroad (particularly in Latin America). Not surprisingly, Castro moved into an even closer relationship with the USSR, and he declared himself a Marxist–Leninist (December 1961). The Bay of Pigs left Kennedy desperate for a foreign policy success, and Khrushchev believing that he could take advantage of a 'soft' and foolish young president.

b) The Berlin Wall

Why Was Khrushchev Anxious About Berlin?

▼ From 1949 to 1958, over 2 million East Germans had fled to West Germany, often via Berlin. In the first six months of 1961, 100,000 fled to West Berlin. The total East German population was only 17.5 million, and many of those who fled were highly skilled workers. The USSR's economy was highly dependent upon East German exports of high-tech goods and machinery.

▼ The emigrants were a public and persistent reminder that the East German regime was unpopular.

▼ The East German regime wanted Khrushchev to stop the haemorrhage.

▼ West Berlin was a centre of espionage and propaganda for the West, and a glittering example of Western prosperity. Khrushchev therefore wanted to decrease contact between West Berlin and East Berlin. Khrushchev desperately needed a foreign policy triumph, and Berlin seemed the best place.

In June 1961, Khrushchev and Kennedy met at Vienna. Encouraged by Kennedy's Bay of Pigs disaster, Khrushchev was patronising and aggressive. He gave Kennedy an ultimatum: something had to be done about Berlin by December 1961, or Khrushchev would hand over the Berlin access routes to East Germany.

Khrushchev's ultimatum greatly increased Cold War tension. In July 1961 the Soviets increased their military budget by 33 per cent. The Americans did likewise. Then, on 13 August 1961, the East Germans sealed off the 100-mile frontier with West Berlin with wire fences, and four days later they erected a 30-mile wall between West Berlin and East Berlin.

The results and significance of the Berlin Wall crisis were great. The Wall closed the frontier, and stopped East Germans getting out of East Germany, thereby helping the Soviet bloc economy. It clearly registered the division of the two Germanys, which increased West German antagonism toward the Soviet bloc. In some ways, it could be said to have brought a certain stability to Germany and Berlin, in that the lines of demarcation were now clearly drawn. On the other hand, the border area itself became very tense, especially when East Germans tried to escape. In some ways, it increased Cold War tensions, in that soon after both the USSR and the USA resumed nuclear testing. Soviet bloc writers claimed the erection of the wall as a triumph, because the West had been unable to stop its construction and continued existence. Some historians suggest that Khrushchev considered it a triumph, and was thereby encouraged to put the missiles in Cuba. Western writers interpreted the erection of the wall as a triumph, because it showed the world that East Germany needed to wall its people in! They felt that it made Khrushchev look rather foolish, after all his bullying and blustering over Berlin. Despite his repeated threats, he did not hand over the West access routes to Berlin to the East Germans. Some historians suggest that Khrushchev did not consider the wall to be a triumph, which was why he resumed nuclear testing for the first time since 1958.

Figure 45 Kennedy and Khrushchev at Vienna (1961).

c) The Cuban Missile Crisis

After the Bay of Pigs, Kennedy warned that if any Western Hemisphere nation failed to withstand Communism, the United States would intervene to protect its security. In August 1962 the US press debated whether or not the Soviets had put offensive nuclear missiles on Cuba. On 4 September 1962, Kennedy warned the Soviets that that would be an intolerable situation. On 11 September, the Soviets announced that they did not need to put offensive missiles in Cuba. However, this was exactly what the Soviets did.

The Kennedy administration was slow to believe and realise what was happening. They were sure that the Soviets would not station nuclear missiles outside their own territory, as they had never done so before. However, the Soviets did just this. On 14 October 1962 a

Why Did Khrushchev Put Missiles in Cuba?

In 1962 the Soviets had 50 ICBMs, the Americans 304. Back in September 1961, the Americans had publicly declared their superiority in this area. Khrushchev was therefore anxious. He felt he had to do something. The Soviets could not afford a massive ICBM programme. It therefore made sense to put shorter-range missiles on Cuba, which was only 90 miles from the US coast. Khrushchev believed that having missiles on Cuba would increase Soviet prestige, and improve his bargaining position on Germany. The Bay of Pigs fiasco and American acquiescence in the construction of the Berlin Wall suggested Kennedy would be a soft touch.

U2 photographed the missile sites in Cuba. On 16 October, Kennedy established a committee to consider the options:

▼ Doing nothing was not an option. If the US did nothing it would be a great Soviet victory.

▼ Something had to be done quickly, as presumably the missiles would be operational soon.

▼ Many of Kennedy's advisers suggested an invasion of Cuba or a 'surgical air strike' to knock out the missiles. The problem with military options was that Soviet technicians and engineers on Cuba would be killed which might trigger off World War III.

▼ A naval blockade of Cuba would give Khrushchev time to think again, although it could also give the time necessary for the completion of the missiles.

Kennedy decided on the naval blockade, but also had planes ready for an air strike, and 100,000 men prepared to invade Cuba. Kennedy announced the blockade on 22 October 1962. He said that the 1930s had taught democratic politicians not to appease. He said that any nuclear missile launched from Cuba constituted a Soviet attack on the US, and the US would have to retaliate against the Soviet Union. He advised Khrushchev to stop this provocative threat to world peace.

As Soviet technicians worked by flare light on the missile sites, American ships waited 800 miles off the Cuban coast. The ships' captains were told that they needed Kennedy's assent before they attacked Soviet ships trying to run the blockade. In order to give Khrushchev more time, Kennedy decreased the blockade line by 300 miles. On 24 October, Soviet vessels approached the blockade line then retreated. Khrushchev backed down because he knew that America's nuclear arsenal and navy were far more powerful than those of the USSR. On 26 October, Khrushchev sent Kennedy a message, promising to get the missiles out, if Kennedy promised never to invade Cuba. On 27 October, Khrushchev upped his demands, no doubt under pressure from others in the Kremlin. He now demanded an American promise to remove missiles from Turkey. Kennedy decided to act as if he had not received the 27 October message, and accepted the earlier offer. Khrushchev broadcast his answer on Radio Moscow, on 28 October. He said he was dismantling the Cuban missiles for the sake of peace. The Voice of America radio station in Europe broadcast US acceptance.

The results and significance of the Cuban missile crisis were great:

▼ The world had come terrifyingly close to nuclear war. It frightened Kennedy and Khrushchev into the installation of a direct 'hotline' telephone link between Moscow and Washington (June 1963), and the first-ever Partial Nuclear Test Ban Treaty (August 1963).

▼ Although both Kennedy and Khrushchev claimed a triumph, most of the world interpreted it as a Kennedy victory. Khrushchev had apparently backed down, and this probably contributed to his fall from power in 1964.

▼ The Soviets were determined that they would never have to back down again. They worked hard and successfully to achieve nuclear and naval parity by the end of the decade.

▼ The Americans felt that they had won some kind of a victory. This led to over-confidence, especially in Vietnam.

▼ It demonstrated the great power of the president, in his capacity as Commander-in-Chief, during the Cold War. The Congressional role in the missile crisis was relatively insignificant.

▼ The crisis hastened and perhaps even began the change from a **bipolar** world to a **multipolar** world. Both sides alienated their allies by their behaviour during the crisis. De Gaulle furiously complained that the US had informed not consulted him. He soon withdrew French troops from NATO. The Chinese were equally furious. Mao felt that Khrushchev had humiliated the Communist world by his climbdown.

> **'BIPOLAR' AND 'MULTIPOLAR'**
> Historians talk of the post-Second World War world as being 'bipolar', that is, dominated by two very different powers, the United States and the USSR. However, during the 1960s, the United States and the USSR found it increasingly difficult to control their allies. France and China in particular moved away from their respective blocs. A new world in which there were several centres of power (a multipolar world) was replacing the old bipolar world in which there were two centres.

ACTIVITY

Look back over all references to Berlin and Germany in this chapter, then plan an essay: 'How and why was Germany important in the Cold War between 1945 and 1961?'

ISSUES:
Why was there Sino-
American tension after
1949? How and why
did relations improve?

7 The United States and the People's Republic of China

When we talk about the Cold War, we tend to concentrate upon the relationship between United States and the Soviet Union. However, the hostility between the United States and the People's Republic of China was also important.

The United States was involved in the Chinese Civil War in the years 1945–8. The US gave aid to Chiang Kai-shek and the Chinese Nationalists in their struggle against Mao Zedong and the Chinese Communists. However, by 1949 the US had abandoned Chiang, who fled with thousands of followers to the island of Taiwan. The US was unhappy at Mao's success in late 1949. Americans feared that other Asian countries might follow China's lead. Nevertheless, when the State Department publicly announced that Taiwan was not strategi-

Figure 46 Cold War China.

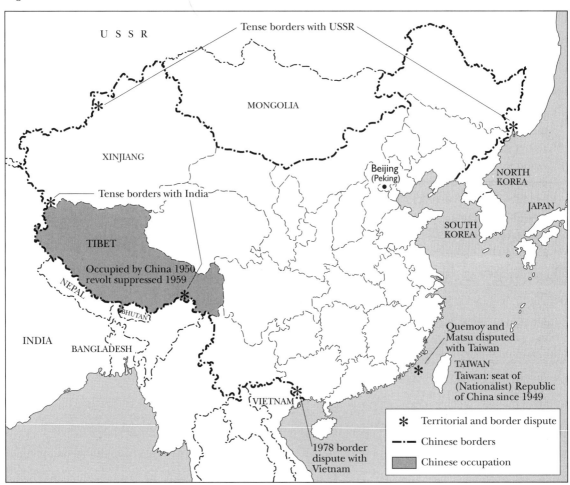

cally important to America (December 1949), it seemed as if America had lost interest in the Chinese Civil War. However, the Korean War changed the US attitude. Truman sent the US 7th Fleet to the Taiwan Straits. Mao declared that America had reinjected itself into the Chinese Civil War. When American and Chinese troops met on the battlefields of Korea, it was the only time that American troops clashed with the troops of one of its great Cold War antagonists.

a) What Were the Causes of the Sino-American Hostility?

▼ The United States hated Communism, particularly resented their erstwhile protégé China becoming Communist, and was convinced that Beijing was Moscow's puppet.

▼ Mao hated capitalism, felt that America was imperialistic, and resented American aid to Chiang (1945–8, 1950 onwards).

▼ The United States interpreted the Korean War as a sign that Chinese-sponsored Communism was expansionist and threatened US security.

▼ China interpreted the Korean War as a sign that America was aggressive, anxious to get a foothold on the Asian mainland, and likely to attack China itself.

▼ After the Korean War, the US put a trade embargo on China and kept it out of the UN. The US also established bases on Taiwan.

▼ The US–Taiwan Defence Treaty (1954) infuriated Mao, who never gave up hope of regaining Taiwan.

▼ In 1955, Communist China shelled the Chinese Nationalist islands of Quemoy and Matsu, which were very close to the Chinese mainland. President Eisenhower hinted in public that he was considering the use of tactical atomic weapons to protect Taiwan. The furious and humiliated Chinese backed down.

▼ In 1958 there was a similar Quemoy and Matsu crisis. Mao threatened, America threatened in return, and Mao backed down.

▼ Dulles insisted that Chinese Communism was more threatening than Soviet Communism. China had more people and great cultural influence and prestige in Asia. There were major Chinese minorities in all Asian nations, and other Asian nations were relatively weak.

▼ Both America and China resented the other's involvement in French Indo-China after 1945 (see Chapter 7).

▼ America was convinced that China was determined to aid revolutions throughout the world, for example, in Vietnam and Malaya. America felt that the Chinese occupation of Tibet and the Chinese invasion of India in 1962 demonstrated Chinese aggression.

DETENTE
In the Cold War context, this means a relaxation of tensions between America and China and/or the Soviet Union.

b) Causes of the Sino-American Detente

During 1969–70, President Richard Nixon relaxed restrictions on trade with and passports for China. The Chinese reciprocated in April 1971, when they invited the American table tennis team to China. Amid much talk of 'ping pong diplomacy', Nixon lifted the 21-year-old trade embargo on China. In February 1972, Nixon visited Beijing, and in 1973 told Congress that there was no fundamental Sino-American clash of interest.

How and why had one of America's leading Cold Warriors brought about this amazing rapprochement? Nixon rightly anticipated that detente with China would make him look like a peace-loving world statesman, and help him win re-election in the autumn of 1972.

As one of America's leading Cold Warriors, Nixon had an impeccable pedigree as far as conservatives were concerned. Many Americans thought that if the old Cold Warrior said that detente was right, it must be! Nixon's conversion to detente deprived the conservatives of their leader. Nixon and his foreign policy adviser Henry Kissinger believed that allowing ideology to dominate foreign policy was a great and unrealistic error. Nixon and Kissinger were aware that US power was in relative decline thanks to budgetary problems, Soviet parity, and the economic rise of the European Community and Japan. Making a friend out of an enemy therefore made sense. By 1968 Nixon had concluded that the Cold War had changed. It was no longer a bipolar world, and therefore America had to adjust her foreign policy. Both America and China found their relationships with their old 'friends' were deteriorating. America was dismayed by West European criticism of the Vietnam War, and Japan was becoming a great trade rival. The Sino-Soviet split meant that America was no longer faced with a monolithic Communist bloc. It therefore made sense to change America's relationship with the two leading Communist nations. Nixon and Kissinger wanted to use China to counter Soviet power, to force Moscow into detente, and to help America win peace with honour in Vietnam. They felt it was foolish and even dangerous to leave a potential superpower such as China outside the community of nations.

Mao believed that China needed detente. Chinese trade and industry needed the stimulus afforded by contact with the West. Furthermore, Mao could see that Nixon was determined to get American troops off the Asian mainland (see page 275). This made the United States less of a threat to China than was the USSR. In a speech in September 1973, China's Foreign Minister Zhou Enlai said it was acceptable to negotiate with the United States, because it was a decreased threat to world peace, having declined in power since the Korean War.

Figure 47 Nixon and Mao (1972).

Despite detente, there were still tensions in the Sino-American relationship. China was resentful when Nixon insisted that he would maintain the close relationship with Taiwan.

c) The Significance and Results of Sino-American Detente

From the Chinese viewpoint, detente was a great success. It greatly increased China's international standing and prestige. In October 1971, the People's Republic of China took its seat in the UN, and Taiwan was expelled. From the point of view of the US and her allies, a dialogue had at last been opened with a potentially dangerous power. However, America and China were still wary of each other, particularly over the Taiwan issue. The tenuous nature of the detente was demonstrated in December 1975, when President Ford got a cool welcome on a visit to Beijing. The Chinese felt that the Soviet–American detente was too successful (see page 236).

Why Was There a Sino-Soviet Split?

There was a historical antipathy between Russia and China, two neighbouring and expansionist powers. After 1917, Communist Russia did little to help the Chinese Communists. Stalin's advice nearly ruined the fledgling Chinese Communist Party in the 1920s. Stalin's ambassador was the last to leave Chiang Kai-shek in 1949. When China became Communist, the Soviet Union feared that it would be a rival for world Communist leadership. Soviet economic aid was minimal. The USSR appeared to let China do all the work in the Korean War, a war that Stalin had helped to unleash. After the war, the USSR made China repay the massive loans borrowed to finance Chinese fighting in the war. Khrushchev recorded a clear personality clash between himself and Mao: 'His chauvinism and arrogance sent a shiver up my spine… The Chinese have little in common with our people'. His memoirs suggested that Khrushchev shared the 'yellow peril' fears of his Russian ancestors. At the 1955 Bandung Conference for Third World nations, Zhou persuasively aligned China with the poorer nations who had suffered at the hands of imperialists, in a way that the Russians never had. Khrushchev was desperately competitive with the United States over the Third World, and was irritated that the Chinese seemed to be muscling in. There were ever-increasing ideological differences between the Chinese and the Soviets. Mao's insistence on the importance of the peasantry in a Communist revolution annoyed the Soviets, who followed the Marxist-Leninist emphasis on the industrial proletariat. Without consulting Mao, Khrushchev criticised Stalin in 1956. Mao considered himself to be the world's leading Communist after the death of Stalin, and resented the lack of consultation. Mao and Khrushchev disagreed about relations with the West. Khrushchev spoke frequently of peaceful coexistence, and thought that Mao's aggressive anti-Western rhetoric was dangerous and provocative. Mao resented the lack of Soviet support during the Quemoy and Matsu crises in 1955 and 1958 and in the Sino-Indian disputes in 1959 and 1962. In 1957 Khrushchev promised Mao that the USSR would help China become a nuclear power. However, the Soviets wanted to control Chinese foreign policy and nuclear warheads, so China worked independently on the atomic bomb. In 1960, the Soviets withdrew 1,390 industrial advisers from China. This damaged Chinese economic development, but made the Chinese more determined to go ahead without Soviet aid. Within the Communist world, one Communist nation (Albania) and several Communist Parties (such as the Australian and Indian) aligned themselves with China rather than the USSR. There were Sino-Soviet border clashes in 1962, and in 1969, 658,000 Soviet troops faced 814,000 Chinese troops in Sinkiang. By this time, China and the USSR regarded each other as the world's greatest threat to peace.

ACTIVITY

Construct an outline of the main phases in twentieth century Chinese history.

8 Soviet–American Detente

During Nixon's presidency Soviet–American relations improved. There was a slightly more relaxed relationship, which became known as detente.

a) Reasons for Soviet–American Detente

By 1968 it suited both superpowers to improve their relationship. Why?

i) The American Viewpoint

▼ Some commentators detected a growing American desire to retreat from international affairs.

▼ Other commentators felt America wanted detente as an alternative approach to the traditional containment policy. Detente was a tactic for controlling the emergence of the USSR as a truly global power.

▼ America hoped to use Soviet friendship to help to extricate the US from Vietnam.

▼ The USSR was gaining in strength so that the USA had to do something. After the Suez crisis (1956) the Soviets had built up their conventional forces. After the Cuban missile crisis (1962) the Soviets had built up their fleet. By the late 1960s, the Soviets were approaching nuclear parity with the Americans.

▼ American weapons were superior to Soviet weapons in quality if not quantity, so the US hoped that detente would serve to preserve that superiority.

▼ There were problems within the Western alliance. There was increasing anti-American feeling within France. This made America uneasy and more inclined toward detente.

ii) The Soviet Viewpoint

▼ The Soviets wanted detente in order to cut their military expenditure, which had left them with great economic problems.

▼ The Soviets wanted more economic contacts with the West because of Soviet technological backwardness.

▼ The Soviets believed they had attained nuclear parity and therefore felt more secure about negotiations.

▼ The Soviets feared China and therefore wanted to decrease tension with the West.

▼ The Soviets wanted to gain recognition of the European status quo, that is, their domination of Eastern Europe.

WHY HAD FRANCO-AMERICAN RELATIONS DETERIORATED?
The French resented American policy during the Suez crisis (see page 220) and American pressure on France to grant independence to Algeria. President De Gaulle (1959–69) wanted to restore his country's international prestige. He doubted that the USA would risk nuclear attack in order to save Western Europe. He worried about the frequent Congressional debates about the wisdom of keeping American soldiers in Europe, and concluded that the United States was an unreliable ally. After the Cuban missile crisis, De Gaulle complained that he had been informed not consulted. De Gaulle disapproved of Lyndon Johnson's Vietnam policy. He resented US domination of NATO and therefore took France out of NATO in 1966.

However, although the Johnson administration was reasonably well inclined toward detente, the prospects were damaged by the Tet Offensive (see page 274) and the 1968 Soviet invasion of Czechoslovakia (to keep it a single party state within the Warsaw Pact). To universal amazement it was Johnson's Cold Warrior successor President Richard Nixon who engineered the first real Soviet–American detente.

Why did Nixon want detente with the Soviets?

▼ Nixon had privately concluded 'there is no way to win the [Vietnam] war'. He knew that decreased involvement in Vietnam would make it easier to improve relations with the Soviets. The Soviets could then be used to put pressure on North Vietnam to agree to a settlement, which would enable the US to get out of Vietnam without losing face.

▼ Nixon and his foreign policy adviser Henry Kissinger were fearful of the USSR's growing military strength. Kissinger stressed that the Soviets needed 'managing' now that they were a truly global superpower.

▼ Nixon and Kissinger knew that the American public and economy made it impossible to counter increased Soviet power by a massive arms race or by increased US global commitments. Containment had to be pursued in a different manner – by making a deal with the enemy.

▼ Nixon and Kissinger believed that the increasing economic and military power of Western Europe and Japan had created a multipolar world wherein America would have to readjust its position and policies.

▼ Kissinger wanted America to forget the old idealistic and legalistic foreign policy style that had sometimes gone against American national interest. He felt America's prime concern should be maintaining a world balance of power, while recognising that American power was limited.

How was Nixon able to bring about detente? He had an impeccable anti-Communist pedigree. That made it harder for American right-wingers to attack his detente policy. Nixon also knew that Americans wanted a safer world, and many trusted his capacity to broker a good deal with the Soviets. He believed his improving relationship with China would frighten the Soviets into greater cooperation with the USA. Finally, Nixon knew that the Soviet leader Brezhnev was desperate for detente because:

▼ Fearful of the Chinese, Brezhnev was beginning to feel in need of friends.

▼ The USSR's economy was in a dire state. Brezhnev wanted US technology and US agricultural produce.

▼ Some of the Soviet Union's East European satellites were trying to gain greater national independence. Brezhnev therefore wanted to stabilise Eastern Europe, which necessitated an agreement with West Germany, which in turn needed US approval.

DETENTE – A TIMELINE

1966 Willy Brandt became German Foreign Minister;
1967 Chinese demonstrators attacked Soviet embassy in Beijing (January);
Johnson met Soviet Premier Kosygin (Glassboro, New Jersey)(June);
1968 US, USSR and Britain signed Non-proliferation Treaty to stop spread of nuclear weapons; US and USSR promised to begin Strategic Arms Limitation Talks (SALT) (July);
Soviet invasion of Czechoslovakia damaged Soviet-American relations and delayed SALT (August);
1969 Nixon's inauguration speech emphasised 'era of negotiations' with the Soviet Union (January);
first of many US troop withdrawals from Vietnam (June);
West German–Polish Treaty of friendship (December);
1971 Four-Power Agreement on Berlin (USA, USSR, Britain and France) (September);
1972 first visit by a US President (Nixon) to Moscow;
SALT signed (May);
US–Soviet grain deal (July);
West Germany and East Germany signed 'Basic Treaty' (December);
1973 Vietnam peace agreement signed in Paris (January);
last US troops left South Vietnam (March);
second Brezhnev–Nixon Summit (Washington) (June);
Helsinki Conference on European Security attended by 35 countries, including US (July);
Middle East war caused Soviet-American tension;
NATO and Warsaw Pact countries' talks on conventional arms reductions started (Vienna); continued for years; unsuccessful (October);
1974 Nixon-Brezhnev third Summit (Moscow) (June–July);
President Nixon resigned (August);
Ford–Brezhnev Summit at Vladivostok laid foundation for SALT II Treaty – signed in 1979, but never ratified (November);
1975 Helsinki Accords.

b) Detente in Europe

Before 1967, no West German politician wanted to admit that Germany was permanently divided, lest the admission lose him votes. However, the West German position changed. Why? By 1967 reunification seemed unlikely. Furthermore, the West Germans were very much aware that they were in the 'front-line' in any Soviet–American clash. Detente would decrease tension. West Germany would then become more secure. German Foreign Minister Willy Brandt was therefore keen to improve relations with the Soviet bloc countries. Brandt believed detente would lead to the loosening of the Soviet grip on Eastern Europe. He hoped that West Germany could massively increase its trade with Eastern Europe, and that detente would bring humanitarian gains, such as more visits between East and West Germans. When NATO agreed that detente was desirable, Brandt set to work.

THE FOUR-POWER AGREEMENT ON BERLIN SAID

▼ The Soviets recognised Western rights of access to West Berlin.

▼ West Berliners would have easier access to East Berlin and East Germany. The agreement conceded the Soviet point that West Berlin was not part of West Germany, and the West's point that there should be a close relationship between West Berlin and West Germany.

THE BASIC TREATY

East Germany and West Germany agreed to set up missions (not embassies) in each other's country, recognise the permanence and validity of each other's frontiers, and to increase economic, cultural and personal contacts. However, West Germany had not given full diplomatic recognition to East Germany (the 'missions rather than embassies' clause made that point clear).

SALT I

Historian Walter La Faber wrote that SALT I 'only placed a few limits on, but did not stop, the arms race'.

Initially, the Soviets were wary of Brandt's policies. Brandt therefore lifted the ban on the West German Communist Party (1968), recognised the post-Second World War Polish acquisition of German territory as permanent, and signed the nuclear Non-Proliferation Treaty (1969), thereby assuring the world that West Germany had no aggressive intent. Problems with China made the Soviets anxious to decrease tensions in Europe, so they responded positively to Brandt's overtures. In September 1971, the USA, USSR, Britain and France at last settled the Berlin problem with a **Four-Power Agreement** on Berlin. When East Germany and West Germany signed a Basic Treaty it seemed that the German problem was finally settled.

There were several reasons for this reduction of tension in Cold War Europe. Two important individuals, Brandt and Nixon, favoured detente. Soviet fears of and preoccupation with China made the USSR keen to reduce tensions in Europe. The NATO powers wanted decreased military expenditure to lower taxes. The American public was tired of paying to defend Europeans and wanted to decrease the number of American troops in Europe. The US economy was in trouble, so Nixon was keen to cut down on defence expenditure. Thus both NATO and the Warsaw Pact countries were willing to recognise the European status quo. The West seemed content to allow Soviet domination of Eastern Europe. The Soviets seemed to lack any desire to destabilise Western Europe. Having recognised that the tensest area in Europe was Germany, both sides were keen to decrease tension in Germany, even if it meant making some concessions.

c) What Were the Consequences and Significance of Detente?

▼ **SALT I** was signed at Moscow in May 1972. This Strategic Arms Limitation Treaty ended the arms race on defensive antiballistic missile systems (ABMs) and froze the number of nuclear missiles possessed by the US (1,054) and USSR (1,600). The Soviet numerical advantage was far outweighed by the US ability to put multiple warheads (which could hit widely separated areas) on one missile.

▼ Soviet pressure on North Vietnam helped bring about the peace settlement there.

▼ Detente helped Nixon win the 1972 presidential election, but barely survived Nixon's downfall.

▼ Both the USA and the USSR continued to struggle to win friends and allies. For example, the September 1973 downfall of the democratically elected Marxist leader of Chile, Salvador Allende, owed much to the CIA.

▼ Once Germany was settled, the road was open to an agreement that decreased Cold War tensions throughout Europe – the **Helsinki Agreement**. The Helsinki Agreement (1975) could be said to be the nearest the victors of the Second World War ever got to making a European peace settlement. Both sides recognised the post-war status quo in Europe. The West thereby implicitly recognised Soviet domination of Eastern Europe. Although some in the West felt the agreement was a sell-out, the human rights provision encouraged agitation for human rights in Eastern Europe and caused the Soviet Union a great deal of international embarrassment.

▼ Detente could not stop an acute Soviet–American crisis arising out of the Middle East war in 1973.

The Helsinki Agreement (1975)

▼ The West recognised the current national boundaries in Eastern Europe.

▼ West Germany renounced its claim to be the sole legitimate German state.

▼ NATO and the Warsaw Pact countries agreed that each should have observers at each other's military exercises.

▼ There would be more trade, and more economic, scientific, and technological cooperation between the Soviet bloc and the West.

▼ There would be a freer exchange of people and ideas.

▼ Both sides put their human rights record to public scrutiny.

---

d) Crises that Demonstrated the Limits of Detente

i) The Middle East Crisis (1973–4)

After Suez (1956), the Soviets rebuilt Egypt's armed forces, while the Americans made Israel the greatest military power in the region. In 1967, feeling threatened by Egypt, Israel launched the 'Six-Day War', and seized territory from Egypt (Sinai), Jordan (West Bank) and Syria (Golan Heights). The superpowers kept out of that war but continued to build up their client states.

Israel steadfastly refused to evacuate the occupied territories she had taken in 1967. Therefore, Egypt and Syria attacked Israel (October 1973). The Israeli counter-attack was so successful that Egypt appealed to Brezhnev for assistance. The Soviets mobilised their conventional forces. Nixon warned Brezhnev not to use those forces, and put US nuclear strike forces on alert. However, Nixon simultaneously restrained the Israelis, while Kissinger initiated an excellent working relationship with the Egyptians. Kissinger then managed to stabilise the region while excluding the Soviets.

The significance of the 1973 Middle East crisis was great:

▼ It demonstrated the West's increasing vulnerability to Arab oil-power. Because the US was supplying weapons to their great enemy Israel, and using NATO bases in Western Europe as transportation points, the Arab nations retaliated by imposing an oil embargo which damaged the American, West European and Japanese economies. As oil prices rocketed, the New York stock exchange shares plummeted.

▼ Under pressure of the oil crisis, Japan and Western Europe became increasingly pro-Arab, which infuriated the USA. This confirmed the dangers of the multipolar world that the Nixon administration had feared, and which had made Nixon seek detente.

▼ The Soviets were embarrassed by their apparent inability to help their Arab allies, and by the Egyptian–American rapprochement.

▼ While the superpowers had concentrated upon improving relations with each other, the crisis revealed that their basic rivalry and antagonism remained, and that the new multipolar world in which they both operated was more unpredictable than the old bipolar Cold War world.

▼ The crisis clearly demonstrated the limitations of detente, particularly when Nixon put the US on full nuclear alert.

ii) Africa

According to a Soviet analyst (1975), 'Peaceful coexistence is a principle of relations between states which does not extend to relations between...the oppressed peoples and the colonialists'. That Soviet interpretation of detente helps explain Soviet involvement in Africa in 1974–5.

In 1974 Portugal's African colony Angola gained independence. Competing Angolese factions struggled for power. America and China supported one faction, the USSR supported the other. The Soviets airlifted thousands of Cuban troops to Angola. Kissinger described that as a dangerous escalation of the Cold War, but failed to persuade Congress to vote for US military intervention. Congress indicated that there must be no more Vietnams. The 'Soviet' faction won in Angola, but then turned to the US for technical aid. The crisis showed that detente had severe limitations and that Third World countries were unpredictable within the Cold War context. They tended to turn to the country, which could offer them the most assistance or advantage, regardless of ideology.

e) Why Did Detente Collapse?

Nixon's successor, Gerald Ford, relied heavily upon Henry Kissinger. Ford and Kissinger agreed with Brezhnev on the basic principles of a SALT II agreement at the Vladivostok Summit (1974). Ford hoped it would help him get elected president in the 1976 election. However, during that election, it was clear that detente had become an embarrassment to Ford's Republican Party. Even Kissinger said detente was 'a word I would like to forget'.

There were several reasons why Americans had turned against detente:

▼ The disgraced President Nixon (see page 298) was associated with detente, so detente lost some credibility along with him. Prior to his presidency, Nixon had been the unchallenged leader of American conservatives and Cold Warriors. Now Nixon was gone, American conservatives spoke of 'appeasement' of the USSR once again.

▼ Detente seemed to necessitate recognition of Soviet domination of the East European countries from whence the ancestors of many Americans had emigrated.

▼ The Communists seemed to be in an expansionist phase in Angola and Vietnam.

▼ American liberals criticised the lack of human rights in the USSR. In 1974, Congress infuriated the Soviets by inserting a clause on human rights in the Soviet–American trade agreement.

▼ Americans had become dissatisfied with SALT I by 1973, as the Soviets caught up with the Americans on multiple warheads.

The Soviets had also turned against detente. President Ford's successor, President Carter, took a moralistic stance in foreign policy. Carter frequently criticised the Soviets' human rights record, which infuriated the Soviets. The Soviets resented their exclusion from the Middle East peace process, which Carter initiated in 1978, and they felt that Carter was too friendly with China. In January 1979 the Americans and Chinese finally established full diplomatic relations. The Soviets blamed Sino-American plotting for the subsequent Chinese invasion of Vietnam (a Soviet ally). The Chinese were buying military hardware from the West and apparently befriending America's ally Japan. As far as the Soviets were concerned, detente had proved unhelpful in isolating the Chinese. Furthermore, the Soviets had hoped that detente would prove helpful for their economy, but their economic situation was worsening. Perhaps worst of all, the Helsinki Agreement had resulted in unrest in Eastern Europe and world-wide criticism of the USSR because of the human rights issue. The Soviets felt that the US was unappreciative of Soviet concessions. In 1979 Brezhnev allowed an exceptional number of Jews to emigrate from the USSR – something the Americans had long demanded. However, Carter responded by conducting a high-profile correspondence with a Soviet dissident. The Soviets retaliated by criticising the US human rights record. They pointed out that widespread racial prejudice, unemployment, and organised crime in the West indicated Western hypocrisy. Although Carter and Brezhnev at the Vienna Summit (1979) had agreed SALT II, the suspicious American Congress refused to ratify the treaty.

CARTER'S FOREIGN POLICY

Under President Carter, US foreign policy went from 'coexistence to conversion', according to historian Peter Boyle.

Congress felt that the Soviets were aggressively active in too many parts of the world, such as Afghanistan. Thus from the Soviet viewpoint, detente brought insufficient gain.

President Carter faced many problems. Detente was unpopular. American national pride was greatly damaged in autumn 1979, when anti-Western Iranian Muslims took hostage Americans in Iran. NATO allies criticised the lack of direction in Carter's foreign policy. In July 1979 pro-Cuban forces in Nicaragua overthrew a pro-American dictator. Carter failed to get any support from the Organisation of American States (OAS). The Soviets seemed to be in an expansionist phase, especially in Afghanistan. All that Carter could think to do was to begin a massive military build-up. Brezhnev was doing the same. Detente was dead.

f) Was Detente a Failure?

If America's aim in detente was to end the arms race, eliminate Soviet–American rivalry, and reform the USSR, then detente was a failure. However, if detente simply aimed to stop superpower differences escalating into dangerous crises, then it could be said to have been a success. In SALT I, the madness of the nuclear arms race was recognised, and the principle of restraint was agreed upon. A notorious Cold War trouble spot, Berlin, was settled. Although the status quo in Europe might not have been desirable to all parties, at least the continent was stabilised and peaceful. Increased East–West contacts eventually played an important part in the downfall of the USSR: the Helsinki Agreement triggered off unrest over the issue of human rights within the Soviet bloc.

The USSR and Afghanistan

In 1979, the pro-Soviet government in Afghanistan was divided into two factions. Tribal risings plagued the government. On 27 December 1979 the Red Army invaded Afghanistan in support of the more moderate faction. Soon 100,000 Soviet troops were there, fighting Muslim guerrillas who opposed the pro-Soviet government.

Why did the Soviets get involved?

▼ Afghanistan was a Muslim state on the southern border of the USSR. As the Soviets had a potentially disaffected Muslim population within their southern borders, they wanted to stop unrest spreading from Afghanistan.

▼ The USSR's southern borders would be endangered if there was another hostile state there (Islamic Iran already disliked the USSR).

▼ The Soviets were losing their traditional influence over the government of Afghanistan.

▼ The Soviets felt encircled by hostile nations and hostile alliances. It seemed important to keep Afghanistan friendly.

What was the significance of the Soviet intervention in Afghanistan?

▼ The war was a long, expensive drain on the Soviet economy. It damaged Soviet morale and the reputation of the USSR throughout the world.

▼ The West interpreted the war as highly significant, believing that the Soviets had entered into a new expansionist phase. This was the first time that Soviet troops had been used outside Eastern Europe since 1945.

▼ The US reaction was hostile. SALT II was not ratified. Carter stopped exports to the USSR, dramatically increased US defence spending, and pledged US intervention if the USSR threatened Western interest in the Persian Gulf. He stopped US participation in the Moscow Olympics (1980).

ACTIVITY

'Detente was never likely to work.' Do you agree?

9 The End of the Cold War

ISSUES:
Was there a second Cold War? Why did the Cold War end?

In his first term (1981–5) President Ronald Reagan worsened the Cold War. In his second term (1985–9) he helped to end it.

a) Reagan's First Term

Some historians talk of a second Cold War, although they disagree over when it started. Kissinger said it was in 1975. From the Soviet viewpoint detente was definitely over by 1979, when Carter seemed very close to the Chinese and excluded the Soviets from the Middle East peace settlement. Whenever the second Cold War started, there is no doubt that it was under way during President Ronald Reagan's first term. During the 1980 presidential election campaign, Reagan made clear his feelings about the Soviet Union: 'Let us not delude ourselves. The Soviet Union underlies all the unrest that is going on [in the world]'. No doubt he genuinely believed that what he called the 'evil empire' (the USSR) was a great threat.

In his first term, Reagan achieved little of note. Despite all his Cold War rhetoric, the economic interests of American farmers led him to end the embargo on wheat exports to the Soviet Union. In retaliation for the Soviet suppression of the trade union movement within Poland, Reagan put sanctions on Poland, which made the

Polish people suffer more. Reagan tried but failed to stop the West Germans purchasing Siberian natural gas. When Kennedy had attempted something similar in 1962, he had been successful, which showed the extent to which American power and influence over her allies had decreased. Reagan's military build-up alienated the Soviets, who stopped participating in arms reduction talks. Reagan was quick to intervene in small countries (such as Lebanon, Grenada, Libya, and Nicaragua), but his aims were rarely totally clear or believable, and the results were never impressive.

So, by the end of Reagan's first term, detente seemed dead and buried, and Reagan's foreign policy seemed to lack constructive direction. In 1987 an independent investigatory committee concluded that President Reagan had frequently failed to supervise and oversee US foreign policy effectively. However, some Americans contend that Reagan's massive defence expenditure helped destroy the USSR, which ruined itself by trying to maintain parity.

Was there a second Cold War under President Reagan? Relations were very tense, but there was nothing comparable to the Cuban missile crisis. Furthermore, the four years of tension were soon forgotten, owing to great changes in the USSR. A common contemporary joke was that the Kremlin was doubling as a geriatric ward and a funeral parlour: the senile Brezhnev died in 1982, and two elderly successors soon followed him. However, in March 1985 the youthful Mikhail Gorbachev became leader of the Soviet Union, and the Cold War was miraculously transformed.

b) Why Gorbachev and Reagan Wanted to End the Cold War

▼ Gorbachev knew that it was vital to cut Soviet military expenditure to revitalise the Soviet economy.

▼ He knew that the USSR had few reliable allies but many reliable enemies. It made sense to decrease the number of enemies.

▼ Gorbachev believed that the traditional Soviet obsession with the USA was an anachronism in the new multipolar world. Believing that the United States was in decline, it made no sense to continue the Cold War.

▼ Reagan was running for re-election in 1984. He needed votes and he knew that one-third of American voters feared his Cold War extremism.

▼ Reagan had lost credibility through some of his misguided foreign policy adventures, so he was desperate for some international success. He was very much influenced by his wife Nancy who urged him to seek his place in history through being a peacemaker.

▼ Reagan knew that he could claim to be negotiating from a position of strength because of his previous massive military build-up.

c) How Reagan and Gorbachev Ended the Cold War

Although both Reagan and Gorbachev wanted to improve relations, the task would have been far more difficult had they not got on so well together. Gorbachev suggested the first summit meeting for six years. They met at Geneva (1985) and agreed in principle to a 50 per cent cut in their armed forces. The second summit was at Reykjavik in Iceland (1986). A contemporary observer, Strobe Talbott, described the meeting as amazing: there was no proper preparation for talks, nor any consultation with allies. As the atmosphere became more euphoric, they were on the verge of agreeing to eliminate all missiles. However, when Gorbachev insisted that Reagan give up his beloved '**Star Wars**' programme, the meeting ended in quite bitter recriminations. However, Gorbachev visited Washington in December 1987 and, for the first time, an entire class of missiles (medium and short range) was eliminated. Reagan's impeccable anti-Communist and right-wing credentials ensured that he met with little or no opposition at home. The relationship prospered with Reagan's visit to Moscow in summer 1988, and Gorbachev's visit to New York in December 1988.

Gorbachev made concessions and changes in other areas. When he said, 'It is inadmissible and futile to encourage revolution from abroad', he decreased world anxiety about Communism. He slowly withdrew Soviet soldiers from Afghanistan and decreased support for left-wing regimes in Angola and Cuba.

d) Bush and the Soviet Union

In 1989 George Bush became president of the United States. He was far more knowledgeable about foreign affairs than Reagan had been, and determined to 'be his own man'. He was therefore less enthusiastic about meeting Gorbachev. He was also puzzled and confused as to what to do about the collapse of Communism in the former Soviet bloc countries during 1988–9.

A minority of informed Americans suggested Bush should give Marshall-style aid to Eastern Europe, but not to the Russians. However, Congress was unenthusiastic. Bush now had greater freedom of international action than any American president had had for a long time. By 1991 the Cold War had clearly ended. One of the main protagonists had lost its empire and collapsed from within. The other was now the world's sole superpower.

STAR WARS
In 1983 Reagan enthusiastically endorsed the Strategic Defence Initiative (SDI), also known as Star Wars. The aim was to shoot down nuclear missiles before they reached their targets. Star Wars never materialised.

PRESIDENT BUSH AND FREEDOM OF ACTION
Bush had disliked being called a wimp because of his inability to get rid of an undesirable Panamanian dictator (General Noriega), and this perhaps inspired his 26,000-troop invasion of Panama in 1989. Bush claimed that the Panama Canal was threatened, that US citizens in Panama needed protecting (a US Marine had been killed there), and that he had to capture the defiant dictator Noriega (an ex-CIA agent). Few people found his explanations convincing, and the venture was disastrous for US–Latin American relations. Bush had similar opportunities for freedom of action during the Gulf crisis of January 1991. In August 1990 Iraq had invaded Kuwait. When Iraq refused to retreat, Bush and the Western alliance used force to make it do so, and there was no opposition worthy of the name in the UN. Gorbachev was totally compliant.

Why and How Did the Soviet Empire Collapse?

In late 1988 Gorbachev rejected the so-called Brezhnev Doctrine, by which the Soviets had asserted their right to interfere in any wayward Communist country. Gorbachev decided the USSR no longer had the strength to keep increasingly restless East European satellites within their orbit. When a democratically elected government came into power in Poland (June 1989), Gorbachev did nothing to stop it. In September 1989 a new Hungarian regime came into being. Hungary relaxed all frontier restrictions, and thousands of East Germans took advantage of this to flee into West Germany. The Communist East German regime lost confidence. In November 1989 the Berlin Wall was dismantled, and in 1990 elections, the East Germans overthrew the Communist regime. In March 1990 Germans from both East and West discussed reunification, and in September the Treaty of Moscow was signed, in which the USA, the USSR, Britain, France, West Germany and East Germany agreed on German reunification. The old Communist regimes in Czechoslovakia, Bulgaria, and Romania also collapsed. During 1990–91, Gorbachev struggled to keep control of the USSR. He resigned on Christmas Day 1991, by which time it was clear that the old USSR could never be revitalised.

---

e) Results of the Cold War

Some commentators have looked back with nostalgia on the Cold War world. They have talked about a 'long peace', when the world was unusually stable. However, for countries such as Korea and Vietnam, the Cold War exacerbated internal conflicts, while there was little personal freedom or prosperity for those under Soviet domination in Eastern Europe. People throughout the world took the prospect of nuclear holocaust very seriously, and were understandably terrified. Furthermore, domestic problems within the United States and the USSR were often ignored because of the preoccupation with the Cold War.

It could be claimed that America saved the world from Communist tyranny, although America's own actions were frequently less than admirable. It could also be claimed that the American military–industrial complex contributed to US economic prosperity during the struggle, or that fear of condemnation from Cold War antagonists helped improve the status of African Americans. On the other hand, America had and still has a large minority of impoverished citizens. The money spent by both the United States and the USSR on the arms race could have been used to improve citizens' standard of living.

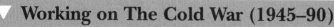

ACTIVITY

Make a Cold War date list, highlighting the causes and consequences of crises and their significance.

▼ Working on The Cold War (1945–90)

You need to be familiar with the chronology of the Cold War, and to be able to list the causes, courses and consequences of great crises (such as the Berlin Blockade and the Korean War) and to recognise their significance.

Answering Extended Writing and Essay Questions on The Cold War

Questions on the Cold War usually focus on the great crises, although some of you might be asked to include the Cold War in an 'overview' question. Typical questions for you to think about are:

1. In what ways did US foreign policy change in the twentieth century?
2. Was the Korean War a 'UN war' or a 'US war'?
3. What were the causes and consequences of the Cuban missiles crisis?

Remember that questions often structure your answer for you. Question 1 suggests you should find several 'ways', each of which could be an essay paragraph. Question 2 suggests you trace US involvement, assessing at each stage the extent to which the UN or allies were involved and/or dependent. Question 3 asks you for two lists, one of reasons, one of results.

Answering Source-based Questions on The Cold War

The attack upon Korea makes it plain beyond all doubt that Communism has passed beyond the use of subversion to conquer independent nations and will now use armed invasion and war. It has defied the orders of the Security Council of the United Nations issued to preserve international peace and security. In these circumstances the occupation of Formosa [Taiwan] by Communist forces would be a direct threat to the security of the Pacific area and to

Source F Statement by President Truman, 27 June 1950.

United States forces performing their lawful and necessary functions in area. Accordingly, I have ordered the Seventh Fleet to prevent any attack upon Formosa.

Source G Official Soviet statement by Foreign Minister Gromyko, 4 July 1950.

The resolution which the US government is using as a cover for its armed intervention in Korea was illegally put through the Security Council in gross violation of the Charter. This was only possible because the pressure of the US government on members of the Security Council converted the UN into ... an obedient tool of the American ruling circles who acted as violators of peace.

Source H Declaration issued by the Government of the Chinese People's Republic, 10 October 1950.

The American war of invasion in Korea has been a serious menace to the security of China from its very start. The American invading forces in Korea have on several occasions violated the territorial air of China and strafed and bombed Chinese people ... Now the American forces are attempting to cross the 38th parallel on a large scale, the Chinese people cannot stand by idle with regard to such a serious situation created by the invasion of Korea by the United States and its accomplice countries and to the dangerous trend towards extending the war.

Source I Margaret Truman, President Truman's daughter, writing in the 1970s.

By now the terrible truth about massive Chinese intervention in Korea was visible to everyone ... Dad ... was meeting the crisis ... with quiet courage. First, he coped with the defeatism of Prime Minister Attlee and his aides ... My father disagreed with the British desire to seat China in the United Nations at this time. It would be rewarding the Chinese for their aggressive, lawless actions in Korea ... On January 13 my father wrote ... MacArthur a long letter, explaining ... the thinking behind his policy to confine the war to Korea. He pointed out how much we would gain from a successful resistance in Korea. We would deflate, as indeed we did, the political and military prestige of Communist China ... We would lend urgency to the rapid expansion of the defences of the Western world.

▼ QUESTIONS ON SOURCES

1. What do the sources reveal about Harry Truman's opinion of Communism? **[3 marks]**

2. Assess the value of Source I to a historian studying Truman's policies during the Korean War. **[6 marks]**

3. (i) To what extent do Sources F and H differ in their interpretations of American actions in Korea? (ii) Why do they differ? **[5 marks]**
4. What evidence is there in the language, tone and content of Sources G and H of anti-American feeling? **[6 marks]**
5. Using the sources and your background knowledge, would you agree that the Americans were the aggressors in the Korean War? **[20 marks]**

Further Reading

Books in the Access to History *series*

Oliver Edwards covers *The USA and the Cold War* and Vivienne Sanders *The United States of America and Vietnam, 1945–75*.

General

There are several good basic books on the Cold War. P. Mooney and C. Bown, *Cold War to Detente* (Heinemann, 1986), is clear and competent, as is Joseph Smith, *The Cold War: 1945–1965* (Basil Blackwell, 1989). Martin McCauley, *Russia, America and the Cold War, 1949–91* (Longman, 1998), is short but stimulating. S.J. Ball, *The Cold War* (Arnold, 1998), is more detailed. The Longman *Companion to Cold War and Detente*, by J.W. Young (Longman, 2000), is an invaluable reference work, with useful date lists, biographies, and brief summaries of crises and conferences. Of the books on particular crises, Peter Lowe's *The Korean War* (Macmillan, 2000), is the most accessible.

7 THE UNITED STATES AND VIETNAM

POINTS TO CONSIDER

Post-Second World War US foreign policy was dominated by the Cold War, in which America's main antagonists were the USSR and the People's Republic of China (see previous chapter). You need to consider how the Cold War context led the United States into a conflict in the small South-east Asian country of Vietnam. You need to think about why America (a) got involved, (b) failed to achieve its aims and (c) got out of Vietnam.

ISSUE:
What were the main themes in Vietnamese history up to 1975?

1 Foreign Interference in Vietnam

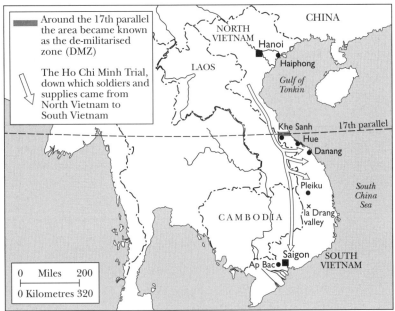

Figure 48 Important places in Vietnam during the American era.

a) Before the Second World War

Throughout their history the Vietnamese people suffered foreign interference and conquest. In the second century BC the Chinese began a series of attempts to conquer and retain Vietnam which lasted until the fifteenth century. The French first became interested in Vietnam in the seventeenth century. By the late nine-teenth century France had conquered Vietnam, Cambodia and Laos, which were collectively known as French Indo-China. Many articulate Vietnamese were unhappy with French rule, although some members of Vietnam's Catholic minority collaborated with their French co-religionists. By the 1930s, a small Vietnamese nationalist group that espoused Communism had grown up in exile under the leadership of Ho Chi Minh.

b) The French and Vietnam, 1940–54

In 1940 imperialist France was itself conquered by Nazi Germany. The fall of France left French Indo-China powerless in the face of Germany's ally, Japan. From September 1940 until Japan surrendered to the United States in August 1945, Vietnam was under Japanese control. The Japanese allowed the French colonial administration to continue the day-to-day running of Vietnam.

Ho Chi Minh

Ho Chi Minh came from a middle-class Vietnamese family. In 1911 he began 30 years of travel, during which time he visited and learned from countries such as France, Britain, the United States, the USSR and China. In France in 1919 he tried but failed to persuade the victorious powers in the First World War to recognise the Vietnamese right to self-government. After 1917 Communism increasingly impressed him, because of its emphasis upon anti-colonialism and economic equality. He established a Vietnamese Communist Party in Hong Kong in 1929. He finally returned to his beloved Vietnam in 1941 in order to fight the Japanese occupation forces.

Figure 49 Ho Chi Minh dining: behind him are portraits of himself and Mao Zedong.

In August 1945, Ho Chi Minh proclaimed the independence of Vietnam. However, the French returned to Vietnam to re-establish their authority. In 1946, Ho and his followers (the Vietminh) began their fight for independence against the French. Ho's Communist forces did well. The French had problems back home and found it difficult to defeat the Vietminh. In 1954, the Vietminh victory over the French at Dienbienphu precipitated a French withdrawal. At an international peace conference in Geneva, France, the Vietminh, China, and the USSR agreed that the war in Vietnam would cease. Ho would retain the lands his forces occupied north of the 17th parallel, while the Vietnamese Emperor **Bao Dai** would rule the south. There would be nationwide elections in 1956. The United States and Bao Dai rejected these agreements.

BAO DAI – THE LAST VIETNAMESE EMPEROR

Bao Dai succeeded his father as Emperor in 1925. He collaborated first with the French, then with the Japanese (1940–45), and finally with the French again (1945–55). Diem drove him from power in 1955, and Bao Dai went to live in France.

THE GENEVA SETTLEMENT, 1954

Ho Chi Minh's Vietnamese Communists agreed with France that:
1. The French and the Vietminh would stop fighting.
2. The Communists would control Vietnam north of the 17th parallel.
3. Bao Dai would govern Vietnam south of the 17th parallel.
4. There would be democratic elections throughout Vietnam in 1956.
5. No Vietnamese were to make military alliances with any foreign power.

c) Roosevelt, Truman and Vietnam

The United States had first become interested in Vietnam in the Second World War. President Franklin Roosevelt could not decide what would be best for post-war Vietnam. At different times he contemplated either returning Vietnam to the French or giving it to China, or having an international trusteeship. After the war, President Harry Truman (1945–53) favoured a return of the French, but he envisaged France steering the Vietnamese towards eventual self-government.

Truman's views on Vietnam were changed by the development of the Cold War (see Chapter 6). From 1944 to 1949 the Soviet–American relationship deteriorated. Truman became concerned about the expansion of Communism, particularly when China was 'lost' to Communism in 1949. In this context, Truman sympathised with the French in their struggle against Ho and his Communist forces. Truman therefore gave the French financial aid ($15 million in 1950) to prosecute their war against Ho.

d) Eisenhower and Vietnam

President Eisenhower (1953–61) continued the financial aid to the French, until the dramatic change occasioned by the **Geneva settlement** in 1954. Eisenhower hated the idea of Communists governing even half of Vietnam. Eisenhower knew that if the proposed nationwide elections were held in Vietnam in 1956 they would result in the election of a Communist government. Eisenhower therefore refused to recognise the Geneva settlement and promoted an anti-Communist South Vietnamese government. The Geneva settlement left South Vietnam under the nominal control of the Emperor Bao Dai. Bao Dai relied heavily upon his Prime Minister Ngo Dinh Diem. Diem soon ousted Bao Dai and became the leader of South Vietnam. In effect, there were now two independent states, North Vietnam and South Vietnam. Diem's government was unpopular and often ineffective. While the Eisenhower administration was aware of this, they failed to see any acceptable alternative. The Eisenhower administration sent military equipment and advisers as well as financial aid to Diem.

In 1957 Ho's supporters in South Vietnam began guerrilla activities to destabilise Diem's regime. Ho stepped up the agitation in 1960, from which time his southern supporters were known as the National Liberation Front (NLF). Diem called the NLF the Vietcong (VC) or 'Vietnamese Communists'.

e) Kennedy, Johnson and Vietnam

Successive American presidents increased US involvement in Vietnam. At President Kennedy's accession (1961) there were 800 American military advisers in South Vietnam. By the time Kennedy died (1963) there were 16,000 American 'advisers' there. US military personnel and equipment were increasingly in evidence: for example, in 1961 a US aircraft carrier brought in 47 US helicopters to Saigon. Kennedy's ambassador Henry Cabot Lodge colluded in the army's overthrow of the unpopular Diem in 1963. However, Diem's successors were equally unpopular.

Figure 50 Diem waving to the crowd in New York City, in a parade in his honour (1957).

President Lyndon Baines Johnson (1963–9) continued and then escalated US involvement in Vietnam. The South Vietnamese government and its Army of the Republic of South Vietnam (ARVN) remained unsuccessful. Johnson wanted to prop up the Saigon regime. That entailed increased US aid. Johnson wanted to protect American personnel in Vietnam so he took a major escalatory step in 1965. He began large-scale bombing of North Vietnam. Within weeks he took another great escalatory step. He sent in American ground troops. By the end of 1965 he had sent in 200,000 American ground troops to South Vietnam. By 1968 there were half a million Americans there. Despite these great American efforts, the Communist forces remained undefeated.

f) Nixon and Vietnam

President Richard Nixon (1969–74) was therefore determined to get US soldiers out. As he withdrew them he built up ARVN ('Vietnamisation') and escalated US bombing of North Vietnam and the Ho Chi Minh Trail, down which the North Vietnamese sent men and materials to South Vietnam. Nixon escalated the bombing in order to persuade Hanoi to agree to peace. In 1973 Nixon achieved a peace settlement that enabled him to extricate America from the war and left South Vietnam's President Thieu in power in South Vietnam. However, within two years North Vietnam had invaded South Vietnam and re-unified Vietnam under Communist rule. Richard Nixon was no longer president and the United States Congress was unwilling to intervene.

Vietnam has been under Communist rule since 1975 although, like China, it has incorporated elements of capitalism in its economic structure. Vietnam and the war remain controversial and uncomfortable topics for many Americans.

ACTIVITY

Construct a date list showing some main themes and events in Vietnamese history, and US interest in Vietnam. Keep this date list alongside you as you read the rest of this chapter. When you construct a date list, it is best to leave several lines in between each entry, as you will invariably want to add more events as your knowledge of the topic increases.

ISSUE:
Why did the United
States get and remain
involved in Vietnam?

2 The Causes of US Involvement in Vietnam

a) Fear of Communism

Americans perceived Communism to be a great threat to the United States. The Communist ideology was anathema to Americans. Americans believed in political democracy (universal suffrage in a multi-party state) while Communists favoured economic democracy. Americans believed in capitalism (with minimal state intervention in the national economy) while Communists advocated state-controlled economies. When, after the Second World War, more nations became Communist, Americans grew increasingly fearful. If the world balance of power titled in favour of Communism, the US might find itself surrounded by hostile powers who might refuse to trade with (and maybe even attack) the US.

i) Truman (1945–53)

American fear of Communism was the reason why the French were able to persuade Harry Truman to give them aid in their struggle against Ho Chi Minh. The French depicted Ho as part of a world-wide movement of Communist expansion. The Truman administration found this believable. From 1945 to 1949 the Soviets had consolidated their hold over Eastern Europe and made what the United States perceived to be aggressive moves in Iran and the eastern Mediterranean. When China 'fell' to Communism in 1949 it confirmed the Truman administration's belief that Communism was on the march and that Ho and his Vietminh were part of a world-wide army directed from Moscow. Some State Department specialists tried to point out that Ho was as much nationalist as Communist. However, Truman's Secretary of State Dean Acheson said it was 'irrelevant' to ask if Ho was 'as much nationalist as Commie'. This would prove to be a crucial and basic misunderstanding that haunted and distorted US policy toward Vietnam. Ho and his followers were always Vietnamese first. Although willing to use Soviet and Chinese aid, they were not puppets.

The strategic importance of Indochina derives from its geographical position as a key to the defence of mainland Southeast Asia; its economic value as a potential large exporter of rice; and its political importance as an example of Western resistance to Communist expansion.

Source A The State Department on why Vietnam was important (March 1952).

Events in 1950 made Truman finally make up his mind to help the French in Indo-China. The Republicans attacked Truman and the Democrats for having 'lost' China to Communism (1949), while Senator Joseph McCarthy aroused the country into a witch-hunting anti-Communist frenzy (see page 285). After Communist North Korea attacked South Korea (see page 211) and the United States moved to defend the latter, it was inevitable that Truman would help the French against Ho's Communist forces. As the United

States fought to stop a Communist takeover of the whole of Korea, it seemed sensible to give aid to the French who claimed to be trying to stop a Communist takeover of the whole of Vietnam.

ii) Eisenhower (1953–61)

Like Truman, President Eisenhower wanted to save Vietnam from Communism. He hoped to be able to do so by paying the French to do the fighting. Eisenhower also wanted to help France in order to help Western Europe. While France was preoccupied with Vietnam, the French could not contribute greatly to West European defences against the Soviet Union.

After the French defeat at Dienbienphu, Eisenhower supported Diem in the creation and sustenance of a new South Vietnamese state. Unaware or unappreciative of the historic Sino-Vietnamese antagonism, Eisenhower and his Secretary of State John Foster Dulles were convinced that the Communist Chinese were fully behind Ho Chi Minh.

Eisenhower articulated the reasoning behind his support of the anti-Communist forces in South Vietnam in his '**domino theory**'. He believed that if he allowed Vietnam to go Communist, then other 'dominoes' suffering Communist insurgency (such as British Malaya and the Philippines) would go Communist too. Thus the world balance of power was at stake. Eisenhower assumed that Communist expansion would deprive America and the capitalist world of vital raw materials, and put millions more people under a tyrannical ideology. America might be left surrounded by Communist countries that might be reluctant to trade with capitalists and might even want to subvert and conquer them.

However, Eisenhower did not want to see American boys fighting on mainland Asia again, so soon after the unpopular Korean War. He feared that American troops might end up fighting Communists all over the world. Furthermore, some of his advisers felt that the loss of a small country like Vietnam to Communism might not lead to other nations following it. So although fear of Communism inspired Eisenhower to help anti-Communist forces in Vietnam, he was not convinced that the United States could or should commit itself more fully. Nevertheless, Truman's policy of containment of Communism and Eisenhower's 'domino' theory had combined to make the small insignificant South-east Asian country of Vietnam highly significant for the United States.

Eisenhower's Domino Theory

You have the specific value of a locality in its production of materials [rice, rubber, coal, iron ore] that the world needs. You have the possibility that many human beings pass under a dictatorship that is inimical to the free world. You have the broader considerations that might follow what you would call the 'falling domino' principle … You have a row of dominoes set up, you knock over the first one, and what will happen to the last one is the certainty that it will go over very quickly.

Source B

The enemy is the Communist system itself – implacable, insatiable, unceasing in its drive for world domination... This is not a struggle for supremacy of arms alone. It is also a struggle for supremacy between two conflicting ideologies: free-dom under God versus ruthless, godless tyranny.

Source C Extract from a Kennedy campaign speech.

iii) Kennedy (1961–3)

President John Kennedy was an even more vociferous opponent of Communism than his two predecessors were. Senator McCarthy was a family friend. McCarthy and the Kennedys were Catholics and their church was particularly anti-Communist (because of Communist atheism). John Kennedy subscribed to the domino theory and emphasised that it was in the emerging nations of the Third World (like Vietnam) that the Cold War would be fought. Kennedy's 1960 presidential election campaign was characterised by militant Cold War rhetoric. Given his Cold Warrior background, it is not surprising that Kennedy continued and escalated the US involvement in the battle against Ho and Communism in Vietnam. It was especially important to Kennedy after his unsuccessful intervention in Cuba (see page 224) and his inability to stop Communist activity in Laos. Perhaps what is surprising is that it was not Kennedy who sent in US ground troops to Vietnam, but his successor, President Johnson.

iv) Johnson (1963–9) and Nixon (1969–74)

Lyndon Johnson was vehemently anti-Communist. He subscribed to the domino theory. He believed that Ho was another Hitler and that Communism was an evil that had to be opposed as fascism had been opposed. He believed that the history of appeasement in the 1930s proved that aggressors needed to be stopped. If Neville Chamberlain had not appeased Hitler, the Second World War might have been avoided. If Ho was appeased, the Communists might gain the confi-dence to expand further and thereby cause World War III. Like Kennedy, Johnson believed that it was China rather than the USSR that was behind Ho.

Soviet and Chinese Aid to the Vietnamese Communists

Both China and the USSR supplied the Vietnamese Communists with weapons and technical advisers. After the Korean War, the flow of Chinese arms increased. The Chinese sent weapons at a rate of 10,000 tons per month by late summer 1953; the Soviets supplied great quantities of heavy trucks. When US involvement increased in 1965, Moscow and Beijing sent in even more. By late 1966, North Vietnam had a sophisticated and deadly air defence system, supplied by the Soviets and Chinese. By 1967, North Vietnam had 250 surface-to-air missile sites. Despite detente (see page 233) Chinese and Soviet aid doubled during 1971 and 1972. Significantly, when President Richard Nixon decided that there was no longer a threatening monolithic Communist bloc (see page 230), he got the United States out of Vietnam.

b) The Quagmire and Stalemate Theories and the 'Commitment Trap'

Historians trying to explain US involvement in Vietnam tend to concentrate either upon the anti-Communist beliefs of successive US administrations or upon the process of escalation. Some historians consider the process of escalation to be the major cause of sustained US involvement. Some call this concentration upon the slow process of escalation the '**quagmire theory**', and others talk in terms of a 'slippery slope', 'investment trap', or 'commitment trap'.

According to the quagmire theory, every escalatory step taken by the United States was taken in the hope that the desired end would be reached sooner. However, instead of leading to a defeat of Communism, each step not only failed to bring victory but also led to far greater investment in continuing and escalating the struggle. Each escalatory step led to a greater commitment of US pride, prestige, money, troops and lives. It began with Truman's commitment to the French. That led to Eisenhower's support of a South Vietnamese state under Diem. Eisenhower left Kennedy with a considerable US investment in Vietnam. Finally Johnson decided that the only way America could win was by sending in tens of thousands of US troops.

Other historians offered a variation on the quagmire theory. They contended that as the United States had committed so much in South Vietnam, successive administrations escalated even as they knew there was no chance of winning, in the hope that they could avoid the humiliation of defeat by at least ensuring stalemate.

In the Cold War climate of vehement anti-Communism it was very hard for any president to claim that his predecessor(s) had made a great error in the commitment to South Vietnam. No president wanted to be accused of being 'soft on Communism' as Truman had been after the 'loss' of China. Kennedy's Secretary of Defence Robert McNamara and Secretary of State Dean Rusk told the President that US withdrawal from Vietnam would lead to a loss of American face. It would 'undermine the credibility of American commitments everywhere'. Johnson frequently doubted that 'Westerners can ever win a war in Asia'. However, he repeatedly said that whenever he thought of cutting down the commitment, he wondered how he would be able to explain to the mothers of dead American soldiers that it had all been a mistake. When in 1972 Nixon mined North Vietnam's ports (which many perceived to be escalation of the war effort) he said,

> If the United States betrays the millions of people who have relied on us in Vietnam... it would amount to renunciation of our morality, an abdication of our leadership among nations, and an invitation for the mighty to prey upon the meek all around the world.

Source D

WHY A 'QUAGMIRE' THEORY?

Much of South Vietnam is covered by rice paddies and wet delta lands. The quagmire image suggests a person who walks into some kind of swamp and gets in deeper and deeper. Thus the quagmire theory seems appropriate in relation to the geography of Vietnam, and also in relation to the ever-increasing US involvement in Vietnam.

HISTORIANS' VIEWS

The most famous writers on the quagmire theory were David Halberstam and Arthur Schlesinger, Jr, and on the stalemate theory, Daniel Ellsberg and Leslie Gelb.

c) Domestic Politics

Each of the four administrations that got and kept America involved in South Vietnam was swayed by what they thought the electorate wanted. Truman was accused of 'losing' China to Communism in the winter of 1949 to 1950. In speedy response to this, he committed the United States to fight a war against Communism in Korea and to help finance a war against Communism in Vietnam in 1950. Both Truman and Eisenhower were under great pressure to be militantly anti-Communist because of the impact of Joseph McCarthy's witch-hunting upon public opinion. Eisenhower knew that Truman's popularity amongst voters had suffered because he had 'lost' China. Eisenhower did not want to be accused of having 'lost' Vietnam. Furthermore, he had promised to 'roll back' Communism in his presidential election campaign. Eisenhower therefore gave money and materials to the French and when that failed he helped to establish a South Vietnamese state with an anti-Communist government. However, Eisenhower did not send in American ground troops. He had just extricated America from what had become an unpopular war in Korea and he wanted to avoid another such war in Vietnam. Therefore his views on what US voters wanted served to restrain him and his commitment in Vietnam.

Kennedy had campaigned for the presidency as a militant Cold Warrior. That militancy probably won him votes. He was keen to counter views that he was young and inexperienced and therefore 'soft'. His earliest foreign policy involvement was the disastrous Bay of Pigs episode (see page 224). Kennedy therefore had to prove he could be tough and successful in order to be re-elected in 1964. Rusk and McNamara pointed out that 'extreme elements' (militantly anti-Communist Republicans) would make political capital out of any retreat. Kennedy's presidential campaign slogan had been 'a time for greatness', and he (or rather a ghostwriter) had written a book, *Profiles of Courage*, the theme of which was that 'great crises make great men'. Thus Kennedy's perception of what he had to do to please the electorate ensured that the United States continued and increased its involvement in Vietnam.

Would President Kennedy Have Got America Out of Vietnam?

The premature and tragic death of Kennedy, coupled with his own and his family's glamour, led many people to idealise him after his death. After his death and after the Vietnam War had become unpopular in United States, some of his friends and advisers claimed that Kennedy would have got America out. They cited conversations in which Kennedy said he would withdraw. Historians still argue about this.

Arguments suggesting Kennedy would not have got America out
1. In September 1963 Kennedy told influential broadcaster Walter Cronkite that it would be 'a great mistake' to withdraw from Vietnam.
2. On the day of his assassination, he had planned to make a speech saying that although involvement in Vietnam was costly, 'we dare not weary of the task'.
3. His Secretary of State Dean Rusk said, 'Kennedy's attitude on Vietnam should be derived from what he said and did while President, not what he may have said during tea table conversations'. What Kennedy did was to increase the number of American 'advisers' from 800 to 16,000 and to initiate secret sabotage missions in North Vietnam.
4. When Kennedy talked of possible troop withdrawals in the near future, it might have been because he hoped that victory was in sight and that American troops would no longer be needed.

Lyndon Johnson became president because Kennedy was assassinated, not because the electorate had voted for him. Johnson therefore thought it constitutionally proper to continue the Vietnam policies of his elected predecessor. Johnson repeatedly said he did not want to be the first president to lose a war. He also wanted to be elected president in his own right in 1964. Johnson was convinced that 'they would impeach a president that would run out, wouldn't they?' When he bombed North Vietnam for the first time, just before the 1964 presidential election, his public approval rating rose from 42 per cent to 72 per cent. Escalation helped Johnson look tough and it helped him to win the election. On the other hand, like Eisenhower, he knew that the voters preferred to get tough without getting hurt. Voters might approve of bombing, but they were glad to hear Johnson assure them that 'We are not going to send American boys away from home to do what Asian boys ought to be doing for themselves'. That promise too played a part in Johnson's victory in the 1964 presidential election, wherein his Republican opponent Barry Goldwater was quite generally perceived to be a trigger-happy hawk. It is significant that increasing evidence that the electorate was anti-war played an important part in causing Johnson to halt escalation in 1968. Anti-war protests and the belief that peace-making would ensure his re-election in 1972 played a very important part in Richard Nixon's extrication of the United States from Vietnam. Thus the politicians' monitoring of public opinion helps explain both escalation and extrication.

MCCARTHY AND VIETNAM

The State Department had been purged of 'Communist sympathisers' under Truman and Eisenhower. Those 'Communist sympathisers' included most of the experts on China. They had predicted that the Communists would win the Civil War and take control of China. Because of this they were accused of being pro-Communist! The loss of these China experts greatly affected US policy toward Vietnam. Without those experienced China-watchers, there were few to remind successive adminis-trations of the historic Sino-Vietnamese antagonism. That antagonism was a good indi-cator that there was no monolithic Communist bloc and that Ho was his own master. So, McCarthy not only helped create the fanati-cal anti-Communism of 1950s America but he also deprived his country of some of the best available information on and insight into South-east Asia. Thus McCarthy inadvertently made a massive contribution to US policy toward Vietnam.

Source F

d) Important Individuals and Pressure Groups

Harry Truman recognised the vital importance of the US president in decision-making when he famously said, 'The buck stops here'. Presidents certainly made the final decisions about American involve-ment in Vietnam, but all of them took advice from other important individuals. Harry Truman himself lacked expertise in foreign affairs when he became president. He relied heavily upon Dean Acheson, his Secretary of State (1949–53). Acheson was a firm believer in standing up to Communism. Like Acheson, Eisenhower's Secretary of State John Foster Dulles (1953–9) was a Cold Warrior. Acheson and Dulles had many supporters in the State and Defence Departments. McCarthyism had forced the State Department into a far more militant anti-Communist posture. **McCarthy** was a good example of an important individual outside of the government who helped create the mind-cast that got the United States embroiled in Vietnam. However, for the most part, it was presidents and their advisers who bore prime responsibility. Kennedy's own anti-Communism was reinforced by the militancy of his Secretary of State Dean Rusk (1961–9) and even more so by his Secretary of Defence Robert McNamara (1961–8). In November 1961, Rusk and McNamara wrote:

> The United States should commit itself to the clear objective of pre-venting the fall of South Vietnam to the Communists. We should be prepared to introduce United States combat forces if that should become necessary for success.
>
> *Source E*

In 1964, Rusk declared himself tired of America's South Vietnamese allies:

> Somehow we must change the pace at which these people move, and I suspect that this can only be done with a pervasive intrusion of Americans into their affairs.

As a non-elected president, Johnson felt it right and proper to keep Kennedy advisers such as Rusk and McNamara. Journalist David Halberstam (who was initially very pro-war) pointed out that all 'the best and the brightest' deserved to share the blame, as they favoured escalation during Johnson's presidency. In 1964, Johnson ordered a Working Group with representatives from the Defence Department, the State Department, the CIA and the Joint Chiefs of Staff to study

Vietnam and suggest policy options. The Working Group favoured escalation to help the weak regime in Saigon.

Occasionally an individual outside the inner circle of government made an important contribution to the American involvement in Vietnam. This was the case with McCarthy and with Kennedy's ambassador to Vietnam from 1963 to 1964, Henry Cabot Lodge. Lodge colluded with the plotters who ousted Diem in 1963. Johnson was convinced that the coup greatly increased American responsibility toward the South Vietnamese people. Johnson had disapproved of US collusion in the overthrow of Diem. However, as the United States had gone along with the coup, Johnson believed it to be the duty of the United States to try to find a suitable replacement to head the South Vietnamese government in Saigon.

As US military involvement escalated, the input from the military establishment increased. Both Kennedy and Johnson found some of America's military leaders frightening. Johnson said Air Force chief Curtis LeMay (who famously wanted to 'bomb Vietnam back into the Stone Age') 'scares the hell out of me'. Naturally, the military men wanted to win the war. They found it frustrating that their political masters never gave them permission to 'go all out'. Instead, army leaders in Vietnam such as General William Westmoreland (1964–8) continually asked for more soldiers with which to do the job and, perhaps more importantly, with which to defend the American soldiers already there. For example, in July 1965, in response to a request from Westmoreland, Johnson increased US troop numbers from 75,000 to 125,000.

In 1965 Johnson still had the vast majority of journalists and the public behind him. In 1965 polls and White House mail showed that 70 per cent of the nation supported Johnson's escalation, 80 per cent believed in the domino theory, and 80 per cent favoured sending US soldiers to stop South Vietnam falling. Forty-seven per cent wanted to send in even more troops than Johnson had sent. Not surprisingly, 200,000 American soldiers were in Vietnam by the end of 1965. When the US casualty rates rose and when that seemed to be of no avail in winning the war, the public and then the press began to turn against the war. However, both press and public probably shared responsibility for US involvement. Perhaps the public could be 'excused' responsibility in that they were dependent upon politicians and the press for their information.

The role of Congress was very important, because it had to vote the money to finance the war. In 1964 Congress passed the Gulf of Tonkin resolution, wherein it gave Johnson a free hand to do as he saw fit in South-east Asia. In May 1965 Congress granted $700 million for the prosecution of the war. The House of Representatives voted 408 to 7 and the Senate 88 to 3 in favour. Johnson warned them that this was no routine grant, but a vote to continue opposing Communism in Vietnam. On the other hand, the Johnson administration was not always straightforward with Congress. Congress passed the **Gulf of Tonkin** Resolution having been given inaccurate information by Johnson on supposed incidents of North Vietnamese aggression in the Gulf of Tonkin. In some ways, then, it could be argued that Johnson's presidency demonstrates that it was important individuals, particularly the president, who bore most responsibility for US involvement in Vietnam. Many contemporaries talked of 'Johnson's war' or even of 'McNamara's war'. On the other hand, his presidential predecessors bequeathed Johnson an unenviable legacy of ever-increasing involvement. One might therefore justifiably contend that it was neither one individual nor necessarily one office that bore responsibility. It was a combination of the Cold War context, people's reactions to it, and the problems of trying to conduct a foreign policy in the interests of the nation while simultaneously trying not to displease the electorate.

The Gulf of Tonkin Incidents

On 2 August 1964 North Vietnamese patrol boats attacked the US destroyer *Maddox* in the Gulf of Tonkin. On 4 August the *Turner Joy* was also supposedly attacked. On 7 August, Congress accepted the Johnson administration's claim that US ships and men had been the victims of unprovoked aggression, and passed the Gulf of Tonkin Resolution. That Resolution gave the president the power 'to take all necessary measures to repel any armed attack against the forces of the United States and to prevent further aggression'. There are several significant points to consider in relation to the Gulf of Tonkin incidents and Resolution:

▼ Those few days in August marked a turning point in US involvement in Vietnam, as the Resolution gave Johnson the power to wage war as he saw fit in South-east Asia.

▼ No one in the House of Representatives and only two members of the Senate opposed the Resolution.

▼ 85 per cent of people polled supported administration policy in Vietnam at this time.

▼ Some people claim that the administration engineered the Gulf of Tonkin crisis.

▼ The *Maddox* was on a surveillance operation near or in North Vietnamese waters.

▼ At the time McNamara denied that the *Maddox* was spying on the North Vietnamese. Subsequently he admitted that he had got the facts 'wrong' but he had been misinformed so he was wrong but 'honest'.

▼ Photographic evidence and physical damage confirm that the *Maddox* was attacked, but there was no photographic evidence of any attack on the *Turner Joy* and no reported physical damage.

▼ Some Americans who were on board or flying above the *Turner Joy* said they were unaware of any incident.

▼ The attack on the *Turner Joy* was either outright fabrication or innocent misinterpretation.

ACTIVITY

Have a class debate. Divide into two groups. One should argue that the presidents were responsible for involvement then escalation, the other against.

Warning Voices Against US Involvement in Vietnam

There were a few influential Americans who warned against involvement and escalation. The most persistent critic of involvement within the Kennedy and Johnson administrations was George Ball. In 1962 Ball warned Kennedy that 'we'll have 300,000 men in the paddies and jungles' within five years. Kennedy responded, 'George, you're crazier than hell. That just isn't going to happen.' Ball was remarkably accurate in that and other predictions. He warned Johnson that the more the United States got involved, the harder it would be to get out. Ball predicted that the public would turn against the war as they had against the Korean War when there were US casualties. He said there was no point in bombing a primarily agricultural country whose industrial needs were served by China and the USSR. He said the United States had no chance of victory against guerrillas in jungles. Ball anticipated that no amount of American intervention could make up for an ineffective government in Saigon. He forecast world hostility to US bombardment of tiny Vietnam. Ball recognised that US involvement in Vietnam would not demonstrate to America's friends that the United States was a reliable ally, rather that the United States was misguided and unwise.

In early 1963, Democratic Senator Mike Mansfield visited Saigon and reported to Congress that after eight years of effort and $2 billion expenditure, US efforts to establish an independent non-Communist South Vietnamese state were 'not even at the beginning of a beginning'. Mansfield subsequently and repeatedly advocated extrication from Vietnam.

ISSUES:
What was the United
States trying to
achieve in and for
South Vietnam? How
did the United States
propose to achieve it?

3 America's Aims and Methods in the Vietnam War

a) Truman (1945–53)

All five of the American presidents involved in Vietnam aimed to stop Communism. In the context of the Soviet takeover of Eastern Europe, the fall of China to Communism, Soviet and Chinese recognition of Ho Chi Minh's Democratic Republic of Vietnam and the Korean War in 1950, it seemed to Truman that the French were holding the line against a world-wide and expansionist Communist movement in Vietnam. Truman aimed to contain Communism and his method was to give financial assistance for the French war effort ($2 billion) and for economic and technical aid to the Vietnamese people ($50 million). Significantly, those figures demonstrate that Truman saw military activity as the most effective method whereby Vietnam could be saved from Communism. In 1950 Truman established the Military Assistant Advisory Group (MAAG), which advised the French on the use of American military hardware. Truman put far less emphasis upon improving the lives of the Vietnamese people and thereby winning the battle for 'hearts and minds'. His successors did the same.

b) Eisenhower (1953–61)

At first, Eisenhower continued Truman's aims and methods. Early in 1954, Eisenhower sent US bombers and 200 US technicians to Vietnam. He also gave the French $385 million worth of armaments to fight the Vietminh, on condition that France promise to grant greater independence to Indo-China. That anti-colonialist aim was similar to Roosevelt's. There was debate within the Eisenhower administration as to the importance of Indo-China to US security and over what, if anything, the US should do there. Thus aims and methods were exhaustively discussed.

Questions Asked about Vietnam Within the Eisenhower Administration

▼ Was South-east Asia vital to US security?
▼ Should the US get involved in Indo-China?
▼ Should the US give financial aid and/or military advice and/or air and/or sea support to the French?
▼ Should the US send ground troops to Indo-China?

▼ Did the US have enough troops to send?
▼ Could the French win in Indo-China with US aid?
▼ Could the US alone win in Indo-China?
▼ Was it worth risking a Sino-American clash in Vietnam?
▼ How much was the US willing to do without support from the UN or US allies?

It was Eisenhower who really changed US aims and methods in Vietnam. Although he refused to help the French at Dienbienphu with an American air strike, he dramatically increased US involvement after the Geneva conference. Between 1955 and 1961 the Eisenhower administration gave $1447 million to Diem. Eisenhower aimed to stop dominoes falling in South-east Asia, to keep South-east Asia with all its economic resources friendly to the US and its ideals of democracy and capitalism. He had new methods. After the Geneva Conference of 1954, Eisenhower tried to create a stable and anti-Communist South Vietnamese state and a NATO-like treaty alliance that would help to protect the new state. The South-east Asia Treaty Organisation (**SEATO**) agreed to protect South Vietnam, Cambodia and Laos. SEATO thereby contravened the Geneva settlement, which had said that the Vietnamese should not enter into foreign alliances nor allow foreign troops on their soil. Thus Eisenhower ignored the Geneva settlement's attempt to neutralise Indo-China in the Cold War world. The Eisenhower administration aimed to make what one cynic called 'a synthetic strongman' out of Diem. Eisenhower poured money and advisers into Diem's South Vietnam. Most of the advisers were military, although some worked on 'winning the hearts and minds' of the people. For example, American advisers urged Diem to gain popularity through land redistribution, a policy Ho Chi Minh used to great effect in the North.

> **SEATO MEMBERS**
> The United States, Great Britain, France, Australia, New Zealand and Pakistan.

c) Kennedy (1961–3)

Kennedy continued with the same aims and methods as Eisenhower and to a lesser extent with the same debates as to whether and how the US should be involved. Although George Ball warned against US policy on Vietnam and Bobby Kennedy suggested it might be time for a dramatic reappraisal, John Kennedy continued and developed the path set out by his predecessors. Kennedy added a variant to his predecessors' aims of halting Communism. Kennedy aimed to concentrate upon combating the ideological foe in Third World countries, which he called 'the lands of the rising peoples'. That inevitably gave Vietnam greater importance. Like Eisenhower,

Kennedy never aimed to bring democracy to Vietnam. In 1954 both Eisenhower and the young Senator Kennedy had rejected the 1954 Geneva agreement's provision for nationwide elections in Vietnam in 1956. Both knew that the Communist Ho Chi Minh would win, and both considered that to be totally unacceptable. Kennedy, like Truman, aimed to please the US electorate by his policies on Indo-China. Truman had toyed with the idea of standing for re-election in 1952, and Kennedy definitely planned to stand in 1964. Both felt they would lose the support of the electorate if they let Vietnam fall to Communism.

Kennedy's methods represented something of a change from Eisenhower's, although both saw the Vietnam problem as something to be solved by the military method. While Kennedy refused to put in US ground troops, he dramatically increased the number of US military advisers in Vietnam, from 800 to 16,000. Many 'advisers' frequently participated in military actions with the ARVN against the VC. In 1962 Kennedy established the 'Military Assistance Command, Vietnam' (MACV) to oversee the increasing American involvement. Fascinated by 'counter-insurgency' (the use of guerrilla-like tactics to counter Communist guerrillas), Kennedy set up a special US counter-insurgency force known as the Green Berets. The Green Berets cooperated with the ARVN. Kennedy put new emphasis on the use of US air power and technology to help defeat the Communists. US pilots used US helicopters to transport ARVN troops, and for reconnaissance and fire support. US helicopters also dropped defoliants on the Vietnamese jungle to facilitate aerial observation. From 1962 the US encouraged Diem to introduce 'strategic hamlets'. These were fortified villages wherein Vietnamese peasants could theoretically be isolated from the VC. Like Eisenhower, Kennedy tried to persuade Diem to make his government more popular by introducing greater political, social and economic equality to South Vietnam. When Diem repeatedly refused, Ambassador Lodge, with no resistance and probably encouragement from Washington, connived in Diem's deposition. Under Eisenhower and Kennedy the US had effectively chosen the government of South Vietnam, a country that the US claimed was a sovereign state.

Figure 51
An American soldier trying to help a South Vietamese child

d) Johnson (1963–9)

Like his predecessors, Johnson aimed to decrease the threat from Communism. Perhaps his emphasis on saving US face by standing by and continuing a commitment to a US ally (South Vietnam) was new. The sense of obligation to a duly elected predecessor was definitely new. Johnson aimed to continue Kennedy's policies: 'I swore to myself that I would carry on. I would continue for my partner who had gone down ahead of me.' Within America itself, Johnson aimed to follow in the footsteps of Franklin Roosevelt and his New Deal and to help develop a 'Great Society'. He talked of doing the same for Vietnam, of aiming to re-make the Mekong Delta in the manner of the Tennessee Valley Authority (see page 116). Johnson had a totally new aim, forced upon him by the development of events in Vietnam. He had decided to teach Hanoi a lesson by bombing North Vietnam in the later months of 1964. US bomber bases and person-nel thus increased in numbers and became increasingly vulnerable. Most governments find it difficult to deal with guerrilla activity and terrorism, and this was a particular problem for an unpopular and inefficient government such as that in Saigon. In February 1965 the VC attacked an American base at Pleiku. When eight Americans were killed and 100 wounded, Johnson aimed to protect them by increasing the air attacks on North Vietnam and the Ho Chi Minh Trail. The bombing was of such intensity that it was called 'Rolling Thunder'. The aim of the bombing was to stop the flow of men and materials from the North to the South and thereby to demoralise Hanoi and revitalise Saigon. However, Johnson aimed to avoid get-ting entangled in the war with China, so he never declared war on North Vietnam and never fully committed America to the struggle. Nevertheless, he continued to aim to protect US personnel in Vietnam. That was what led him to send in ground troops in spring 1965, after Westmoreland asked for marines to protect the US bomber base at Danang.

Thus Johnson's main method of support for South Vietnam was escalation of US involvement. He sent in around half a million US ground troops and stepped up the air war against the Communists.

> **TERMINOLOGY FOR THE VIETNAMESE COMMUNISTS**
> Ho established the Vietnamese Communist Party in 1930. In 1941 Ho set up the League for the Independence of Vietnam, more commonly known as the Vietminh. After the Geneva Conference, Ho's supporters in South Vietnam were known as the National Liberation Front (NLF). The North Vietnamese army (NVA) was also known as the People's Army of Vietnam (PAVN). PAVN was raised and trained in the North and sent South to fight. The vari-ety of military forces of the NLF were collectively known as the People's Liberation Armed Forces (PLAF), but Diem called them the Vietcong (VC). The Americans preferred to use the name VC. The VC consist-ed of both South Vietnamese and North Vietnamese.

e) Nixon (1969–74)

US aims and methods were not always clear, and frequently changed. Much depended on the situation in America, in Vietnam and the rest of the world. Richard Nixon decided that the world had changed and that the Communist threat had changed. He therefore aimed to get the United States out of Vietnam as soon as possible, while still leav-ing President Thieu in power in a well-armed South Vietnam. Nixon's favourite method consisted of heavy bombing of North Vietnam, the Ho Chi Minh Trail, and supposed Communist enclaves in neighbouring Cambodia. More than half the total tonnage dropped on Vietnam was dropped in Nixon's first term. Nixon used one unique method, his so-called 'Madman Theory', whereby he was content that the North Vietnamese should consider him to be an unpredictable and fanatical Cold Warrior who might well put his hand on the nuclear button. Nixon was convinced that that would give America an advantage at the Paris negotiating table (in operation intermittently from May 1968).

Different Americans favoured different aims and methods. In 1967 an influential Defence Department figure privately declared US aims as

Source G

> seventy per cent to avoid a humiliating US defeat (to our reputation as a guarantor). Twenty per cent to keep South Vietnamese (and the adjacent) territory from Chinese hands. Ten per cent to permit the people of South Vietnam to enjoy a better, freer way of life.

The military men, such as Curtis LeMay and Westmoreland, wanted to use the military method on a far larger scale. Some Americans wanted greater emphasis upon winning the hearts and minds of the people. Although Johnson in particular paid lip service to that aim, it turned out to be a relatively little-used American method.

4 Why Was the United States Unable to Win in Vietnam?

a) Failure to Win Hearts and Minds

Successive US administrations and soldiers often failed to comprehend and care about the Vietnamese people. Eisenhower was determined that there would not be the nationwide elections demanded by the Geneva agreements for 1956. Eisenhower knew that the Communists would win any such election and he did not want the Vietnamese to make their own democratic choice of government if it was the 'wrong' choice! In April 1965 Johnson was convinced that if he promised Ho economic aid, Ho would agree to peace on US terms: 'Old Ho can't turn me down'. Americans could not quite understand how anyone might truly want and be suited to Communism. When President Thieu told Johnson that the Communists would win any elections, Johnson said, 'I don't believe that. Does anyone believe that?'

US policies were frequently based on a misunderstanding of the Vietnamese people and their culture. Kennedy was shocked when members of the Buddhist majority in South Vietnam protested against the discriminatory policies of the Diem regime in 1963. Diem favoured the Catholic minority (of which he and his family were a part). When 10,000 Buddhists protested, Diem sent in soldiers who killed seven protesters. When Buddhist priests burned

> ### ACTIVITY
>
> Re-read this chapter so far. Imagine *you* have written it as an examination essay. Either mentally or in pencil, add extra dates wherever possible. For example, the first time Dienbienphu is mentioned in this chapter, the date is given. Add the date to any subsequent mention of Dienbienphu. Examination answers require good knowledge of dates, so this should be good practice!

> ### ISSUE:
>
> Who or what was to blame for the American failure in Vietnam?

themselves to death in protest, Kennedy asked, 'How could this have happened? Who are these people? Why didn't we know about them before?' It is possible that Kennedy was pleading ignorance to escape blame. However, if he was genuinely ignorant of the fact that most South Vietnamese were Buddhist it suggests dangerous limitations in US knowledge and cultural empathy. Sometimes the lack of understanding was tragi-comic. For example, Robert McNamara toured South Vietnam in 1964. After careful coaching, he was able to shout 'Viet Nam Muon Nam' to every crowd that greeted him. McNamara thought he was saying, 'Long live South Vietnam'. He was unaware that Vietnamese is a tonal language, and that what he was really saying was, 'The southern duck wants to lie down'.

American soldiers, frustrated because they could not distinguish VC from non-Communist Vietnamese, frequently mistreated South Vietnamese civilians. The most famous instance was the 1968 massacre of women, children and old people in the village of My Lai. A major part of the US military strategy consisted of bombing parts of South Vietnam that were considered to be Communist. South Vietnamese villages were sometimes destroyed, which served to alienate many Vietnamese from the Saigon regime and its American allies. Thus when an American officer said, 'We had to destroy [the village of] Ben Tre to save it', he inadvertently summed up a major reason for the US failure in Vietnam.

Figure 52 A GI with his Vietnamese girlfriend.

While the Saigon regime was corrupt and inefficient, Ho's Communist regime won over many Northerners and some Southerners. Ho's followers had for years put as much if not more emphasis upon the political indoctrination of the peasantry as upon warfare. Some Vietnamese favoured Ho because he seemed to be a Vietnamese nationalist, in contrast to successive US-dominated Saigon regimes. Communist soldiers usually behaved better towards the peasantry than ARVN or US soldiers. It made sense for Communist guerrillas to keep in with the local population upon whom their safety would frequently depend. The Communist policy of fairer land redistribution naturally appealed to poorer peasants throughout Vietnam. The Americans did try to urge Saigon to introduce social, economic and political reform. However, the United States needed the military cooperation of leaders such as Diem (1955–63) and Thieu (1967–75) and for the most part therefore refrained from putting intolerable pressure upon them. Because the United States put greater emphasis on military methods to achieve the salvation of Vietnam, it proved impossible to win the hearts and minds of the Vietnamese people. The Americans thereby helped ensure their lack of success in Vietnam.

b) Inappropriate Military Tactics

The United States ought perhaps to have learned a military lesson
from the French, whose conventional forces had struggled to defeat
the Vietnamese Communist General Giap's army and guerrillas.
General Tran Van Don recalled how in November 1954 he and other
ARVN leaders suggested to MAAG that ARVN use guerrilla tactics to
combat the Communists. However, his advice

> fell on deaf ears. The Americans evidently put us in the same mould
> as the Koreans whose army they had organised and trained, and they
> seemed to think that our country was similar to the Korean peninsu-
> la. They believed, I suppose, that what would work for Korea would
> certainly work for Vietnam ... The Americans were organised to fight
> a war in which there are well-defined front lines with relatively
> secure rear areas ... and where the overwhelming fire superiority of
> American weapons could bring decisive results.

Source H

As Eisenhower poured money and sent military advisers into
Diem's South Vietnam, the VC stepped up their guerrilla warfare
therein. The Kennedy administration recognised the importance of
counter-insurgency and began the introduction of the Green Berets
to South Vietnam. The Green Berets specialised in guerrilla-like tactics to combat the VC in South Vietnam. However, for the most part,
conventional US forces (theoretically) dealt with VC guerrillas.

Under Johnson, US troops engaged in 'search and destroy' missions, wherein they would try to clear an area of VC. It is notoriously
difficult to try to wipe out a guerrilla movement, particularly when
the guerrillas are sent in from another 'state' (North Vietnam) and
when the guerrillas have a sympathetic, supportive or simply apa-
thetic reaction from the local community. Frequently, US troops
would 'clear' an area of VC. However, as soon as the Americans
moved out, the Communists would move back in. A famous example
of this is the bloody battle for 'Hamburger Hill' (so-called because of
the bloody carnage) in 1969. The Americans 'won', but the ground
was quickly re-taken by the VC when the Americans left.

The United States relied heavily on superior technology. During
the Kennedy years the United States contributed increasing numbers
of helicopters and bombers to Saigon's cause. Bombing was a
favourite tactic during the presidencies of Johnson and Nixon.
Under Johnson, the US bombed North Vietnam, the Ho Chi Minh
Trail and South Vietnamese villages suspected of Communist sympathies. From 1966–8, an average of 800 tons of bombs fell on North
Vietnam each day. Under Nixon, the bombing was dramatically

extended in North Vietnam, and also in areas of neighbouring Laos and Cambodia, where it was believed that the VC had their head-quarters. However, the bombing served only to alienate many South Vietnamese and many Americans back home. It did not damage North Vietnamese morale, nor did it stop the flow of men and materials coming down the Ho Chi Minh Trail from North Vietnam to South Vietnam. Warnings about the lack of impact (for example from the CIA and an independent think-tank in 1966) were not acted upon by the Johnson administration.

Years later, McNamara admitted that US tactics were wrong, that it was unwise to use a high-tech war of attrition against a primarily guerrilla force that never considered giving up their war for independence. McNamara's successor Clark Clifford (1968–9) recalled that it 'was startling to me that we had no military plan to win the war'. General Westmoreland hoped to be able to meet the VC in conventional set-piece battles in which US firepower would be decisive. However, his 'search and destroy' missions usually failed to find VC and the ratio of destruction was usually six South Vietnamese civilians for every VC soldier. The large-scale use of helicopters and the blasting of the zones where they were to land was not conducive to searching out guerrillas, who simply went elsewhere upon hearing all the noise. In Operation Cedar Falls in 1967, 20 American battalions entered an area north of Saigon. Defoliants, bombing and bulldozers cleared the land. Six thousand peasants were evacuated and their homes and lands destroyed. Thus 'friendly' civilians were made hostile to Saigon and its American ally. Only a few VC were found. During 1967–8 fewer than 1 per cent of the 2 million small unit operations undertaken by the Americans or ARVN led to any contact with the enemy.

What If...

Americans, particularly ex-soldiers, frequently debate what might have happened if the United States had done things differently in the Vietnam war.

What if President Johnson had gone beyond limited war and declared war on North Vietnam? Could the United States have won? The war might have become even more unpopular. The USSR and China might have entered the war, something Johnson was determined to avoid. He clearly did not think South Vietnam was worth World War III, and the American public certainly would not have thought so. Congress would probably not have declared war for South Vietnam.

What if, as General Bruce Palmer contended in 1986, the United States had cut South Vietnam off from Communist infiltration, thereby giving South Vietnam time to build itself up into a viable state?

That 'cutting off' might have been possible in flatter terrain as in Korea. However, to 'cut off' the jungles and mountains on the Cambodian and Laotian borders would have been impossible. Furthermore, the PLAF would have been 'trapped' inside South Vietnam, and would have continued their guerrilla warfare. The strategic hamlets had been infiltrated by Communists, which proved that it was impossible to isolate the South Vietnamese population from South Vietnamese (or North Vietnamese) Communists. In 1967 the CIA established that most of the supplies used by the Communists originated in the South, so 'cutting off' supplies would have been difficult.

What if the United States army had worked harder to win the hearts and minds of the people, as Andrew Krepinevich suggested in 1986?

Richard Hunt pointed out in 1995 that this would have taken too many American soldiers too long, and that the American public would have run out of patience. One commander pointed out that if he and his men became 'mayors and sociologists worrying about hearts and minds', they would not be much use if they had to fight the Soviets!

c) The Soldiers' Performance

The VC fought with the tenacity and determination of people fighting for their independence and their ideology. North Vietnamese troops poured down the Ho Chi Minh Trail, carrying supplies and switching to another part of the Trail if US planes bombed them. The VC had a determination that the Americans lacked. In the Battle of Ia Drang in 1965, 3,561 North Vietnamese and 305 Americans died. Both sides thought they had won, believing that the other side would not be able to sustain such losses. Ultimately, it was the VC who were right.

US forces were weakened by several factors. Americans usually despised the military capacities of their **ARVN** ally. There was often jealousy, disunity and poor communication between the American service branches. As the anti-war protests back home in the United States increased, the US forces' morale sank. This was particularly obvious from June 1969 when President Nixon withdrew the first 25,000 troops. As Nixon slowly withdrew thousands more, those soldiers left in Vietnam wondered why they were risking their lives in a

ARVN

The American forces admired their VC enemy far more than their ARVN ally. The ARVN was often ineffective, sometimes content to rely upon the Americans, sometimes reluctant to commit itself. At Ap Bac in 1963, 2,000 ARVN soldiers supported by American-operated helicopters, bombers, and armoured personnel carriers, refused to attack 310 lightly armed VC. ARVN was not always totally loyal to the Saigon regimes. Diem was faced with a rebellion from within the army in 1960 and an army coup resulted in his death in 1963. In late 1967, ARVN outnumbered the American soldiers, but the latter killed twice as many of the enemy. General Westmoreland was reluctant to use ARVN, preferring where possible to use his own American troops, as at Khe Sanh in 1968.

conflict from which their country was withdrawing.

The American foot soldier or 'grunt' served for one year, which meant that units rarely achieved the camaraderie characteristic of the Second World War. The conditions faced by the grunt in battle zones were exceptionally unpleasant. It was hard to tell whether a Vietnamese was friend or foe. There were VC booby traps and mines all around. They accounted for 11 per cent of American combat deaths. The heat, rain and insects often felt unbearable. And all for what? One disillusioned soldier recorded how

> The American people had been told that we were defending a free democracy. What I found was a military dictatorship rife with corruption and venality and repression. The premier of South Vietnam openly admired Adolf Hitler. Buddhist priests who petitioned for peace were jailed or shot down in the streets. Officials at every level engaged in blatant black-marketeering ... at the expense of their own people.

Source I

Black grunts were resentful because they felt they constituted a disproportionate number of the ordinary soldiers in the front line (they constituted 10.6 per cent of active duty military personnel and 12.5 per cent of combat deaths). Black and white grunts resented the relative facility with which middle-class whites avoided the draft. One-quarter of grunts came from families with incomes below the poverty line. Officers only served six-month tours of duty. Grunts resented that fact. The officer class was often unpopular and criticised for inexperience and affection for 'desk jobs'. Forty-three thousand officers ranked major or above served in Vietnam but only 201 were killed in action. Thousands of military personnel were involved in desk jobs or logistical support. Supplies were stored at large US bases and men were needed to unload, distribute and guard them. In 1967, there were 473,200 troops in Vietnam, but only 10.46 per cent of them were part of the combat force.

President Nixon felt the United States had made an error in trying to make its soldiers' lives too comfortable. Nixon felt it softened them up. Some American soldiers in Vietnam were able to take advantage of frequent R and R (rest and recuperation), 357 libraries, 159 basketball courts, 90 service clubs, 85 volleyball fields, 71 swimming pools, 55 softball fields, 40 ice-cream plants, and 30 tennis courts. A swift helicopter ride could take soldiers from the front line to a relatively luxurious base in Saigon. The result was often disorientation and dissatisfaction:

> It was weird, really; you'd be out in the bush for two or three weeks or longer and come in … You could have a cookout… see movies at night. It was almost like being back [in the United States]… I personally could never get used to that, and to me, it was one of the problems. We were deceiving ourselves. If we were going to fight the war and win it, let's fight the war and win it and go home. But this artificial living … was beyond me. It may have kept the troops entertained, but it prevented them from focusing on what we were there for.

Source J

UUUU

American soldiers frequently painted UUUU on their helmets. The initials stood for 'the unwilling, led by the unqualified, doing the unnecessary, for the ungrateful'. Black soldiers often wrote on their helmets 'NO GOOK [Vietnamese] EVER CALLED ME NIGGER'.

Drug abuse became common during the Nixon years and army discipline deteriorated dramatically. South Vietnamese politicians such as Ky and Thieu made a fortune out of the drugs trade.

In many ways, the US military was asked to do the impossible in Vietnam. Many American commanders complained they were being told to fight a war with one hand tied behind their back. Washington's aims, tactics and commitment were nowhere near as clear, attainable and appropriate as those of the Communist opposition. Not surprisingly then, Communist soldiers fought more effectively than American soldiers.

d) Unrealistic US Aims

It could be argued that US aims were unrealistic and unattainable. The underlying aim (initially) was to stop Communism. While that aim might have been realistic, the choice of Vietnam as a major battleground to achieve it was probably a mistake. It soon became clear that it would be very difficult to stop Communism in Vietnam. Then US aims changed. After the Bay of Pigs and the Vienna summit, Kennedy said 'we have a problem in making our power credible, and Vietnam is the place'. In 1965 Secretary of State Dean Rusk said that failure in Vietnam would lead 'the Communist world' to 'draw conclusions that would lead to our ruin and almost certainly to a catastrophic war'. The aim of saving US face had become entangled with the aim of containing Communism.

Truman aimed to 'save' Vietnam by working through the French, but despite American largesse the French were incapable of defeating the Vietnamese Communists. In the post-Second World War world, the tide of nationalism in the the Third World proved impossible to turn back. This was particularly the case for tired colonial powers such as France. Eisenhower aimed to contain Communism by colluding in the establishment of a South Vietnamese state. From the first, this state was not a genuinely viable alternative to Ho Chi Minh and Communism. As Eisenhower admitted, the Communists would have gained 80 per cent of the votes in any nationwide election held in 1956. Eisenhower's three successors found themselves trying to prop up a series of unpopular and ineffective regimes in Saigon. The Saigon regimes' association with the United States further increased their unpopularity. In the context of Vietnam, the United States was aiming for the unattainable in trying to sustain a South Vietnamese government that lacked a leader of the calibre of Ho Chi Minh. Not surprisingly, when the Americans withdrew after the peace settlement of 1973, the whole of Vietnam was united under a Communist government within two years.

Had the United States ever gone 'all-out' to win in Vietnam, then US aims might have been attainable. However, Johnson knew that if he used all available military power in South-east Asia, the Chinese and possibly the Soviets were likely to intervene. Johnson did not aim to contain Communism in Vietnam at the cost of provoking World War III. Given the relative popularity of the Vietnamese Communists and the unpopularity of the Saigon regimes, the US aim of halting Communism by using limited military force was unattainable.

SOUTH VIETNAMESE LEADERS

1955–63	Diem;
1963–4	General 'Big' Minh;
1964–5	General Khanh;
1965	Quat;
1965–7	Ky;
1967–75	Thieu.

e) A Divided Home Front

After the first 3,500 marines landed at Danang beach in March 1965, it was inevitable that there would be US casualties and that the US media would increase coverage of the American war effort. As the media covered not only US casualties but also the unpleasant aspects of the Saigon government and the war, popular support for the war decreased. Division on the home front contributed to the US inability to win the war. Divisions damaged the morale of some of those who fought in Vietnam. Divisions and protests were important in causing Johnson to halt the escalation of the war in spring 1968. This American uncertainty improved North Vietnamese morale and inspired the Communists to put up with what Americans considered to be unacceptable hardship. (See also section 5 below.)

ACTIVITY

Write an essay discussing the following assertion: 'It was the Americans who lost the war, rather than the Communists who won it'.

Figure 53 The massive anti-war protest outside the Pentagon, October 1967. The 'war criminal' is President Johnson.

ISSUE:
What was the main factor in the US decision to stop the escalation and get out of Vietnam?

5 Why Did the United States Get Out of Vietnam?

a) The Failure to Win

The United States was unable to sustain a viable South Vietnamese government, despite colluding in coups (such as Diem's overthrow in 1963) and pouring in ever more money, materials and men. Influential figures in the Kennedy and Johnson administrations believed for years that sending in more men would effect victory but it was difficult to see progress being made. By August 1967, the NLF controlled 3,978 of South Vietnam's 12,537 hamlets. The Johnson administration remained publicly optimistic, claiming in 1967 that the 'crossover point' had been reached: American and ARVN troops were supposedly killing the enemy faster than they could be replaced.

Media coverage of Hanoi's massive Tet Offensive in South Vietnam in January 1968 convinced many Americans that they were losing this war and unlikely to win it. American troops restored the status quo within a few weeks but American TV crews had captured the dramatic scenes as the Communists took temporary control of the US embassy in Saigon. This shook the faith of the American public, many of whom had believed government claims that they were winning the war. The failure to make real progress, coupled with increasing domestic opposition to the war, led influential people to advocate withdrawal. In autumn 1967 a demoralised Secretary of Defence Robert McNamara advocated halting the escalation. In March 1968 the 'Wise Men' (a group of senior advisers that included Dean Acheson) advocated a retreat. The 'Wise Men' had originally been firm advocates of escalation. With their defection and increased anti-war media coverage and protests, Johnson lost his nerve and prepared for retreat.

CONTROVERSY: DID THE MEDIA LOSE THE WAR FOR AMERICA?
Some Americans, particularly Vietnam war veterans, blame unsympathetic media coverage for the United States' failure to win in Vietnam. Initially, the media were pro-war. However, as the lack of progress became evident to reporters in Vietnam, the media began to turn against the war. Tet accelerated that process. While the media did not cover Communist atrocities, reporters saw enough of South Vietnam and the war to know that there was something wrong with the Saigon regime and that American policy in supporting it was not always admirable.

The Tet Offensive (January 1968)

▼ Tens of thousands of Communist forces attacked cities and military installations in South Vietnam.

▼ Hanoi hoped to 'liberate' South Vietnam or at least demonstrate such strength that the United States would give up and get out.

▼ Tet was a great Vietnamese holiday – the South Vietnamese and Americans were preoccupied with the festivities.

▼ It took 11,000 US and ARVN forces three weeks to clear Saigon of Communist forces.

▼ 3,895 Americans, 4,954 ARVN, 14,300 South Vietnamese civilians, and 58,873 Communist military died.

▼ In the city of Hue, 17,134 houses were totally destroyed, 3,169 were seriously damaged.

▼ The Communists were disappointed that the South Vietnamese had not risen up to welcome them.

▼ It took Hanoi several years to get over this great effort.

▼ Many Americans were convinced that the United States had failed (even the US embassy in Saigon was not safe).

▼ Tet played a great part in Johnson's decision to halt escalation and Nixon's decision to get out of Vietnam.

Johnson halted the escalation but left it to Nixon to finish the job. As president, Nixon viewed the war very differently from his predecessors, and Nixon's interpretation of the situation was vital to the US exit from Vietnam.

b) Richard Nixon

Richard Nixon had made his name as a Cold Warrior. Nevertheless he extricated the United States from Vietnam. Although in 1967 he criticised anti-war protesters as traitors, he was determined by 1968 that the United States should get out of Vietnam. The turning point for Nixon was Tet. He began to emphasise that the South Vietnamese would have to win the war for themselves, otherwise 'they cannot be saved'. Nixon was also very much aware that the Cold War world had changed. Previous presidents had escalated the involvement believing that the Soviet Union and China represented a monolithic Communist bloc and consequently a tremendous threat. As the 1960s progressed, the Sino-Soviet split became increasingly evident, culminating in large-scale border clashes (see page 232). Nixon concluded that there was no longer any need for the US to try to contain Communism in Vietnam in the context of this new multipolar world. Nixon hoped to improve US relations with both the USSR and China and play the two Communist powers off against each other. Thus US security could be guaranteed by old-fashioned balance-of-power policies instead of by containment of Communism in Vietnam.

What stopped Nixon withdrawing immediately was concern for the United States' image. He wanted 'peace with honour'. He insisted that America's ally Thieu had to remain in power in an independent South Vietnamese state.

Nixon was always very concerned about the anti-war protesters. When his Cambodian offensive of spring 1970 caused massive student unrest, Nixon quickly withdrew US troops from Cambodia. It is difficult to tell whether he would have taken the US out of Vietnam

---

DID THE PROTESTERS 'LOSE THE WAR'?

Yes

Most historians think the protests helped bring the war to an end. A retired US air force officer, Colonel Joseph Martino, said 'America lost because of its democracy. Through dissent and protest it lost the ability to mobilise the will to win.' Protests certainly made politicians stop to think.

No

Had America been winning the war or had the waging of war been beyond reproach, there might not have been protests. Johnson halted the escalation in 1968. Until that time it was mostly students who protested. Only 10 per cent of higher education institutions had serious anti-war disturbances, and within those 10 per cent, fewer than 10 per cent of students participated. Some historians (for example, Gerard DeGroot) argue that the students simply alienated the majority of Americans, for example, their 1967 March on Washington had a 'hippy' character that irritated many older Americans. The 1969 Moratorium Day brought a quarter of a million protesters of all ages and classes to Washington DC, and there were simultaneous demonstrations in 500 towns and cities nationwide. However, this greatest of the anti-war demonstrations occurred *after* Johnson decided to halt the escalation.

without the protests. Nixon might conceivably have continued the involvement in Vietnam to save American face.

c) The Unpopularity of the War

Although protests began in American colleges in 1964, Johnson seemed at that stage to have most of the nation behind him in his Vietnam policies. Congress passed the Gulf of Tonkin Resolution and Johnson had a landslide victory in the presidential election. Once US ground troops went in (1965) and casualty lists went up, the protests escalated. During 1965 the number of American troops in Vietnam rose from around 20,000 to around 200,000 and there were widespread protests. In April 1965, 25,000 protesters marched on Washington and one congressmen reported 'widened unrest' among colleagues.

In 1966 Johnson's Democratic Party suffered bad defeats in the mid-term elections, which caused congressmen to urge the president to end the war. American politicians were naturally sensitive to the unpopularity of the war, and that clearly played a very important part in the final US decision to cease escalation and get out.

The war necessitated higher taxes. These were unpopular. In 1967 there were more protests in cities throughout America. Seventy thousand protesters converged on Washington DC. The media began to turn against the war, but it was after the Tet Offensive (1968) that a majority of newspapers and television stations became hostile. The United States seemed to be falling apart, with race riots and anti-war protests. In this situation, Johnson decided to halt the escalation.

The protests continued under Nixon. In October 1969 the largest anti-war protest in US history occurred. There were protests in every major city. Millions participated. 1970 saw more protests. By this time the number of US troops in Vietnam was decreasing dramatically. As it became clear that the United States was really getting out, the protests decreased.

d) Financial and Economic Problems

US involvement in Vietnam was very expensive. In the year General Westmoreland took charge of MACV (1964) the war cost the US taxpayer under half a billion dollars. When Westmoreland left Vietnam (1968) it cost $26.5 billion. The war was the main contributor to the government's $25 billion deficit and to rising inflation in 1968. The Treasury warning that the war could not go on, coupled with taxpayer resentment, helped to convince Johnson that the escalation must stop and Nixon that the war must end.

THE SILENT MAJORITY

Throughout all the protests, polls showed that what Richard Nixon called the 'silent majority' did not want to get out of Vietnam. Although they might not like the war, they felt that America had to finish the job properly.

ACTIVITY

Consider the factors contributing to the US withdrawal: (a) failure to win; (b) changing international situation; (c) unpopularity; (d) cost. Remove each factor individually – for example, remove (a) and decide whether the US would have withdrawn if the war had been successful, then reinsert (a) and instead remove another factor. Do this with all the factors. Decide which factor you consider to have been most important.

6 The End of the Story

a) How Did the United States Get Out of Vietnam?

After Tet and the advice from the 'Wise Men', Johnson halted the escalation. Peace talks began in Paris in May 1968, but a settlement looked unlikely as the United States demanded North Vietnamese withdrawal from South Vietnam while the North Vietnamese were insistent that they participate in the government of South Vietnam. Richard Nixon worked to achieve this unlikely settlement by a combination of diplomatic pressure, bombing and 'Vietnamisation'.

Nixon introduced direct (but secret) Washington–Hanoi negotiations that excluded South Vietnam, in April 1969. Detente with the Soviets and Chinese seemed to pay off, as Nixon had hoped. Moscow and Beijing urged North Vietnam to stop insisting upon the removal of President Thieu. The Soviets made little fuss about the massive escalation of US bombing of North Vietnam even when four Soviet merchant ships were sunk in Haiphong harbour in 1972. Nixon also made concessions to the North Vietnamese. By late 1972 the US had agreed that North Vietnamese forces should stay in South Vietnam after the Americans had left. A peace was signed in Paris in January 1973. Hanoi rightly thought that so long as they could get the Americans out, they could bide their time and take South Vietnam eventually. As it turned out, they reunited Vietnam within 27 months.

b) Results for the United States of Involvement in Vietnam

▼ The US could argue that it had contained Communism by its efforts in Vietnam. Outside Indo-China, no other South-east Asian state became Communist.

▼ The US military showed it had recovered from Vietnam in an impressive performance in the Gulf War (1991). President George Bush (Senior) crowed, 'We have kicked the Vietnam syndrome once and for all'.

▼ Vietnam made the American public and Congress far more inclined to monitor any future crises that looked likely to lead to 'another Vietnam'.

▼ Over 50,000 Americans died in Vietnam, 300,000 were wounded, and among survivors there was a disproportionate percentage of alcohol and drug-related problems and suicides.

▼ US economic troubles during Nixon's presidency owed much to expenditure on the Vietnam War.

▼ The Vietnam War caused and still causes a great deal of tension within the United States. When Bill Clinton was first elected president, his Vietnam War 'draft dodging' was controversial. In the last year of his presidency, Clinton visited Vietnam and stirred up old memories and some antagonisms in the United States.

ACTIVITY

Look at American movies on the Vietnam War. Are they of any use to the historian?

▼ Working on The United States and Vietnam

The two most important debates over the US involvement are (a) Why America got involved and (b) Why America could not achieve its aims in Vietnam. When you are asked about questions such as this in an examination, you will be more impressive if you can persuasively conclude that one cause or factor is more important than the others. There is no right answer to 'most important cause' questions, but when you re-read this chapter, try to construct a case for a 'most important cause' in the two great debates.

Answering Extended Writing and Essay Questions on The United States and Vietnam

Think about this question: 'To what extent should previous presidents share responsibility for President Johnson's Vietnam policy?' Examiners frequently use the phrase 'to what extent'. They mean 'give me arguments for and against' a proposition. In this case, you would give arguments that suggest Johnson bears responsibility for aspects or all of his Vietnam policy, and then arguments that balance this by demonstrating how his predecessors had bequeathed an undesirable legacy to him.

Answering Source-based Questions on The United States and Vietnam

It is fashionable in some quarters to say that the problems in Southeast Asia are primarily political and economic rather than military. I do not agree. The essence of the problem in Vietnam is military.

Source K General Earle Wheeler, Chairman of the Joint Chiefs of Staff, November 1962.

The President reviewed the situation in South Vietnam with US Ambassador Taylor ... The new government [in Saigon] was making a determined effort to strengthen national unity, to maintain law and order, and to press forward with the security programme, involving a combination of political, economic and military means to defeat the Vietcong insurgency ... The strength of the armed forces of the Government was being increased by improved recruiting and con-scription, and by the nearly one hundred percent increase in the combat strength of the Vietnamese Air Force. Also the Government forces continue to inflict heavy losses on the Vietcong ... On the economic front ... agricultural output was continuing to increase with US assistance in fertilisers and pesticides playing an important role. On the other hand ... the Vietcong is interfering to some extent with commerce within the country, and recent typhoons and floods in central Vietnam have destroyed a large percentage of the crops and livestock in that region. The Vietnamese Government, with US assis-tance, has moved promptly to organise a programme which is bring-ing relief and rehabilitation to the stricken areas ...

The meeting reviewed the accumulating evidence of continuing and increased North Vietnamese support of the Vietcong ... The President reaffirmed the basic US policy of providing all possible and useful assistance to the South Vietnamese people and Government in their struggle to defeat the externally supported insurgency and aggression being conducted against them.

Source L White House briefing for the press, 1 December 1964.

We seek an independent non-Communist South Vietnam ... Unless we can achieve this objective in South Vietnam, almost all of Southeast Asia will probably fall under Communist domination.

Source M Secretary of Defence Robert McNamara's report to the president, 16 March 1965.

Clark Clifford: A substantial build-up of US ground troops would be construed by the Communists, and by the world, as a determination on our part to win the war on the ground. This could be a quagmire.

CLARK CLIFFORD

Clark Clifford was a respect-ed lawyer and international commentator, whom Johnson made Secretary of Defence in 1967.

It could turn into an open-ended commitment on our part that would take more and more ground troops, without a realistic hope of ultimate victory... I don't think we can win in South Vietnam. If we send in one hundred thousand men the North Vietnamese will meet us. If North Vietnam runs out of men, the Chinese will send in volun-teers. Russia and China don't intend for us to win the war. I can't see anything but catastrophe for my country.

George Ball: We cannot win, Mr President. The war will be long and protracted. The most we can hope for is a messy conclusion. There remains a great danger of intrusion by the Chinese. But the biggest problem is the problem of the long war. The Korean experience was a galling one ... As casualties increase, the pressure to strike at the very jugular of North Vietnam will become very great. I am con-cerned about world opinion. If we could win in a year's time, and win decisively, world opinion would be all right. However, if the war is long ... then we will suffer because the world's greatest power can-not defeat guerrillas. Then there is the problem of national politics ... The enemy cannot even be seen in Vietnam. He is indigenous to the country. I truly have serious doubts that an army of Westerners can successfully fight Orientals in an Asian jungle ... The least harmful way to cut losses in South Vietnam is to let the government decide it doesn't want us to stay there ...

President Johnson: Then you are basically not concerned by what the world would say about our pulling out?

George Ball: If we were actively helping a country with a stable gov-ernment, it would be a vastly different story. Western Europeans look upon us as if we got ourselves into an imprudent situation.

President Johnson: But I believe that the Vietnamese are trying to fight.

George Ball: Thieu spoke the other day and he said the Communists would win the election ...

Dean Rusk: If the Communist world found out that the United States would not pursue its commitment to the end there was no telling where they would stop their expansionism.

Henry Cabot Lodge: I feel that there is greater threat to start World War III if we don't go in. Can't we see the similarity to our indolence at Munich? I simply can't be as pessimistic as Ball. We have great sea ports in Vietnam. We don't need to fight on roads. We have the sea. Let us visualise meeting the Vietcong on our own terms. We don't have to spend all our time in the jungles.

Source N Minutes from a meeting, 21 July 1965.

Admiral McDonald: First supply the forces [General] Westmoreland has asked for. Second, prepare to furnish more men, one hundred thousand in 1966. Third, commence building up air and naval forces and step up air attacks on North Vietnam …

General McConnell: If you put in these requested forces and increase air and sea effort, we can least turn the tide to where we are not losing any more.

Source O Report of a meeting between the President and the Joint Chiefs of Staff, 22 July 1965.

▼ QUESTIONS ON SOURCES

1. (a) By which theory is McNamara influenced in Source M? **[1 mark]**
(b) What did George Ball mean when he described the 'Korean experience' as 'galling'? **[2 marks]**
2. To what extent do the descriptions of the South Vietnamese government in Sources L and N differ? **[5 marks]**
3. Bearing in mind the language, tone and content, how persuasive is George Ball? **[5 marks]**
4. How useful is Source L to the historian interested in the progress of the American war effort? **[7 marks]**
5. Using the sources and your own knowledge, explain why the United States was unable to win in Vietnam. **[30 marks]**

Further Reading

Books in the Access to History series
The United States and Vietnam, by Vivienne Sanders.

General
A useful short account is Kevin Ruane, *War and Revolution in Vietnam, 1930–75* (UCL Press, 1998). Journalist Stanley Karnow's *Vietnam: A History* (Penguin, 1991), is a fascinating read. Gerard DeGroot's *A Noble Cause? America and the Vietnam War* (Longman, 2000), is good on all the important controversies. Robert Schulzinger, *A Time for War* (Oxford, 1997), is excellent, as is R.J. McMahon's *Major Problems in the History of the Vietnam War* (DC Heath, 1995). A good documentary collection is *Vietnam and America,* edited M. Gettleman et al. (Grove Press, 1995).

ISSUE:
Who were the most
successful presidents
during the period
1945–90?

POINTS TO CONSIDER

The USA emerged from the Second World War as the richest and
strongest nation on earth. According to historian James Patterson,
most Americans had Grand Expectations. This chapter examines the
extent to which those expectations were realised after 1945. To get a
broader picture, you must also read chapter 5 which deals with civil
rights and Chapters 6 and 7 which examine US foreign policy.

ISSUE:
How successful were
the presidents during
the 'age of affluence'?

1 The 'Age of Affluence': the USA, 1945–60

a) The US Economy and Society

In 1945 the USA, with 140 million people, had 7 per cent of the
world's population but 42 per cent of the world's income and over 50
per cent of the world's manufacturing output. Its per capita income
was twice that of any other country. This state of affairs continued
post-1945 as the USA enjoyed a tremendous economic boom. The
major growth areas were aircraft, electrical goods, chemicals, tobacco, food processing and cars. The building industry also flourished as

---

Demobilisation

In August 1945 the USA had some 12 million men in its armed
forces. By mid-1946 only 3 million remained in uniform. The
USA demobilised quickly and humanely. Thanks to the GI Bill of
Rights (1944), huge sums of money were made available for ex-
servicemen who wanted help with education costs. Nearly 8 million veterans benefited. The result was a massive increase in colleges and universities.

After 1945 US industry quickly converted from the production
of war materials to the production of consumer goods. During the
war Americans had postponed buying major items such as cars and
houses. With savings of over $150 billion, they were eager to spend.

new suburbs sprang up. Federal and state government spending (for example, on road building and schools) remained high.

During the 1950s there was rising per capita income, no inflation and little unemployment. By the mid-1950s 60 per cent of the population enjoyed a 'middle-class' standard of living and white-collar (salaried) workers outnumbered blue-collar (hourly wage) workers for the first time in US history. Home ownership rose dramatically and houses were filled with all the latest appliances. New developments in air transport meant that foreign travel became accessible to millions of Americans. For those who stayed at home, new tourist attractions such as Disneyland were established. A new social group – teenagers – was 'discovered' and encouraged to spend money on 'rock 'n' roll' records and clothes. Television had a huge impact. By 1960 most homes had one.

The Car

In the 1950s the car 'ruled'. Freeways, multi-storey car parks, out-of-town shopping malls and drive-in restaurants, cinemas and banks catered to the motorist. Cars became a status symbol. By 1960 one in seven US workers was employed in a job either directly or indirectly connected to the automobile industry.

BIG BUSINESS
Big business grew bigger. After 1945 a wave of mergers occurred. Dominant corporate giants appeared in every major industry. More and more Americans worked for fewer and fewer firms.

In 1946 2.2 million couples wed – a record. Although divorce rates reached record highs in 1945–6, they dropped sharply thereafter, reversing what had been a trend since 1900. The baby boom was the most amazing social trend. The US birth rate had been declining throughout the early twentieth century. In the 1930s it was below 20 per thousand of the population a year. In 1947 it shot up to 26.6 and remained at 24 or higher until 1959. In 1946 3.4 million babies were born: in 1947 3.88 million. It became the norm for Americans to marry younger and thus start families sooner. Family life was portrayed as being idyllic by advertisers and the media.

THE GROWTH OF SUBURBS
New suburban housing estates provided a pleasant environment for many families. However, most of those who moved to the suburbs were affluent whites. poor, often black, Americans were left behind in inner-city areas.

The Role of Women

Historians debate the extent to which the period was one of gender discrimination or a wonderful era of domesticity. It was generally thought that women's role was at home and in the kitchen. Women's rights were, according to President Truman, 'a lot of hooey'. Feminism had little support among women. The prevailing view was that women could achieve fulfilment by accepting their natural functions as wives and mothers. Nevertheless, many married women worked to keep up with the Joneses and/or to

THE FLIGHT FROM THE FARMS
New technological advances in agriculture reduced the need for manual labour. Some 20 million Americans left the land for the city between 1940 and 1970.

provide for the basic needs of their families. Gender-segregated employment was the norm. Women were usually paid less than men, even when they did the same work.

b) President Truman

In April 1945, following the death of Franklin Roosevelt, Harry Truman became President. He had little experience and was not seen – nor did he see himself – as FDR's obvious successor. Awed by his rapid elevation, he coped with that awe through an outward aura of confident command. Convinced that the USA was the world's best hope for peace and prosperity, he believed that hope could best be realised if the USA developed a political and social system that was an example to the rest of the world. He was aware that life was not good for all Americans. Intending to extend the scope of the New Deal, he proposed sweeping laws in 1945 providing for healthcare and low-cost housing. His most immediate concern was the matter of employment. He pinned his hopes on the Full Employment Bill which had been introduced in Congress in 1945. This bill declared employment to be a right and required the government to ensure that sufficient jobs were available. Truman supported the bill and reinforced it with measures of his own – increased dole, a higher minimum wage, farm price supports and a public works programme. Congress passed the Employment Act but watered down many of Truman's proposals.

The end of the war fuelled inflation. Union leaders, determined to increase the purchasing power of their members, called a number of major strikes in 1945. Truman called a special labour-management conference in November 1945 to try to smooth over differences but it ended without agreement. In April 1946 the United Mine Workers struck for a pay increase. In May the railroads were hit by strikes. Truman now took firm action. He announced that he would conscript the railroad workers and have the army run the railroads. He also called for legislation that would restrict the right to strike against the government and would impose severe penalties on violators. He did not have to implement his threat because the rail strike was called off. Truman had made it clear that labour could not count on his automatic support.

Truman soon faced major political difficulties. The 1946 mid-term elections resulted in a Republican majority in both houses of Congress, the first time since 1928. Republicans saw this as a mandate for the revision of the New Deal. Intent on cutting back the federal government's involvement in social welfare, they supported tax reductions and the restoration of the market economy. The 1947 Taft–Hartley Bill made labour unions liable for violations of contracts and prevented them from insisting that all workers must join a union as a condition of employment. Truman, unwilling to lose the support of labour, vetoed the bill but Congress passed it over his objections.

The Republicans, confident of success, chose Thomas Dewey as their presidential candidate in 1948. Truman was the Democrat candidate but his party split into warring factions. Henry Wallace, a former vice-president of FDR, set up the Progressive Party. Strom Thurmond, a southern conservative, disliking Truman's support for civil rights (see page 172), also stood against Truman. Most opinion polls agreed that Dewey was favourite to win. But Truman fought back. In 1948 he called Congress into special session and tried – unsuccessfully – to pass various New Deal-type measures. He then went on a 30,000 mile whistle-stop tour of the USA, defending his record and attacking the Republican 'do-nothing Congress'. In one of the biggest electoral surprises of the century, he won a majority of over 2 million (303–189 electoral college) votes. The Democrats also regained control of Congress.

Figure 54 Truman defeats Dewey! The *Chicago Daily Tribune* famously got it wrong.

THE FAIR DEAL

In 1949 Truman declared that 'Every segment of our population and every individual has a right to expect from our Government a fair deal'. He called for a raft of new welfare measures. In his second term he did succeed in raising the minimum wage, extending the Social Security Act and passing an act to aid slum clearance and to provide housing for the poor. But Republican and Democrat conservatives blocked many of his reform proposals.

c) McCarthyism

In the late 1940s and early 1950s the USA was gripped by the fear of Communism. Concern about Communist subversion affected all areas of public life. Senator Joseph McCarthy was the most notorious 'witch-hunter'. His anti-communist activities gave rise to a new word in the vocabulary of US politics, McCarthyism. Why did this phenomenon occur? To what extent should McCarthy be blamed for it?

The USA had long been anti-Communist. There had been a Red Scare in 1919. In 1942, at a time when the USA was allied with the USSR, 50 per cent of Americans favoured a law outlawing membership of the US Communist Party. The onset of the Cold War (see Chapter 6) increased American fears. Despite its atomic monopoly, the USA was unable to stop the Soviet domination of Eastern Europe. Then, in 1949, China went Communist and the USSR exploded its own atomic bomb. Many believed that there had been a deliberate mishandling of the post-war challenges by Communist sympathisers. This view was fuelled by a number of revelations.

▼ In 1946 a Canadian spy ring, which sent atomic secrets to the USSR, was uncovered.

▼ In 1948 Alger Hiss, a former State Department official, was accused by Whittaker Chambers, a confessed Communist agent, of being a Soviet agent and of passing on secrets. Hiss was tried in 1949. In 1950 he was convicted of perjury in relation to the charge and sentenced to five years' imprisonment.

▼ The arrest in 1950 of British physicist Klaus Fuchs on charges of atomic espionage seemed to confirm the worst fears of those who were intent on finding proof of guilt in high places. Fuchs' testimony led to the conviction and execution (in 1953) of Julius and Ethel Rosenberg for passing atomic secrets to the Russians.

Some of Truman's advisers argued that opposition to the USSR abroad had to be combined with vigilance at home. In 1947 a Loyalty Review Board was set up to investigate government employees. 'Communists shall not work for the government', said Truman, 'and our vigilance shall be unremitting'. Some 300 were dismissed: 2,500 left their jobs of their own accord. J. Edgar Hoover, head of the FBI, was given extra resources to weed out Communists. Eleven leading Communists were convicted on the grounds that they advocated the violent overthrow of the US government. Meanwhile, Congressional committees were set up to investigate the Communist threat in the film industry and in education. In 1950 Congress passed the McCarren Internal Security Act. Communist organisations now had to register with the Justice Department and provide a list of their members. Communists were excluded from employment in defence agencies and from holding passports. Some Republicans realised that political capital could be made from charges of disloyalty. Richard Nixon, for example, won elections in California by suggesting his Democrat opponents were 'red' sympathisers.

Joseph McCarthy had taken an anti-Communist stance since being elected a Republican Senator for Wisconsin in 1946. However, his Senate record was mediocre and he had re-election fears. In February 1950 McCarthy's fame began when he announced at Wheeling, West Virginia, that he possessed a list of names of 205

Communists who were working in the State Department. He repeated his charge in other speeches. (The numbers of his alleged 'card-carrying' Communists changed almost daily.) His sensational claims aroused huge press interest. Many veteran anti-Communists were surprised at how little McCarthy actually knew. But through a monumental bluff, he had placed himself at the centre of the anti-Communist movement. A Senate Committee, headed by Senator Tydings, examined McCarthy's allegations and concluded that his charges were a 'hoax'. But McCarthy had won great publicity and many Americans believed him. Fear of Communist infiltration increased with the start of the Korean War in June 1950 (see Chapter 6). The war strengthened McCarthy's position. In 1950 he was able to ensure the defeat of Senator Tydings in Maryland. The political lesson was clear: do not attack McCarthy.

Figure 55 McCarthy witch-hunting in 1954.

McCarthy used the Senate floor, where he enjoyed congressional privilege, to name names. Most of those named were investigated and cleared. Yet for four years McCarthy and his supporters continued to level charges at individuals and to conduct inquisitions of public institutions. Honourable men, such as General Marshall, Truman's former Secretary of State, were defamed. McCarthy had the support of other politicians, several leading newspapers and radio stations, and many ordinary Americans who saw him as an heroic crusader. Republican leaders realised they could use McCarthyism to attack Truman and the Democrat Party. Republicans claimed that the New Deal and Fair Deal were evidence of 'creeping socialism' and accused the Democrats of harbouring Communists.

The 1952 Election

Truman chose not to run in 1952. Instead, the Democrats chose Governor Adlai Stevenson of Illinois. The Republicans opted for General Dwight D. Eisenhower – affectionately known as 'Ike'. He was an excellent candidate. Born in humble circumstances, he had risen by his own efforts and ability. After a brilliant record in the Second World War, he became Supreme Commander of NATO. Given that the Korean War was still in progress, the choice of a war hero as presidential candidate made sense. Korea, Communism and corruption were the main issues. Ike disliked McCarthy but realised that anti-Communism was a vote-winner. He used his young vice-presidential candidate, Richard Nixon, as his 'hit man'. Nixon, who had a strong anti-Communist record (he had successfully prosecuted Alger Hiss), declared that the Truman administration was 'soft on Communism'. Ike won 34 million popular and 442 electoral college votes to Stevenson's 27 million popular and 89 electoral college votes. However, the Republicans only won slender majorities in the House and Senate. Thus Ike needed the support of McCarthy (who was re-elected) and other anti-Communists.

ACTIVITY

Consider the question: To what extent was Joseph McCarthy responsible for McCarthyism?
Suggested line of response:
▼ Stress that anti-Communism was strong in the USA pre-1950.
▼ Examine the impact of McCarthy between 1950 and 1954.
▼ Stress that anti-Communism existed post-1954.

McCarthy's witch-hunt was at its height in 1953–4. In January 1954 a poll indicated that 50 per cent of Americans had a generally favourable opinion of him. However, McCarthy's position was less secure after 1952. Eisenhower detested him and distanced himself from his activities. McCarthy's fall came about through his own self-exposure. In 1954 he determined to investigate subversion in the army. In the televised hearings, McCarthy showed himself to be rude and malicious. As public opinion turned, Congress moved against him. He was censured by the Senate in 1954 by 67 votes to 22 and virtually silenced thereafter. (He died in 1957.) 'McCarthyism', said Ike 'had become McCarthywasm'.

McCarthyism transcended the actions of a single man. In some respects McCarthy became a scapegoat: there were others like him who were not castigated to the same extent. Moreover, he reflected the general mood of the US public. Anti-Communism was strong before he rose to prominence: it retained its vigour after his fall. Given that there were some significantly placed Communist cells in the USA, it has been claimed that McCarthy was wrong in details but right in essentials. However, the fact remains that he was unable to unmask a single Communist in the government. Virtually all historians agree that he was a blot on the US landscape. That said, the so-called 'age of fear' does need to be seen in context. In the USA hundreds of people lost their jobs and some books were removed from library shelves, but there were no deaths (the Rosenbergs apart) and no prison camps. In the USSR and China, by contrast, millions of people were put to death or imprisoned for their political views in the 1950s.

d) President Eisenhower

Many contemporary liberals thought of Ike as a cautious conservative, a do-nothing president who spent his time playing bridge, poker and golf. They assumed he represented the interests of big business. His cabinet was composed, for the most part, of millionaire businessmen, three of whom had worked in the car industry. ('New Dealers', said Adlai Stevenson, 'had given way to car dealers.') He was blamed for showing little sympathy for civil rights and for paying little attention to rural poverty and urban decay. Ike's critics also claim that he showed no great ability in foreign affairs, failing to roll back Communism or to improve relations with the USSR. However, recent historians have been more positive. Most see him as a safe pair of hands who made things look deceptively easy. Historian Stephen Ambrose thinks he 'was a great and good man…one of the outstanding leaders of the western world of this [twentieth] century.' He is praised on a number of scores.

▼ He chose an able team, delegated well, and had a good record as a mediator. 'You do not lead by hitting people over the head', he said. 'Any damn fool can do that but it's usually called 'assault' – not 'leadership'… I'll tell you what leadership is. It's persuasion and conciliation and education and patience. It's long, slow, tough work. That's the only kind of leadership I know or believe in or will practice.' Historians refer to Ike's 'hidden-handed' presidency: he knew where he wanted to go and steered the country in that direction.

▼ He was a shrewd political operator and exploited his reputation for vagueness and muddle. (It was an act: he often went to press conferences, intending to be vague and evasive.) He worked well with a Congress that for most of his presidency was Democrat-controlled.

▼ A middle-of-the-road Republican, Ike called his programme 'dynamic conservatism'. This meant being 'conservative when it comes to money and liberal when it comes to human beings'. He favoured lower taxes, less bureaucracy, reducing the budget deficit and stopping the 'drift towards statism'. He was committed to 'finding things the government can stop doing rather than new things for it to do'. Even so, he accepted that the federal government should have some responsibility for the welfare of its citizens and that it should promote economic growth. Benefits for the poor were increased and a growing number of people were covered by social security. Huge sums of money were spent on

completing the St Lawrence Seaway, linking the Great Lakes with the Atlantic, while the Interstate Highway Act (1956) provided $33.5 billion to build a national network of roads.
▼ He generally decreased the role of government. He ended wage and price controls and reduced farm subsidies.
▼ He skilfully managed foreign policy (see Chapters 6 and 7).
▼ He was popular with most Americans. Although he suffered a heart attack in 1955, he stood again for the presidency in 1956, defeating Stevenson by an even bigger majority than in 1952.

e) The 1960 Election

Vice-President Richard Nixon was the Republican candidate. The two main Democratic contenders were Hubert Humphrey and John F. Kennedy (JFK). Humphrey was experienced and well-respected. The much younger JFK had a playboy-type image. (Most were unaware of the extent of his playboy activities: he may well have slept with hundreds of women.) First elected to Congress in 1946, he had a poor Congressional record and was not popular with leading Democrats. Many liberals regarded him with suspicion because he had failed to vote in the censure of McCarthy in 1954 and showed little interest in civil rights. However, helped by his family's wealth, JFK saw off the Humphrey challenge, winning first the key primaries and then the Democrat convention.

Nixon – 'Tricky Dicky' – had the advantage of experience. Moreover, as vice-president he could claim to be the successor of Ike who had presided over eight years of peace and prosperity. The fact that JFK was Catholic was felt to be to Nixon's advantage. The USA had never had a Catholic president. But JFK also had some advantages. Son of one of the richest men in the USA, he appeared youthful (at 43 he was four years younger than Nixon), had both looks and style, a glamorous wife, and an excellent campaign team which included his brother Robert Kennedy. He was also helped by a general sense of unease. Although the 1950s had brought a rising standard of living, the apparent complacency of Ike's administration had begun to cause disquiet. Communism seemed to pose a growing threat. In 1957 the USSR launched the first space satellite Sputnik. Then, in 1959 Castro seized power in Cuba. To many Americans the nation seemed to be drifting, without much sense of purpose. They wanted a change. JFK promised a 'New Frontier' – although he never made it very clear what this meant. He would also 'get the country moving again' and beat Communism.

Television played a crucial role in the election. Commercials were used to some effect. More importantly, Nixon and JFK agreed to four televised debates. The first debate was on 26 September. Those who

WHY WAS JFK MORE IMPRESSIVE IN THE TV DEBATES?

Most historians agree that, while Nixon debated better, JFK looked better! Nixon had been ill. He still looked unwell, and perspired profusely. Viewers found his 'five o'clock shadow' unattractive. JFK, although physically far less fit than Nixon, looked to be brimming with vigour and good health.

only heard the debate on the radio believed that Nixon had won. But those 70 million who watched the debate on TV were more impressed with JFK. Although Nixon did better in the next three debates, there were fewer floating voters: the damage had been done. Nixon had other problems. He made the mistake of campaigning in all 50 states. (Alaska and Hawaii had joined the Union in 1959.) JFK, by contrast, concentrated on the well-populated states. Nixon was also unfortunate in that Ike, whose health was in some doubt, only began actively campaigning for the Republicans in the last few days of the election.

Before 1960 JFK had shown little interest in civil rights issues. Then, in October 1960, Martin Luther King was arrested for trying to desegregate a restaurant in Atlanta and sentenced to four months' imprisonment. JFK telephoned King's wife, expressing his sympathy and support. Meanwhile, Robert Kennedy used his influence to obtain King's release. The Kennedys' intervention was well publicised and helped secure JFK black support.

The election, the closest since 1888, gave JFK a majority of just 118,574 popular votes. (He won 303 to Nixon's 219 electoral college votes.) There was evidence of corrupt practices in Illinois and Texas and if the voting had been different in these states, Nixon would have won. Not wishing to destroy US credibility in the world, Nixon accepted the result. JFK won the support of most traditional Democrat voters. Although he probably lost some Protestant votes in the South, the fact that he retained – or won back – Catholic support was more important. The religious issue may thus have helped him.

Figure 56 President John F. Kennedy – a new presidential style for a new generation of Americans.

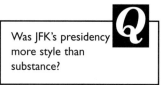

Was JFK's presidency more style than substance?

f) The Thousand Days

Few presidents in the twentieth century ruled for a shorter time than JFK – yet few are so well-known or have such a high reputation. How good a president was he? Although he gave the impression of being a man of principle, he prided himself on his pragmatism and refused to be tied down by theory. His image was one of energy and youth (although in reality, his health was quite poor). He undoubtedly had style. He was highly articulate and displayed considerable wit and disarming casualness. He seemed to be in a powerful position. His party had majorities in both houses of Congress. However, little was achieved. Some think this was because JFK was politically inept. Others have questioned his liberal aims. Although he gave the impression that he intended to promote social justice for all, he did little, focusing his attention on foreign, not domestic, affairs. His defenders claim that he was sincere in espousing liberal goals. They think the problem was that he faced a hostile Congress in which Republicans and southern Democrats held the whip hand.

CONSPIRACY OR LONE GUNMAN?

Historians continue to debate whether JFK was killed by a lone gunman – Lee Harvey Oswald – or whether Oswald was just part of a much larger conspiracy (and possibly just the fall guy). The fact that Oswald was murdered (by Jack Ruby) within two days of his arrest suggests a conspiracy, possibly by the Mafia. But serious Congressional investigations have invariably reached the conclusion that Oswald acted alone.

The lack of a clear, coherent programme hindered JFK when it came to securing the passage of legislation through Congress. His piecemeal proposals were easily blocked by conservatives. Efforts to reform the tax system, provide health insurance for the elderly, and give more money for education all failed. However, he did increase the minimum wage and did provide funds for urban renewal. JFK had a mixed record on the civil rights front. Before 1963 he was somewhat hesitant, largely because he did not wish to alienate conservative Southerners whose votes he needed for other measures. However, by 1963 he had committed himself to the cause of racial equality and sent a strong Civil Rights bill to Congress. Like many of his measures, it got stuck in committee. JFK did have some success in space. In 1961 he announced that it was his intention that the US would land a man on the moon 'before the decade is out'. Huge resources were given to Project Apollo, ensuring that the US did indeed land a man on the moon in 1969.

JFK was largely image but image was – and is – important. When he spoke people listened. It is probably fair to say that he aroused expectations but had too little time to deliver. A great deal of important legislation was working its way through Congress in 1963. His assassination in Dallas in November 1963 enhanced the Kennedy myth. People asked what might have been. Given that the early 1960s were a prosperous time for many Americans, JFK probably left the USA a better place than he found it.

ISSUE:

Why were the 1960s and the 1970s such troubled decades for the USA?

2 The Troubled Decades: 1963–80

a) President Lyndon B. Johnson and the Great Society

JFK was succeeded by Lyndon B. Johnson (LBJ). A greater difference in style between the two men would be hard to imagine. Whereas JFK was articulate and charismatic, LBJ was a poor speaker and lacking in charm. What he possessed, that JFK lacked, was a deep concern for the have-nots in society and the political skills necessary to push his liberal measures through Congress. In January 1964 he declared: 'Unfortunately, many Americans live on the outskirts of hope … some because of their poverty and some because of their colour, and all too many because of both'. In order to 'help replace their despair with opportunity', LBJ continued, 'this administration today … declares unconditional war on poverty'. The 'war' began when LBJ submitted the Economic Opportunity Bill to Congress in March 1964. Among its provisions were plans to aid disadvantaged children. In May LBJ called for the creation of a 'Great Society'. He envisaged the federal

Figure 57 President Johnson signs the Medicare Bill in 1966. Vice-President Humphrey gives a helping hand.

government taking action to eliminate poverty, improve education, further civil rights, ensure full employment, and enhance health care. This vision was approved by the electorate in the 1964 election. Running against Senator Barry Goldwater, a conservative Republican, LBJ won a landslide victory, polling 61 per cent of the popular vote.

LBJ now moved to enact the Great Society into law at a pace unseen since 1933. In quick succession Congress passed bills providing healthcare for the elderly and poor, $1.5 billion in federal aid to schools, $2.9 billion for urban renewal, and $1.1 billion to help the depressed Appalachian region. In total Congress enacted 435 bills in the period 1964–6. Thereafter, as the Vietnam War began to take more of his time, LBJ found it hard to provide the leadership which was necessary for further legislative success. Without his direction, the move towards a Great Society slowed down. There was also growing opposition. On the right, critics argued that the programmes were too expensive, led to the creation of a huge, inefficient bureaucracy, and failed to produce the desired results. On the left, critics could not agree about the best means of achieving the goals defined by LBJ. The outbreak of riots in many of the USA's cities in the late 1960s (see Chapter 4) has often been used as evidence that the Great Society was a failure. Arguably, it aroused expectations which it was then unable to deliver. But for all the criticisms levelled at the Great Society, millions benefited from its education and healthcare programmes.

b) The 1968 Election

In March 1968 LBJ, worn down by the Vietnam War, declared that: 'I shall not seek and I will not accept the nomination of my party for another term as your President'. This decision, together with the assassination of Robert Kennedy in June, left the way clear for Vice-President Hubert Humphrey to secure the Democratic nomination. Divisions within the Democrat convention at Chicago, and violent scenes outside the convention hall as police battled with left-wing protestors, suggested that the party was in disarray. Closely identified with the policies of LBJ, Humphrey campaigned to continue the war in Vietnam and to pursue the objectives of the Great Society. The Republican candidate Richard Nixon tried to appeal to 'Middle America' by championing the cause of people disillusioned with the Great Society and worried by the black riots. He also promised 'peace with honour' in Vietnam. Ex-governor of Alabama, George Wallace, who ran as an independent, was also critical of the Great Society. He proposed tough action against black rioters and even tougher action against North Vietnam. Nixon defeated Humphrey by some 500,000 votes, a margin of 1 per cent. (Nixon won 302 electoral college votes to Humphrey's 191.) In the best showing of a third-party candidate since 1924, Wallace won 10 million votes – 13.5 per cent of the total – mainly from white Southerners.

c) President Richard Nixon

In 1968–9 Nixon promised to 'bring Americans together again'. He faced major problems.
▼ The USA was still fighting the war in Vietnam.
▼ The country had major economic and financial problems. Spending on the Vietnam War and the Great Society programmes contributed to the inflationary pressures that were being generated by an expanding world economy. By the late 1960s the USA's economic pre-eminence had been reduced and her manufacturing growth lagged behind that of Japan and western Europe. There was a growing trade gap and rising unemployment.
▼ Nixon was the first president since 1849 to face a Congress in which both chambers were controlled by the opposition party.
▼ US society was deeply divided. Many young Americans questioned traditional values and institutions. University campuses were seething with discontent. Older Americans were concerned at the rising crime and the growing sense of permissiveness.

Nixon's background was lower middle class. He had risen by his own hard work and talent. Something of a loner, he lacked the grace and wit of JFK and Ike and was more admired than loved. He tended to see conspiracy at work against himself and the USA, and liked to conspire in turn. He relied more on three assistants – Chief of Staff Bob Haldeman, domestic adviser John Ehrlichman and foreign adviser, Henry Kissinger – than on cabinet officials. Nixon's main interest was foreign policy. The fact that the Democrats controlled Congress meant that there was little likelihood of him being able to do much on the domestic front.

Nixon was conservative. Fearing that the traditional family unit might be undermined, he was suspicious of the growing feminist movement and opposed abortion, which won him Catholic support. He also took a tough stance on law and order. In general, he hoped to win the support of the 'forgotten' Americans who were weary of big government in civil rights and welfare. Nixon, determined to be re-elected in 1972, aimed to forge a Republican majority from the working class, the suburban middle class, and the Southern whites who had voted for Wallace in 1968. He thus showed little interest in civil rights. His so-called 'southern strategy' was consistent with the general aims of his domestic policy. At the centre of his approach was the belief that federal government had grown too large and needed trimming. However, he had no wish to destroy the welfare state. The innovative Family Assistance Plan (FAP), which Nixon submitted to Congress in 1969, aimed to streamline the bureaucracy created by the Great Society programmes. Rather than receive a range of different benefits, the FAP proposed paying poor families a direct grant of $1,600. FAP was defeated in Congress by a (strange) alliance of Republican right and Democrat left. Even more strangely, during Nixon's presidency, there was a more rapid rise in spending on social programmes than had been achieved by LBJ. While Nixon was trying to trim the federal government, Congress was passing laws which added to the bureaucracy's size.

Nixon faced a worsening economic situation. At first he tried to stem inflation by cutting government spending, supporting higher interest rates, and persuading business to curb price increases and labour unions not to ask for wage increases. This had little effect. Therefore, in 1971 Nixon imposed a 90-day wages and prices freeze, a reduction in income tax and a repeal of excise tax on cars. His aim was to spur the purchase of consumer goods. In October 1971, just before his 90-day freeze ended, he initiated 'phase two' of his programme, setting up a Pay Board which limited wage increases to 5.5 per cent and a Price Commission which limited price increases to 2.5 per cent. In 1971 he also devalued the dollar. This helped stimulate a boom, just in time for the 1972 election.

> ### 'FORGOTTEN' AMERICANS
> As K. Phillips noted in his book *The Emerging Republican Majority* in 1969, most Americans were 'unpoor, unyoung, unblack, middle-aged, middle-class and middle-minded'.

Feminism

A strong feminist movement, partly inspired by the civil rights movement and partly by Betty Friedan's best-selling *The Feminine Mystique* (1963), arose in the USA in the 1960s. Friedan criticised the ways in which the cult of domesticity had stifled women's creativity and opportunities for personal growth. Middle-class homes, said Friedan, had become 'a comfortable concentration camp'. In 1966 the National Organisation of Women (NOW) was founded and campaigned for passage of an Equal Rights Amendment to the Constitution. It also spearheaded efforts to end job discrimination, to legalise abortion and to obtain government support for childcare centres. In the early 1970s Congress and the Supreme Court advanced the cause of sexual equality. For example, under Title 1X of the Educational Amendments Act (1972), colleges were required to institute 'affirmative action' programmes to ensure equal opportunities for women. An increasing number of women entered professions which had once been perceived as male preserves such as law and medicine. The two-career family began to replace the traditional pattern of male breadwinner and female housekeeper. However, the women's movement was not totally successful. It was essentially middle class: few working-class women showed much interest. There was also a major division between moderate and radical feminists. While the Equal Rights Amendment Act passed Congress, it was not ratified by the states. Moreover, the success of NOW's efforts to change the abortion laws generated a powerful reaction, especially among Catholics and fundamental Protestants.

Differing Views of Women, 1956 and 1963

A special issue of *Life* magazine in 1956 featured the 'ideal' middle class woman, a 32 years old 'pretty and popular' suburban housewife, mother of four, who had married at age 16. She was described as an excellent wife, mother, hostess, volunteer, and 'home manager' who made her own clothes, hosted dozens of dinner parties each year, sang in the church choir ...' Of all the accomplishments of the American woman', the *Life* cover story proclaimed, 'the one she brings off with the most spectacular success is having babies.'

Source A From *A Narrative History* by
G.B. Tyndall (Norton, 1988).

The problem lay unburied, unspoken, for many years in the minds of American women. It was a strange stirring, a sense of dissatisfaction, a yearning that women suffered in the middle of the twentieth century in the United States. Each suburban wife struggled with it alone. As she made the beds, shopped for groceries, matched slipcover material, ate peanut butter sandwiches with her children, chauffeured Cub Scouts and Brownies, lay beside her husband at night – she was afraid to ask even of herself the silent question – 'Is this all?'

Source B Betty Friedan: *The Feminine Mystique* (1963).

ACTIVITY

How do the two sources help explain the changes that took place in women's position in the USA in the 1960s and 1970s?

Youth Rebellion

▼ Nixon's Vietnam policies (see page 265) revitalised the anti-war movement. In October 1969 some 2 million people took to the streets demanding an end to the Vietnam War. Students were at the cutting edge of the anti-war movement. In May 1970 at Ohio's Kent State University, students protested at the invasion of Cambodia. National Guardsmen opened fire on a peaceful rally: four students were killed. Hundreds of other campuses experienced risings in the wake of Kent State.

▼ Many young Americans seemed alienated from mainstream society. Long hair, 'outlandish' dress, rock music, drugs and cooperative living arrangements were part of a new 'hippy' counter-culture. This was summed up by the Harvard professor Timothy Leary: 'Tune in, turn on, drop out'. The main counter-culture event came at the Woodstock Festival in August 1969, attended by some 400,000 people. For a few the new way of life brought a sense of fulfilment. For most it was a case of sowing wild oats. In general, American youth displayed little interest in politics.

▼ The New Left, which Nixon saw as a major threat to the 'American way', was massively divided. A small minority advocated revolutionary terrorism. The Motherfuckers and Crazies urged anarchy. The Weathermen advocated random violence against almost anyone. In 1969–70 they were responsible for scores of bombings. These slowed down when three Weathermen accidently blew themselves up. Nixon, who exaggerated the internal threat, used the FBI and CIA to subvert left-wing organisations.

▼ The New Left, youth rebellion and student unrest sparked off a conservative backlash which helped Nixon.

d) The 1972 Election

The Democrats chose Senator George McGovern of South Dakota as their candidate. Third-party candidate George Wallace had the potential to attract conservative votes away from the Republicans and was thus a potential threat to Nixon. This threat was removed when Wallace was shot and paralysed. Nixon was now in a strong position. He branded McGovern as a wild radical and pledged to end 'the age of permissiveness'. Visits to both the USSR and China in 1972 enhanced his prestige. The Vietnam War seemed to be coming to an end and the economy seemed to be improving. Nixon won 47 million votes to McGovern's 29 million and won every state except two – the greatest electoral triumph ever achieved by a Republican candidate. However, the Democrats still had majorities in both houses of Congress.

e) Watergate

On 17 June 1972 five men associated with the Committee to Re-elect the President (CREEP) were caught as they tried to break into the Democratic National HQ at the Watergate Hotel in Washington DC They were hoping to tap the phone of the Democratic National Committee Chairman. (Two other men were also subsequently arrested.) Whether Nixon knew in advance of the plan is unclear: he always denied he did. He succeeded in deflecting attention from the affair during the election campaign by using the CIA (illegally) to stop an FBI investigation. It was implied, quite wrongly, that national security secrets might be exposed if the FBI pursued its leads. In August Nixon declared that White House Counsel John Dean had 'conducted a complete investigation' and found that 'no one in this administration presently employed, was involved in this very bizarre incident'. It was only after Nixon's re-election that the full story of Watergate broke.

In January 1973 the seven men involved in the Watergate break-in were found guilty of conspiracy and burglary. Sentencing was delayed to give the defendants a chance to cooperate in exchange for mitigation. In March James McCord, former head of security for CREEP, informed Judge Sirica that high-ranking government officials were involved in the affair. John Dean panicked and began to talk to prosecutors, negotiating for immunity. He testified that former Attorney General Mitchell, with the knowledge of Haldeman and Ehrlichman, had authorised the break-in and that Nixon had approved the cover-up. Mitchell, Haldeman and Ehrlichman denied the accusations. So did Nixon. In April he fired Dean and accepted the resignations of Haldeman and Ehrlichman. In May a Select Senate Committee began televised hearings into the affair. Howard Baker, the leading Republican on the Committee, repeatedly asked: 'What did the President know, and when did he know it'.

When it emerged that Nixon's conversations in the White House had been taped, special prosecutor Cox tried to obtain the tapes hoping to establish the extent of Nixon's involvement. Nixon refused to comply and ordered Cox's dismissal. In October 1973 Attorney-General Richardson and his deputy resigned rather than execute the order. A year-long legal battle for Nixon's tapes ensued. By late 1973 Watergate was undermining Nixon's presidency. Vice-President Agnew's resignation on charges of income tax evasion and of accepting bribes, was a further embarrassment. Gerald Ford became the new vice-president.

In March 1974 the Grand Jury charged seven men close to Nixon, including Haldeman and Ehrlichman, with obstruction of justice and with perjury. Meanwhile the House of Representatives voted to authorise its Judiciary Committee to determine whether Nixon should be impeached. In July the Supreme Court ruled that Nixon should hand over all the tapes to the Judiciary Committee. The tapes established beyond any doubt that six days after the Watergate break-in, Nixon had ordered a cover-up. The House Judiciary Committee now voted to recommend three articles of impeachment. Nixon was accused of obstructing justice through the withholding of evidence, abusing federal agencies like the FBI to deprive citizens of their constitutional rights, and unconstitutionally defying the subpoenas of the Judiciary Committee. Moderate Republicans joined with Democrats in supporting the impeachment proceedings. Before the House as a whole could vote on the articles of impeachment, Nixon – on 8 August – resigned.

Nixon, the first president in US history to resign, was generally castigated for bringing the office into disrepute. Perhaps he was unlucky. Most US presidents since the 1930s had 'stretched' the powers of their office. Nixon had some achievements, not least in foreign policy (see Chapters 6 and 7). But it is difficult to feel much sympathy for him. He had abused power more than most previous presidents. He was supposedly committed to law and order, but no fewer than 25 of his aides were indicted for criminal activity.

Q How serious a crime was Watergate?

f) President Gerald Ford

Ford was an accidental president. Amiable and honest (if not particularly able), he restored some confidence in the presidency. Unlike Nixon, he delegated considerable power to his cabinet members. Although he made some initial efforts to work with the Democrat-dominated Congress, his pardon of Nixon ended the honeymoon period. Thereafter, relations between Ford and Congress were to be characterised by conflict. During his two years as president, Ford vetoed 66 bills, beating Hoover's record.

The main focus of conflict between Ford and Congress was the US economy. By 1974 the US was suffering from both high inflation and a high rate of unemployment – 'stagflation'. There was also an energy crisis. The USA, like many countries, suffered when the Organisation of Petroleum Exporting Countries (OPEC) quadrupled the price of oil in December 1973. Ford, deciding to concentrate his efforts on curbing inflation, advocated a reduction of government spending and higher taxes. Most Congressmen, in contrast, wanted tax cuts and an increase in government spending, hoping to reflate the economy and reduce unemployment. As the rates of inflation and unemployment continued to worsen in 1975, Ford changed his priorities. He recommended an anti-recession programme to Congress which included both a tax cut for low earners and a plan for public-service employment. This '179 degree' turn did little for Ford's reputation. It also had little effect. At the end of 1976 the inflation rate was 9 per cent while the unemployment rate stood at 8 per cent.

With the economy performing so badly, Ford came close to being rejected by his party for the Republican nomination in 1976. He was only just able to beat off a strong challenge by Ronald Reagan. Jimmy Carter, ex-Governor of Georgia, won the Democrat nomination. He was helped by being an outsider – untainted by the current collapse of confidence in political leaders. The liberal-inclined Carter promised full employment, national healthcare, welfare reform, aid to the cities, a new energy policy and more 'openness' in government. 'I will never tell a lie to the American people', he declared. Carter won 40,180,000 popular votes to Ford's 38,435,000, and 297 electoral college votes to Ford's 240. Carter, the first president from the Deep South since Taylor in 1848, seemed to be in a strong position because the Democrats had large majorities in both Houses of Congress.

g) President Jimmy Carter

At the start of his presidency Carter took several steps to bring a 'common touch' to the office. After his inauguration, he walked down Pennsylvania Avenue instead of riding in a limousine. He also dressed informally when giving televised 'fire-side chats'. Such gimmicks could not disguise the fact that he was often out of his depth. Inexperienced and a poor communicator, he never conveyed a sense of leadership. Nor, lacking the wheeling and dealing skills of LBJ, did he establish a sound working relationship with Congress. His sanctimonious moralising irritated most Congressmen.

Carter's promise of national healthcare, welfare reform, etc. were largely left on the campaign trail. His main priority was to restore the USA's economic strength. He determined to tackle the unemployment, rather than the inflation, component of stagflation. His methods of dealing with the problem were the same as those used by Ford and Nixon: tax cuts and increased public spending. In 1977, an economic stimulative package was passed by Congress. In that year the unemployment rate declined from 8 to 7 per cent. By 1978 it was down to 5.7 per cent. But the rate of inflation began to spiral out of control, reaching 10 per cent in 1978. Fearful of the consequences, Carter increased interest rates and tried to delay the implementation of the 1977 tax reductions and public spending programmes. This helter-skelter approach to economic management did not solve the problem of stagflation. By 1980 the unemployment rate stood at 7.5 per cent, the inflation rate at over 12 per cent and interest rates at a historic high of 20 per cent.

In 1977 Carter set up a Department of Energy and proposed strict conservation of fuels and heavy penalties on organisations which wasted energy. However, Congress failed to pass legislation based on his plan. His problems were compounded in 1979 when OPEC raised the price of a barrel of oil by 55 per cent. There was suddenly a fuel shortage in the USA. Motorists were forced to queue for petrol and Carter's standing in the polls dropped to an all-time low. He spent ten days at Camp David with his closest advisers trying to find a solution to America's problems. When he emerged, he could only talk about a need for 'a rebirth of the American spirit'. Few people were reassured by such generalities.

By 1980 the USA appeared to be in the middle of a deep crisis:
▼ The economy was plagued by stagflation.
▼ The social programmes of the 1960s and 1970s were largely discredited. Poverty and social deprivation remained only too evident in most US cities.
▼ In foreign affairs, Soviet expansionism in Africa and Afghanistan fuelled criticism of detente, while the Iranian hostage crisis seemed evidence of US impotence. Each evening in 1980 newscasters finished their broadcasts by reminding their viewers of the number of days that the US hostages had been held captive in Teheran.
▼ The rising crime rates, the spread of pornography, an increase in the divorce rate, together with Supreme Court decisions which legalised abortion and prohibited prayer in schools, led to the rise of groups committed to defending traditional values. Commonly identified as the New Right, these groups included religious organisations, such as the Moral Majority and anti-abortion groups. (By 1977 70 million Americans described themselves as born-again Christians.) Many yearned for a leader who could offer the USA a new sense of direction and who could restore its faith in itself.

h) The 1980 Election

The Democrats nominated Carter. The Republicans chose Ronald Reagan. Reagan had established a reputation for patriotic nationalism and for his support of the reduction of the role of government.

Democrats tried to make Reagan's age and right-wing views the central issues in the campaign. But Reagan was able to focus attention on Carter's abysmal record. At the end of the final television debate on 28 October Reagan asked the audience the decisive question: 'Are you better off than you were four years ago?'. Most Americans felt not and Reagan won 51 per cent to Carter's 41 per cent. Independent candidate John Anderson, a former Republican, gained most of the rest. The Republicans won the Senate for the first time in 25 years and made sufficient gains in the House to ensure that a conservative coalition of Republicans and Southern Democrats would have a majority.

ISSUE:
How good a president was Reagan?

3 The USA: 1980–90

-Profile-

1911 born in Illinois;
1932 worked as a radio sports
–7 reporter;
1937 worked as a movie actor in
–65 Hollywood;
1947 collaborated with the investiga-
–52 tion of Communist subversion in Hollywood;
1947 (and 1956–60) president of the
–52 Screen Actors Guild;
1966 elected Governor of California: cut taxes and took strong stand on law and order;
1970 re-elected Governor;
1980 defeated Carter in presidential election;
1984 re-elected President.

RONALD REAGAN

Reagan has generally had a bad press in Britain. Yet arguably he was one of the USA's greatest presidents. Unpretentious and free from pomposity, he radiated warmth and charm. Even Tip O'Neill, a Democratic adversary in Congress, found Reagan to be 'an exceptionally congenial and charming man. He's a terrific storyteller, he's witty, and he's got an excellent sense of humour.' He had many other skills. Intelligent, articulate, tough-minded, decisive and well-informed, he proved to be a strong president who moved the USA in the direction he had chosen.

Figure 58 Jimmy Carter watches from the wings as Ronald Reagan is sworn in as president. Nancy Reagan looks on proudly.

a) President Ronald Reagan

Historians' views on Reagan are divided. Some still see him as an age-
ing, empty-headed, grade-B movie actor who somehow stumbled into
the White House. Others think that he rates with FDR as the greatest
US president of the twentieth century. Reagan was the opposite of a
workaholic. He enjoyed his vacations at his Californian ranch and had
a relaxed attitude to political power. Some questioned whether he fully
understood, never mind controlled, events. But he had clear goals and
a stubbornness to achieve them along with a capacity to compromise
when it was necessary to do so. A great TV performer, Reagan was
believable because it was obvious that he believed what he said. He
appointed an able cabinet and gave its members considerable freedom. He deliberately did not get bogged down in details: this enabled
him to keep his eye on the wider picture. His laid-back style did not
mean he was ineffective: indeed, it enabled him to be effective.
Delegation ensured his sanity; it also made possible the 'Teflon' (non-
stick) factor: if things went wrong, he was less likely to be blamed.

Reagan's main mission on the domestic front was to reduce the
size and role of the government. 'Government is not the solution to
our problems', he declared in his inaugural address: 'government is
the problem.' He promised the American people a 'new beginning'
and attacked a 'tax system which penalises successful achievement
and keeps us from maintaining full productivity'. It was a declaration
of war on the philosophy of the New Deal and the Great Society.
(Ironically Reagan had been an admirer of FDR in the 1930s.)

In 1981 Reagan 'hit the deck running', mastering Congress and
enjoying a great deal of legislative achievement. The Economic
Recovery Tax Act (1981) cut personal taxes by 25 per cent across
the board. The Omnibus Budget and Reconstruction Act (1981)
reduced the level of federal spending (particularly for health, education and housing programmes) for 1982 by $35.2 billion. Reagan
hoped that tax cuts would stimulate economic growth and reduce
unemployment. This would then reduce the amount of social security payments and also bring more people into the tax net. The
economy did improve. Thanks largely to a fall in world oil prices,
the rate of inflation fell from 12 per cent to 2 per cent in 1983.
Although the level of unemployment remained high in 1981–2,
thereafter it fell. This was partly due to the great increase in
defence spending. (By 1984 some $1.5 trillion had been spent.)
'Defence is not a budget item … You spend what you need', said
Reagan. His defence spending had two main side-effects: it created
jobs and it helped to fuel the economic recovery which the USA
enjoyed from 1983–8. It also enabled the USA to win the Cold War
(see pages 242–3).

ATTEMPTED ASSASSINATION
In March 1981 Reagan was severely wounded in an assassination attempt. He showed wit and courage ('Honey, I forgot to duck', he told his wife Nancy on the way to hospital) and made an amazing recovery. This enhanced his reputation.

BUDGET DEFICIT
When Reagan took office in 1981 the budget deficit was $79 billion or 2.7 per cent of the USA's Gross National Product (GNP). By 1982 it was $128 billion or 4.1 per cent of GNP. Over the next two years it continued to grow. By 1984 it was $203 billion or 5.7 per cent of GNP. The Reagan adminis-tration thus ran up almost as much debt in its first term as had been run up in the pre-vious 200 years of the USA's existence.

Concern about the size of the growing budget deficit dominated the political agenda after 1981. Both Reagan and Congress accused each other of irresponsible behaviour. Reagan criticised Congress for failing to cut spending on domestic programmes. Congress criticised Reagan for his spending on defence. However, those who believed that the large budget deficit would cause major problems were proved wrong. The USA continued to enjoy economic growth throughout the 1990s.

Reagan aimed to shift responsibility for welfare from the federal government to state governments. He was critical of the power of federal regulatory agencies (he claimed they were costly and stifled initiative) and he managed to reduce regulation in areas such as consumer protection and the environment. The result was a renewed vitality in local government as states and cities sought their own solutions to problems. For the first time since the New Deal, power began to shift away from Washington. Reagan did little on the civil rights front and opposed affirmative action programmes which gave job preference based on race or gender. He supported traditional family values (despite being the first divorced president), was an opponent of abortion, and said and did little about AIDS (the first documented case was in 1981). He favoured a tough stance on law and order. By 1989 over one million Americans were in prison and the conservative Supreme Court supported the death penalty.

> ## THE 1984 ELECTION
>
> By 1984 the country was doing well economically and there was a 'feelgood' factor. US success in the 1984 Los Angeles Olympic Games helped Reagan's cause. Using the slogan 'America's Back Again', Reagan won a landslide victory over Democrat Walter Mondale, securing 59 per cent of the popular vote and losing only two states.

b) Irangate

Reagan was anxious to help the Contra guerrillas fighting against the Marxist Sandinista government in El Salvador. However, Congress refused to give him financial support. His administration thus devised several ways of circumventing the spirit, if not the letter, of the law. Colonel Oliver North devised a plan to sell arms (illegally) to the Iranians and use the profits from the sales to finance the Contras. News of the Iran–Contra link broke in 1986. National Security Advisor John Poindexter was forced to resign and North was relieved of his duties. Reagan denied direct knowledge of the affair and appointed a commission under former Senator Tower to investigate. The 1987 Tower Commission's Report placed much of the responsibility for the scandal on Reagan's loose management style. Meanwhile, both the Senate and the House of Representatives set up investigative committees. North and Poindexter testified that they never told Reagan precise details of what they had done. In November 1987 a Congressional select committee report concluded that if Reagan had not known what was going on, he should have known. Congress, aware that most Americans were not disturbed by the 'crime', did not go further in attacking a popular president.

Figure 59 Edward Sorel cartoon.

Was Reagan just lucky?

North and Poindexter were both tried and sentenced but not harshly punished. Later both men said that Reagan knew and encouraged everything.

c) Conclusion

'We meant to change a nation, and instead we changed a world ... All in all, not bad, not bad at all', said Reagan as he bowed out in 1989. His popularity (his rating stood at 70 per cent in 1989) and impact was reminiscent of his early idol, FDR. By 1989 he had achieved many of his aims: victory in the Cold War; prosperity at home; the reduction of federal taxes to the lowest rates since the 1920s; and the reversal of some of the liberal programmes. He had challenged the assumptions upon which the New Deal had been based: the extension of the role of the federal government was no longer taken for granted. He had also revitalised the presidency after the disgrace of Nixon and the ineffectiveness of Ford and Carter. He proved that the American system worked: the presidency was not the impossible job that it had seemed. Above all he restored Americans' self-confidence. There was no doubt that the USA felt better about itself in 1989 than it had done in 1981.

Reagan passed the presidency on to his Vice-President George Bush. Bush defeated Democrat Michael Dukakis in 1988, polling 53 per cent of the vote. In office, he abandoned the conservative programmes on which he was elected and moved to the ideological centre. In 1990 he retracted his 'no new taxes' pledge in an effort to reduce the budget deficit. He lacked Reagan's clear-cut resolve and never commanded similar respect. In 1992 he was defeated by Democrat candidate Bill Clinton. Clinton presided over a prosperous America and triumphed again in 1996.

▼ Working on Domestic Politics: 1945–90

Draw up a timeline covering the period from 1945 to 1990. It should include all the presidents, the parties to which they belonged, and the main domestic events of the period.

Answering Extended Writing and Essay Questions on Domestic Politics: 1945–90

Consider the following question: 'Why was the period from 1968 to 1980 so difficult for the USA?' Assuming you accept the notion that the years were 'difficult' (and it is possible to question the notion), this chapter will provide some information about the presidents and the political, economic and social problems they faced. However, you will also need to use information from Chapters 5, 6 and 7. Devise an introductory paragraph. Then plan seven or eight further paragraphs – the 'meat' of the essay. Finish by writing a conclusion of seven or eight sentences, pulling together your thoughts and answering the question!

Answering Source-based Questions on Domestic Politics: 1945–90

There is a new voice ... being heard across America. It is different from the old voices, the voices of hatred, the voices of dissension, the voices of riot and revolution. It is the voice of the forgotten Americans, those who did not indulge in violence, those who did not break the law, people who pay their taxes and go to work, people who send their children to school, who go to their churches, people who are not haters, people who love their country.

Source C Richard Nixon's inaugural speech, 1969.

Throughout the years of protest on the left, political activism and countercultural experimentation with drugs and alternative living styles had gone hand in hand, the one providing reinforcement for the other. But with a growing sense of resignation and frustration about the efficacy of political activism, the two strands began to diverge, with more and more people convinced that political expression was useless, and that building a new life with different values, mores and institutions provided the only answer. Appropriately, one of the factions of SDS [Students for a Democratic Society] articulated most clearly this way of thinking. 'What we are trying to say', the 'Up Against The Wall Motherfuckers', declared, 'is that the whole fucking struggle isn't anti-imperialist, capitalist, or any of that bullshit. The whole thing is a struggle to live. Dig it? For survival. The fucking soci-

Source D From William Chafe:
*The Unfinished Journey: America
since World War II* (OUP, 1999).

ety won't let you smoke your dope, ball your woman, wear your hair
the way you want to. All of that shit is living, dig, and we want to live,
that's our thing.'

Source E (Figure 60)
Woodstock poster.

▼ QUESTIONS ON SOURCES

1. Examine Source E. Why is the Woodstock Festival regarded as an
important event? **[3 marks]**

2. How do the three sources reflect the problems of the New Left? **[7
marks]**

3. Using all the sources and your own knowledge explain the divisions and
tensions within American society in the late 1960s. **[15 marks]**

Further Reading

The following are among the best general texts: *Grand Expectations* by J. Patterson (OUP, 1996), *Years of Discord: American Politics and Society, 1961–1974* by J. Morton Blum (Norton, 1991), and *The Unfinished Journey: America since World War 11* by W.H. Chafe (OUP, 1999). On specific presidents try: *The Truman Years 1945–1953* by M.S. Byrnes (Longman, 2000), *The Presidency of Dwight D. Eisenhower* by C.J. Pach and E. Richardson (University Press of Kansas, 1991) *Kennedy* by H. Brogan (Longman, 2000), *The Presidency of L.B. Johnson* by V.D. Bornet (University Press of Kansas), *The Presidency of Richard Nixon* by M. Small (University Press of Kansas, 1999) and *Ronald Reagan and the American Presidency* by D. Mervin (Longman, 1990).

INDEX